Medicine
and
Health
1990

GROLIER INCORPORATED, DANBURY, CONNECTICUT

Jean Paradise, *Group Editorial Director*
Robert Famighetti, *Executive Editor*
Zelda Haber, *Design Director*

EDITORIAL STAFF

Christine Martin Grove, *Senior Editor*
Irene Gunther, *Senior Editor*
Richard Hantula, *Senior Editor*
Christopher Kenny, *Senior Editor*

Terrence Adolph, *Editor*
Ingrid Strauch, *Associate Editor*
Carol R. Nelson, *Assistant Editor*
Ann Leslie Tuttle, *Editorial Assistant*
Laura Girardi, *Clerical Assistant*

John P. Elliott, *Adjunct Editor*
Jacqueline Laks Gorman, *Adjunct Editor*
Kathryn Paulsen, *Adjunct Editor*
Elizabeth Roberts, *Adjunct Editor*
AEIOU Inc., *Indexing*

ART/PRODUCTION STAFF

Joan Gampert, *Associate Design Director*
Gerald Vogt, *Production Supervisor*
Marvin Friedman, *Senior Designer*
Marc Sferrazza, *Designer*
Adrienne Weiss, *Designer*
Joyce Deyo, *Photo Editor*
Margaret McRae, *Photo Editor*
Marjorie Trenk, *Photo Editor*
Michele Carney, *Senior Production Assistant*
David Salinas, *Clerical Assistant*

Medicine and Health is not intended as a substitute for the medical advice of physicians. Readers should regularly consult a physician in matters relating to their health and particularly regarding symptoms that may require diagnosis or medical attention.

FEATURE ARTICLES

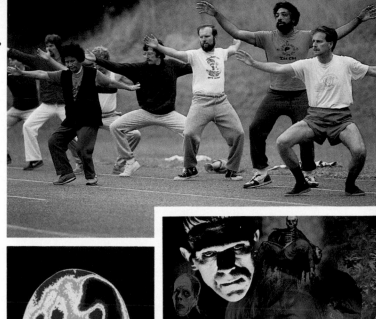

Page 4

Page 28   Page 104

Contents Continues

SPOTLIGHT ON HEALTH

A series of concise reports on practical health topics.

Health and Medical News

DIET ROUNDUP

Eleanor R. Williams, Ph.D.

ILLUSTRATION BY RICK BROWN

Dieting has long been a national obsession in the United States. A 1985 Gallup poll noted that 90 percent of Americans would like to be thinner, and the 1985 National Health Interview Survey found that one out of four men and nearly half of all women were trying to lose weight. These numbers may not be surprising given the prevalence of obesity in the United States: according to the National Institutes of Health, 30 percent of adult females and 25 percent of adult males are obese—at least 20 percent above desirable weight.

It is not, however, only the obese who diet. Thinness, too, has become something of an obsession, and many people whose weight is well within the ideal range—as well as many who carry around some excess pounds but are not overweight enough to be considered obese—feel the need to reduce.

Some people are engaged in a never-ending struggle to attain what they see as the perfect body image—an image more than likely based on role models seen in fashion magazines, on television, and in movies. Others go on an occasional diet to shed a few pounds, perhaps to look good for a special occasion.

In response to public interest in weight control, a multimillion-dollar industry has sprung up, offering a perplexing array of weight-loss diets and programs. Few people know enough about the basic principles of weight control to choose a suitable program or diet. This article is aimed at helping dieters to find their way through the morass and guide them

5

Readily available and fairly inexpensive, fast food is also high in fat and calories. Too much of it can lead to obesity in both youngsters and adults.

toward programs or diets that will allow them to lose weight without risk to health and—just as important—to maintain their new weight permanently. Contrary to the claims of some diet plans, there is no magic formula for instantly, safely, and permanently shedding unwanted pounds. Whatever the amount to be lost, the basic approach to dieting should be the same: a slow weight loss achieved with a balanced diet that contains all the nutrients the body needs. And maintaining weight loss requires more than just going on a diet for a few weeks—it involves a permanent change in eating and other habits, in particular, incorporating regular exercise into one's life-style.

Obesity and Its Complications

Appearance aside, obesity is cause for concern because it increases one's chances of developing many diseases. Obese people are more apt than those of normal or near normal weight to develop high blood pressure (hypertension), high levels in the blood of cholesterol and the fats called triglycerides, coronary heart disease, diabetes, respiratory problems, gallbladder disease, certain cancers, and gout. They are also at greater risk for complications if they require surgery or anesthesia. Moreover, for many of the conditions mentioned above, the mortality rate among obese people is higher than that of people of normal or close to normal weight. The good news is that bringing weight down closer to normal—and keeping it there—decreases the risks for most of these disorders.

Causes of Obesity

What accounts for obesity—and why is it so prevalent? We know that people accumulate extra body fat when they consume more calories than they use up. Calories are used up by the *lean* tissues in the body to keep organs such as the heart, lungs, liver, and kidneys functioning. The rate at which the body uses up, or metabolizes, calories when one is at rest is called the resting metabolic rate (RMR). Calories are also burned up to support muscular exercise. The higher the body's proportion of lean tissue to fat tissue and the greater the amount of exercise one does, the more calories one uses up. Any intake of calories over the amount needed to support the RMR and the body's physical activity is nearly always stored as fat.

People who earn their living through long hours of intensive labor must eat large amounts to balance their energy expenditure and keep their weight normal. But today physical activity generally is low, and highly palatable, easily prepared, high-calorie foods are widely available. It is hardly surprising, then, that many people consume more calories than they expend and become obese.

After young adulthood, the RMR gradually declines, and often, so does physical activity. Therefore, people who continue to take in the

Eleanor R. Williams is an associate professor in the Department of Human Nutrition and Food Systems at the University of Maryland.

same number of calories as they did in their youth will gradually accumulate an excess of fat—the familiar "middle-age spread." An additional factor can contribute to obesity in women. If a mother does not breast-feed, the fat normally accumulated during pregnancy remains in the body after childbirth. As a result, many women become heavier with each pregnancy.

What about the people who maintain normal weight for years, hardly giving a thought to how much they eat and somehow having no difficulty matching their caloric intake to caloric expenditure? Why are some people able to do this while others cannot? Many researchers believe that people who maintain normal weight have efficient physiological controls for hunger and satiety (the feeling of having had enough), while some obese people have faulty controls and will eat even when caloric needs are satisfied. Researchers are looking at factors that may give people the urge to eat or induce them to stop eating.

A tendency toward obesity may be inherited; at least some people who are prone to obesity appear to be less efficient than some lean people in metabolizing extra calories. Some lean people appear to burn off excess calories from overeating and dissipate them as heat, while some obese people appear unable to do so and instead store such calories as fat. It is not as yet known whether this is a common problem among the obese.

Emotional and behavioral factors also affect eating habits. Many

HOW MUCH SHOULD YOU WEIGH?

The tables below show the weights at which people live longest, sometimes called ideal weights, according to current research. The weights listed are for people age 25–59, of small, medium, or large frame. All weights include 5 pounds of clothing for men and 3 for women; heights include shoes with 1 inch heels.

MEN				WOMEN			
Height	**Small**	**Medium**	**Large**	**Height**	**Small**	**Medium**	**Large**
5' 2"	128–134	131–141	138–150	4' 10"	102–111	109–121	118–131
5' 3"	130–136	133–143	140–153	4' 11"	103–113	111–123	120–134
5' 4"	132–138	135–145	142–156	5' 0"	104–115	113–126	122–137
5' 5"	134–140	137–148	144–160	5' 1"	106–118	115–129	125–140
5' 6"	136–142	139–151	146–164	5' 2"	108–121	118–132	128–143
5' 7"	138–145	142–154	149–168	5' 3"	111–124	121–135	131–147
5' 8"	140–148	145–157	152–172	5' 4"	114–127	124–138	134–151
5' 9"	142–151	148–160	155–176	5' 5"	117–130	127–141	137–155
5' 10"	144–154	151–163	158–180	5' 6"	120–133	130–144	140–159
5' 11"	146–157	154–166	161–184	5' 7"	123–136	133–147	143–163
6' 0"	149–160	157–170	164–188	5' 8"	126–139	136–150	146–167
6' 1"	152–164	160–174	168–192	5' 9"	129–142	139–153	149–170
6' 2"	155–168	164–178	172–197	5' 10"	132–145	142–156	152–173
6' 3"	158–172	167–182	176–202	5' 11"	135–148	145–159	155–176
6' 4"	162–176	171–187	181–207	6' 0"	138–151	148–162	158–179

Source: Metropolitan Life Insurance Company

Low in cholesterol needn't mean low in appeal. Here, caterers prepare an appetizing array of low-cholesterol dishes.

people overeat when under stress, or when they are bored, lonely, anxious, or excited. However, obesity is not necessarily the result of overeating—many obese people seem not to eat more than those of normal weight. For such people, lack of physical activity and/or a low metabolic rate caused by a relatively low proportion of lean tissue to fat tissue, or (rarely) by hormonal influences, may be important contributing factors.

Losing Weight Wisely

People try to lose weight in different ways. Some go about it by dieting on their own, cutting out whatever they see fit; others prefer to follow a specified diet, perhaps one contained in a best-selling book; still others turn to structured weight-loss programs for help. Some well-known diets, such as Weight Watchers and Optifast, are offered only through membership in a program. Whatever the approach, and whether the goal is to lose 5 pounds or 50, the basic principles of sensible dieting apply.

The Yo-Yo Syndrome. Overweight people are often tempted by quick-weight-loss diet plans that promise to remove inches in days or weeks. But experts know that people who lose large amounts of weight quickly by dieting are almost always unable to keep it off. In fact they frequently gain not only all of the lost weight—but more. Gaining weight, losing it on a diet, then regaining—a cycle called the yo-yo syndrome—may be worse than not losing weight at all. Those who lose

SAMPLE MENUS OF APPROXIMATELY 1,200 CALORIES

Breakfast

- ½ cup orange juice
- ½ toasted English muffin
- 1 tsp. soft tub margarine
- 1 cup coffee or tea
- ½ cup skim milk

Lunch

Sandwich of 2 slices whole wheat bread, 2 oz. tuna (in water), chopped celery and pimento, 1 T. mayonnaise, and 2 lettuce leaves
- ½ carrot, cut into sticks
- 1 apple
- ½ cup skim milk

Dinner

- 2 oz. flank steak (cooked in red wine)
- ½ cup brown rice
- ⅔ cup steamed broccoli
- 1½ cups tossed salad (romaine lettuce; ½ small carrot, grated; ½ celery stalk, sliced; 3 fresh mushrooms, sliced; 1 T. regular Italian dressing)
- 1 cup skim milk yogurt
- 1 pear

Breakfast

- 1 cup fresh blueberries
- 1 cup plain nonfat yogurt
- 1 English muffin with 1 tsp. margarine

Lunch

Chef's salad (2 cups lettuce; 1 tomato, cut up; ½ cup shredded carrot; 1 oz. turkey; 2 oz. lean ham; 1 oz. low-fat cheese; 1 T. French salad dressing)
- 6 saltines
- 2 fresh plums

Dinner

- 3 oz. roast chicken breast
- ½ cup steamed asparagus spears
- ½ cup steamed yellow squash
- 1 roll with 1 tsp. margarine
- 1 fresh peach

Note: tsp. = teaspoon, T. = tablespoon.
Menu 2 reproduced with permission from *Dietary Treatment of Hypercholesterolemia: A Manual for Patients*, 1988. Copyright © American Heart Association.

weight rapidly on a low-calorie diet lose lean tissue as well as fat, but what they gain back is chiefly fat. The loss of lean tissue slows the metabolic rate, resulting in a lowered need for calories. Consequently, dieters are apt to gain weight faster and faster each time they go off the diet—and must cut calories progressively lower to lose it again. Obviously they are fighting a losing battle. This is why experts stress *slow* weight loss to minimize loss of lean tissue and increase the likelihood of maintaining the lower weight permanently.

The Right Way to Diet. A sensible diet is one that furnishes all the vitamins, minerals, and dietary fiber needed and is low enough in

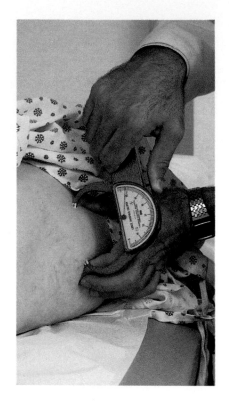

Pinching inches: a skinfold caliper is used to measure body fat.

calories to bring about slow weight loss. For most people caloric intake should be between 1,100 and 1,800 calories a day, depending on the individual case. This level is likely to provide adequate nutrition while promoting weight loss of 1 to 1½ pounds a week—which results in minimal loss of lean tissue and thereby avoids the problems that arise when the resting metabolic rate is lowered.

Calories should be properly distributed among protein, fat, and carbohydrates. Experts recommend that 20 to 30 percent of total calories should be taken in as fat, 15 to 25 percent as protein, and the remainder as carbohydrates (chiefly from starchy, not sugary, foods). The box on page 9 contains sample one-day menus of about 1,200 calories that include acceptable proportions of fat, protein, and carbohydrates.

To ensure the nutritional adequacy of a diet, foods should be chosen daily from each of the following four groups: vegetables and fruits; whole grain and enriched bread, cereals, pasta, and rice; legumes, meats, poultry, and fish; milk and milk products. High-calorie items such as fried foods, candy, cakes, pies, and cookies should be limited. For many people, however, such a diet contains many more vegetables, fruits, and whole-grain products than they are used to eating, and they may need support to make the necessary changes in their dietary habits. For these people, joining a weight-loss program that offers such support may be a good choice. Permanent changes in dietary patterns are more apt to occur if the diet fits individual tastes and preferences. A good weight-loss program will show participants how to substitute one food for another so as to prevent monotony and add variety to their diet. The kind of diet just described can be turned into a long-term maintenance diet simply by increasing the caloric intake just enough to prevent weight loss.

A Look at Some Popular Diets

Many popular weight-loss diets differ markedly from the sensible diet described above. Although popular diets will bring about short-term weight loss if they provide fewer calories than the dieter needs, they often fail to meet the requirements of an ideal diet.

Fad Diets. Often, diets that claim to have found a new key to quick weight loss achieve tremendous popularity for a short time. Such fad diets proliferate because they bring quick profits to authors and to book and magazine publishers. Well aware that most people want to lose weight instantly and painlessly, the promoters attract people through well-tested marketing techniques, such as the use of a famous name or the claim that the diet is based on a "new scientific discovery." Fad diets frequently formulate rules or restrictions that have no purpose other than to distinguish them from other diets. For example, a diet may limit or omit an entire food group, such as milk, promote specific foods, such as grapefruit, or set rules for combining foods. Some mislead consumers by false claims, for example, saying that the body cannot digest certain food combinations, that calorie reduction is not needed for weight loss, that people are fat because of "overworked glands," or that enzymes in specific foods bring about weight loss.

Fad diets include diets that advocate fasting or are very low in calories (less than 800 calories a day) and diets that are very low in carbohydrates or fat. Many of them fail to supply sufficient vitamins and minerals either because of their restrictions on food choices or because of their very low calorie levels. (Food restrictions also can make it impossible to keep to the diet in many social situations.) Some diets induce fatigue and other discomforts, and by far the majority fail to produce permanent weight loss because they do not establish viable new eating patterns.

Fasting and Very-Low-Calorie Diets. Fasting can be extremely dangerous, and any program that requires it should be avoided. Responsible physicians no longer advocate fasting, even for patients who are very closely supervised in a hospital setting, because life-threatening imbalances of sodium, potassium, and magnesium in body fluids can develop, and death can result from malfunctions of the liver and heart. Fasting patients frequently develop headache, nausea, and dizziness. Moreover, they rapidly regain their lost weight when they resume eating.

The popularity of very-low-calorie diets goes back to the early 1970s, when physicians tried to help severely obese patients by giving them diets of only 400 to 500 calories a day that were high in protein derived from meat, poultry, and fish. Later, diets were prescribed in which patients consumed only a specially formulated liquid containing high-quality protein from milk or eggs. Rapid weight loss resulted from both these types of diets—but also some negative consequences. In

A hospital nutritionist gives patients counseling to help them reach—and maintain—their optimal weight.

1976 a popular book promoted a very-low-calorie liquid diet, called the Last Chance Diet, in which the drink contained protein derived from cowhide. The product was very widely used, with and without medical supervision. In 1978 scientists reported that at least 60 deaths had resulted from use of this and similar products. Investigation revealed that the protein in these diets was so low in some essential amino acids that the heart muscle was inadequately nourished. In addition, the liquid diets were deficient in minerals including calcium, sodium, potassium, and magnesium, leading to often fatal disturbances of the heart rhythm.

Today's very-low-calorie diets differ from those of the 1970s in that they contain high-quality protein and make provision for supplying the necessary amounts of vitamins and minerals. Currently, some hospital, clinic, and other diet programs use very-low-calorie diets that provide 500 to 600 calories a day to treat severely obese adults. Some of these diets, like Optifast, the much-publicized one that helped Oprah Winfrey lose nearly 70 pounds in a few months, are all-liquid. Others, like the Rotation Diet, are not entirely liquid. To ensure that patients receive appropriate medical supervision, the Optifast diet is made available only through official Optifast programs, which are routinely monitored by the manufacturer of the diet.

Very-low-calorie diets are inappropriate for people who are less than 40 percent over desirable weight (although many programs accept people who are as little as 15 percent over). And they are safe only if the protein used really is of high quality (that is, provides all the amino acids needed), if individuals remain on the diet for less than three months, if they have no disease complications, and if they receive

Regular exercise is a key component of a weight-loss program, helping prevent the loss of lean tissue. As a bonus, physical activity also brings a sense of well-being.

careful, competent medical supervision and the necessary vitamin and mineral supplements. These low-calorie diets result in large weight losses, but the lost weight usually is rapidly regained. The rapid weight loss from either fasting or very-low-calorie diets lowers the resting metabolic rate. In addition, many people go on eating binges when they stop fasting or go off a very-low-calorie diet. Proponents of these diets claim that the use of behavior modification techniques can lead to greater success in maintaining the new lower weight; however, many programs lack such a component.

Low-Carbohydrate Diets. Low-carbohydrate diets became popular in the 1960s and 1970s because they brought about quick weight loss. Proponents claim—incorrectly—that the loss is due not to a decrease in calories, but to low carbohydrate intake. Dieters are told they can eat all the meat and high-fat foods they want as long as they take in a very small amount of carbohydrates. The problem is that such diets work by causing ketosis. This is a condition in which the body's stores of fat are broken down faster than the liver can use them for energy, resulting in the accumulation in the blood of substances called ketones and their subsequent excretion in the urine. Excretion of ketones demands increased excretion of water, so that the dieter at first loses weight rapidly as a result of water loss. But ketosis also causes headache, dizziness, bad breath, nausea, and high levels in the blood of uric acid (the last increases the risk of gout). And, to their surprise, dieters find that they are unable to eat large quantities of meat and fat because of some loss of appetite. (The direct cause of the appetite loss is unclear.) They consequently consume fewer calories than they expend, and—after the initial water loss—they begin to lose lean tissue as well as fat.

The loss of lean tissue occurs because it is crucial for the body to maintain its blood glucose levels. When the liver is deprived of the carbohydrates from food that it normally converts to glucose, it uses instead amino acids obtained from the breakdown of lean tissue. The loss of lean tissue then lowers the metabolic rate, decreasing the body's need for calories. Another serious problem with low-carbohydrate diets is that they are high in fat and cholesterol, and a high-fat diet is known to increase the risk of heart disease and possibly of cancer. Examples of low-carbohydrate diets are the Atkins and Stillman diets.

Very-Low-Fat Diets. Although restricting fat in the diet to 30 percent of calories is currently recommended for the general public, diets in which less than 20 percent of calories come from fat may be too extreme. One such diet, the Pritikin diet, provides 700 calories a day, of which only about 10 percent comes from fat. It requires extreme changes in both the choice of foods and the way foods are prepared (very little meat, no added fat, and no nuts or seeds are permitted); it is thus difficult to adhere to and to convert to a weight-maintenance diet.

Choosing the Right Weight-Loss Program

If you are strongly motivated to lose weight, a responsible, supervised weight-loss program may be the answer. You have a better chance of reaching your goal if you can accept a slow weight loss—not more than a pound to a pound and a half each week—assume complete respon-

People often succumb to eating binges when they go off very-low-calorie diets.

13

WEIGHING UP A WEIGHT-LOSS PROGRAM

Measure any program you are thinking of entering against the criteria below. The more "yes" answers, the better the program.

	Yes	No
ASSESSMENT		
Do qualified professionals assess such factors as physical health, motivation, eating and exercise habits, emotional problems with food, prior dieting experience?	❏	❏
DIET		
Does the diet offer at least 1,100 calories a day?	❏	❏
Is it based entirely on everyday, readily available foods?	❏	❏
Does it include foods from all four main food groups?	❏	❏
Does it allow for individual food preferences?	❏	❏
Can it be used for weight maintenance?	❏	❏
Does it provide 20–30% of calories as fat, 15–25% as protein, the remainder as carbohydrates?	❏	❏
RATE OF WEIGHT LOSS		
Is the weight lost slowly—no more than 1–1½ pounds a week?	❏	❏
MAINTENANCE OF WEIGHT LOSS		
Are there provisions for helping you maintain your new lower weight?	❏	❏
RESPONSIBILITY		
Does the program teach you to take responsibility for keeping to your diet and exercising regularly?	❏	❏
Do qualified personnel help you by suggesting changes in your life-style and your approach to food?	❏	❏
EXERCISE		
Is an exercise program provided?	❏	❏
If so , is medical screening required before you begin the exercise program?	❏	❏
Is the program designed so it fits easily into your life-style?	❏	❏
SUPPORT		
Is individual or group support available?	❏	❏

sibility for controlling your food intake, and commit yourself to exercising regularly.

Weight-loss programs are offered by registered dietitians and licensed nutritionists in private practice, by hospital-based clinics (some, but not all, of these offer commercial programs), by spas or residential health facilities, and by commercial enterprises. Since the offerings vary widely, you should thoroughly evaluate a given program to see if it meets your specific needs. Prices vary, and you should be clear about what is entailed before signing any contract.

The most effective weight-loss programs individualize treatment as much as possible. A good program should help you improve your health, lose a reasonable amount of weight, and establish a life-style that will result in permanent maintenance of the lower weight.

Begin With an Assessment. Before choosing a program, you should see your doctor to determine the extent to which you have a weight problem and whether you have any medical conditions that make it inadvisable for you to go on a rigorous diet. Some programs begin with a medical examination, as well as an appraisal of your eating and exercise patterns and a psychosocial assessment to single out factors that may help or hinder your ability to adhere to a weight-loss program. You should probably postpone entering a weight-loss program if you are under a great deal of stress.

Changing Behavior. Besides providing a suitable diet, a good program will suggest ways to help you stick to it. It will encourage you, for example, to set realistic goals and help you change your eating patterns and your approach to food to make dieting easier. Beneficial behavior changes include sitting down to eat in only one suitable place (for example, at the dining room table—not in front of the TV), not stocking foods that tempt you to overeat, putting appropriate-sized servings directly onto the plate (rather than placing large serving dishes of food on the table), and eating slowly and savoring the food.

One suggestion for dieters: Eat at the table, not in front of the TV.

The Importance of Exercise. A good program should also emphasize regular exercise. Suitable forms of exercise include walking, jogging, and cycling, generally undertaken three or four times a week, but the program should advise you on the kind and amount of exercise that is best for you. Exercise helps prevent the loss of lean tissue and lets you take in more calories, thus improving the nutritional value of your diet. Moreover, increased physical activity brings a feeling of well-being. Exercise also helps you to deal with tension and stress and can be used as a substitute for snacking or other problematic eating habits. If, however, you are obese and have specific medical problems, you should check with a physician before beginning an exercise program.

Support Along the Way. Many good weight-loss programs provide either individual counseling or support groups to encourage adherence to the program and to prevent regain of lost weight. Take Off Pounds Sensibly (TOPS) and Overeaters Anonymous are support groups only; members are expected to obtain nutritional guidance elsewhere. Other groups, such as Weight Watchers, provide weekly support meetings as well as guidance on diet, exercise, and behavior changes. Some people do better with individual counseling, others prefer group support. □

SUGGESTIONS FOR FURTHER READING

The following books contain diet plans that meet the criteria described in this article for ideal weight-loss diets. The regular Weight Watchers diet (but not the "quick start" diet, which is too low in calories) also meets the criteria.

CONNOR, SONJA L., AND WILLIAM E. CONNOR. *The New American Diet: The Lifetime Family Eating Plan for Good Health.* New York, Simon & Schuster, 1986.
DEBAKEY, MICHAEL E., et al. *The Living Heart Diet.* New York, Raven Press, 1984.
GRUNDY, SCOTT, M.D., AND MARY WINSTON, eds. *American Heart Association Low-Fat, Low-Cholesterol Cookbook.* New York, Times Books, 1989.

The Martial Arts

Christine Martin Grove

*I*f you've ever seen a kung fu movie, you may have trouble thinking of the martial arts as a form of exercise for ordinary folk. In such movies the image is of spectacular leaps and kicks, grunts, groans, and blood-curdling cries, fancy spins, vicious punches—so much action and so much violence, in fact, that it's difficult to imagine any of the participants coming out alive, much less in better shape than before they started.

Over the past few years many Americans have found that behind the violent image lies a disciplined, orderly world with a wide range of offerings to suit men, women, and children of all ages, shapes, and sizes, those looking for vigorous workouts and those looking for a gentler form of exercise, those looking for a purely physical workout and those looking for a little more. They have discovered that what the martial arts really are has little relation to the popular image.

What They Are

The term "martial arts" is used loosely to cover systems of hand-to-hand fighting that developed in Asia, with perhaps the best known being karate and judo. These systems are all based on ancient combat skills. Activities like archery and fencing, based on ancient Western battle skills, are not covered by the martial arts umbrella. The difference is that the Eastern arts, at least as they were originally conceived, were seen as more than ways of fighting—they were means by which participants could develop not only the physical but also the spiritual and mental aspects of their lives. Not all of today's participants in the martial arts give equal weight to the same aspects of the arts—for some they are simply a way of keeping fit, for others they are recreation, or a method of self-defense, or a form of meditation, or a way of learning discipline and focus, or any combination of the above. Nevertheless, it is the mental/spiritual aspects of the martial arts that give them their distinctive status.

Their History

The origins of the martial arts are shrouded in mystery. Tomb paintings and carvings suggest that the actual physical fighting skills of some go back 2,000 years or more. Many scholars believe that it was in the sixth century that the martial arts gained the extra dimension that made them more than practical fighting systems. According to one legend, in A.D. 525, Bodhidharma, a Zen Buddhist monk, traveled from India to a Buddhist temple in China called Shaolin, where he began to teach the monks and nuns his beliefs. He soon found they were so physically unfit that they were falling asleep while he was instructing them. Convinced that the monks and nuns could never become spiritually strong if they were physically weak, Bodhidharma set out to teach them physical and mental exercises and breathing techniques that would help them reach the state of spiritual enlightenment to which they had dedicated their lives.

The legend does not describe in detail any of the exercises that Bodhidharma might have taught his followers, but it is possible that one of them was Horse-Riding Stance, a basic exercise in the martial arts today; it is known at least to have been practiced at Shaolin at a slightly later date. In Horse-Riding Stance, Horse Stance for short, the legs are held apart, with the knees bent and the back straight—just like

The martial arts are based on ancient Asian combat skills, but with a twist.

Christine Martin Grove is a staff editor.

To the monks and nuns of Shaolin temple, the fighting skills they developed in hours of daily practice were not important in themselves but were an aid in their journey toward spiritual enlightenment.

riding a horse, except there's no horse to sit on. The exercise both develops the sense of balance and strengthens the legs. If, as in some martial arts styles today, the monks and nuns were required to stand in Horse Stance for an hour at a time, it must also have taught them to endure pain (try the stance for yourself) and to endure in general, for an important part of the exercise is that nothing is allowed to interrupt it—whatever happens, one concentrates hard on a single thought and holds still.

Whether the legend of Bodhidharma is true or not, by the seventh century Shaolin monks and nuns were renowned for their fighting skills, based on a formidable combination of patience, self-discipline, strength, and balance. Over the years they improved their methods so that strength became less important than technique and everyone, big or small, old or young, male or female, could practice them successfully. The same principle—that technique is more important than strength—holds true today.

The fighters of Shaolin never forgot that, however well-developed their fighting skills, they were first and foremost Buddhist monks and nuns whose ultimate aim in life was to reach spiritual enlightenment and for whom practicing their fighting skills was principally a matter of practicing "meditation in motion." Fighting was never seen as an end in itself—it was to be used only for self-defense or to help others, never for personal gain, revenge, or show. And if one ever had to fight, the rule was to do no more damage to one's opponent than was absolutely necessary.

In time the new art spread beyond Shaolin to other parts of China, where it became an important means of self-defense during centuries of civil turmoil. Many historians believe that various versions were also taken to other areas, such as Okinawa, Korea, and the Japanese main islands, where they became the basis of new systems of martial arts adapted to the needs and wants of the different cultures. Others believe that different arts developed independently in different parts of Asia. Whatever their origins, at times the arts were forced underground by rulers who saw them as threats to their own power. In 1730, for example, the Manchu emperors of China passed a law forbidding the practice of the Chinese martial arts. They survived anyway, as parents secretly passed down their knowledge to their children. And when the need for them as day-to-day methods of defense had passed, new forms were developed that put renewed emphasis on spiritual values.

Most of the martial arts were not well-known in the West before World War II. Exceptions were judo and jujitsu, which were brought to Europe and America by Japanese immigrants at the end of the 19th century and the beginning of the 20th. President Theodore Roosevelt

Some karate styles base their moves on the defense systems of animals such as the eagle (left), the crane (center), and the tiger (right). (Moves demonstrated by June Castro of Los Angeles, who has a 5th degree black belt in Shaolin kenpo karate.)

took judo lessons in the White House, and some of the English suffragists learned jujitsu—and used it in their confrontations with British police during the campaign to win the vote for women.

In the 1940s and early 1950s, however, U.S. soldiers stationed in Japan and Korea saw and studied judo, tae kwon do, karate, aikido, and other martial arts and brought them back to the United States. And in the 1960s, as Chinese emigrated to the United States in large numbers, Americans for the first time found Chinese masters willing to pass on their knowledge and skills to non-Chinese students in the New World.

Over the past few years about 10 percent of Americans have tried the more popular martial arts, among them karate, tae kwon do, judo, aikido, and tai chi (full name, tai chi chuan). Each of them has something different to offer in terms of technique and fitness benefits.

Karate and Tae Kwon Do

The term "karate" was originally used by the people of Okinawa to mark the fact that their fighting style was heavily influenced by the Chinese. "Kara" was the character used to refer to the Tang rulers of China and "kara-te" meant, essentially, "China hands." In the 1930s, however, when karate had become very Japanese, the character meaning "Tang" or "China" was altered to mean "empty," to better reflect what karate actually is—empty-handed fighting. (Interestingly enough, as both characters are pronounced the same, the change didn't show up in English at all.)

Americans by the thousands were inspired by a movie, The Karate Kid, *to try the martial arts for themselves.*

Today, "karate" is used to describe the hundreds of martial arts styles that emphasize kicking, punching, parrying, and blocking. Some karate styles place more emphasis on punching; others on kicking. When Americans talk about karate, they usually mean some variant of the Okinawan-Japanese karate brought to the United States after World War II. Another kind of karate was later brought over from Korea. This is tae kwon do (which lays a heavy emphasis on sometimes spectacular kicks). Tae kwon do has its own schools and associations, quite separate from those for other kinds of karate.

A typical karate or tae kwon do class starts with a warm-up period—running or jumping in place for a few minutes, followed by strength-building exercises such as sit-ups and push-ups. Next come stretching exercises to loosen up various joints and muscle groups. Practice of single techniques—stances, kicks, punches, strikes, or blocks—comes next, with 50 or so repetitions of each.

Following single-technique practice, students go on to forms, or formal fighting exercises, which have been called the grammar of karate. Each style of karate has its own forms, but they all consist of defensive and offensive moves put together in stylized combinations that follow preset patterns. Forms include all of a style's hand and foot techniques and call for rapid changes not only in technique but also in speed, balance, position, and breathing. Some forms are done alone against an imaginary opponent, others are done in pairs. Forms range from the very simple to the very complex and have more than one purpose. Besides teaching students how to turn, pivot, and move

21

backward, forward, and sideways at different speeds, all while carrying out hand and foot techniques properly, they are a means of physical conditioning: through endless repetition of the forms, students develop balance, muscular coordination, and endurance. And the forms serve as a sign of the student's level of achievement—the more advanced the student, the more complex the form. A bonus is that, to the onlooker, a group of people performing a form well is like a group of dancers performing a beautiful, synchronized dance routine.

After the forms comes free sparring, in which pairs of students spar with each other, changing partners every few minutes so that they can get experience fighting people of all sizes and skill levels. In free sparring students use what they learned in single-technique practice and forms. They do not actually land their kicks and punches for the aim is not to hurt the opponent but to practice techniques. If students are studying an increasingly popular form of karate called contact karate, of course, this will not be the case—the aim is to make contact as often as possible following very specific rules.

Students might also practice kicking or punching boards or heavy

Free sparring is an important part of a karate class. Changing partners every few minutes, students get a chance to practice their techniques on people of all sizes and skill levels.

bags hung from the ceiling. This helps them develop speed and accuracy along with strength in their arms and legs, as well as giving them an idea of what it's like to have a real target.

A Word About *Ki*, or *Chi*

Most martial arts teach that you have an inner strength, called *ki* (Japanese) or *chi* (Chinese), centered in a spot just below your navel. This inner strength, it is taught, can be developed with special breathing and meditation exercises, so that you can learn to focus your energy and increase the force behind every kick, punch, or strike. Some martial arts practitioners regard *ki* as a metaphysical or spiritual force, while others see it as a practical matter of learning to concentrate and to breathe properly. However you look at it, *ki* is the power behind the so-called karate chop that is used to break bricks, boards, and stones. In spite of the popular image, breaking boards is hardly ever used in day-to-day training. It's done more for demonstration purposes, to show outsiders that the human body is capable of more than most of us suppose. Another manifestation of *ki*—the *kiai*, the ferocious yell that sometimes accompanies a karate strike or kick—is part of everyday training, for the simple reason that a strong exhale as you punch acts like an extra source of energy, making the punch more powerful.

Judo

Judo, developed in Japan in the late 19th century, was based on the centuries-old combat art of jujitsu. Judo's creator, Jigoro Kano, kept what he regarded as of greatest value in the old art while getting rid of violent techniques suitable only for life-and-death situations. In judo, the "gentle way" or "way of yielding," a basic principle is that you yield to, or move with, a physical force directed against you rather than meet it with more force. This principle, bolstered by the scientific principles of gravity and leverage, resulted in an art in which students learn to turn opponents' strength against themselves so that they can be put off balance, thrown, and immobilized by locking of the joints or pressure on vital organs.

A typical judo class is similar to a karate class in structure. A warm-up period of stretching and strengthening exercises is followed by practice of techniques. In judo this means plenty of practice in falling every which way—very important in an art in which the main aim of opponents is to throw each other—and in learning how to make opponents lose their balance so they can be thrown. Mat work, that is work on holds, chokes, and locks (with very specific rules about what is and is not permitted, to prevent injury), is also important. Practice in forms, in which there is one set of prearranged moves for the attacker, another for the defender, is important in many judo classes, but not in all, just as the development of *ki* is important in some judo classes and virtually disregarded in others.

In free play, students practice on each other the techniques they have been learning. This activity is called free play, rather than sparring or

BOWING

Americans visiting a judo, karate, tae kwon do, or aikido class for the first time are sometimes taken aback by the bowing that goes on. To Americans, bowing to someone else means that you are acknowledging the other's superiority. To Asians, bowing is a form of greeting and a sign of respect, and it is the Asian meaning that is at work in the martial arts. Two students bowing to each other before and after free sparring are acknowledging that they are not there to hurt each other but to perfect their techniques. Students bowing to the teacher are showing respect for the teacher's years of hard work, knowledge, and skills. Teachers bowing to students are showing respect for the efforts and dedication of the students as they work their way up through the ranks.

23

Practice Makes Perfect

Beginning tai chi students in Oregon (right) and more experienced practitioners in a Shanghai park (left) practice the movements that, when done well, resemble formal dances in slow motion.

fighting, in recognition of the basic judo ethic that partners protect each other from hurt even while executing throws, holds, and chokes.

Aikido

Aikido is sometimes called the nonfighting martial art because it is almost exclusively defensive. In theory, it would be impossible for two aikido players to fight each other because each would be waiting for the other to make the first move. Aikido was created in this century in Japan by Morihei Uyeshiba, who had studied over 200 martial arts and was a master of many of them. Uyeshiba wanted a martial art that could be used to defend the individual against violence—but without using violence in return. The development of *ki* is very important in aikido (which means "the way of bringing together one's *ki*") and is stressed from the beginning.

An aikido class begins with exercises for developing *ki*. These include breathing and meditation exercises intended to teach concentration and the channeling of energy. Other warm-up exercises make the wrists stronger and more flexible—many aikido techniques use the wrists for holds and locks—while still others teach tumbling and falling.

Next comes work on techniques. These are unlike karate techniques in that there are no punches or kicks; they are unlike judo techniques in that there is no grappling with an opponent. Instead, students learn to slip around an attacker's lunges and then "lead" the attacker to the floor by applying pressure to the arms or neck. The attacker, once down, is kept down, not with sheer physical force but with a simple arm lock.

In an aikido class there will also be free play, in which one student

will stand in the middle of the floor and take on the other students one by one. Any forms that are done, usually by the more advanced students, make use of swords and staffs.

Tai Chi

Tai chi is a kung fu art. Many people think that kung fu is the showy, hard-edged, flying-leaps-and-all art often seen in the movies, but kung fu is actually a Chinese phrase meaning "something that takes a long time to accomplish" and is used outside China to mean all the Chinese martial arts. (In China itself they are called *wu su*.) Although a kung fu school might teach any of hundreds of kung fu styles, from tai chi to the wing chun style made famous by martial arts superstar Bruce Lee, tai chi is so distinctive and popular that it is often taught in separate schools (listed separately in telephone directories).

Tai chi chuan means "supreme ultimate fist," which reflects its origins as a fighting art, but at first glance it looks anything but belligerent. Tai chi stresses smooth, graceful movements, deep breathing, and relaxation. At its heart is the solo exercise, a series of beautiful, flowing movements that look more like a formal dance done in slow motion than the series of fighting moves they actually are. For most practitioners today—including those who can be seen practicing early every morning on the streets and in the parks of China—the self-defense aspect of tai chi is secondary to the wish to keep fit, in both mind and body.

Central to tai chi is the idea that softness and flexibility mean strength, as in the case of the willow tree that survives a storm because it bends in the wind. And as in aikido, the development of *ki*, or *chi*, is very important and emphasized from the beginning.

A typical tai chi class begins with a standing meditation exercise, in which breathing and mental exercises are combined in an effort to "awaken one's *chi*." Then comes practice in the solo exercise, or form. (Stretching and strengthening exercises are not done before the form because the form itself is considered to include all necessary exercise.) The form uses all 700-plus muscles in the body, and by the time students have done all the twists and turns, and the leg, arm, and waist movements, while keeping perfect control and balance, they have had a complete workout.

As students become more proficient, they move on to working in pairs. One of the most common exercises done in pairs is called push hands, and in it the partners face each other with their wrists and forearms touching. Keeping in contact all the time, they practice yielding and pushing, yielding and pushing, until they develop the ability to sense what the partner is going to do ahead of time and foil the intended move. The objective is not to meet force with force but to quickly yield, providing no resistance, so that the force loses its intended power and the other person's momentum can be used to topple him or her with only a slight push or pull.

At more advanced levels, students learn forms with swords, spears, and staffs, two-person forms, and faster, more acrobatic solo forms.

Clothing and Equipment

Clothing for the martial arts is simple. For tai chi, students wear loose clothing that allows them to stretch, twist, and bend with ease. Some participants wear soft shoes, also. For karate, tae kwon do, and judo, pajama-like uniforms are worn and for aikido either the same kind of uniform or *hakamas*, wide flowing pants that look like long skirts. In judo, karate, and tae kwon do a special belt is tied around the uniform (as it is at some aikido schools), with the color of the belt showing what rank the student has reached.

Different styles and schools of the martial arts use different progressions of belt colors, but they generally progress from light to dark. According to one legend, this is because at one time students were not allowed to wash their uniform belts. Over years of sweat and toil the belts, which had started off colorless, gradually got darker, making it easy for everyone to see who had been practicing—and presumably perfecting—the martial arts the longest. When colored belts were introduced in the 20th century, it was decided that the same light to dark progression would be used, ending with black. (Although most people think a "black belt" is an expert martial artist, this is not necessarily so. There are many ranks of black belt and the first one means only that a student is an experienced beginner.)

Benefits

An official of the Taekwondo Union has been quoted as saying that a 75-minute tae kwon do class is the equivalent of 45 minutes of aerobics, 45

A good martial arts class provides a thorough physical workout.

minutes of calisthenics, *and* 45 minutes of yoga. Not all physical fitness experts agree that the martial arts have what is called aerobic benefit—the conditioning of the heart and circulatory system that generally comes from at least 30 minutes of uninterrupted vigorous exercise several times a week. They do agree, though, that the martial arts will make you strong and flexible while improving coordination and balance, with the level of each kind of benefit varying according to the art. In tae kwon do, for example, the legs and hips become particularly strong, and in karate, where hand techniques are stressed, the strength and grace of the wrists are developed. Tai chi and aikido, while they provide a less vigorous workout than the others, develop especially good muscle tone, flexibility, grace, and balance. With any of the arts, you can get a thorough workout from a good class, for you'll be using muscles from every part of your body, including some you didn't know you had.

Beyond the physical conditioning, say martial arts enthusiasts, are the mental benefits to be gained. Not only do the martial arts develop amazing powers of concentration, advocates say, they teach patience, humility, and respect for others; they teach endurance, both physical and mental; and they teach mind and body to work in harmony so that, when the situation calls for it, you are able to respond with lightning-quick reflexes. And if that isn't enough, the martial arts can play the same role as any other sport or exercise in relieving stress, can provide hours of enjoyment—and can arm you with self-defense techniques.

Finding the Right Class

Once you've decided that the martial arts—or a particular type—is for you, you should learn as much as possible about available classes. (Taking class three times a week is recommended to get the full benefits of the martial arts.) A local Y, college, or recreation center may give classes, and they will certainly be cheaper than the commercial schools. Before you sign up with a commercial school, ask if you can watch a class, or even take a free introductory class. Move on if you're not allowed to observe—you can't tell whether a class is right for you without seeing it in action first. When observing a class, watch both teacher and students. Does the teacher explain clearly what is to be done, rather than merely demonstrate and leave students to copy? Is the teacher patient and encouraging with the students? Are the students enthusiastic? Do they help each other? Is the atmosphere friendly and polite? If you are investigating a school for a son or daughter, check that the teacher is watching students carefully enough to intervene in time if the children become too aggressive.

If you can, choose a school that has been in business for at least three years—nearly 75 percent of new schools fail in their first year. Make sure that the instructor has several years of experience (black belt experience in the arts that use the belt system) and that the person you observed will actually be doing the teaching. Rates at commercial schools vary greatly. Try to find a school that allows you to pay by the month rather than making you sign a long-term contract, in case you want to drop out or change schools. □

Mental benefits, say advocates, can range from improved powers of concentration to greater patience and humility.

Looking Into the Body

William R. Hendee, Ph.D.

People are living longer than ever before. In the United States life expectancy has increased by nearly 30 years since 1900. Partly this reflects improved sanitation, immunization against childhood diseases, better working conditions, and the adoption of healthier diets and lifestyles. But progress in treating disease and injuries has also played a major role. And the success of that role has depended largely on advances in detecting and diagnosing health problems. Doctors now have tools enabling them to actually see the state of things within the body.

These remarkable devices avoid the risks—and pain—associated with exploratory surgery. Some, like the flexible slender fiber-optic instruments called endoscopes, still require entry into the body through openings such as the mouth or anus. But others yield images from inside the

A CT scanner with the monitor showing a "slice" of the patient's head

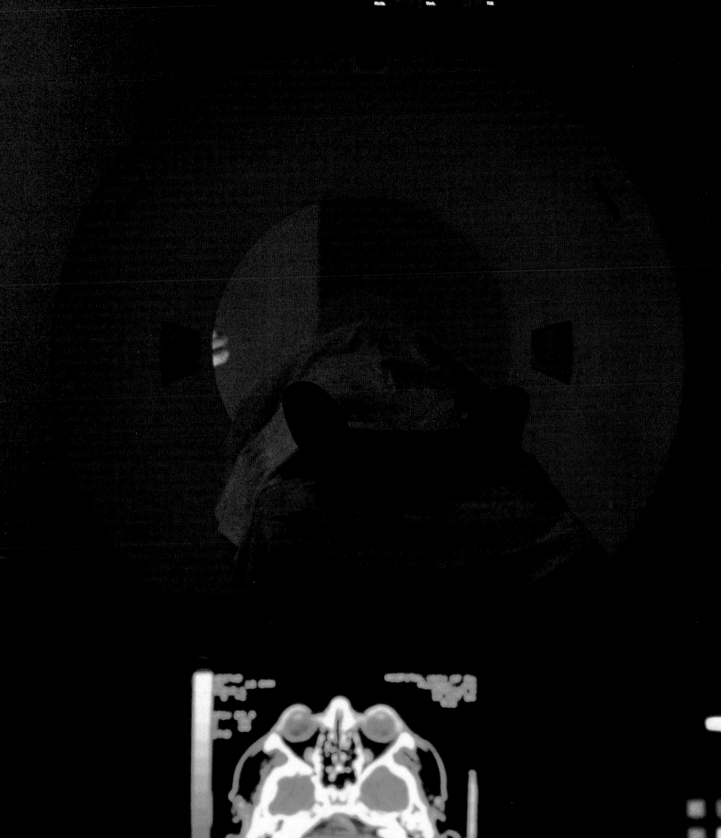

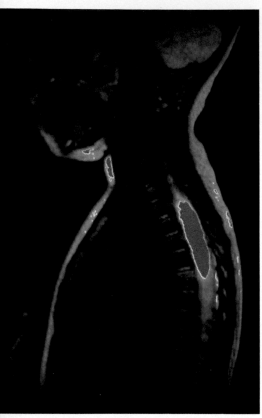

This magnetic resonance scan of a four-year-old girl has been color enhanced; the long, red object is a tumor growing in her spinal cord.

body in a manner that may not be "invasive" at all. They rely on various technologies. One—computed tomography, or CT scanning—is a sophisticated variation on conventional X rays, while ultrasound, or sonography, uses sound waves; a third technology, magnetic resonance imaging, is borrowed from chemistry, and a fourth, nuclear imaging, draws on research on radioactivity. In some cases these imaging techniques can show not only how an organ looks but how it is functioning. They have evolved rapidly over the past two decades, and one or more are now included in the medical "workup" of almost every patient admitted to a hospital or examined elsewhere for a medical complaint. Advances continue to be made in all areas of imaging, and the ultimate contribution of the techniques to medical practice will be limited only by researchers' ingenuity and the resources available to support them.

X Rays: The First Breakthrough

Even today, diagnosing an illness or injury can sometimes challenge the most experienced doctors. Before the turn of the century, a diagnosis was often more of a guess than a certainty. Besides the patient's complaints, the physician relied on observation of external signs such as fever, abnormal skin color, and chest sounds, measurements of pulse and breathing rate, and a general knowledge of infectious diseases prevalent in the community. There was no way to look into the body. Frequently, unable to identify the cause of a health problem or a method for treatment, the physician could offer little more than relief of symptoms.

A major breakthrough came in 1895 when the German physicist Wilhelm Conrad Roentgen discovered X rays. These were a form of radiation that could penetrate the human body and produce photographic images showing internal tissues. Word of Roentgen's discovery spread quickly, and by 1900, X rays were being used in many parts of the world to diagnose various illnesses and injuries. Physicians finally had a way to peer into the body to identify the cause of a patient's ailments. The discovery, however, was followed by the finding that radiation, in large quantities, could damage tissue. During early research on X-ray properties a few experimenters developed burns and skin ulcers, some of which progressed to cancer.

For several decades after 1900 doctors used X rays for imaging without major changes in equipment or procedures. There were some advances, of course. New X-ray tubes produced more intense beams. Dyes capable of absorbing X rays were introduced to help make blood vessels and the intestinal tract stand out. Image intensifiers were developed to increase the images' brightness.

William R. Hendee is vice president for science and technology of the American Medical Association, adjunct professor of radiology at Northwestern University School of Medicine, and clinical professor of radiology and biophysics at the Medical College of Wisconsin.

Tomography: Slices of the Body

The early 1970s saw a new breakthrough, reflecting a change in thinking about how images could be produced by X rays. When X rays pass through the body and strike a photographic film, they yield an image consisting of shadows cast by internal body structures. The darkness of each structure's shadow depends on the extent to which the structure absorbs X rays. Structures on top of each other in the body cast overlapping shadows on the film, sometimes making it hard for doctors to distinguish each structure's exact features. Subtle features of anatomy may be hidden that are important for making an accurate diagnosis.

Several decades ago a technique known as tomography was devised to try to detect such subtle features. In tomography the X-ray tube and film are moved during exposure in order to focus on a specific slice—a single plane—of the body. This approach can remove overlapping shadows if the structures producing them are not oriented parallel to the motion of tube and film. Tomography is far from perfect, however, and great skill is required in interpreting the resulting images.

In the early 1970s a new form of X-ray tomography was introduced. Since it requires a computer, it is called computed tomography, or CT. (The name "computerized axial tomography," or "CAT scanning," has also been used.) Today, it is difficult to imagine the practice of medicine without the help of computed tomography. The impact of CT scanning in providing images of the central nervous system (the brain and spine) has been especially remarkable. Yet it was less than two decades ago that the technology first became available.

In CT a thin fan-shaped beam of X rays is directed through the patient from a number of points lying in a plane that intersects the body at a right angle. Hundreds of thousands of measurements of X-ray transmission are obtained with small detectors positioned around the patient. A computer analyzes the data to produce an array of numbers representing the extent of absorption of the X rays at points on this cross section of the patient's body. Each number is assigned a certain brightness in a black-and-white television display, resulting in a "gray-scale" image of varying brightness that reveals subtle differences in X-ray absorption, and therefore anatomical composition, in the patient. Color images can also be produced, but most doctors find color more of a handicap than a help in interpreting images.

CT has added a new dimension to doctors' ability to detect and diagnose disease and injury in virtually every region of the body. It is particularly helpful in detecting small density differences in the brain caused by cancerous lesions, accumulations of blood (hematomas) following head injuries, and abnormalities in the supply of blood. It is frequently the preferred method for examining the spine, being especially useful for locating and identifying the causes of back and leg pain. CT can often provide informative images of the chest, abdomen, and pelvis in cases where traditional X-ray imaging fails.

During a CT scan the patient lies on a table surrounded by a machine shaped like a large doughnut. The patient ordinarily experiences no physical reaction during the examination, because X rays do not

One or more imaging techniques are now used on almost every patient admitted to a hospital.

stimulate any of the senses. (In some cases a small amount of dye is injected to enhance the visibility of blood vessels or the spinal canal; occasionally the dye causes the patient to have a fleeting hot flash.) The amount of radiation to which the patient is exposed usually is no more, and is sometimes less, than that administered during other medical examinations employing X rays. The chances are very small that so little radiation will ever cause the patient to develop cancer, and the risk is greatly outweighed by the benefits of the examination.

Although a few seconds suffice to acquire the data for each CT image, a typical examination might take a half hour or so because many images are obtained. Since the price of a scanner can be hundreds of thousands of dollars or more, and since it takes several specially trained

persons to operate a CT unit, a typical CT procedure can cost several hundred dollars. Usually there are two charges: a facility charge for the use of the equipment and the time of the people who operate it and a physician charge for interpretation of the results.

Traditional CT scanners are too slow to capture the details of fast-moving structures like the heart or to analyze the function of joints such as the knee. A new CT scanner capable of producing images in milliseconds has been developed to analyze these moving structures. Called an ultrafast CT scanner, it is available today in a few medical centers, with more expected to acquire it in the future. These scanners offer no special advantages for most CT applications but are very helpful in looking at fast-moving structures.

LIFESAVING IMAGES

Both Joe Silvers (left) and young Ryan Petersen suffered severe seizures. They were saved by surgery after a magnetic resonance scan showed a tumor (here colored yellow) in Joe's brain and a PET scan revealed minimal activity in the left half of Ryan's brain.

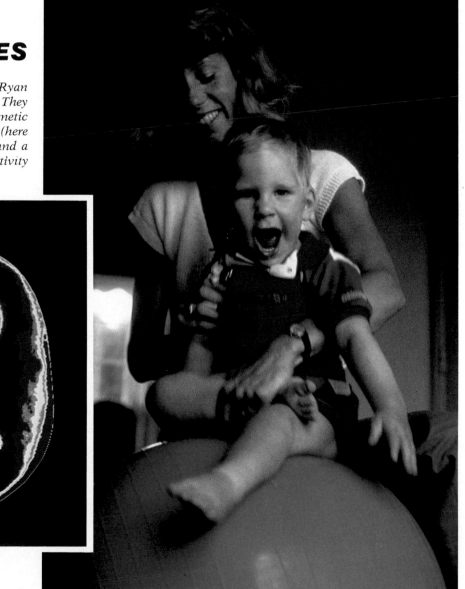

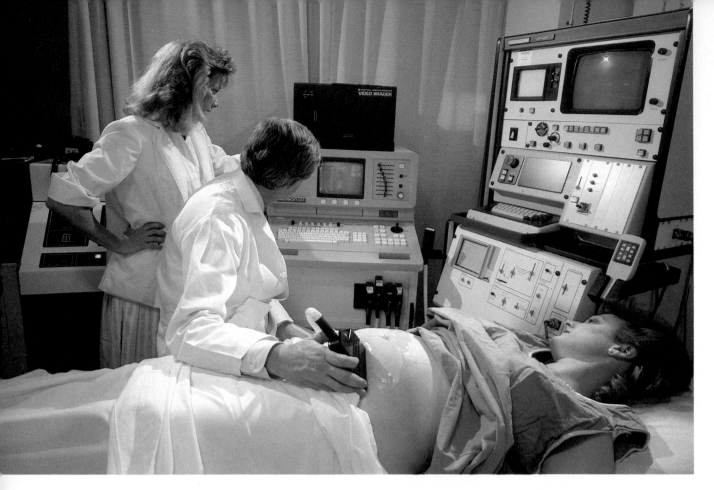

The impact of computed tomography on diagnostic imaging goes beyond improved visualization of anatomy. The introduction of the computer as an integral part of the imaging process has led to major advances over the past 15 years in nuclear, ultrasound, and magnetic resonance imaging. These advances have made diagnostic imaging one of the most rapidly changing areas in medicine.

Ultrasound

World War I brought the use of sound waves for detection of underwater objects, and by World War II sound waves (sonar) had become an essential part of naval warfare against submarines. The wartime effort required a large amount of electronic equipment, much of which was declared surplus at the war's end, with some finding its way to researchers interested in imaging the human body. Their work helped move sonography into the position of prominence that it holds today in medicine.

Sound waves are vibrations that move through a material, such as a body tissue, when a source of sonic energy is placed on or near it. The human ear can detect waves that have a frequency of 20 to 20,000 hertz (or cycles per second). Vibrations with a higher frequency are called ultrasound waves. Sonographic imaging uses frequencies of 1-20 million hertz, most commonly between 2 million and 7 million hertz. The patient experiences no sensation on exposure to ultrasound, feeling only a slight pressure on the skin as the probe ("transducer") producing the sound waves is moved on the skin surface. Ultrasound at the

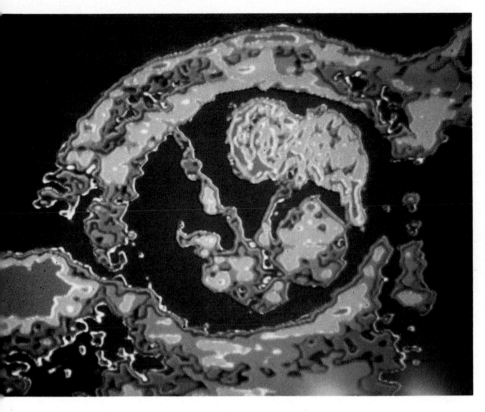

PICTURES OF PREGNANCY

The safest technique for scanning a pregnant woman is ultrasound. On the opposite page the doctor is obtaining a sonogram of a woman in her sixth month of pregnancy. The "transducer" he is holding on her abdomen emits sound waves; they are reflected by the fetus back to the transducer, which converts them into electrical signals for processing. The color-enhanced scan at left shows twins at ten weeks.

intensities employed for diagnostic purposes presents no risk to the patient.

During a sonogram the transducer directs a thousand or so small bursts of ultrasound into the body each second. As each burst encounters a boundary between tissues, some of the energy is reflected back to the transducer, where it produces a tiny electrical signal. By timing the interval between the release of a burst and the arrival of an echo, the depth of the boundary below the skin can be estimated. The sonographic equipment uses this information, together with the angle at which the transducer is oriented, to position a flash of light on a display. The flash corresponds to the location of the tissue boundary producing the echo. The intensity of the light flash depends on the amount of ultrasound energy reflected at the boundary. By compiling light flashes for various boundaries between tissues, an image is constructed of tissues under the skin surface. This image (sometimes called an echogram) can provide an excellent view into the body.

In the 1950s and 1960s ultrasound imaging techniques were rather primitive, but their evolution speeded up in the early 1970s with two major developments: gray-scale imaging and real-time sonographic techniques. The former made images more realistic by increasing their ability to depict the intensity of reflected ultrasound energy in an exact fashion. The latter enhanced the ability of ultrasound to depict moving structures by providing television-like images. These developments were made possible in large measure by the addition of a computer to ultrasound equipment.

Ultrasound is now used to depict structures in many parts of the body. One of its most common applications is to image the unborn baby, or fetus, during pregnancy, primarily in order to identify problems that might arise in the birth process and to find ways to avert these problems—for example, a cesarean delivery might be called for. A sonogram also can help detect difficulties that might compromise the health of the mother or baby during pregnancy and can be used to monitor the success of efforts to reduce these difficulties. Today in the United States most women under the care of a physician receive at least one sonogram during pregnancy. A major advantage of ultrasound in pregnancy is that it does not use X rays or other forms of radiation that might be hazardous to the fetus.

Another major application of ultrasound in medical diagnosis is in echocardiography, to evaluate how well valves and chambers in the heart are functioning and whether surgical intervention in functional problems has been successful. Sonography is also helpful in examining abdominal and pelvic organs such as the gallbladder, kidneys, liver, prostate, and uterus. It is normally of little help in the chest, because sound energy is not transmitted well through the chest wall and into the lungs. The adult brain also is not accessible to sonographic examination, because the skull prevents transmission of sound energy. Brain imaging is possible, however, in infants, whose skulls offer "windows" to ultrasound.

A relatively recent innovation is Doppler sonography, which provides measurements of the velocity of moving fluids, primarily blood, superimposed on ultrasound images. Often the measurements are depicted in color, making it easier to detect obstructions to blood flow indicating the presence of possibly dangerous buildups of plaque within arteries or abnormal vessel configurations that are hazardous to the patient. Color Doppler sonography is being used increasingly to replace more invasive procedures such as angiography (X-ray imaging after injection of a dye) for detection of blood vessel abnormalities.

A wide variety of ultrasound instrumentation exists, much of it relatively inexpensive. Sonography is widely available in clinics and physicians' offices as well as hospitals. Most examinations are relatively low in cost compared with CT scans and other more complex imaging methods.

Magnetic Resonance Imaging

The nuclei of atoms of hydrogen and a few other elements have magnetic properties and tend to line up in one direction when placed in a magnetic field. This orientation can be disturbed by subjecting the nuclei to a short pulse of radio waves of a certain frequency. When the pulse is finished, the nuclei tend to realign with the magnetic field and in so doing radiate a weak radio signal of a frequency that depends on the chemical composition of the material containing the nuclei. By detecting and analyzing this signal, the composition of the material often can be determined. This technique, known as nuclear magnetic resonance, has been widely used in analytic chemistry for decades.

An abundance of hydrogen is present in body tissues, especially in water and fat. In the mid-1970s researchers explored the possibility of

Magnetic resonance imaging can provide exquisitely detailed scans.

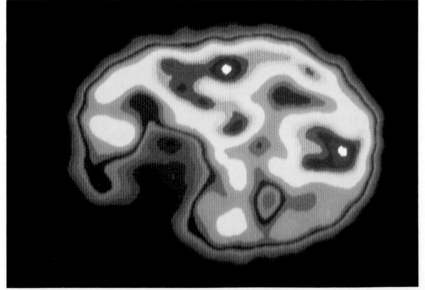

THREE KINDS OF BRAIN SCANS

The PET image at left uses particles emitted by a radioactive material. CT scanning, based on X rays, produced the computer-generated three-dimensional view at lower left; the red object is a tumor, and the white surface is the skull. Below is a color-enhanced magnetic resonance scan.

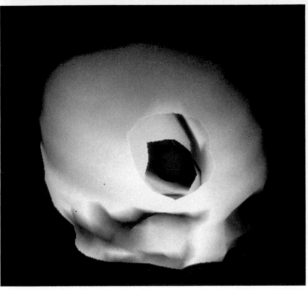

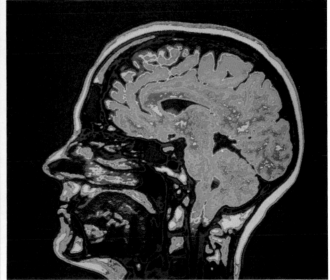

producing images of the body using radio signals released by hydrogen-containing tissues. Skeptics claimed the signals were so weak that useful images would never be produced. Yet by the end of the decade it was clear that magnetic resonance imaging, or MRI, was a promising method for looking into the body.

MRI is now used to examine many regions of the body, providing exquisite black-and-white images. In the brain it can depict various conditions, such as multiple sclerosis plaques and subtle hematomas, that are invisible even to computed tomography. Ruptured and bulging intervertebral disks in the spine are often studied with MRI using special equipment designed for imaging shallow structures. Fast-scan methods have been developed to image the heart, and pictures can be obtained of pelvic structures that are hard to portray with X-ray techniques because they are shielded by dense bone.

MRI is a complex new technology, and mastering it presents a challenge to physicians and scientists. Many experts believe that up to now doctors have merely sampled the ultimate potential of MRI for medical diagnosis. Researchers would like, for example, to combine medical images with information about the chemical composition of tissues obtained through the use of magnetic resonance spectroscopy.

During an MRI examination, which may require a half hour or longer, the patient lies on a table inside a tunnel surrounded by a massive piece of equipment not unlike a CT unit in appearance. No sensation is felt other than a soft thumping noise caused by shifts in secondary magnetic fields used to locate the origin of the weak radio signals coming from the patient. Many patients fall asleep during the examination.

MRI has no known biological effects, and the procedure is considered entirely safe. Occasionally a patient may experience claustrophobia because of the close physical surroundings of the imaging device, but this reaction is rather rare, even in people who have a propensity for claustrophobia. Of course, one should not undergo MRI while wearing metal objects that could be affected by the powerful magnetic field. Nor should the procedure be undergone by a person in whose body objects are implanted or embedded that could be moved or disrupted by the magnet—such as surgical clips, a cardiac pacemaker, or shrapnel.

MRI units are sophisticated electronic devices that are expensive to purchase and operate. Since a high-field-strength unit may cost up to $2 million, not every hospital can offer MRI, although some smaller hospitals may be able to afford to rent a mobile unit on a part-time basis. But MRI often provides information that is not available by other means or is obtainable only by more invasive procedures. In such cases the cost of an MRI examination usually is justifiable, and the patient, if at a hospital not offering MRI, may be referred to another institution for the examination.

Nuclear Imaging

In most imaging methods tissues are displayed by exposing them to radiation from an external source. But nuclear imaging, also referred to as nuclear medicine or scintigraphy, uses an internal source. A radiation-emitting material is taken into the body (by injection, ingestion, or inhalation), and the radiation from inside the patient is then measured by detectors outside the body. The radiation-emitting material, or "radiopharmaceutical," should have radioactive atoms that emit gamma rays. The chemical composition of the radio-pharmaceutical determines the organ or region of tissue where it localizes inside the body, and hence the part of the body that can be analyzed.

Although a few experiments were conducted in the 1930s, nuclear imaging really started after World War II, when nuclear reactors became available to produce the radioactive atoms needed for radiopharmaceuticals. The early 1960s saw the advent of new sources of radioactive elements for medical use and the introduction of "scintillation" cameras to produce rapid images from radioactivity

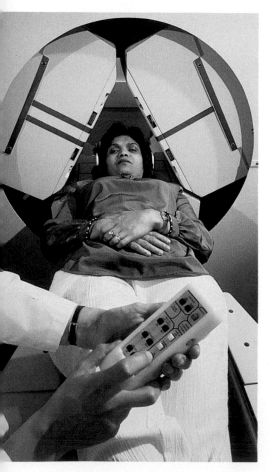

A patient lies in a SPECT scanner. Like PET scanning and other forms of nuclear imaging, SPECT scanning can be used to show not only what the body, or at least some part of it, looks like but also how well it is working.

inside the body. In the mid-1970s computers began playing an essential part in nuclear imaging, and imaging studies of the heart in action became a mainstay of nuclear medicine.

Today, almost every organ in the body is accessible to nuclear imaging, and doctors use nuclear techniques to detect many types of cancer, locate metastases, or secondary tumors, identify the causes of breathing difficulties, see functional difficulties in internal organs, and observe obstructions in vessels carrying blood, urine, and bile. In many cases the information provided by nuclear imaging is not obtainable by other means, because nuclear methods depict how organs function as well as their anatomy.

Two new approaches recently entered nuclear medicine. One—single photon emission computed tomography, or SPECT—displays tomographic images based on the distribution of radioactive atoms inside the patient. The images are obtained by collecting measurements at various orientations around the body and then processing this information with a computer. The result is an image of radioactivity in a single plane through a selected organ or region of tissue in the body. Often this tomographic image reveals abnormal conditions that would not be visible in conventional nuclear medicine images of the patient.

The second approach—positron emission tomography, or PET scanning—employs special radioactive atoms that emit positrons (positive electrons). The positrons are quickly annihilated inside the body by combining with ordinary electrons. As they combine, electromagnetic radiation is released. Detection of this radiation and its analysis by sophisticated computer methods yield PET images.

Positron emission tomography is an exceptionally promising method for studying the functioning of various organs, including the human brain. PET images showing stages in the body's metabolism of the sugar glucose reveal differences depending on the patient's emotional state, the type of stimuli to which the individual is exposed, and whether the person is experiencing a mental or emotional disorder such as dementia or depression. Through PET imaging researchers in the neurosciences hope to learn more about various mental illnesses, emotional states, and behavior patterns, including anxiety, drug dependency, aggression, rage, and criminal behavior. Largely thanks to PET scanning, the 1990s appear destined for significant advances in understanding of the human nervous system and the causes of abnormal emotional states and behavior.

Nuclear imaging methods offer many benefits. Because they use radioactive materials, exposing the patient to radiation, they carry a certain risk. But the risk is very small, since the doses involved are tiny and little radiation remains in the body after a day or so. Individuals undergoing nuclear imaging procedures experience no discomfort other than that which might occur upon administration of the radiopharmaceutical. Nuclear procedures are intermediate in cost between most X-ray examinations and examinations conducted with a CT or MRI scanner. Almost all hospitals of at least intermediate size offer some form of nuclear imaging. PET scanning, however, is available primarily only in large research centers. ☐

Nuclear imaging uses tiny doses of radioactive material, with little radiation remaining in the body.

Pesticides

Lucio G. Costa, Ph.D.

Editor's Note: *Recent extensive media coverage has focused the public's attention on the pesticides and food additives used in our food. What are these chemicals? Why are they used? Are there risks associated with their use? What would be the consequences of not using them? This article presents the analysis of a prominent environmental scientist, Lucio G. Costa, who teaches environmental health at the University of Washington.*

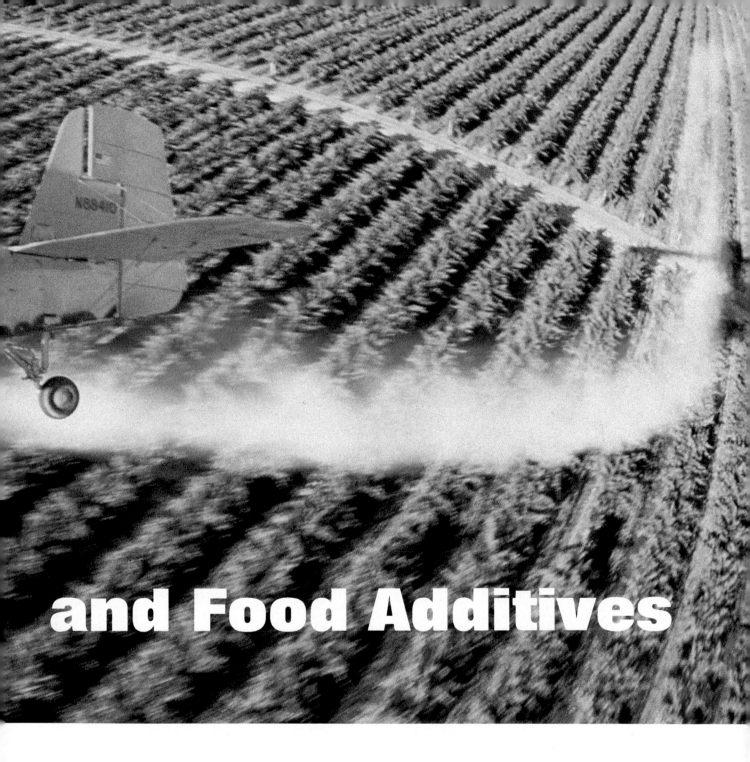

and Food Additives

The use of chemicals has made it possible to increase the amount of food that farmers can raise, to preserve and store foods for extended periods of time so that they can be distributed over wide areas, and to give foods the sensory and aesthetic characteristics that people find appealing. Two major classes of chemicals that have helped make these goals a reality are pesticides and food additives. Both remain under continuous scrutiny for potential adverse effects on the health of consumers.

41

FOOD ADDITIVES

Food additives are usually defined as substances other than basic foodstuffs that are present in foods as a result of any aspect of production, processing, storage, or packaging. This definition encompasses both direct food additives—those added intentionally for a functional purpose—and indirect food additives, such as the residue of a plasticizer that leaks into food from its packaging.

Direct food additives are used by the food industry to aid in the processing of foods, to enhance their appearance, to retard spoilage and maintain freshness, and to provide nutritional supplements. The intentional use of food additives can be dated back to more than 2,000 years ago, when salt was widely used as a preservative. The rapid development of the food industry in the 20th century led to a great increase in the use of food additives. Currently, about 2,800 substances are used as direct food additives in the United States. A handful of them (sucrose, corn syrup, dextrose, and salt) represent 93 percent, by weight, of the total quantity used.

Several additives are intended to aid in the processing of food. For example, humectants, such as the propylene glycol added to shredded coconut, keep foods from drying out. Emulsifiers, such as the algin in

Concern about pesticides has increased. Below, a farmworker gathers organically grown tomatoes produced without pesticides. Right, organic baby foods meet with approval.

salad dressings, allow liquids and solids that usually separate out to stay mixed.

Flavoring, appearance, and texturing agents are used to enhance or add flavor to food as well as to improve its appearance and its texture or consistency. Nonnutritive sweeteners like saccharin and aspartame (NutraSweet), the starches used to thicken soups and dessert mixes, and the pectin used to thicken jams are among the compounds that serve these purposes. So are natural or synthetic flavoring agents, from spices to fruit juices. Food colors serve only an aesthetic purpose, helping to satisfy society's demand for foods that are appealing to the eye in addition to having a pleasant taste, texture, and smell.

Some compounds are added to foods to prevent their deterioration during storage and to increase their shelf life. (Of the four basic food groups—dairy products, meats, cereals, and fruits and vegetables—three are highly perishable; only cereals have some stability when stored.) Antioxidants such as butylated hydroxyanisole prevent or retard chemical reactions that produce a rancid flavor in fatty foods, while preservatives such as sodium benzoate, nitrites, and sulfites destroy or inhibit the growth of microorganisms.

Besides improving the look, taste, and texture of foods, additives can aid in their processing, make them more nutritious, and retard spoilage.

Governmental and International Regulation

A number of federal laws regulate the safety of food additives in the United States. The most important of these is the Food, Drug, and Cosmetic Act—passed in 1938 (and since amended) to ensure that the foods sold in the United States are pure, safe to eat, and produced and packaged under sanitary conditions. The Food Additives Amendment of 1958 prohibited the use of any substance as a food additive until the producer provides evidence of its safety. (Exempt from this ruling were a number of substances already in use that were "generally accepted as safe" by qualified scientists at the time. Many of them have never undergone the kind of testing that is required of new additives.) The Color Additive Amendments of 1960 gave the U.S. Food and Drug Administration authority to ensure that coloring agents used in foods (and in cosmetics and drugs as well) are safe.

A section of the 1958 and 1960 amendments known as the Delaney clause states that "no additive shall be deemed to be safe if it is found to induce cancer when ingested by man or animal." Such additives, therefore, would not be allowed in foods. There are exceptions to this rule, however. For example, as a result of special congressional legislation, saccharin is still widely used, although research has shown that it can cause bladder cancer in laboratory animals when administered at very high doses. Because it is not reasonable to suppose that such high doses would be consumed by people, numerous committees of experts have concluded that saccharin consumption is no cause for concern. Every product containing this sweetener, however, must carry a label stating that saccharin has been shown to produce cancer in laboratory animals.

Since international trade in food products is increasing, problems can arise if a food additive is allowed in one country but banned in another. Several international agencies, such as the United Nations Food and

Agriculture Organization and the World Health Organization, are involved in the complex task of reconciling national and international laws regulating food additives. Generally speaking, U.S. regulations take into consideration the work of these two bodies.

Public Concerns

Among all the natural and synthetic chemicals introduced into the environment, current safety records rank food additives in a low-risk category. Nevertheless, questions about the safety of food additives are recurrent in the press and the general population. Are these fears always justified? A few examples will address some of the most controversial issues related to food additives.

Aspartame. The artificial sweetener aspartame, known by the brand name NutraSweet, is suspected by some scientists of being toxic to the nervous system when consumed in large amounts. When consumption is kept below the level of 40 milligrams for every kilogram, or 2.2 pounds, of body weight (a dose established as an Admissible Daily Intake by the World Health Organization), there is no significant risk of an adverse neurological effect. (To reach his ADI, a 165-pound man consuming aspartame only in soda would have to drink 16.3 cans a day.) However, while the estimated aspartame intake in a group of 2,000 households was found to be below the WHO's Admissible Daily Intake, certain individuals, children for example, might exceed their ADIs because they consume so much sweet food and drink. Animal studies have not shown aspartame to have any effect on behavior, but further clinical studies, stimulated by several case reports of aspartame-related neurotoxicity in humans (headaches, seizures, dizziness, or mood changes), are now being carried out. It is known that people who have a genetic defect known as phenylketonuria, which involves the inability to metabolize phenylalanine, a constituent of aspartame, must avoid consumption of the artificial sweetener. Thus, while concern by the general public about aspartame appears inappropriate, the potential health implications of its consumption are still under investigation.

Nitrites. A controversy also exists over the potential hazards of nitrites, which are used in the curing of meats such as bacon. Under certain conditions nitrites can combine with other chemicals to form cancer-causing agents in animals. Epidemiological studies, however, have not established an association between cancer and exposure to nitrites in humans.

Dyes and Flavorings. Yet another controversy involves artificial food coloring and flavoring agents. In the 1970s some of these additives were said to be possible causes of childhood hyperactivity and learning disabilities. It was claimed that the "Feingold diet," which eliminated the additives, alleviated hyperactive symptoms. Studies that tried to confirm these claims, however, failed to detect any effect of food colorings on the behavior of children. On the other hand, several compounds used in the past as food dyes have been removed from the market because of serious concerns about their toxicity over the long-term, especially their ability to cause cancer.

Among the additives that have caused controversy are artificial sweeteners, nitrites, and artificial coloring and flavoring agents.

Responding to consumer concern, some food stores have begun stocking produce that is certified free of pesticide residues.

The sign in the image reads:

Ralphs Puts Its Produce to the Test!
NutriClean, an Independent Certification Company is now laboratory testing random samples of selected shipments of
Ripe Bananas
for the presence of pesticide residues
You can count on Ralphs for Top-Quality, Wholesome and Nutritious produce!

.55 LB.

A Commonsense Approach

The overall approach to food additives should be that of a benefit-versus-risk analysis. For some additives, this analysis is rather straightforward. Thanks to preservatives, bacterial food poisoning from consuming spoiled canned food is now so rare as to make the front pages of newspapers. The benefit of artificial sweeteners for people with diabetes and others unable to consume sugar is also easily understandable. For other additives, the analysis might be more difficult. Information for adequately evaluating risk is still missing in certain cases. Most important, better means of assessing benefits need to be developed. A very reasonable approach for the decision maker, suggested by the late biochemist Philip Handler in 1979, remains applicable today: "A sensitive guide would surely be to reduce exposure hazard whenever possible, to accept substantial hazard only for great benefit, minor hazard for modest benefit, and no hazard at all when the benefit seems relatively trivial."

PESTICIDES

The term "pesticides" refers to several classes of chemicals deliberately introduced into the environment to control pests—plants, animals, and microorganisms regarded as undesirable. Pesticides are not new—for centuries farmers have used a variety of natural poisons such as arsenic, lead, and copper. Nor are concerns about their side effects new; over a century ago, journalists were writing about the dangers of pesticides. But the public largely ignored such concerns until synthetic pesticides, including perhaps the best-known, DDT, came into widespread use following World War II. After the publication in 1963 of Rachel Carson's *Silent Spring*, which pictured the natural world ravaged by pesticide poisons, scientists and government officials in the United States became increasingly alarmed at possible health threats from pesticides. Federal regulations controlling their testing and use were strengthened, and in 1972, DDT was banned. The use of pesticides in agriculture continued to grow, however. By the early 1980s ten times the pesticides (by weight) were being used compared to 40 years earlier.

The types of pesticides used most often today are insecticides, fungicides, rodenticides, and herbicides. Insecticides and rodenticides kill animal pests. Fungicides are used to control plant diseases, and herbicides are used to control weeds. Unfortunately, the great majority of these substances are extremely toxic, not only to their targets but also to human beings who are exposed to them. Insecticides are often toxic to the nervous system, and some rodenticides interfere with blood coagulation. (Perhaps not surprisingly, insecticides or rodenticides are the poisons of choice in murder or suicide attempts.)

People who work in the manufacture and application of pesticides are concerned about the potential long-term effects of prolonged exposure on the body's nervous system, immune system, and reproductive system. In addition, some pesticides are suspected of being carcinogenic, that is, of causing cancer. Pesticides linked to one or more of these effects are insecticides (particularly the widely used

Children consume much more fruit and fruit juice than do adults, raising fears that they are especially at risk from any pesticide residues in these products.

organophosphates such as parathion), herbicides (especially phenoxy herbicides such as 2,4-D), and fungicides. As far as the general population is concerned, exposure is likely to be to extremely minute amounts of pesticides present as (regulated) residues in food supplies; knowledge about the potential health effects of this kind of exposure is very limited.

Necessary Evils?

Considering all the possible problems associated with them, why are pesticides used? The principal benefits are in the realms of economics (to increase agricultural production), health (to prevent the transmission of disease by insects), and aesthetics (to avoid damaged food). More than 1 million species of insects and 250,000 species of plants are known to inhabit the earth; most are beneficial to people. Still, farmers must cope with pest insects or weeds for every crop they grow. It has been estimated that without the use of pesticides, world production of major agricultural crops would decrease by anywhere from 24 percent (for wheat) to 45 percent (for rice). This is unacceptable, particularly in Third World countries where the nutritional needs of fast-growing populations already exceed food production. In the developed nations, clean, good-looking food is synonymous with healthful food. Few people in these countries have been willing to eat grapes full of insect pieces or apples with maggots.

Without pesticides, world production of major crops would decrease by 24 to 45 percent.

Government Regulations

Pesticides are regulated in the United States by two laws, the Federal Insecticide, Fungicide, and Rodenticide Act of 1947 and the Food, Drug, and Cosmetic Act of 1938. In 1970 the U.S. Environmental Protection Agency was created to respond to growing concerns about the effect of pesticides on the environment. The EPA is responsible for reviewing all scientific data prior to registration or reregistration of pesticides. (A special review process is currently being conducted by the EPA to reevaluate information on pesticides registered before 1972, when less stringent requirements were in force.) The agency establishes the maximum levels of pesticide residues that can be present in raw food. This tolerance level is generally set by establishing an acceptable daily intake based on results derived from toxicological studies in animals or, more rarely, in humans. In deciding what is acceptable, the agency uses a "negligible-risk" standard—that is, a negligible risk is deemed to exist if the pesticide residue will cause no more than one additional cancer case per million people.

The EPA also sets what are called food additive tolerances, which come into play for a processed food when the concentration of a pesticide in the product (such as apple juice) exceeds that found in the raw food (apples). If the pesticide is a potential carcinogen, the Delaney clause, which forbids *any* level of a potential cancer-causing agent in food, is triggered. However, as applied to regulation of pesticides, the Delaney clause has been criticized in recent years for being rigid and unrealistic. A bill aimed at abolishing the Delaney

AND WHAT ABOUT DIOXIN?

One chemical that has generated great concern in the United States recently is dioxin. Chemical analyses conducted in the mid-1980s suggested that virtually everyone in Western industrialized societies has traces of the chemical in their body, so widespread is its impact.

In earlier years dioxin, a known carcinogen in animals, was produced as an unwanted by-product in some herbicides as they were manufactured, and thus could contaminate cropland and groundwater. (It was present in the defoliant Agent Orange used in the Vietnam War.) These herbicides are no longer used, and it is a different type of dioxin that is causing concern today, 2,3,7,8 TCDD. TCDD is released into the air by municipal and hazardous waste incinerators and, again, can end up on cropland and in groundwater. And, it has been discovered recently, it is formed during papermaking—the chlorine process used to bleach wood pulp in manufacturing paper products leaves traces of dioxin in paper. Paper products used to package or prepare food can then contaminate the foods with dioxin. The two major sources of such contamination appear to be milk cartons and coffee filters. The EPA is coordinating a federal interagency effort to assess the risks of dioxin in paper. The agency is expected to announce in 1990 whether it will propose regulations limiting dioxin in paper or refer the problem for further study. In the meantime, the U.S. paper industry is implementing manufacturing changes meant to limit dioxin residues in paper.

clause in favor of a negligible-risk policy was introduced in the U.S. Congress in 1989. The reasoning behind the controversial proposal was as follows. The overall lifetime cancer risk in the United States is now about one in four, or 0.25 (that is, one in four Americans will develop some type of cancer at some point). Adoption of the negligible-risk standard for a pesticide would raise the risk to 0.250001. Backers of the bill believe that this risk is trivial compared to the cancer risks associated with other factors, such as smoking. Opponents, however, claim that even a slight increase of cancer cases is unacceptable. Both sides have an array of scientific, political, and emotional arguments to back their views.

Recent Scares

Widely publicized events related to the presence of pesticide residues in food have occurred over the past ten years. For example, ethylene dibromide, which was used as a fumigant in grain, has been banned recently because of its high cancer risk for consumers. Several episodes of acute food poisoning by the insecticide aldicarb occurred as a result of contamination of watermelons and cucumbers. Besides the gastrointestinal symptoms associated with food poisoning (pain, nausea, diarrhea), aldicarb can cause blurred vision, seizures, and unconsciousness.

Perhaps the most notorious recent case involving a pesticide residue was that of Alar in apples. Strictly speaking, Alar is not a pesticide but a plant-growth regulator, which alters a plant's growth patterns. It is, however, regulated as a pesticide. Alar has been used for years on certain apples (and occasionally on other fruits, although in smaller amounts) to regulate ripening, increase firmness, and enhance their red color. Alar is a systemic chemical—it penetrates the skin and leaves residue throughout the flesh of the fruit. Thus, the residue cannot be removed by washing or peeling. In 1989 an environmental group alleged that residues of Alar in apples, and particularly in apple juice, would result in an increased cancer risk. Children in particular would be at significant risk—they consume larger quantities of fruit than adults do and consume more of such apple products as applesauce and apple juice; in addition, they eat more relative to their body weight than adults do, so that potentially harmful substances like food additives and pesticides are more concentrated in their bodies.

Confusion and fear soon became widespread; school administrators removed apple products from lunch menus, and sales of apples and apple juice plummeted. Meanwhile, a harsh debate began among scientists, consumer advocates, and politicians. Was Alar really a significant threat to the health of children?

Alar itself is not a carcinogen. However, a breakdown product of Alar, unsymmetrical dimethylhydrazine (UDMH), is a proven carcinogen in mice. Levels of UDMH in apple juice made from Alar-treated apples may reach 20 parts per billion (ppb). By comparison, a peanut-butter sandwich contains about 2 ppb of aflatoxin, a naturally occurring carcinogen present in corn and peanuts. Aflatoxin's carcinogenic potency is about 1,600 times higher than that of UDMH.

To encounter the same theoretical risk presented by a single peanut butter sandwich, one would have to consume about 26 glasses of apple juice. Thus, although Alar may present a small theoretical cancer risk to the consumer, the magnitude of the risk should be put into perspective. Avoiding apples, and thus missing out on the beneficial nutrients they contain, would not seem to be the solution. In any event, in response to pressure from the public and from the apple industry, which needed to shed the negative image it had acquired as a result of the Alar scare, the chemical—which had in fact been used on only about 5 percent of the U.S. apple crop—was voluntarily withdrawn from the U.S. market by its manufacturer in June 1989.

ASSESSING THE RISKS

Some misconceptions exist in our perception and judgment of the risk associated with pesticides and food additives. Driving a car or being exposed to cigarette smoke is much riskier than exposure to minimal levels of pesticide residues or additives in food. Contrary to widespread belief, people are probably safer today than ever before in history. Yet, we have the luxury to worry about subtle hazards that, centuries or even decades ago, would have been given a very low priority. This is not to say that potential problems associated with the use of pesticides or food additives should be ignored or overlooked. What is desirable is a more reasoned approach to these issues, an approach that takes into consideration the benefits as well as the risks associated with the use of chemicals. Increased knowledge and information appear to be the key factors both for toxicologists and regulators, who must decide what chemicals are allowable and at what levels, and for the general public, which needs to make informed choices.

Efforts are also being directed toward identifying new methods of food production and conservation that could reduce dependency on agricultural chemicals. Integrated pest management (IPM), for example, is being proposed as an approach to pest control that would be more friendly to the environment. This is a technique in which biological, physical, and chemical methods are used in combination to control pests. Among other things, crops are rotated, natural predators of insects known to destroy specific crops are introduced into the fields, the breeding areas of certain pests are cleaned out, and crops are monitored closely to determine when insecticides are likely to do the most good. Besides protecting crops, IPM aims to reduce environmental pollution, to cut down on the number of pests developing resistance to chemicals, and to avoid the harmful effects of chemical pesticides on organisms not targeted for treatment. Recent developments in genetic engineering add a new dimension to attempts to cut back on chemicals. Inserting specific genes into plants can allow them to become resistant to attack from insects or disease-causing viruses. These and other advances in biotechnology appear very promising for agriculture. They will not become reality, however, until they are proven effective and cost efficient for farmers and safe for people and the environment. ☐

In assessing food additives and pesticides, both the benefits and the risks associated with their use must be considered.

49

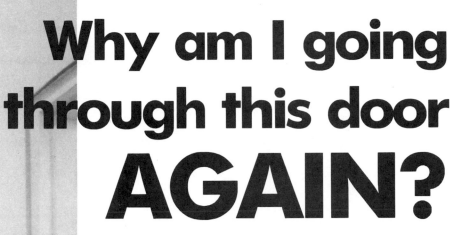

Why am I going through this door AGAIN?

Lorrin M. Koran, M.D.

Jennie cannot be sure that her stove is turned off, even after checking it six times. Her persistent doubt is an obsession; her checking the stove, a compulsion. Michael thinks that a bump he passed over in the road may have been a child's body. He has to drive around the block several times to reassure himself, and even then he may call the police on arriving home to make sure that no fatal accident has been reported along his route. His gnawing fear is an obsession; his circling the block is a compulsion. Both Jennie and Michael suffer from obsessive-compulsive disorder, a puzzling affliction whose victims are tormented by recurrent irrational ideas and feel compelled to engage in repetitive, often ritualistic actions.

The Symptoms

Obsessions are recurrent, persistent thoughts, fears, doubts, images, or impulses that are experienced as senseless, repugnant, or absurd. They are difficult—often impossible—to suppress or ignore. Unlike ordinary worries or anxieties, obsessions usually do not concern possibilities that the person regards as realistic. *Compulsions* are irrational behaviors that a person feels forced to perform repeatedly or according to certain rules, usually to prevent an imagined catastrophic future event or to restore a sense of being clean, innocent, or free of tension. Unlike gambling, or drinking alcohol, or eating excessively, the compulsions of obsessive-compulsive disorder bring no pleasure.

Many people worry a bit too much about cleanliness or have to check the door locks twice before going to sleep, but they do not have obsessive-compulsive disorder. Pathological obsessions or compulsions occupy an hour or more a day and cause significant emotional distress or interfere with the individual's ability to function.

Obsessions. The range of obsessions is wide. They usually center on aggressive or violent acts, contamination, religion, or sex. They may also involve hoarding, needing to know or remember something, lucky or unlucky numbers, superstitions or fears of becoming ill with dread diseases like cancer or AIDS. Aggressive obsessions include fearing that one may act on an aggressive impulse, shout obscenities, or be responsible for a catastrophic event through taking insufficient care. For example, a woman may experience a recurring impulse to stab a friend, poison her spouse, or even kill her infant. She may be unable to prepare food for fear that she will allow a piece of glass to fall into the food unnoticed. An individual affected by an obsessive need to know may have to reread a sentence or a paragraph several times to be sure of understanding it.

Contamination obsessions revolve around feeling fouled by dirt or germs, bodily secretions such as urine or feces, environmental contaminants such as asbestos or radiation, household items such as cleansers or solvents, or ill-defined sticky substances. Religious or moral obsessions involve persistent doubt and intricate analysis to determine whether some thought or action was blasphemous or immoral. The individual may wonder, "Was it sinful to want more?" "Am I entitled to take communion?" "Does God know that I sometimes doubt His existence?" This excessive concern is termed "religious scrupulosity." Sexual obsessions take the form of intrusive thoughts or images of sexual acts that are usually reprehensible. Hoarding obsessions prevent the affected person from discarding scraps of paper, newspapers, or

mail because they just might contain some important bit of information. The obsession may be so severe that the person's entire home becomes filled with these materials.

Compulsions. Cleaning rituals are the most common form of compulsion, followed by checking behaviors, but compulsions can also take the form of counting, repeating thoughts, words, or actions, touching objects, arranging objects symmetrically, hoarding, or having difficulty starting or completing tasks because of a need to carry them out extremely carefully. Compulsions are usually preceded by related obsessions. Cleaning compulsions such as excessive hand washing, showering, bathing, or toothbrushing are usually designed to remove contamination from dirt, germs, or bodily secretions. Affected individuals may avoid touching doorknobs, shaking hands, and using public telephones. They may wash their hands so often that they damage the skin and require medical attention. They may have to wash telephones and other objects used by others, or even the walls and floors of certain rooms. At times, they may feel compelled to discard clothing, small tools, or even furniture that they feel have become irreversibly contaminated.

The next most common form of compulsion is checking. By checking the stove, electrical outlets and light switches, an obsessive-compulsive individual seeks to calm fears that a fire may start as a result of carelessness. By repeatedly retracing the path from home to the local market, the individual seeks reassurance that nothing was dropped along the way.

Repeating and counting compulsions may be linked to superstitious fears or may need to be continued until the individual "feels right" and can stop. The individual may have to pass through a doorway exactly three times, or get in and out of a chair until the motions seem to have been completed exactly right.

Obsessive-compulsive individuals find it hard to resist their compulsions (although they may try, at least initially). If they are prevented from carrying them out by circumstances or by a family member or friend, they experience intense and growing anxiety and discomfort. These feelings may persist for an hour or more before beginning to subside.

About 70 percent of individuals with obsessive-compulsive disorder have both obsessions and compulsions. About 25 percent have obsessions

Lorrin M. Koran is professor of psychiatry (clinical) at Stanford University Medical Center and acting medical director of Charter Hospital at Stanford. He does research on the treatment of obsessive-compulsive disorder.

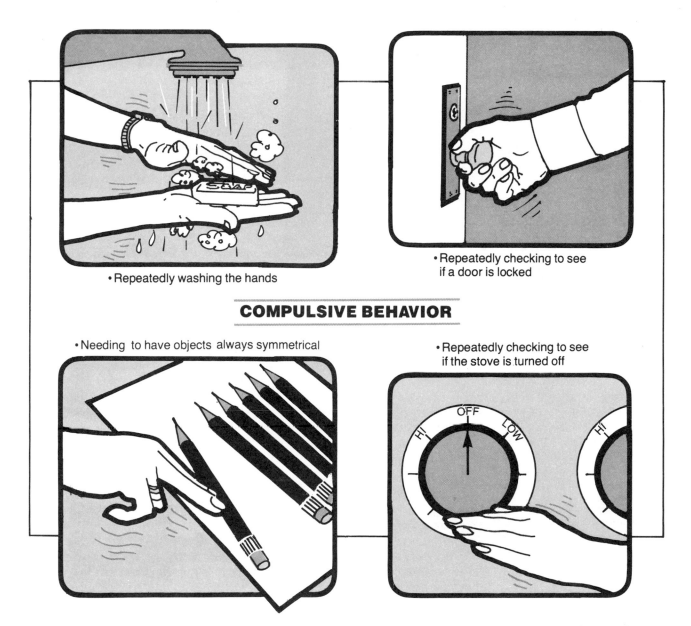

• Repeatedly washing the hands

• Repeatedly checking to see if a door is locked

COMPULSIVE BEHAVIOR

• Needing to have objects always symmetrical

• Repeatedly checking to see if the stove is turned off

alone, and around 5 percent have compulsions without obsessions. Frequently an individual's symptoms change over time, so that someone who was initially troubled by checking behaviors may later develop counting rituals or a need to reread.

How Common Is the Disorder?

Until recently, obsessive-compulsive disorder was thought to be rare, largely because those who suffer from it tend to conceal their symptoms and rarely seek out help. Scientists were therefore surprised by the results, reported in 1988, of a survey of households in five cities, involving more than 18,000 Americans. The survey revealed that in a one-year period, between 1.4 and 2.3 percent of the individuals surveyed had symptoms of the disorder.

Generalized to the United States population, this prevalence translates into 3 million to 5 million affected adults. Moreover, a questionnaire survey of 5,000 high school students in New York uncovered 20 cases of obsessive-compulsive disorder, or 1 in 250 students. This suggests that as many as a million children and adolescents in the United States are affected.

The five-city survey revealed that few participants with this disorder had gone to psychiatrists or psychologists for treatment. Most sufferers had kept their symptoms completely secret, and many had avoided seeking help because they were afraid that they would be labeled "crazy." Others feared that nothing could be done to help them.

The discovery that this disorder was much more prevalent than had been thought—25 to 60 times

Howard Hughes, the eccentric American billionaire/ aviator/movie producer/entrepreneur, suffered from cleanliness compulsions.

more prevalent than previous estimates, according to the five-city study—led to a great deal of media attention, including articles in national magazines and appearances on national radio and television programs by patients, physicians, and researchers. Such attention let individuals with obsessive-compulsive disorder know that they were neither alone nor crazy, and that effective treatments exist.

Who Is Affected?

Obsessive-compulsive disorder has been recognized for more than 400 years in the literature on religious scrupulosity. An early literary description appears in Richard Flecknoe's *Enigmaticall characters, all taken to the life from several persons, humour, and dispositions* (London, 1658). Flecknoe describes

obsessional thinking in a character he terms "an irresolute Person":

> he hovers in his choice, like an empty Ballance with no waight of Judgement to incline him to either scale. . . . Every thing he thinks on, is a matter of deliberation . . . and he does nothing readily, but what he thinks not on. . . . When he begins to deliberate, never makes an end. . . . Has some dull *demon* cryes, *do not, do not* still, when hee's on point of doing any thing. . . .

Modern studies show that obsessive-compulsive disorder afflicts people from all walks of life, although women are slightly more likely to be affected than men. Well-known sufferers have included the U.S. billionaire Howard Hughes and the 18th-century English lexicographer and writer Samuel Johnson. The disorder frequently begins early in life: some cases have begun as early as age 2, and two-thirds of cases begin before age 25. Only about one in seven cases begins after age 35, and one in twenty after age 40. When obsessive-compulsive disorder begins in childhood, the symptoms resemble those seen in adults. Thus, affected children may wash their hands excessively, have counting rituals or insist on ordering things in a particular, symmetrical way. Early in the course of the disorder, the child may be able to control the symptoms in public settings like school but may feel compelled to give in to them when at home.

Related and Unrelated Disorders

The American Psychiatric Association's *Diagnostic and Statistical Manual of Mental Disorders (Third Edition-Revised)* groups obsessive-compulsive disorder with the anxiety disorders. These include phobias, which are irrational fears of particular things or situations, and panic disorder, which is characterized by sudden episodes of intense fear accompanied by physical symptoms such as shortness of breath, accelerated heart rate, and sweating. In the five-city household survey, 47 percent of the individuals with obsessive-compulsive disorder were affected by phobias at some time in their lives and 14 percent were affected by panic disorder. The same survey found that 18 to 24 percent of obsessive-compulsives abused alcohol or other drugs. Whereas panic disorder and phobias tended to precede obsessive-compulsive disorder, alcohol and substance abuse tended to begin afterward, suggesting that the affected individuals may have been using drugs or alcohol in an attempt to ease their symptoms.

Between 30 and 40 percent of individuals with obsessive-compulsive disorder also suffer at some time in their lives from a form of depressive disorder termed major depression. Obsessive-compulsive disorder usually precedes the major depression by one or more years and tends to be chronic, whereas the depression is episodic, usually lasting less than a year.

Despite their somewhat similar names, obsessive-compulsive disorder is not the same as compulsive personality disorder. A personality disorder is defined as a maladaptive and inflexible pattern of perceiving, relating to, and thinking about one's environment and oneself, which leads either to significant impairment in social or occupational functioning or to personal distress. Individuals with compulsive personalities have difficulty expressing warm emotions, are perfectionists, insist on being in control of others, are excessively devoted to work, and have trouble making decisions. They may also be excessively conscientious, moralistic, judgmental, and frugal. True obsessions and compulsions are not part of this disorder. Few methodologically sound studies of personality disorders in obsessive-compulsive patients have been conducted, but available research does suggest that patients with obsessive-compulsive disorder rarely have a compulsive personality.

The irrational, unwanted thoughts that typify schizophrenia may appear similar to symptoms of obsessive-compulsive disorder. However, patients with obsessive-compulsive disorder do not appear to develop schizophrenia more often than the general population, nor is schizophrenia more prevalent among their family members, which suggests that the two disorders are not closely linked. Psychiatrists make a distinction between obsessions and the irrational thoughts (delusions) seen in schizophrenia. Delusions are experienced as coming from someone or somewhere else and are not resisted or recognized by the patient as irrational. Obsessions, on the other hand, are recognized as coming from one's own mind, are resisted to some degree, and are recognized as irrational. In severe cases of obsessive-compulsive disorder, however, patients may lose sight of their irrationality.

The relationship between obsessive-compulsive disorder and Tourette's syndrome is currently the subject of intensive study. Tourette's syndrome is a rare, chronic disorder characterized by recurrent, involuntary, and repetitive motor and vocal tics. Although the vocal tics involve a variety of sounds, in more than half of affected patients they take the form of an irresistible urge to utter obscenities. Many Tourette's patients have obsessions and compulsions, and obsessive-compulsive disorder appears to be more common in their relatives than in the general population. However, Tourette's syndrome is not more common in the relatives of obsessive-compulsive patients. It is hoped that the discovery of the cause of one of these disorders may shed light on the cause of the other.

Recent research has suggested that a disorder called trichotillomania may be related to obsessive-compulsive disorder. Individuals with trichotillomania—mainly women—feel an irresistible urge to pull out the hair on their heads, arms, eyebrows, and eyelashes, often creating bald patches or becoming completely bald. Although no large-scale treatment studies have been conducted, this disorder has been shown, in initial tests, to respond to drugs that have been helpful in relieving the symptoms of obsessive-compulsive disorder. At present, however, trichotillomania is classified as a disorder of impulse control.

Some Theories About Causes

Janet. The cause of obsessive-compulsive disorder is unknown. Several theories have been advanced, but none has yet been accepted as definitive. In 1903 the French psychiatrist Pierre Janet theorized that obsessive-compulsive disorder was one manifestation of what he called psychasthenic illnesses, all of which began with feelings of incompleteness and insufficiency. As the higher mental centers of the brain became depleted of psychic energy, he hypothesized, lower centers, with more primitive modes of thinking, took control. Obsessions and compulsions arose in the third stage of the illness, after a stage of excessive and repetitive mental, emotional, and behavioral exertions. In contrast to current diagnostic thinking, which considers obsessions and compulsions as illnesses in themselves, Janet considered these symptoms as only one possible final result of severe psychasthenia.

Freud. In 1907, Sigmund Freud, the founder of psychoanalysis, began the year-long treatment of a young university student who had suffered from obsessions since childhood. The case is known as the "Rat Man." The student was obsessed with the thought that rats would bore into the anus of his father and of a woman whom the patient loved. He was also obsessed with impulses to commit suicide, by cutting his throat with a razor, for example. Freud traced his obsessions primarily to guilt over wishes to see attractive women naked and to aggressive wishes toward his father and toward his beloved's mother. From this case and his evolving theories of the mind, Freud developed a theory of the origins of obsessive-compulsive disorder that dominated American psychiatry until the 1980s.

Freud theorized that the mind of the obsessive-compulsive patient, faced with conflicts between unacceptable wishes and the demands of conscience and reality, returns to early childhood modes of functioning that characterize what he termed the anal-sadistic phase of psychosexual development. In this phase, the ego, or conscious portion of the mind, tends to engage in magical thinking, that is, believing that thinking about something can make it happen in the external world. For example, a 43-year-old television repairman believed that if he had an evil thought while walking through a doorway, the thought might become reality unless he reentered the doorway while holding "good" thoughts in his mind. As a result this man often felt compelled to reenter doorways. In the anal-sadistic phase, the id, or mental storehouse of instinctual drives and desires, exhibits an ambivalent style of thinking, for example, being alternately in favor of and against a course of action. In the obsessive-compulsive patient this ambivalence causes chronic doubt and indecision and creates the urge to undo many actions. The television repairman's compulsion to retrace his steps is an example of the need to undo. According to Freud, the superego, or conscience—the part of the personality that incorporates societal moral standards into thoughts and actions—is also functioning at the more primitive level. This causes patients to regard many everyday thoughts and acts as taboo and to criticize themselves for infractions of minor rules. The television repairman felt it was wrong, for example, to sit facing directly toward any major compass point or toward a clock.

Freud's theory is useful in organizing the phenomena of obsessive-compulsive disorder. Its validity as a causal explanation for the disorder, however, has been questioned for several reasons. First, psychotherapy based on this theory does not seem to cure this disorder or to ameliorate it greatly. (Psychotherapy can, however, help patients cope with or overcome related depressions or tendencies toward isolation.) Second, drug treatments that do not depend on psychoanalytic understandings or techniques are proving moderately to markedly effective for many patients. Finally, studies of patients with obsessive-compulsive disorder are uncovering biological abnormalities in their brains. Whether these abnormalities cause or simply accompany the disorder is as yet unknown.

Biological Explanation. The biological abnormalities found in people with obsessive-compulsive disorder involve both brain anatomy and brain physiology and center on three related brain regions: the caudate nucleus, the orbital frontal cortex, and the cingulate gyrus. (Each of these regions exists on both sides of the brain.) The caudate nucleus is a structure deep within the brain located at a point just in front of the top of the earlobe. The caudate and the basal ganglia of which it is a part are believed to be involved in regulating and integrating bodily movements into smooth, effective motions. Recently, animal experiments have suggested that the basal ganglia also play a role in regulating the flow of sensory information to the cortex, or outer layer of the brain, where conscious and unconscious thinking and problem-solving processes occur. The orbital frontal cortex is located just above the bony cavity containing the eye. This brain region is thought to be involved in anxiety, impulse control, meticulousness, the inhibition of behavior, and excessively repetitive behavior. The cingulate gyrus, among its other roles, connects the frontal cortex to the basal ganglia.

Child psychiatrist Judith Rapoport and her colleagues at the U.S. National Institute of Mental Health used a brain-imaging technique known as computerized tomography (CT scanning) to study brain anatomy in obsessive-compulsive patients. Their study revealed that the caudate nucleus is smaller in patients with obsessive-compulsive disorder than in healthy control subjects.

Other investigators have found that the caudate nucleus in obsessive-compulsive patients metabolizes glucose (burns sugar for energy) at an abnormally high rate. Using a brain-imaging technique called positron emission tomography (PET scanning), Lewis Baxter and his colleagues at UCLA Medical Center reported abnormal rates of glucose metabolism in the head of the caudate nucleus and in the orbital frontal cortex. The abnormality in the frontal cortex—but not in the caudate nucleus—diminishes or disappears when patients are treated with medications. Investigators at the National Institute of Mental Health have confirmed the abnormal glucose metabolism in the orbital frontal cortex but not in the caudate nucleus, perhaps because of differences in the scanning techniques employed.

A number of other observations suggest that the three brain areas discussed above play a role in the production of obsessive-compulsive symptoms. As mentioned earlier, obsessive-compulsive symptoms are common in patients with Tourette's syndrome, and this syndrome is thought to be related to dysfunction of the basal ganglia. Another disorder thought to involve damage to the basal ganglia, Sydenham's chorea, is also associated with (usually transient) obsessive-compulsive symptoms. Finally, for reasons unknown, severe, otherwise intractable cases of obsessive-compulsive disorder have been ameliorated when portions of the cingulate gyrus, connecting the frontal cortex and the basal ganglia have been surgically severed.

Rapoport and her colleagues used these observations of biological abnormalities to formulate an ethological theory of obsessive-compulsive disorder. (Ethology is the scientific

Hoarding obsessions compel some people to hold on to useless objects such as decaying newspapers, junk mail, or shoes that no longer fit. The clutter may fill every available space in the home.

study of behavior patterns in animals.) Rapoport noted that in their uniformity many compulsions resemble the unlearned motor behaviors of animals, such as grooming, nest building and defensive behaviors. In some species, these behaviors are "hard-wired" into the brain's circuitry (that is, innate rather than learned). In humans, such hard-wired behavioral "packages"—if they exist—may reside in the caudate nucleus and other portions of the basal ganglia and may be regulated by cortical nerve cells, including those in the frontal cortex. Rapoport speculates that obsessive-compulsive symptoms may result when hard-wired behavioral packages escape from the control of higher mental centers of the brain because of malfunctioning of the basal ganglia. In some aspects, her theory is a modern biological analogue to the psychological speculations of Janet.

Treatment Alternatives

Both behavioral and drug treatments have been found effective for obsessive-compulsive disorder. However, about one-quarter of patients are too anxious to be able to cooperate with behavioral treatments, and more than a third do not respond to drug treatments or cannot tolerate the drugs. Still, there is much more hope for patients today than some 15 years ago, when a scientist who reviewed treatment studies concluded that no treatment influenced the outcome of obsessional illness.

Behavioral Treatments. Behavioral treatments are most effective for compulsions; obsessions respond less well. Behavioral treatment was first used in 1966 in an uncontrolled study of ten people who were compulsive cleaners. The patients were exposed repeatedly for a period of two weeks to two months to the situations in which they felt they became "contaminated" and were encouraged to avoid washing for longer and longer intervals. This technique, which combines exposing patients to the situation and preventing them from responding, has become the mainstay of behavior therapy for obsessive-compulsive disorder. In the mid-1970s, S. J. Rachman and his colleagues at the Maudsley Psychiatric Institute in London and E. B. Foa and her colleagues at Temple University Medical School in Philadelphia began a series of carefully controlled studies that conclusively demonstrated the effectiveness of the technique. In a 1984 summary of the research, Foa reported that of 200 patients

with obsessive rituals treated with this technique, 50 percent were either free of symptoms or much improved at the end of treatment, 40 percent were moderately improved, and only 10 percent showed no benefit. In follow-up evaluations carried out six months to three years or more after the end of treatment, 75 percent were much improved or improved and 25 percent showed no benefit.

In a related technique, Foa and her coworkers have shown that exposure in the imagination to the feared situation—for example asking patients to imagine "contaminating" their hands by touching the doorknob in a public bathroom without performing the associated compulsive ritual, handwashing—combined with actual exposure produces better long-term results than using only one of those methods. Prolonged exposure—say, for 80 minutes—to the actual situation was found to be more effective than exposure in eight 10-minute sessions. However, patients who hold a strong conviction that their fears are realistic and those who have symptoms of severe depression are less likely to benefit from behavioral treatment.

Thought stopping and satiation are among behavioral treatments that have been tried for obsessive ruminations. In thought stopping, the patient is instructed to relax and then think the obsessive thought. When this occurs, the therapist shouts, "STOP!". The hope is that, with much repetition, the therapist's shouted command will be incorporated into the patient's thought pattern and will bring the obsessions to a halt. In the few studies reported to date, improvement has been observed in only 27 percent of patients. In the satiation technique, patients are instructed to ruminate intensively on their obsessions or to write them out daily for an hour. The intent is to make the obsessions become boring and less able to arouse anxiety. This technique helped two of seven patients in one reported study.

Drugs. At least one drug has been shown to be effective in treating obsessive-compulsive disorder, and several others show promising results. In a small, uncontrolled study published in a Belgian medical journal in 1968, it was reported that clomipramine—one of a class of drugs called tricyclics that was used originally to treat depression—had benefited 10 out of 15 obsessive-compulsive patients. In 1980 several well-designed studies comparing clomipramine to a placebo (an inactive substance) gave more convincing evidence of its effectiveness. Subsequently, several investigators demonstrated that clomipramine was more effective than other tricyclic antidepressants in treating obsessive-compulsive disorder, leading to speculation that the way the drug affects the brain might hold clues to abnormal brain physiology involved in the disorder.

One nerve communicates with another in the brain by releasing molecules—called neurotransmitter molecules—that travel across the minute gap that separates one nerve cell from another and attach themselves to receptors on the second cell. However, many of these neurotransmitter molecules are reabsorbed by the nerve cell that released them, in a normal process called reuptake. Clomipramine differs from other tricyclic antidepressants in that it blocks the reabsorption of a neurotransmitter called serotonin. This has given rise to a new theory about the cause of obsessive-compulsive disorder, namely that it results from abnormal serotonin functioning. Based on this theory, investigators have begun testing other drugs that block the reabsorption of serotonin to see if they are effective against obsessive-compulsive disorder. Researchers have also begun to study serotonin functioning in obsessive-compulsive patients.

Several drugs that block the reabsorption of serotonin show promise. Fluvoxamine has been found to be more effective than a placebo in two studies, one of 19, the other of 42 patients. Fluoxetine (brand name, Prozac) and sertraline appear to be effective and are now the subject of carefully controlled studies. Although conflicting data exist with regard to the antianxiety drug buspirone (brand name, Buspar), some investigators are considering its use and the use of lithium carbonate (marketed as Eskalith or Lithobid) to heighten the effects of drugs that block serotonin reabsorption. Other drugs have been reported to help individual patients, but no data are available about their effects on large groups of patients.

In December 1989 the U.S. Food and Drug Administration (FDA) approved the use of clomipramine (brand name, Anafranil) for the treatment of obsessive-compulsive disorder. Anafranil was already available in Canada, where it has been marketed as an antidepressant. Fluoxetine has been approved by the FDA for the treatment of depression and many physicians are making it available to their patients with obsessive-compulsive

disorder. Data on its safety and effectiveness for this use are being gathered by the manufacturer. Fluvoxamine and sertraline are not yet marketed, but clinical trials to measure their effectiveness in treating depression and obsessive-compulsive disorder are under way.

About 60 percent of patients treated with clomipramine, fluoxetine, fluvoxamine, and sertraline have been reported to improve. However, about one in six of these patients develop unacceptable side effects, so that only 50 percent ultimately benefit. Usually their symptoms occur only half as often as before—or less—but do not completely disappear. Improvement begins to be noticeable after about 3 to 4 weeks of drug treatment and reaches its peak after 12 weeks or more.

Only a few studies have examined what happens when the successfully treated patient stops taking medication. In a study of 16 patients who had benefited from clomipramine for four months, 15 relapsed within two months when switched to a placebo. A study of patients who had been treated with fluoxetine for at least a year was more promising: three-quarters of these patients maintained their gains for a year after they stopped taking the drug. Long-term treatment may be needed to consolidate whatever biochemical changes the drugs are bringing about. □

SOURCE OF FURTHER INFORMATION

The OCD Foundation, P.O. Box 9573, New Haven, CT 06535. Tel: (203) 772-0565.

SUGGESTIONS FOR FURTHER READING

INSEL, THOMAS, ed. *New Findings in Obsessive-Compulsive Disorder.* Washington, D.C., American Psychiatric Press, 1984.

JENIKE, MICHAEL, LEE BAER, AND WILLIAM MINICHIELLO. *Obsessive-Compulsive Disorders.* Littleton, Mass., PSG, 1986.

RAPOPORT, JUDITH. "The Biology of Obsessions and Compulsions." *Scientific American*, March 1989, pp. 82-89.

RAPOPORT, JUDITH. *The Boy Who Couldn't Stop Washing: The Experience and Treatment of Obsessive-Compulsive Disorder.* New York, Dutton, 1989.

RAPOPORT, JUDITH, ed. *Obsessive-Compulsive Disorder in Children and Adolescents.* Washington, D.C., American Psychiatric Press, 1988.

STEPFAMILIES

Anne C. Bernstein, Ph.D.

ILLUSTRATIONS BY DOUG JAMIESON

"We were going to be the ideal unit," recalled Marilyn, thinking back more than 20 years to the time when she, the divorced mother of two boys, married Bob, a widower with three daughters. "My feeling was that the boys would have a real father, a person they respected and loved. And that I was going to be a second mother to these girls who had lost their mother. That's how we made a terrible mistake," she continued. "We pretended that nothing had happened in the children's past, that because the strength of our marriage was so obvious, so good, we were starting over. The girls didn't talk about their mother. The boys didn't talk about their father."

Marilyn and Bob are not alone. Like other remarrying couples of their generation, they believed that their love would be a new beginning for them and for their children and that they would recreate one big happy family from the pieces of two families fractured by divorce or death. Not until the 1970s, when professionals and stepfamily veterans began to write about how remarriage creates families different in structure and "feel" from the families that develop from a first marriage, did romantic visions like those of Marilyn and Bob come to be seen as unrealistic, hindering rather than helping the creation of new bonds among remarrying parents and their children.

Because stepfamilies typically come about through family loss— whether by divorce or bereavement—it takes time for the wounds of the past to heal and for supportive new relationships to develop.

Children often must come to terms with having a mother and a stepmother, a father and a stepfather, while all the adults involved may have to deal with one another to ensure the best interests of the children. Moreover, role definitions are fuzzy— there may be "extra" grandparents, aunts, uncles, and cousins—and financial arrangements can be difficult and complex. All of these factors can cause stress and resentment.

Members of a stepfamily household may not even agree about who they consider part of the family. A recent study of stepfamilies found that 15 percent of the stepparents who took part did not include a stepchild as "part of your family," even when the child lived with them. Stepchildren were even more exclusive about bestowing family membership, with 31 percent excluding a live-in stepparent from their list of who was in the family.

Stepfamilies on the Rise

Stepfamilies make up a large and growing segment of all American families. Approximately 60 percent of divorced adults have children, and each year since 1972 more than a million children have seen their parents divorce. More than 80 percent of all divorced men and more than 75 percent of all divorced women eventually remarry, often creating stepfamilies. In the past stepfamilies more frequently resulted from marriages cut short by the death of a spouse. Today, given the 111 percent rise in the U.S. divorce rate since 1970, in most stepfamilies a stepparent supplements rather than replaces a child's natural parent. By the mid-1980s nearly 10 percent of all households in the United States consisted of couples in which at least one member had remarried after a divorce. An additional 3 percent of all marriages included a widowed partner. More difficult to estimate is the number of stepfamilies formed by the marriage of a previously unwed parent. While approximately one in five children is currently born to an unmarried mother, and 80 percent of these mothers do marry

before the child is grown, there is no way of calculating how many of these marriages are to the children's fathers.

Demographer Paul Glick estimates that the U.S. divorce rate has reached a point where one child in three will encounter a parental divorce before reaching the age of 18. About two-thirds of these children will see the parent with whom they live remarry, so that close to one child in four will grow up having more than two parents. If children whose noncustodial parent remarries are included, and also children who acquire a stepparent through the marriage of a never-wed parent or the remarriage of a widowed parent, the number of children who will have a stepparent during some part of their growing-up years becomes even greater. Glick projects that by the year 2000, stepfamilies will be the single most common kind of family in the United States.

All Stepfamilies Are Not Alike

Stepfamilies are different right from the beginning. In *Love and Power in the Stepfamily*, Jamie Keshet contrasts nuclear families with stepfamilies. In a harmonious nuclear family, acceptance of children by their parents and vice versa is automatic, love and affection immediate, and authority inherent in the role of parent. In the stepfamily, acceptance takes time, authority must be acquired, love may never be strong, and affection grows only gradually. Stepfamilies that look to the ideal nuclear family as their model often add unnecessary hurdles to the already challenging task of creating a household in which all members can feel at home.

When a couple have a child together, they are a twosome before they become a threesome. In a stepfamily, a parent and child may be the original twosome; then the stepparent, as the newcomer, tries to find a place in the family without feeling like an intruder, the stepchild is reluctant to let the stepparent in for fear of being excluded, and the remarrying parent feels like the rope in a tug-of-war between the other two. Stepparent and stepchild have to figure out how they will behave with one another, especially when the child has a biological parent in another household.

Such "territorial" struggles tend to be most severe when one group (or individual) moves into a home long occupied by the other—some members feel invaded and others unwelcome. Therefore, most

---

Anne C. Bernstein is a clinical psychologist in private practice in Berkeley, Calif., and on the faculty of the Wright Institute, where she teaches family therapy. She is the author of Yours, Mine, and Ours: How Families Change When Remarried Parents Have a Child Together.

experts recommend that stepfamilies move into a new household when at all feasible, or at least convert the use of existing space so that all stepfamily members share a fresh start.

New stepparents often feel as if they have been put to work without a job description. They may never have lived with children before; they have no legal standing as stepparents; and society provides them with no well-defined role. Those who are marrying for the first time are also giving up the dream of starting a family from scratch. Stepchildren who still feel the pain of losing a parent or fantasize about their parents getting together again may not want to be part of a new family. Torn by their loyalty to their other parent, living or dead, and to their original family, they are loath to accept a stepparent and chafe at having to live with a situation not of their own choosing. Often they have membership in two households, requiring them to get used to two different sets of rules and standards and to deal with the stress of going back and forth between two homes in which the rest of the family are full-time residents.

A parent often feels like the rope in a tug-of-war between child and stepparent.

Both children's desire to remain close to the parent with whom they live and their loyalty to an absent parent make it difficult for them to open up to a step-parent— even one they like. Many families report that children who got along well with a parent's new partner during courtship became "difficult" when either marriage or living together made the new couple more of a fact of life to be reckoned with daily. Since more than three-fifths of all divorced people remarry within two years, children have to come to terms, within a relatively short period, with a second major change not of their own making. "You guys decided this," said Judith at age nine, protesting the "rubber band life" created by her parents' divorce and her father's remarriage. "We didn't get to vote." When George's after-school program was discussing parental separation, another nine-year-old announced that "the worst thing was when my father walked out the door." "No," George countered, "the worst thing is when your mother marries another man."

Some children have a harder time than others,

Many books are available for adults and children to help them cope with new relationships.

and there can be variations in children's ability to adjust even within the same family. The daughter who was closest to her late mother may have the most difficult time in accepting a stepmother; the son who identifies most with his father may be the one to avoid his stepfather. But ambivalence about accepting a stepparent is a given for every stepchild. Four-year-old Jessica would calmly maintain that she could not stand her stepfather, even as she sat on his lap and hugged him.

A stepparent who does not acknowledge the changes that have occurred in the household may seem even more of an intruder to the child. At 11, Paul, sees his stepmother as having taken over his father's household: "I don't like things so that if you look at them you'll be blinded by the shine. She kind of just stepped into my house when she and my father married, and she kind of like possessed everybody in the house. All we do whenever we're there is work."

Even when changes are not dramatic, it's hard for children to figure out how to relate to a stepparent. Jason, a 14-year-old, reveals the confusion he feels in trying to reconcile having both a stepmother and a mother: "You have another woman who's living with your father, and obviously has some responsibility of the house, and of you. It's hard to understand why she's there, and what she's doing to be there. It's been hard for me to completely understand what her role is. Oftentimes that's why there are fights and stuff like that."

Stages of Stepfamily Development

Psychologist Patricia Papernow has described several stages that a group formed by remarriage goes through before it begins to feel like a family. During the "Early Stages," parents and stepparents try to enact the myth of an instant family, making whole what had been broken, healing with their love the wounds of loss, and rescuing children they see as traumatized, neglected, or abused. Children, however, hang on to the fantasy that their own parents will somehow get back together again, and thus the stepfamily will come to an end.

Later, as reality sets in, stepparents become aware that they are still outsiders, separated from parent and children by the life history of a family they were not a part of. As they alternate between attempting to join the family and retreating in exhaustion, frustrated stepparents blame themselves for the failure to form a cohesive unit. Parents face a different dilemma: as the ones to whom everyone turns—and to whom everyone's unhappiness is expressed—they feel that the success or failure of the remarriage rests on their shoulders alone. It takes time for stepfamily members to become aware that the problems they have in feeling like a family are built into the situation and are not a reflection of personal failure.

The "Middle Stages" of remarriage can be a pretty tumultuous time. This is when the stepparent tries to bring about changes that lead to inclusion in the family and recognition of his or her authority as an adult family member. This is also when one-to-one relationships need to be developed between different pairs in the stepfamily, especially between stepparent and stepchild, so that members of the new family do not feel that they have simply been thrown together.

When it is successful, this effort produces a couple that works as a partnership of equal insiders and a family in which each adult can be with each child without calling in a third person as an ally. Papernow estimates that it takes five to seven years—and courage, understanding, and lots of support—for stepfamilies to reach this last state, "Established Remarriage," in which intimacy and authenticity have been achieved in the various new relationships.

Different Ages, Different Reactions

The earlier a stepparent comes into a child's life, the greater the possibility for a relationship that approximates that of parent and child. Infants, because of their helplessness, are masters at evoking the affection and the nurturing instincts of an adult, and they readily accept and feel affection for a stepparent. Unlike, for example, a young stepmother who enters the life of a teenager, the stepparent who is with a child from the earliest years will earn authority by providing care and attention before asking for obedience. Although they may test limits, toddlers and preschoolers are more ready than older children to accept that adults—all adults—are, of necessity, in charge. Family therapist David Mills proposes that it takes sharing a household for half the child's lifetime for a stepparent to develop a parental relationship with a young stepchild. For example, it will take one year with a one-year-old, four years with a four-year-old, six years with a six-year-old, and so on.

In contrast, the needs of a teenager to be more independent of the family are at variance with the stepfamily's goal of forming a new family unit. The authority that a stepparent can expect to attain with an adolescent is therefore limited, and the stepparent needs to be less of a parent and more of an older friend. Flexibility and tolerance are required to deal with the differing needs of stepfamily members of different ages.

Babies know how to win a new stepparent's affection and readily give their own in return.

Types of Stepfamilies

While all stepfamilies deal with some similar challenges, there are so many kinds of stepfamilies that the problems and rewards of one variety may differ markedly from those of another. There are eight different stepfamily formations based on whether each partner is unmarried, divorced, or widowed. If we also consider whether it is the man, the woman, or both who bring children to the remarriage, whether those children live with the new family or not, and whether the remarrying couple go on to have a child together, the number of possible types of stepfamilies rises to 64.

The transition to being a stepparent is smoother for an adult who is a parent and therefore experienced in living with children. When both adults bring children to the new marriage, they will share the experience of being both a parent and a stepparent. Each knows firsthand that love for a child is not competitive with love for a new spouse. Each is concerned as a parent that his or her own children are treated fairly by their stepparent, while being aware, as a stepparent, how hard it is to gain acceptance and authority with a stepchild. Because each adult occupies both roles, their empathy for each other can be greater.

In this type of stepfamily, both Mom's kids and Dad's kids have a stepparent who is another child's parent and a parent who is another child's stepparent. Each child is aware of having an edge with one adult while knowing that with the other adult another child has the advantage. While children want their stepparent to treat them the same way he or she treats their stepsiblings, they don't want to feel that their parent loves their stepsiblings as much as the parent loves them. Accepting differences in attachment is a great challenge for all stepfamilies. Another equally formidable challenge is to make sure that differences in attachment do not lead to prejudicial treatment. Even if they don't feel the same way about each one, stepparents must be committed to treating all the children fairly.

Some stepchildren lead a "rubber band life," shuttling between two homes and two sets of rules.

The children an adult brings to a new marriage frequently are faced with the difficult task of getting along with stepsiblings. Sociologist Larry Bumpass estimates that 40 to 50 percent of children entering stepfamilies acquire stepsiblings. For many of these children, this means having to adapt to a change in family role or position. For example, an oldest child may become a middle child, an only child may have to share a room, toys, and a parent's attention for the first time, and the baby of the family may need to yield that position to a stepparent's still younger child. While rivalry cannot be eliminated, it can be reduced when the children are assured that their space in the family—both special access to their own parent and protection of their physical space and possessions—will be preserved, despite the need to accommodate to a larger household. Giving children time to get to know one another without the unrealistic expectation that stepsiblings will become best friends will allow them to make connections based on what they do have in common.

One study of stepsiblings revealed that the children were generally ready to like each other. Even when there were feelings of hostility, they were generally directed toward a particular stepsibling, rather than toward the whole sibling group. Poor relations between stepsiblings were blamed on differential treatment by parent and stepparent (a frequent complaint of college-age interviewees). Because the quality of each relationship within a family is inextricably bound to each of the others, when stepparent and stepchildren have a good relationship, stepsiblings are more likely to get along with each other.

Where Children Live Makes a Difference

The amount of time children spend in the stepfamily is an important factor in how relationships develop between stepparent and stepchild, parent and child, and stepsiblings and/or halfsiblings. Stepfamily members who share a home most of the time have more opportunity to become close and more opportunity to fight than those who see each other only occasionally. When children are a regular part of the household, routines become established, and new family traditions can develop.

On the other hand, children who spend time only occasionally with a stepfamily have less opportunity to develop new rituals and fall into family routines. It therefore takes special effort to prevent visiting stepchildren from feeling like intruders. Having a space of their own, whether it is a room, a bed and chest of drawers, or a closet, can help children feel that their emotional territory in the family is protected even over long absences. Reentry rituals, such as spending one-to-one time with their parent before joining the larger family group, can also ease the transitions that children and adults alike find stressful.

Yours, Mine, and Ours

The remarried couple who adds a child of their own to a stepfamily typically has both hopes and fears. They hope that the baby they have together will strengthen family bonds, demonstrate their love and commitment to one another, and provide a ticket of entry to the stepparent who may feel excluded from the parent-child relationship that preceded the remarriage. They fear that the older children, especially if they are not full-time residents, will feel replaced and will resent yet another change.

Having a child in remarriage can help to make a stepfamily feel more permanent. One stepfather described feeling indissolubly connected to his stepson "because my daughter is his sister." The new child can create a bridge between two sets of stepchildren, since the halfsibling is the only member of the family to whom everyone is related.

Timing has a lot to do with whether the child contributes to stepfamily integration or, rather, has a negative effect. The birth of a baby before stepparent and stepchild are secure in their relationship can distract the stepparent from the task of establishing authority and developing a relationship of mutual acceptance and affection with the stepchild. Because any change can be stressful, it is helpful to give all family members time to accommodate to the changes brought about by remarriage before demanding that they adjust to a new baby.

The birth order of other children also influences their response to a new halfsibling. Because their position in the family remains unchanged, oldest and middle children seem to have an easier adjustment than do youngest and only children. Age, too, makes a difference. Children between 10 and 13 seem to enjoy a baby the most, whereas children aged 6 to 9 show the most negative feelings. Preschoolers tend to show the ambivalence toward a new baby that is characteristic of children of their age in first-marriage families. Relations between halfsiblings separated by two to five years most resemble ordinary sibling relationships. This is especially true when the children share a home and there are only two children.

Stepfathers Versus Stepmothers

Family therapists who work with remarried families have long noted that families in which the stepparent is female—stepmother families—are more likely to seek out help than families in which the stepparent is male—stepfather families. This is despite the fact that stepfather families are much more common. Researchers who compare stepmothers with stepfathers agree with therapists' impressions that stepmother families seem to exhibit greater stress than stepfather families.

One possible explanation for this phenomenon is society's differing expectations of male and female parents. In most families—stepfamilies included—women still take the major responsibility for nurturing children. This means that women and their stepchildren have more contact than men and their stepchildren, and more contact—especially when it entails the traditional tasks of socialization—makes for more opportunities for

Getting used to stepsiblings can be difficult; an only child might have to share a room— and a parent's affection— for the first time.

conflict. The relationship between stepparent and stepchild tends to be most conflictual when both are female.

Stepfathers, for their part, tend to see themselves as less adequate and competent than their wives and stepchildren see them. Such a sense of inadequacy, perhaps combined with the guilt of not living with their own children, leads stepfathers to withdraw from involvement with their stepchildren. In one study, more than half of the stepfathers did not perceive mutual love and respect between themselves and their stepchildren, and only slightly more than half felt parental or saw themselves as helping to raise their wives' children.

Girls Versus Boys

Studies of children of divorce have identified boys as more likely to have emotional problems during the single-parent phase of family transition. But the picture changes once a parent remarries. Recent research indicates that girls whose divorced parent remarried were more likely than their brothers to show a wide range of emotional and behavioral symptoms of stress. These findings are in accord with a more general pattern of females being more critical about the quality of familial relationships and demanding more intimacy from such relationships.

Family Networks

For children whose parents have separated, home spans two households, so that a stepfamily is only a part of a larger system of linked families. How divorced spouses manage their continuing relationship as parents affects the degree to which children feel at home in both households and find an identity that integrates their inheritance from both parents. Children fare best when the adults in their lives display civility and mutual concern for the children and accept the shifts in household composition that often characterize stepfamily life. When emotional divorce has not accompanied civil divorce and marital attachment and hostility continue even after remarriage, children are caught in the middle, and new partnerships are endangered by old entanglements. Unresolved mourning for a deceased partner and parent also impedes new attachments, making affection for a stepparent or the welcoming of a new baby a symbol of disloyalty to the original family.

Enduring intimacy between ex-spouses can also impede the consolidation of the new stepfamily. After undergoing family therapy occasioned by battles between his new wife and his pubescent son, one 40-year-old remarried father who had continued to make all of the decisions about the boy with his mother, excluding both her new husband and his new wife, came up with this advice to others in his situation: "While you have a commitment to the mother of your child, when you get married you have a commitment to your wife that should be primary. You have to be clear about where your alliances are." For this man, being more connected as a parent to his ex-wife than to his new partner had led to "a terrible mixup."

Children need to feel that "it's OK with Daddy" to accept a stepfather and that "it's OK with Mommy" to embrace as a brother Daddy's new baby. When children are confident that their other parent, remarried or not, is happily settled in his or her own life, they feel free to relax into the remarried family. Having one apparently miserable parent enlists children's protectiveness, and in this situation to embrace stepfamily life with the other parent smacks of disloyalty.

Bonnie comes from a family in which both parents remarried after divorce. In her 20s now, she is clear that the "negatives have never been nearly as strong as the positives. I don't think there is really anyone in the family who would say, 'Oh, wouldn't it have turned out better if the parents hadn't gotten divorced and remarried.' The relationships in the family are good, and they're strong. Everyone generally likes each other and is happy to be a part of the family."

"My parents are still friends," said 15-year-old Pamela, both of whose parents have remarried and had more children. "They still think highly of each other. My father still thinks my mom is wonderful and that she's pretty. And my mom thinks highly of my dad. I've seen them sit down at a table and be happy together. As far as I can see, they really did love each other. And it's not like one or the other of them got hurt, it's just something that happened. It's not like there was a positive period in my life and a negative period in my life; it's just my life. I don't know that it would have been any better if they had been together. I would hope that if I ever got divorced, I could do as my parents did. Basically what happened was the best solution for everyone involved." Bonnie and Pamela and children like them whose parents manage to rebuild separate homes so that all are satisfied in their life apart are at a tremendous advantage.

The ex-spouse is not the only family member who influences the quality of stepfamily relationships. Grandparents, especially, and other kin affect how children come to terms with their stepparent and with any new children in the remarriage. A grandparent who is a self-appointed protector of a grandchild against the inferred wickedness of a stepparent can do tremendous harm. On the other hand, the grandparent who welcomes the parent's new spouse implicitly gives the grandchild permission to accept a stepparent as a family member.

Stepgrandparents vary enormously in how fully they accept their child's stepchild as a grandchild. The amount of contact between the generations greatly affects the relationship, and opportunities to get to know each other are often hindered by custody arrangements. But even when grandparents make sincere efforts to avoid distinctions between children, they do not necessarily feel a sense of kinship. While it is important not to create situations that make children feel bad—such as giving one child an expensive Christmas present and the other a trinket—even the best disposed stepgrandparents may feel more bonded to the grandchildren they have known since birth.

Building a Strong Foundation

The strength of the remarriage is the foundation on which any stepfamily is built. A loving, enduring marriage gives solidity to the stepfamily and provides security for all the children. Couples whose first source of emotional solace and companionship is each other have a better chance of creating a stepfamily that will endure. Solidarity on the marital front also gives parents the ability to be loving to their children without being overly possessive, since their own needs for closeness are met by another adult. ☐

SUGGESTIONS FOR FURTHER READING

For Adults:

BERNSTEIN, ANNE C. *Yours, Mine, and Ours: How Families Change When Remarried Parents Have a Child Together.* New York, Scribner's, 1989.

BURNS, CHERIE. *Stepmotherhood: How to Survive Without Feeling Frustrated, Left Out, or Wicked.* New York, Harper & Row, 1986.

KESHET, JAMIE KELEM. *Love and Power in the Stepfamily: A Practical Guide.* New York, McGraw-Hill, 1987.

ROSIN, MARK BRUCE. *Stepfathering: Stepfathers' Advice on Creating a New Family.* New York, Simon & Schuster, 1987.

VISHER, EMILY B., AND JOHN S. VISHER. *How to Win as a Stepfamily.* New York, Dembner Books, 1982.

For Children:

BERMAN, CLAIRE. *"What Am I Doing in a Stepfamily?"* Seacaucus, N.J., Lyle Stuart, 1982. (Ages 4-10.)

BOYD, LIZI. *The Not-So-Wicked Stepmother.* New York, Viking Kestrel, 1987. (Ages 4-9.)

BRADLEY, BUFF. *Where Do I Belong? A Kids' Guide to Stepfamilies.* Reading, Mass., Addison-Wesley, 1982. (Ages 7-14.)

GETZOFF, ANN, AND CAROLYN McCLENAHAN. *Stepkids: A Survival Guide for Teenagers in Stepfamilies.* New York, Walter, 1984. (Ages 11 and up.)

LEWIS, HELEN COALE. *All About Families—The Second Time Around.* Atlanta, Peachtree, 1980. (Ages 6-12.)

STENSON, JANET SINBERG. *Now I Have a Stepparent, and It's Kind of Confusing.* New York, Avon, 1979. (Ages 4-10.)

Breast Cancer

Detection and Treatment

Susan Love, M.D.

Breast cancer is one of the most common health concerns of American women. Almost every week, the media feature a story on this disease: new findings about possible contributing causes, new stories about how a well-known actress or political figure has dealt with it. Breast cancer frightens women on two scores: first because it has become nearly epidemic (it is the most common cancer in American women and the second most common cancer *killer* of American women), and second, because it has frightening implications in terms of body image. Modern treatments are addressing both of these aspects of the disease.

The most frequent symptom of breast cancer is a lump—though most lumps are not cancer but benign cysts or fibroadenomas (benign tumors). Not all breast cancers show up as lumps, however. In some cases the telltale symptom is breast swelling, dimpling of part of the breast, redness of the skin, spontaneous and bloody discharge from one breast, or flaking of the skin around the nipple.

Once a patient has been diagnosed with breast cancer, doctors try to determine whether the cancer has metastasized, or spread to other parts of the body—such as the liver, the bones, or the lungs, which are the areas breast cancer most typically moves to. A breast cancer in another organ remains breast cancer, with the particular properties of that

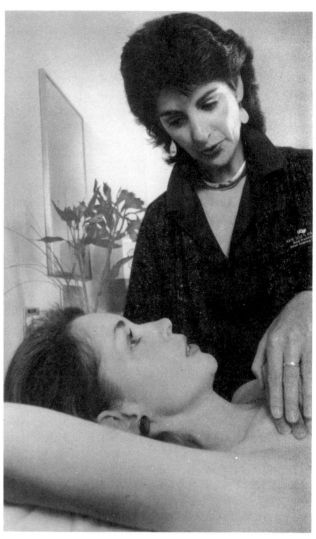

A woman receives instruction from a nurse on how to examine her breasts.

disease. For example, when breast cancer is found in the liver, it is still breast cancer, not liver cancer, and the drugs used to treat it are selected accordingly.

The process of determining the spread of breast cancer is called staging. Doctors have come up with four categories to define the extent of and characterize the seriousness of breast cancer spread.

A stage one cancer is one in which the lump is small—less than 2 centimeters across at its widest part (a centimeter is about two-fifths of an inch)—and there is no evidence of spread to underarm lymph nodes. (Lymph nodes are part of the lymphatic system, which circulates a fluid called lymph throughout the body and plays a role in defending the body against disease. Cancerous cells in the lymph nodes indicate to doctors the strong possibility that there are also microscopic breast cancer cells in other parts of the body.) A stage two cancer is a tumor up to 2 centimeters with "positive" nodes—that is, evidence of cancer in the lymph nodes—a tumor of 2 to 5 centimeters with positive or negative nodes, or a tumor of more than 5 centimeters with negative nodes. A stage three cancer includes a tumor of more than 5 centimeters with positive underarm nodes, or a tumor that has spread to the chest wall, the skin, or distant nodes. A stage four cancer is one that is known to have spread to other organs.

Surgery is generally the initial form of treatment for breast cancer, sometimes alone, sometimes accompanied by radiation, chemotherapy (anticancer drugs), or hormone therapy. According to the U.S. National Cancer Institute, women with stage one breast cancer have an 85 percent survival rate at five years after diagnosis; with stage two, 66 percent; with stage three, 41 percent; and with stage four, 10 percent. However, the increasing use of chemotherapy following surgery is likely to alter these statistics.

Detection

As the above statistics show, the earlier the stage at which breast cancer is detected, the better are a woman's chances of surviving it. Some cancers are discovered during routine checkups by doctors. Others are found on mammograms (X rays of the breast). By far the greatest number, however, are discovered by the woman herself, either when she happens to notice a lump that was not there before or when she detects one during breast self-examination.

Breast Self-Examination. Regular breast self-examination (BSE) is a useful way for a woman to know what her breasts usually feel like, so that she can be aware of any possible changes. Self-examination should be done every month, at a consistent time. The best time for a woman in her

menstruating years is at the end of her period; otherwise, a day that is easy to remember should be chosen, such as the first day of the month.

To begin her regular breast self-examination, a woman should look in the mirror for obvious changes—an unfamiliar dimpling of the breast or a newly inverted nipple. Rarely, a lump will be visible. Or there might be what appears like eczema on the nipple: this can be real eczema, but it can also be a sign of a cancer called Paget's disease. Or the woman might notice some nipple discharge that has not resulted from squeezing her breasts. (If a breast is squeezed hard enough, it will usually produce some kind of discharge. The time to be concerned is when discharge appears spontaneously.) Or the veins may be suddenly prominent (in a pregnant woman, however, this prominence is probably related to her pregnancy). None of these signs will be subtle.

It is easiest to see changes in the breasts by putting the arms up to stretch the tissue out, and then putting the hands on the hips and pushing in, contracting the pectoral (chest) muscles.

The second part of BSE involves palpating the breasts, or examining them by touch. Some women prefer to do this while they are soaped up in the shower—the soap makes the skin slippery, and it is easy to feel what is beneath it. To begin this part of BSE, the woman should put the hand on the side she wants to examine behind her head. This makes the breast tissue under the arm accessible by shifting it over the chest wall and sandwiching it between the skin and the chestbone. The breast should then be examined with a firm, but not rough, touch: too soft a touch will not reveal what is in the tissue, while too hard a touch will cause one to feel bone rather than tissue. Then the breast should be explored in a pattern that ensures that all the tissue will be felt. The pads of the fingers—the fingerprint part—should be used, not the fingertips, and the skin should be pressed, not grabbed.

There are several possible patterns. One popular technique is to think of the breast as a clock, with

Susan Love is the director of the Faulkner Breast Centre, assistant clinical professor in surgery at Harvard Medical School, and clinical associate in surgical oncology at the Breast Evaluation Center of the Dana Farber Cancer Institute. She is the author of Dr. Susan Love's Breast Book.

Breast Self-Examination

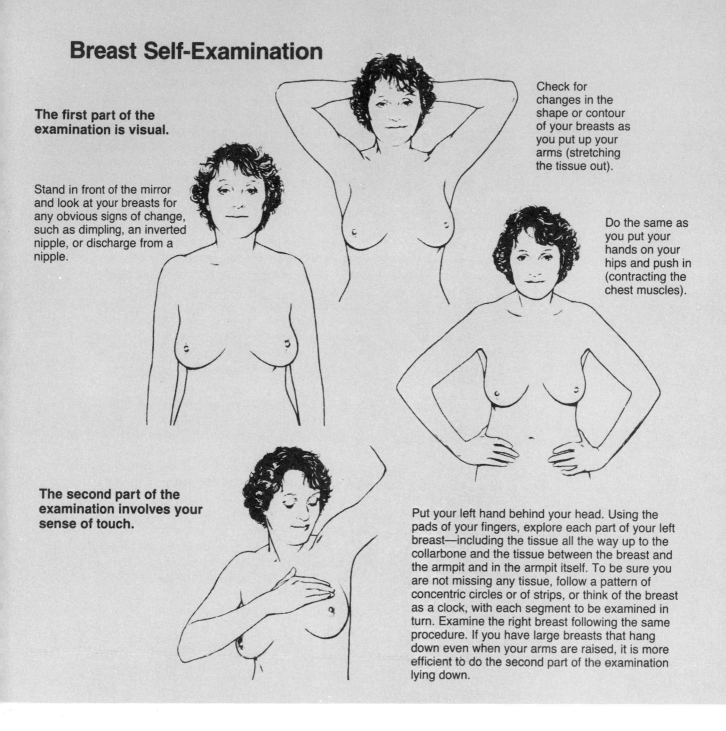

The first part of the examination is visual.

Stand in front of the mirror and look at your breasts for any obvious signs of change, such as dimpling, an inverted nipple, or discharge from a nipple.

Check for changes in the shape or contour of your breasts as you put up your arms (stretching the tissue out).

Do the same as you put your hands on your hips and push in (contracting the chest muscles).

The second part of the examination involves your sense of touch.

Put your left hand behind your head. Using the pads of your fingers, explore each part of your left breast—including the tissue all the way up to the collarbone and the tissue between the breast and the armpit and in the armpit itself. To be sure you are not missing any tissue, follow a pattern of concentric circles or of strips, or think of the breast as a clock, with each segment to be examined in turn. Examine the right breast following the same procedure. If you have large breasts that hang down even when your arms are raised, it is more efficient to do the second part of the examination lying down.

the nipple as its center, and to go through each hour of the clock in turn. (The breast is not, however, a perfectly round clock, and it is important for the woman to include the tissue above the breast itself, which is up below the collarbone.) Another pattern is to examine in concentric circles. Yet a third pattern is to examine in strips, beginning from the top of the chest and going all around the breast, strip by strip. It does not matter which pattern a woman chooses, as long as she picks one and sticks

with it. Each breast in turn should be examined in the same fashion.

Women with very large breasts might find that examining them standing up does not completely work: even with the arm raised, the breast may still hang down. In this case, it is probably better to do BSE lying down, using the same basic method just described. If a woman's breasts are so large that even in this position they hang out over the side of her chest, she can put a pillow under one shoulder, shifting her body to the other side and thus shifting the breast tissue toward her chest wall.

If a woman is doing regular breast self-examination, she should have a doctor examine her breasts yearly. Many women, however, are uncomfortable with BSE and prefer to have their doctor examine them every four to six months.

Mammograms. Another useful detection tool is the breast X ray procedure known as mammography. Originally, mammograms were used only in diagnosis: the doctor suspected a woman had breast cancer and wanted to get more of a sense of the shape of the lump and to see whether other lumps were also in the breast. Over the past two decades, mammograms have been increasingly used as an early detection tool as well. Usually a lump can be felt only after it has been present in the breast for a number of years. But a lump can often be detected on a mammogram before it has grown large enough to be palpable.

Mammograms have, however, engendered some controversy in the medical field. Almost all physicians agree that they are useful as a screening device in women over 50, and not in women under 40. (Breast tissue in a woman under 40 is too dense to allow the radiologist to see most abnormalities. If she has a lump her doctor thinks may be dangerous, though, she probably should get a diagnostic mammogram, to see if any further information can be gained.) Doctors have disagreed about whether they should be done in women between 40 and 50. Although this is still controversial, a number of medical organizations—including the American Medical Association, the National Cancer Institute, and the American Cancer Society—have adopted interim guidelines saying that after 40, every woman should have a mammogram every year or two. After 50 she should have one every year. These recommendations will undoubtedly be revised as

The breast X ray, or mammogram, is a useful early detection tool. It can often reveal a lump before it has grown large enough to be felt.

Some hospitals and cancer centers arrange for patients to meet with several staff specialists so that all possible treatments can be discussed in advance.

more data become available. The radiation dose involved in today's mammogram is so low that any cancer risk from the mammogram itself is considered negligible in women 40 or over.

Diagnosis

Once a questionable lump has been found, the next step should be a needle aspiration to determine whether the lump is a cyst, which is a harmless, fluid-filled sac. This procedure is less invasive than a biopsy. It involves the insertion of a needle into the lump: if fluid comes out, the lump is a cyst. If no fluid comes out, it may still be a cyst, or another type of harmless lump, but now a biopsy is needed to determine the nature of the lump.

The biopsy can be done under either local or general anesthesia. Depending on a number of factors, the doctor will do either a fine-needle biopsy, removing only a few cells, or an open biopsy, removing the whole lump or a piece of it. In any case, the tissue removed will then be sent to a laboratory for a pathologist's examination.

Sometimes a woman will be asked to sign a form before the biopsy, giving her consent, if cancer is found, for an immediate mastectomy (surgical removal of the breast). Fortunately, this practice has become less and less common over the years. The patient should be aware that, if such a

procedure is suggested, she is well within her rights to refuse it and to ask the doctor to follow the now more usual procedure of discussing treatment options after a diagnosis of breast cancer has been made.

Treatment

Treatment options are somewhat more varied than they were years ago. To begin with, the old radical mastectomy—which involved removal of the breast, the two layers of chest muscles underneath it, and all the nearby lymph nodes, from the armpit to the collarbone—is virtually never performed any more because studies have shown that survival rates are no better than those associated with less extreme treatments. The radical mastectomy was developed at the end of the 19th century in response to what doctors then knew, or thought they knew, about how cancer spread. They thought at that time that the lymphatic system played a major role in the spread of cancer. The cancer, they believed, started in the breast, got slowly bigger, spread in orderly fashion (via lymph draining out of the breast) to nearby lymph nodes—and then spread quickly to other parts of the body. Therefore, they reasoned, when cancer was diagnosed, it was necessary to hurry and get it out before it had time to spread beyond the breast and the nearby nodes (hence the practice of doing a mastectomy immediately after a biopsy showed cancer) and, to make sure that no cancerous cells would be left behind, to do the drastic surgery involved in a radical mastectomy.

The belief that speed and drastic surgery were essential held until the late 1970s, when ideas about how cancer spread underwent a major re-evaluation. A new view held that though the lymphatic system may play some role in the spread of breast cancer, the bloodstream is a much more likely agent. Thus, the radical mastectomy was not necessarily the key to survival. An allied theory held that the average breast cancer actually grows much more slowly than anyone had thought. The average doubling time for a breast cancer cell is 100 days—that is, it takes 100 days for the first cell to become two cells, and another 100 days for those two to become four, those four to become eight, and so on. Thus, by the time there are enough cells to form a lump—about 100 billion—the cancer has probably been in the breast for eight to ten years. The idea that no cancer cells have gotten out of the breast in eight to ten years, and yet that they will suddenly get out right away unless surgery is immediately performed, is a bit naive. If the cancer is, as doctors now suspect, growing so slowly, a few days or even weeks between the diagnosis and the surgery will not make any real difference in the woman's likelihood of survival. But it *will* make a difference in her ability to decide, based on facts and not a hypothetical situation, what surgical treatment best meets her particular needs.

Surgery. Today there are two basic forms of surgery for breast cancer. Which of the two is done usually depends on the size of the tumor compared to the size of the breast. The first kind, the modified radical mastectomy, involves the removal of the breast and some of the lymph nodes in the armpit. (The lymph nodes are removed to help the physician decide what stage a cancer is at, which helps determine what kind of postsurgical treatment will be needed.) The muscles behind the breast are left intact. The operation is not as disfiguring as the radical mastectomy, and it does not permanently weaken the arm, as the old procedure did.

Also, women today have the option—which did not exist in the past—of breast reconstruction. This can be done either at the time of the mastectomy or any time afterward. It involves the creation of an artificial breast that looks similar to the breast that was lost. The artificial breast has little or no sensation, and of course, it cannot be used to breast-feed. But it can be cosmetically, and thus psychologically, very helpful to the woman who fears feeling deformed. There are a number of different reconstructive procedures, some more complex than others; generally, the more intricate procedures create the most realistic-looking breast. Of course, many women who have mastectomies do not feel a need for reconstructive surgery and are quite content with the various sophisticated prostheses that can create a thoroughly convincing appearance of a breast beneath clothing—even beneath fairly revealing swimsuits. A small percentage of women choose not to use any method to conceal their mastectomies.

The other surgical option, one that has become more and more popular, is the lumpectomy followed by radiation. This operation, also known as a partial mastectomy and axillary dissection, removes only the lump itself, an area of surrounding tissue, and a few lymph nodes. It is less severe surgery than the modified radical mastectomy, and most women find it more cosmetically pleasing. The radiation treatments are necessary to kill any cancer cells that might be left behind after surgery.

Although studies have indicated that the survival rate for women who have lumpectomy plus radiation is the same as that for women who have mastectomies, many women still prefer the mastectomy. There are a number of reasons for this. The radiation treatments last for six weeks and they can be very tiring; some women simply

THE STAGES OF BREAST CANCER

Stage One
Cancerous growth is smaller than 2 centimeters and has not spread to nearby lymph nodes.

Stage Two
Growth is any size up to 5 centimeters and has spread to nearby lymph nodes, or is 2 centimeters or larger and has not spread to nodes.

Stage Three
Growth is larger than 5 centimeters and has spread to nearby nodes; or growth of any size has grown into the chest wall or skin or spread to distant lymph nodes.

Stage Four
Growth has spread to other organs of the body.

Basic Data: National Cancer Institute

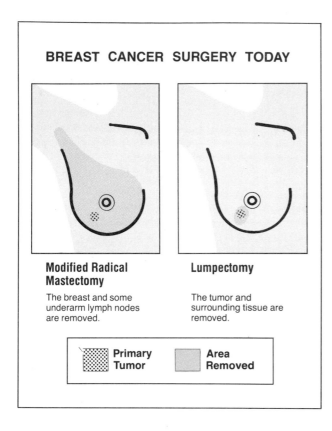

BREAST CANCER SURGERY TODAY

Modified Radical Mastectomy

The breast and some underarm lymph nodes are removed.

Lumpectomy

The tumor and surrounding tissue are removed.

Primary Tumor	Area Removed

feel a need to get on with their lives as soon as possible. Others feel more secure knowing the breast that has harbored a cancerous lump has been removed (although, of course, that does not alter the possibility of cancer occurring elsewhere in the body or in the other breast, and as previously noted, the survival rate is actually the same with either option).

However, increasing numbers of women are opting for the lumpectomy/radiation alternative, feeling that the time and energy expenditure is worthwhile. It is a very subjective choice, and the important thing is that a woman know what her options are and decide for herself which one best meets her own particular needs.

Chemotherapy and Hormone Therapy. Some cancer cells get out of the tumor early on, but the body's immune system detects and destroys them most of the time. Doctors must try to determine how well this has been done. One indication that there might be cancer cells elsewhere is if the lymph nodes removed during surgery are cancerous. In this case, treatment that reaches the body as a whole—systemic treatment—will be needed. For premenopausal women, this will usually be 4 to 12

months of chemotherapy. For most postmenopausal women, hormone therapy—which involves taking the drug tamoxifen for at least 5 years—has been found to work as well. In reality, the systemic treatment of breast cancer is more important than the local treatment. Unlike cancers that affect vital organs—lung cancer or liver cancer, for example—breast cancer *in the breast* is never fatal. It is only when the disease has spread to vital organs that it kills its victims.

Virtually all doctors agree that when lymph nodes are positive, systemic treatment is called for. But there is much controversy surrounding the best treatment when examination of the lymph nodes turns up no cancer cells. In about 20 percent of cases in which microscopic cancer cells are present elsewhere, there will be no evidence of this in the lymph nodes. Thus, many experts believe that all premenopausal women with breast cancer should be given chemotherapy. But chemotherapy often has very uncomfortable, and sometimes permanent, side effects, such as hair loss, nausea, vomiting, and low white blood cell count (which can lead to infections). There is a sharp division in the medical profession over whether the risks of giving unneeded chemotherapy outweigh the risks of missing a cancer that has spread until the cancer has advanced too far for the patient to be saved. Current research is attempting to find a more precise marker of cancer spread than the lymph node analysis; when that marker is found, the controversy over who does and does not need chemotherapy will be resolved. Until then, the breast cancer patient whose lymph nodes are clear of cancer should familiarize herself with the various positions on the subject and decide for herself which course seems best to her.

Risk Factors

For some types of cancer, there are one or two obvious risk factors. For example, it is well-known that the largest cause of lung cancer is smoking. For the general population, this is comforting: one knows that avoiding a certain behavior will dramatically decrease one's susceptibility to the cancer. Sadly, there are no such factors with breast cancer.

There are some factors that can increase one's risk, but the majority of women who get breast cancer have no risk factors at all. Furthermore, breast cancer is a multifactoral disease: it can have many causes that interact with one another in ways doctors do not yet understand.

The biggest risk factor for breast cancer is family history—a woman whose mother had it is likelier to get it than a woman whose mother did not have it. But even that risk is variable. There seem to be two ways in which breast cancer runs in families. In some families, there appears to be a dominant gene that causes many women in each generation to get the disease. There have been rare cases in which every woman in a family got breast cancer. More commonly, however, where breast cancer seems to run in a family fewer women get it.

Besides family history, hormones play a part in one's likelihood of getting breast cancer. Hormones are chemicals that affect many body processes, including menstruation, pregnancy, and menopause. For reasons not yet understood, the younger a woman is at her first period and the older she is at menopause, the more likely she is to get breast cancer. Pregnancy may also affect vulnerability to

the disease. Women who have never been pregnant appear to be more at risk than women who have had a child before 30, but less at risk than women who have their first child after 30. (This does not apply to pregnancies terminated by abortion or miscarriage, which do not seem to affect risk.)

There are various theories about what causes these hormonal risk factors, but so far there are no conclusive findings. It does appear, however, that between her first period and her first pregnancy, a woman is especially vulnerable to some factors that can increase her risk of developing breast cancer later. For example, some carcinogens, such as the high doses of radiation once associated with treatment of various conditions, including acne, are more dangerous at that time of life than they are later on. This has led some experts to suggest that efforts be made to delay the beginning of menstruation, which can sometimes be done by vigorous exercise in adolescence. And indeed there are some data indicating that women who were athletic during their high school and college years

Three days after reconstructive surgery, a breast cancer patient, with her mother and daughter looking on, listens as the surgeon explains some of the exercises she must do during the recovery period.

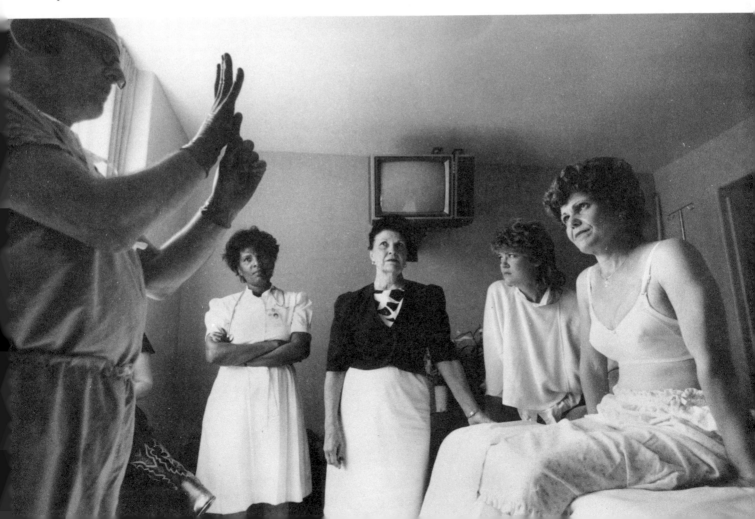

have a lower breast cancer rate than women who were not.

Recently, studies have suggested that the amount of fat in a woman's diet may affect her vulnerability to breast cancer. Unfortunately, these studies are somewhat contradictory, and they do not clearly indicate whether the danger is associated with all fats, animal fats alone, animal and vegetable fats combined, or even just the calories that come with high fat intake. It is known that countries where the diet tends to be high in fat, such as the United States and the Netherlands, have higher breast cancer rates than countries where people tend to have a low-fat diet, such as Japan and Iceland. Studies also suggest that fat consumption during adolescence may be more dangerous than it is in adult life. But even the most convincing studies suggest that only about 27 percent of breast cancers are likely to be related to fat intake.

Alcohol consumption is another recently discovered possible risk factor. It appears that consuming even moderate amounts of liquor may increase susceptibility to breast cancer. Again, it appears that the greatest danger may be during the younger years, with alcohol consumption then increasing one's risk of developing breast cancer later. Alcohol consumption after 30 does not seem to affect breast cancer risk as much. And again, the studies are not yet conclusive.

There are a number of other risk factors. Research reported in 1989 indicated that taking birth-control pills for over ten years before a first pregnancy may heighten a woman's breast cancer risk. Finally, the fertility drug DES has been shown to increase the risk of those who took it.

It is important here to address something that is not a risk factor, because so many women have mistakenly been told that it is. This is so-called fibrocystic disease. The term is a catchall, used by a number of doctors for a variety of unrelated and mostly harmless conditions, such as lumpy breasts, breast pain, nipple discharge, dense breast tissue that shows up on mammograms, and a number of harmless microscopic entities appearing in pathologists' examinations of biopsied breast lumps. None of these constitutes any sort of disease, and none of them leads to cancer. (Unfortunately, doctors have compounded their error by inventing cures for the nonexistent fibrocystic disease, such as taking vitamin E or eliminating caffeine from the

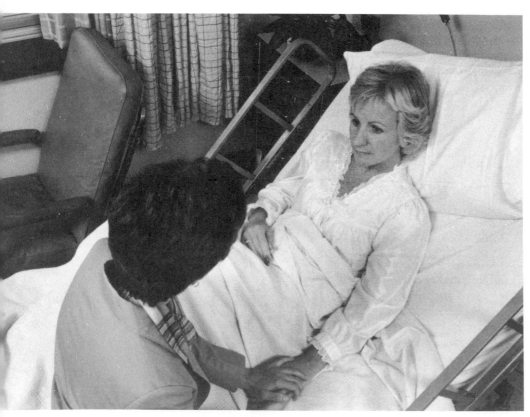

A breast cancer patient in the hospital for surgery is given one-to-one emotional support from a woman who has been through the ordeal herself.

diet. The latter has led some women to believe that drinking coffee increases their risk of breast cancer, but there is absolutely no valid evidence to back up this notion.)

There is one condition, however, that has been included under the phrase "fibrocystic disease" that, when combined with family history, may increase one's risk of cancer—probably because it is a sign that breast tissue already may be on the way to becoming cancerous. The condition, which involves abnormal changes in cells, is called atypical hyperplasia, and it can be detected only under the microscope.

Screening mammography has led to the detection of other precancerous conditions, such as ductal carcinoma in situ and lobular carcinoma in situ. Neither condition is a guarantee that the woman will get breast cancer, but the presence of either greatly increases that possibility. Researchers are now trying to determine the best ways to treat them.

It is important when evaluating reports of increased breast cancer risk to put them in context. Doctors say that one in ten women will get breast cancer in her lifetime. But they are talking about an artificial figure. It refers to a mythical group of ten women, some of whom are at higher risk than others, who are followed from age 25 to age 110. Statistically, one of these women will get breast cancer. A better figure is the age-related risk. A woman between the ages of 30 and 35 has a 1:5900 chance of getting breast cancer in a given year. For a woman between 40 and 50, the figure is 1:1200; for a woman between 70 and 75, it is 1:330. Among women with no risk factors the chances of getting breast cancer at some point in life are 1:30. So if a woman reads that, because she has one of the known risk factors, she has double the risk of a woman with no known risk factors, it does not necessarily mean a jump from a 1:10 to a 2:10 chance of getting the disease; for a given woman, it may mean a jump from a 1:30 to a 2:30 chance, which is less alarming.

Rehabilitation

Facing any cancer—or any other life-threatening disease—can be emotionally devastating. With breast cancer, there is often an added component—concerns about sexuality and physical attractiveness, the sense that one has lost part of one's womanhood. For many women, it is very helpful to work with a psychotherapist or a support group both during the treatment time and afterward.

The patient will also have to deal with some side effects of her treatment. The removal of lymph nodes can cause a problem called lymphedema—a swelling of the arm that can range from barely noticeable to huge and elephantine. It can be temporary or permanent. There are precautions the doctor can suggest that will lessen the likelihood of lymphedema.

Exercises can help alleviate other symptoms, such as the stiff shoulder that is often experienced after breast cancer surgery. In addition, it is useful during recovery for a woman to resume whatever types of exercises she was used to doing before the surgery.

Breast cancer is a frightening disease, but in some ways it is less frightening than many other cancers. Most breast cancers are not fatal, especially if they are detected early on. With the advent of screening mammography, and the constant development of new drugs for the treatment of breast cancer that has spread to other parts of the body, there is every reason to hope that the number of deaths due to breast cancer will soon be on the decline. And with today's treatment alternatives—lumpectomy instead of mastectomy, as well as the option of breast reconstruction following mastectomy—the basis for the old terror of disfigurement has been greatly lessened. □

SOURCES OF FURTHER INFORMATION

American Cancer Society. Contact your local chapter.
National Cancer Institute, Building 31, Room 10A24, Bethesda, MD 20892.

SUPPORT GROUPS

Encore. A YMCA discussion and exercise program. Check with your local Y.
Reach to Recovery. An American Cancer Society hospital visitation program. Check with your local ACS chapter.
Y-Me. Telephone counselors who have had breast cancer. (800) 221-2141 from 9 A.M. to 5 P.M. central time on weekdays; (312) 799-8228 after hours and in Chicago.

How the Arts Are Used in Therapy

David Read Johnson, Ph.D.

John, a 35-year-old lawyer, had tried three different psychotherapists in an effort to improve his self-esteem and get to the roots of his depression. A highly intellectual person who understood psychoanalytic theory, he had talked endlessly about his childhood traumas, his passive aggressive interpersonal style, and his tremendous need for approval. But the flood of verbal self-analysis had little apparent effect on his state of mind. Then, after reading an article about therapy using dance and movement, he decided to give it a try. Though at first he felt awkward, he grew to enjoy moving around the room, sometimes to music he selected, at other times in silence. He developed "dances" that expressed his depression, his intellect, his feelings about his father and mother, and with

Two artworks done a year apart reflect the shifting self-image of a patient hospitalized for major depression and substance abuse. In the pastel drawing above, done a week after his admission to the hospital, a centrally placed butterfly-man depicts the patient's entrapment in his addiction and his absorption in himself, with little awareness of his environment. The acrylic painting on the right was done after the patient had gradually gained more freedom to move around the hospital and its grounds; it depicts butterflies in a more natural setting but a still static manner, reflecting the patient's new sense of confinement by external forces rather than his own problems.

Under the guidance of an art therapist and a drama therapist, a woman with multiple personality disorder created the three puppets above to represent her conflicting identities and used them to convey feelings she could not express directly. In this way she felt she was controlling the personalities rather than being controlled by them.

the therapist he was able to analyze every nuance of these dances in detail.

Especially striking was his "dance of depression," full of tense, angular movements in which he lurched forward with arched back and twisted neck. He said he felt particularly uncomfortable doing it. The therapist then decided to dance it for him. As she moved, he became visibly upset, and then he said that he suddenly remembered how his mother had looked getting out of her hospital bed during a serious illness she had had when he was a child. His dance of depression looked just the same. John said he felt sick to his stomach, just as he had as a child watching her emaciated body. When the therapist then asked him to perform the dance again, he did so with great intensity and emotion and in complete silence. He observed later, "My God, she is still with me." During the six months of his dance/movement therapy, he improved steadily and rapidly.

Human beings have always used the arts to express such feelings as pain, fear, and joy, to communicate to others about the world, and to celebrate the acts of their communities. In this diversity of uses lies a common purpose—a healing of the psychic stress inherent in all human

David Read Johnson is an associate clinical professor in the department of psychiatry at the Yale University School of Medicine, chief of the inpatient unit of the National Center for Post-Traumatic Stress Disorders at the Veterans Administration Medical Center in West Haven, Conn., and chairperson of the National Coalition of Arts Therapy Associations.

life, even on the happiest occasions. When we were put to sleep as infants by our mothers' soft singing, it was healing; when we wrote forlorn poetry late at night during our adolescence, it was healing; and when we danced together in the midst of our families at our weddings, it was healing. The past 20 to 30 years have seen the development of a new profession—the creative arts therapies—that attempts to build on the natural healing fostered by the arts to create a therapeutic tool with a scientific psychological basis.

The creative arts therapies encompass the intentional use of art, music, dance and movement, drama, and poetry by trained therapists in psychotherapy, counseling, special education, and rehabilitation. Approximately 15,000 trained creative arts therapists practice in the United States, and several thousand in other parts of the world. They are trained in specialized university programs, most leading to four-year bachelor's degrees or two-year master's degrees. (Several Ph.D. programs also exist.) Before beginning their training as therapists, all are required to have substantial training in the particular art form they want to use in therapy; such training may come either in university courses or through professional experience as an artist, dancer, actor, or musician. Then they study psychology, learning theory, and psychotherapy and are trained in the special theories, techniques, and methods that have been developed to integrate the art forms with the healing process. Each therapist learns how to analyze what the client does or produces in a particular artistic medium: the art therapist learns what different colors, lines, forms, patterns, and placements mean; the dance therapist learns how to assess different movement patterns, energy levels, and uses of body parts; and the music therapist learns how rhythm, harmony, pitch, timbre, and meter reflect different personality characteristics and emotions. Each discipline has developed sophisticated assessment procedures that give the therapist important information about clients and diagnoses.

Creative arts therapists work in many different settings. Many work in institutions such as psychiatric hospitals or outpatient mental health clinics, where they serve as members of a treatment team. In some locations, their services are routinely part of the treatment; in others, clients are referred to them on an as-needed basis. Creative arts therapists also work in special education programs for the emotionally disturbed and mentally retarded, where their work may be one of several supplementary services offered the client. Increasingly, creative arts therapies are being employed in settings that provide physical rehabilitation for people with traumatic brain injuries, for the physically handicapped, or for substance abusers. Many creative arts therapists also work in nursing homes and geriatric centers. Finally, more and more of them are working independently in private practice, where they act as primary therapists.

Creative arts therapists are also doing increasing amounts of clinical research. Studies reported in the eight professional journals in the field have compared the effectiveness of creative arts therapies with traditional treatments; identified warnings of suicidal potential revealed in artwork; measured the impact of music therapy on heart rate, blood pressure, and hormone secretions; assessed the effects of

Creative arts therapists learn to analyze what the client does or produces in a particular artistic medium.

drama therapy on flashbacks in Vietnam veterans; and identified signs, in body posture and gestures, that a patient has been a victim of sexual abuse.

A Product of the 1940s

The beginnings of the creative arts therapies as a profession in the United States go back to the 1940s when a number of psychotherapists and artists began collaborating in the treatment of severely disturbed clients. The introduction into the United States of psychoanalysis, with its emphasis on the unconscious and its belief that art could reflect the inner thoughts and feelings of its creator, had stimulated many psychotherapists to study the artwork of their patients. Since many severely disturbed patients were unable to express themselves in the highly verbal way required by psychoanalysis, nonverbal forms of communication seemed to hold much promise. Emigrés from Europe who brought their rich traditions in both psychiatry and the arts became leaders of this new field. Creative arts therapies were nurtured in a few long-term psychiatric hospitals (such as St. Elizabeth's in Washington, D.C., Menninger in Topeka, Kan., and Chestnut Lodge in Rockville, Md.) and by psychiatrists, such as Jacob Moreno, who had introduced action-oriented techniques into psychotherapy.

Development of the field of activities therapy continued in the 1950s. The National Association for Music Therapy was formed in 1954. During the 1960s the general atmosphere of social consciousness, the number of opponents of the Vietnam War seeking alternative service, and a dearth of jobs in the arts brought many artists into the health field. By the late 1960s the field of creative arts therapies was in full swing, with university programs developing rapidly. A national dance therapy association was formed in 1966, and an art therapy association in 1969. A second music therapy group and drama and poetry therapy associations were formed in 1971, 1979, and 1981, respectively.

By the 1980s creative arts therapists had diversified their interests well beyond psychoanalysis into behavior therapy (which concentrates on changing clients' behavior rather than on increasing their self-knowledge), special education, and humanistic approaches (which attempt to support a client's natural tendency toward personal growth). They had also become integrated into the established structure of healthcare. Despite their similarities, the creative arts therapies developed relatively independently of the encounter group or New Age movements and should not be confused with them. Creative arts therapists who have completed the training required by their national association are designated as "Registered" or "Certified." In some U.S. states, they are also licensed as professional counselors.

A Typical Session

What happens in a session with a creative arts therapist? Of course, therapists have a wide range of approaches and styles, but a few basic elements can be described. A typical session, whether the client is an individual, a couple, a family, or another kind of group, begins with

Creative arts therapies were developed to help disturbed patients who could not express themselves verbally.

84

HELPING TO PROMOTE HEARING

The creative arts therapies have found a place in many special education programs. Deaf children can often perceive and interpret music more easily than speech, and active participation in music and dance therapy can help to promote the use of their residual hearing. The deaf students at the left are performing a musical play under the guidance of a dance therapist, while those below, led by a music therapist, are playing single-stringed instruments.

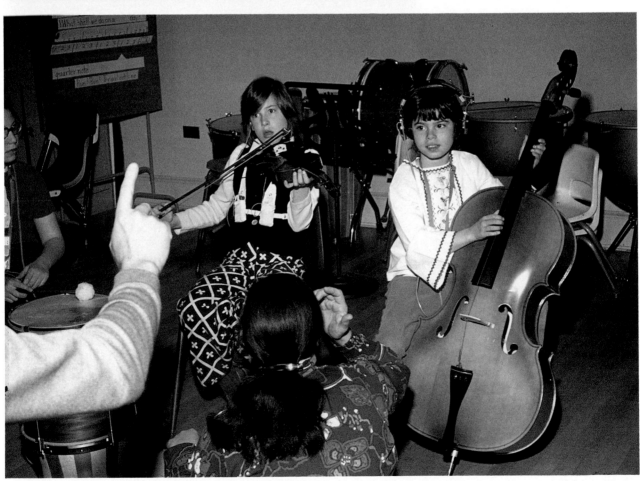

A patient's drawings of his imagined reflections in a mirror show he blames himself for childhood abuse by his father.

discussion about the client's feelings and what problems the client has been facing or is concerned about. Then, instead of exploring these issues by continued discussion, the therapist guides the client into the use of a particular art medium—such as painting, dancing, role-playing, or listening to or creating poetry or music—as a means of working on the problem. Often the therapist will lead the client in warm-up or relaxation exercises to help prepare for the work. For example, in art therapy the client may be asked to draw or scribble randomly on a sheet of paper; in dance/movement therapy the client may be guided through slow breathing exercises, stretching, or even running around the room; in music therapy the preparation may include listening to music, singing a familiar song, or making random noises on an instrument. These activities typically indicate to the therapist the client's mood and level of tension, which can then be explored. In the art therapy session, for example, the therapist may ask the client to look at one of the scribbles and see if it triggers any memory, and then to develop a picture from it.

The main part of the session is spent participating in the art medium. Sometimes the therapist participates with the client, sometimes not. Sometimes the problem is worked on directly; for example, when a man is having trouble dealing with his boss, a drama therapist may take on the role of his boss and enact a scene with the client. At other times the client merely draws, sings, or improvises, and the work of the therapist and client is then to analyze what comes out. For example, an art therapist may ask a client to draw a picture of her mother, or a picture of her feeling of anger, or her perception of her cancerous tumor. A music therapist may help a client to produce a "Song of Myself" or, in a blues style, a song such as "Been Down So Long Since My Divorce Came Through." A poetry therapist may suggest that a client write and then read a poem written as a letter to a dead buddy in Vietnam, or to his father in heaven. In each of these activities, in addition to the conscious thoughts about the subject that arise in the client, the presence of the rhythms, melodies, colors, and actions of the art medium enhances the possibility that new aspects of the situation will emerge.

Often the therapist will leave it up to the client to make observations about what the artwork means and the feelings it arouses. At other times the therapist may facilitate the client's exploring by asking questions about the poem, drawing, or song. Some therapists will in time offer their own ideas about what the artwork might mean for the client.

In institutions, the course of therapy will be determined by the length of stay of the client. In outpatient situations the length of therapy may be as brief as six to eight weeks, when a particular problem can be focused on, or it may involve a long-term commitment of six months to several years.

While many creative arts therapists are familiar with several art media, generally a therapist specializes in one or two. In most cases the client's selection of a particular medium is based on personal preference—some people like to draw, some to sing, some to act roles. However, in institutions where creative arts therapists work in teams, more sophisticated assessments have been developed that help the team select the best medium for the client and suggest shifts from one to another. For example, in working with people with post-traumatic stress disorder, such as Vietnam veterans or the sexually abused, art is the best medium to begin with because the drawings will elicit the visual aspects of the repressed images. Drama or poetry therapy is preferable in the later stages of therapy, when the client has become aware of the traumas and wishes to rejoin the world by expressing to others what happened.

A Multiplicity of Goals

Art was never really "invented"; rather, it emerged naturally out of who human beings are. Even though today we think of art as something produced by a talented few, in early civilizations dancing, singing, enacting stories, and drawing were common means of communicating and healing. Not only tribal shamans but entire peoples found that these ways of expression were able to help them cope with their fears, disappointments, triumphs, and sorrows—that they could be moved by and changed through participation in these rituals.

Nowadays the creative arts therapies are conceptualized with greater precision, but essentially they are being used for the same purposes. Like all psychotherapy and counseling, creative arts therapies attempt to (1) alleviate distress, (2) increase understanding, (3) improve relationships, and (4) change physiological responses.

Alleviating Distress. Much of healing involves simply helping the person express pain, fear, anxiety, or disappointment. The need to get it off your chest, to confess, to unburden yourself is strongly felt by most people. For many, merely talking to a friend, a member of the clergy, or a verbal psychotherapist is sufficient. For others, however, the process is not so easy. Perhaps the pain is so deeply hidden that the person doesn't even know it's there. This is often true of people who have been sexually abused or suffer from post-traumatic stress disorder arising from combat or a natural disaster. Perhaps the person cannot use words well. This is particularly true of people with learning disabilities, schizophrenia, mental retardation, or Alzheimer's disease. Or perhaps the person is so good at words that he or she talks all around the distress but cannot seem to feel it. This is often true of highly intellectual and otherwise high-functioning people.

Because artwork involves the use of one's unconscious, the creative arts therapies can help people express inner pain that their conscious minds cannot

In depicting herself in fragments surrounded by waves representing her obsessive thoughts of dependency, fear, and hopelessness, the woman who drew the sketch below was able to begin accepting and sharing her painful emotions instead of acting them out in self-defeating ways.

recognize or put into words. Sexually abused children often "tell" first through their pictures or in their puppet play. Putting something into physical action helps to achieve a catharsis of feelings.

For example, a ten-year-old girl named Mary was brought to a child guidance clinic because of learning problems, angry and negative behavior at home, and frequent crying spells. She refused to speak with her counselor and instead looked lackadaisically at the toys in the room. She was referred to the art therapist, with whom she also refused to speak. When the therapist put a sheet of paper in front of her, however, she immediately drew a picture of a girl on top of a mountain. The therapist, a male, asked, "What is her name?" and without speaking she wrote "Sandy" on the page. The therapist responded, "I'm Sandy, and I'm on top of the mountain!" Mary immediately threw the sheet onto the floor and began drawing another picture, with Sandy on top of the mountain and a boy, a very ugly boy, being thrown off it. She wrote "Bozo" next to the boy. The therapist said, "Oh, no! I'm Bozo, and Sandy just threw me off her mountain! Ahhhhhhh!" Mary laughed out loud and gleefully began another picture. For several weeks Mary and the therapist interacted through these pictures, dozens in each session, in which Sandy subjugated many people and triumphed over the world. Soon Mary joined in the narration of the stories, which increasingly centered on Sandy's abuse of a little girl named Marie. Within a few months the full story of Mary's physical abuse by her mother emerged. The therapist and Mary continued to use pictures for the entire year of therapy, even after Mary was able to talk about her life directly.

Increasing Understanding. Instead of just talking with the client, creative arts therapists ask, "Show me." When the client draws a picture, writes a poem, dances, makes up a song, or acts out a drama, internal experience—otherwise so shifting and murky—is made real: the conflict or issue now is "out there," where it is easier to see, to understand, and to try to deal with. The client gains perspective on the problem by becoming his or her own audience. Particularly for patients with schizophrenia or other forms of psychosis, this insight can be extremely helpful.

Daniel was a 22-year-old with catatonic schizophrenia. He was beset by conflicting thoughts that often left him paralyzed. Asked by his dance/movement therapist how he was feeling, he only said, "Zigzag." When the therapist then asked him to show through movements or gestures what he zigzagged between, he made one motion that was rigid and tense, another that was soft and swaying. The therapist next divided the room into two parts and had Daniel move between them. One side Daniel named "Uptight"; the other he called "Loving." The clear spatial separation of these feelings helped Daniel control his thinking. He was able to talk about how the uptight feeling was related to his father, who had called to tell him that he was divorcing his mother; the loving side represented his mother and the marriage before it had broken up, an event that Daniel felt his illness was responsible for. Seeing his divided feelings literally laid out in this way allowed Daniel to talk very clearly without any psychotic thinking for the entire session. As a result of this work in dance/movement

The conscious mind often cannot recognize inner pain or put it into words.

therapy, Daniel was able to make significant gains in his interactions with other people and reintegration into society.

The achievement of greater self-awareness can also be crucial for highly verbal people like John, the patient mentioned at the beginning of this article, whose articulateness seems to block them from feeling things directly.

Improving Relationships. Many people come to therapy because their relationships with other people, particularly their family, are poor and seem stuck in the same old patterns. A husband and wife, for example, become so familiar with each other's styles, arguments, and counterarguments that their interactions can become like broken records. All that is positive in the relationship seems to have been drained out of it. The creative arts therapies can help alleviate these problems in several ways. First, by engaging people in art media they place them on unfamiliar territory, where they are no longer sure of their own or others' behavior. Second, the arts bring out previously hidden thoughts and feelings, letting each person know that there is much more to others than is apparent on the surface. Finally, since the creative arts therapies often involve spontaneity, humor, and play, they tend to illustrate to people ways in which they can have a positive effect on each other. All in all, the creative arts therapies provide new opportunities for clients to air their frustrations about their relationships and better understand what is happening in them.

Bob and Trish, for example, came to a drama therapist for couples therapy. They had been married for 15 years and had two children. Since the children were born, Bob had distanced himself from Trish, and Trish had become increasingly angry with and critical of him. She wanted a more intimate relationship and felt Bob had lost interest in

Art therapy has helped many veterans of the Vietnam War, like those in the California hospital above, to heal the long-lasting stress disorder stemming from their combat experiences.

89

her sexually. For his part, Bob felt that she was too demanding and that he couldn't do anything to please her. So he tried to stay out of her way, a tactic that enraged her. In the initial session with the therapist these problems were amply demonstrated: as Trish attacked Bob mercilessly, Bob refused to interact but made indirect demeaning comments about her to the therapist. Discussion of their problems inevitably resulted in this pattern. Then the therapist asked them to role-play several situations. When they played themselves, no matter how benign the situation, they soon turned it into the same old arguments and stances. After they noticed and agreed that they were locked in a pattern, the therapist then asked them to play these scenes with reversed roles. Each of them exaggerated the other's position so much (Trish playing an inarticulate wimp, and Bob a monstrous, teeth-gnashing amazon) that they would alternatively interrupt a scene with "That's not fair!" or break out laughing. The therapist helped them to give names to the various stances that they took ("Wimp City," "ManEater"), and soon their interactions and arguments became much more playful. The therapy sessions provided a place where they could exaggerate the circumstances of their relationship beyond believability. Finally, the therapist encouraged them to improvise scenes in which they played entirely different characters, such as animals or Supreme Court justices. In one scene, Trish played a dwarf who found a huge egg (Bob). She sat on it until it hatched, and Bob emerged as a giant Godzilla and stomped around the room decimating villages and office buildings (like the one where he worked). Then he came back and picked up Trish (now a beautiful maiden) and carried her off. Both of them expressed tremendous relief that treasured parts of themselves reflected in these roles had been only suppressed, and not lost.

Changing Physiological Responses. Changing the body's responses to stress, infection, and pain has become an increasingly important part of therapy today. The use of relaxation and imagery techniques to lower stress, to reinforce new healthful behavior patterns, and possibly to strengthen the body's autoimmune response is receiving much attention. Creative arts therapies, especially music and dance, are being used to enhance a person's relaxation and physiological self-regulation skills, which can be helpful in controlling hypertension and symptoms of chronic conditions like lupus and arthritis.

Music and dance/movement therapies have also been used to treat people with traumatic brain injuries. In addition to providing the basic physical stimulation used in traditional care for such injuries, these therapies utilize what may be special pathways toward healing. It is possible that rhythm and melody are processed by different parts of the brain or through different neural pathways than are verbal or purely physical stimulation, and thus they may at times offer a means of intervention when these other channels are closed. A related phenomenon has been studied in patients with dementia, where certain aphasias (impairments in the use and understanding of language) have been caused by damage to the left (dominant) hemisphere of the brain. Since music and spatial relationships are processed largely by the right hemisphere, sometimes it is possible to improve an elderly person's understanding through the use of music, art, or gesture.

Ann, a 78-year-old woman referred for music therapy in the nursing home where she lived, had suffered a left-hemisphere stroke and was experiencing severe aphasia, a loss of memory, and a lack of concentration. Because of her disabilities she often sat in her wheelchair with her head down, muttering nonsense words. The music therapist first made a comprehensive assessment of her communication abilities and music preferences and discovered that she responded to music of specific rhythm, pitch, and meter, in addition to familiar songs from her past. She was then brought into a music therapy group, where the participants sang songs as the therapist used physical objects (such as scarves, mirrors, and fruit) and hand-holding to stimulate attention and awareness. After a few minutes in the group, Ann became far more responsive, lifting her head up and enjoying the music of the others. On certain songs she began to sing along, using the correct words. After each song she said, "Thank you," and once, she said, "You see, I'm not crazy."

During the treatment it became clear that Ann was suffering from a depression that was making her impairments in thinking worse, for she was increasingly able to make normal remarks during the music structured by the therapist. The therapist then attempted to build on this foundation. Ann loved the song "Oh, Susanna," and after singing it several times with the regular words the therapist sang, "Oh, oh, Anna, now don't you cry for me, For you've come from far away, with a smile upon your face." Ann grinned broadly and applauded. With the therapist's help she then sang, one line at a time, the following version: "Oh, oh, Anna, now don't you cry for me; I'm just an old, old hag, with nothing left to say." Following this method, the therapist was able to get Ann to talk about several topics, most of which confirmed that her self-esteem was very low. She was given antidepressant medications, which helped her depression somewhat. As she continued in music therapy, her level of participation increased, as did her level of orientation and alertness.

The client must bring out new things from within the self.

Revealing the Inner Self

The creative arts therapies are powerful primary or supplementary treatments, but they cannot work miracles. As in all rehabilitation, the best results come from a client who is strongly motivated to change, a therapist who is warm and understanding, and a good match between them. Nevertheless, the creative arts therapies have an important element that distinguishes them from other forms of treatment: nonverbal and aesthetic modes of expression. Engaging in the spontaneity of creating—drawing, telling a story, playing with puppets, making a clay sculpture, or writing a poem—the client must bring out new things from within the self. This process, while at times anxiety provoking, is usually enlightening and relieving, as the demons inside are revealed to be merely parts of the self. Creative arts therapists are guided by scientific and scholarly principles and schooled in rigorous training programs. But like the shamans of old, they help people grow and solve problems by reaching the source of their own creativity and inner life.   □

TEA
THE CUP THAT CHEERS

Irene Gunther

"Thank God for tea! What would the world do without tea?—how did it exist? I am glad I was not born before tea."

So wrote the 19th-century English essayist Sir Sydney Smith. Today, more than a hundred years later, about half the world's population might echo that sentiment. Tea is the most popular nonalcoholic beverage in the world and, aside from water, also the least expensive. In the United States, for example, the average cost of a cup of tea made at home is about 3 cents.

Many people drink tea simply because they enjoy its refreshing, astringent taste and perhaps the feeling of well-being a cup of tea can provide. Those suffering from a mild ailment—a cold or sore throat—often drink it for its soothing "chicken soup" effect. Since tea has only about half the caffeine of coffee, some people who find coffee too stimulating turn to tea instead. Even those who are trying to avoid virtually all caffeine can still enjoy a cup of tea, since decaffeinated varieties are now available.

A tea plantation in Java, Indonesia

In colonial America, tea became the symbol of British oppression. Here, in the Boston Tea Party of December 1773, colonists disguised as Indians board British tea ships and dump their cargo into Boston harbor.

A Very Old Story

No one knows exactly when people first began to drink tea. Chinese legend has it that tea was discovered around 2737 B.C. by the mythical Emperor Shen Nung, when leaves from a nearby tree fell into his campfire pot of boiling water and gave off a delicious aroma. Modern scholars believe that tea cultivation began in the Chinese province of Sichuan around 350 B.C. and that the tea plant was introduced into Japan toward the end of the 6th century. Tea drinking did not, however, become popular in Japan until the 13th century. In China the leaves of the tea plant—or *Camellia sinensis*, an evergreen shrub or small tree of the family Theaceae—were at one time steamed and crushed, then molded into a kind of cake, which was boiled; the technique of infusing tea leaves in hot water was developed during the Ming Dynasty (1364-1644).

In the 17th century, tea was introduced into Europe from China by Dutch traders. It was at first the drink of the rich (ordinary people, who could not afford it, continued to drink their cheap wine and ale). The British East India Company, a trading company established in 1600 and given a charter by Queen Elizabeth to trade directly with the East (and not incidentally to collect customs duties for the British Crown) was responsible for bringing tea to the masses in England. By the 18th

---

Irene Gunther, a staff editor, is English-born and a lifelong tea lover.

century the company had a virtual monopoly on the import of tea from China and was bringing tea into London in large quantities. Prices fell, and in Britain tea eventually surpassed coffee as the country's favorite drink. Some of the tea was reexported—after the import duty had been paid—to other European countries and to Britain's American colonies.

In the 1800s, clipper ships, designed and built for speed by American shipbuilders, were transporting tea to England and North America and racing one another for prizes that amounted to thousands of dollars. The most famous race was the Great Tea Race of 1866, in which the two top contenders, the *Ariel* and the *Taeping*, covered the 16,000 miles from China to London in 99 days—and arrived only minutes apart.

By the 19th century, India had joined China as a major tea producer and London had become the world's most important tea trading center. In 1834, auctions were established in Mincing Lane in the City of London, where teas from all over the world could be examined, tasted, bought, and sold. Today, London remains one of the world's major tea trading centers.

From the Tea Garden to the Tea Table

The tea plant is a versatile plant that will grow in both tropical and subtropical climates. Besides India and China, major tea-producing countries now include Kenya, Tanzania, and Malawi in Africa; Sri Lanka (formerly Ceylon), Japan, Indonesia, Bangladesh, and Taiwan (Formosa) in Asia; the Soviet Union; Turkey; and several South American countries. Tea grows in open fields or on terraced hillsides, at low altitudes or as high as 6,000 feet. In the wild state, the plant may reach a height of 30 feet, but under cultivation it is pruned to a shrub of about 3 to 5 feet tall; this causes it to produce more shoots and makes it easier for pickers to harvest the leaves.

It is fairly easy to grow tea, less easy to obtain good quality, since the plant, much like the grapevine, is affected by factors such as soil quality, rainfall, and elevation. Tea grown at higher altitudes is of better quality because its slower growth improves the flavor. But slow growth means smaller yields, and thus makes the tea more costly.

Most tea is made from "two leaves and a bud," a classic phrase in tea lore that refers to the tender young leaves and the small unopened leaf bud found at the end of new shoots. (Coarser leaves from lower down the stem can also be used, but they produce a poorer quality of tea.) It takes some three to five years before a young plant can produce its first "flush"—leaves of a quality suitable for harvesting. In hot climates, trees may be ready for flushing, or plucking, every seven or eight days; in cooler areas twice as much time may be needed, and in colder weather plucking may slow down further or stop altogether. Tea is plucked by hand, mainly by women; expert pluckers can pick 40 pounds of leaves a day, snapping them off with thumb and forefinger and tossing them into tall baskets as they move between the rows.

Processing and Blending. Tea comes in endless varieties and can look, smell, and taste entirely different depending on where it is grown, how it is blended, and most important, the way it is processed. The extent of fermentation—an oxidation process that turns the green leaves

THE ART OF TEA TASTING

Tea is bought and sold at great auction centers around the world, most of them in tea-producing countries (London is an exception)—Calcutta in India, for example, Jakarta in Indonesia, or Colombo in Sri Lanka. Tea companies are represented at these auctions by tasters, who sample different batches and make recommendations.

Tea tasting is an art, and one that can take years to acquire, partly because there are so many varieties of tea and partly because seasonal variations can be observed only over time. Tea-tasting procedures are precise and carefully followed. Each sample is weighed on a scale—the amount used is the weight of an old silver sixpence, or about 3 grams—then brewed in a special cup that separates the leaves from the liquid. Tea tasters use many senses to judge the quality; the color and aroma of the brewed tea as well as its taste are taken into account, and the appearance and smell of the dried leaves and the infused ones. Tasters sniff and inhale the liquid, swoosh it around in their mouths (often noisily) spray it onto their palates, and spit it out rather than swallow it. Then they pronounce on its characteristics, using terms such as raw, bright, coppery, colory, thin, malty, flaky, pungent, or brisk. An expert taster can identify as many as 1,500 varieties and can tell the exact origin of a tea (even, at times, naming the specific garden, or plantation), at what season of the year it was picked, and how it was processed.

a bright copper color and gives them a stronger, more aromatic flavor—is what determines the three main types of tea: black, green, and oolong. Black tea—by far the most widely consumed type in the West—is fermented, while oolong tea is partially fermented. Green tea, favored in China and elsewhere in the Far East, is not fermented at all.

Processing of black and oolong teas involves several steps: withering, rolling, fermenting, and finally drying. In the first step the green leaves are spread on racks in withering lofts so as to remove most of their moisture. They are then rolled to break up the cells and release the aroma, laid on racks again in cool, humid fermenting rooms, and finally machine-dried using hot air. Green tea is processed somewhat differently. Instead of going through the withering stage, the leaves are put into a large steamer and heated, which softens them and prevents oxidation. They are then rolled and dried. The leaves remain green and produce a tea with a light taste and a green-gold color.

A complicated terminology is used to classify teas, which may be more confusing than enlightening to the average consumer. For example, familiar terms such as Orange Pekoe, Pekoe, and Broken Orange Pekoe refer to the size, or grade, of the leaves and whether they are broken or unbroken, and not to their flavor or quality. (Broken grades account for the largest proportion of tea used throughout the world, and are the only kind suitable for use in tea bags.) Other names describe the tea's origin, for example, Darjeeling, Assam, or Formosa Oolong (which some experts rate as the finest tea in the world), and still others refer to the blend. Among the latter are English Breakfast, a blend of Indian and Ceylon teas, and Earl Grey, a blend of China and Indian teas flavored with bergamot. Most of the teas drunk in the West are blends, often of 15 to 20 or even more varieties. In Britain special blends are created to be sold in different parts of the country to take account of the water, since water strongly affects the taste of the brewed tea.

Tea Around the World

Tea is many things to many people. It is prepared and served differently in different parts of the world and has acquired special ritual and cultural meanings in various countries. Moroccans generally like to drink their tea sweet and to flavor it with mint; Russians and Eastern Europeans generally prefer it strong, usually serve it in a glass, and often flavor it with lemon. Tea has remained popular in most of Britain's former colonies, in particular, Australia and New Zealand. The "billy" referred to in the Australian song "Waltzing Matilda" is the tin can used by the "swagman" (vagabond) to make his tea.

In China, believed to be the world's largest consumer of tea, the beverage is drunk on all occasions by all classes, both in the home and in teahouses. It is served in little cups without handles, and without the addition of milk, sugar, or lemon. In Japan, another big tea consumer, tea plays a significant role in ritual and ceremony. By custom, the Japanese offer tea to their ancestors on arising and serve it to their parents before partaking themselves. The Japanese tea ceremony, an ancient institution rooted in Zen Buddhism, is related to

---

FOR A BETTER BREW

How good your tea tastes depends to a large degree on how you make it. Following a few simple steps—and above all being sure that your water is at boiling point when the tea is made—will help you extract the most flavor from your tea. To make tea from scratch, experts suggests that you:

1. Fill your kettle with cold tap water, freshly drawn.

2. Brew in a teapot rather than in a cup. Warm your teapot by rinsing it with hot water, so that the tea will stay hot while brewing.

3. Use one tea bag or one teaspoonful of loose tea per cup. (Traditionalists add one for the pot.)

4. Pour the water over the tea as soon as it comes to a full boil.

5. Brew for three to five minutes, then stir before pouring.

If the tea is too weak, Increase the amount of tea, not the brewing time. If too strong, add hot water.

For iced tea, use 50 percent more tea, since it will be diluted by melting ice.

the concept of worshipping the beautiful in everyday life. Valued as an aesthetic way of entertaining guests, the ceremony is performed in accordance with strict rules of etiquette, and a separate structure—or if that is not possible, a separate room—is set aside for the purpose.

A National Institution. Tea is to England what hot dogs and hamburgers are to America—a national institution. In the cool, damp climate the hot beverage is a source of warmth and comfort—"a nice cup of tea" is likely to be the first remedy offered for whatever ails you, whether it is a broken heart or a bad day at the office.

Over the years, tea has inspired writers, poets, and philosophers. William Cowper, the 18th-century poet, celebrated it in a phrase that became part of the language: "cups that cheer but not inebriate." Boswell, Samuel Johnson's biographer, reported that the great man was a prodigious tea drinker prone to "swallowing his tea in oceans." According to G. K. Chesterton,

> *"Tea is like the East he grows in*
> *A great yellow Mandarin*
> *With urbanity of manner*
> *And unconsciousness of sin."*

Above: green leaves are spread out in withering lofts to dry. Below: in a tea factory near Kyoto, Japan, leaves are dried and cleaned, and sorted according to quality and size.

More recently, the popular British television series *Upstairs, Downstairs* often showed both the gentry in the drawing room and the staff in the kitchen drinking tea, although the upstairs people would be sipping it from fine porcelain cups while downstairs had to make do with more humble crockery.

Afternoon tea, perhaps Britain's most famous tea ritual, was originated around 1840 by Anna, the seventh Duchess of Bedford, who served her guests tea with cakes around 5 o'clock to tide them over

until a late dinner. Today, afternoon tea might also include dainty sandwiches, buttered scones, sometimes served with thick cream and strawberry jam, and cookies. High tea, another British custom, is (despite its name) decidedly unaristocratic. Served in late afternoon, high tea is actually a light supper that generally includes one hot dish plus the cakes, bread and butter, or sandwiches.

Britain is the Western world's biggest per capita consumer of tea; Britons drink about twice as much tea as coffee, or on average about three cups a day. But consumption has fallen—in the mid-1960s they drank, on average, six cups of tea to one of coffee—and in recent years, coffee has been steadily gaining in popularity, especially among younger people. The change has been variously attributed to tea's staid image, the generation gap, and the fact that in a faster-paced society few people have time for the leisurely afternoon tea ritual.

A Symbol of Oppression. Tea came to America in the 17th century, introduced, it is thought, by the Dutch to their colony of New Amsterdam, where it became fashionable among society, despite the fact that it initially cost the equivalent of $30 to $50 a pound. English colonists in Massachusetts took to tea in the late 1600s, and the beverage increased in popularity in America as in Britain as its price came down. But in 1773 an event took place that was to give tea a bad name. That year, in a protest against the East India Company's monopoly on legal tea imports and the British government's tax on tea, a group of colonists dressed as Indians boarded British ships in Boston harbor and dumped more than 300 chests of tea into the sea. Besides helping precipitate the American Revolution, the Boston Tea Party made tea a symbol of oppression. Although Americans continued to drink tea, it never quite recovered from this image, and in time coffee took its place as the favorite American drink.

Taking Tea the World Over

In England (left) afternoon tea is usually accompanied by cakes, cookies, or sandwiches. The Japanese tea ceremony (right) is an aesthetic ritual passed on from generation to generation. Below: In the Soviet Union people boil water for tea in samovars.

99

The Americanization of Tea. Just as they shaped the English language to their own purposes, Americans transformed the English national beverage to suit the needs of a different culture and a different climate. Americans were the first to replace loose leaves with tea bags; iced tea was created in the United States; and the instant teas that dispensed with both leaves and bags, as well as ready-to-drink iced tea sold in cans, were other steps toward convenience. (Tea bags account for some two-thirds of tea sales, instant mixes for most of the rest.)

The invention of the tea bag, which has almost completely replaced loose tea in the United States, was an accidental one. In 1904, Thomas Sullivan, a New York tea and coffee merchant, started sending tea samples to his customers in small silk bags instead of the usual tins—and began to receive orders for tea packaged in that convenient way.

HOW MUCH CAFFEINE?

PRODUCT		CAFFEINE (milligrams)	
		Average	Range
TEA (5 oz. cup)	Brewed, major U.S. brands	40	20–90
	Brewed, imported brands	60	25–110
	Instant	30	25–50
	Iced (12 oz. glass)	70	67–76
	Decaffeinated	4	—
COFFEE (5 oz. cup)	Brewed, drip method	115	60–180
	Brewed, percolator	80	40–170
	Instant	65	30–120
	Decaffeinated, instant	2	1–5
SOFT DRINKS* (12 oz. can)	Cola		30–46
	Dr. Pepper		30–46
	Orange, lemon-lime (clear)		0
	Root beer		0
	Ginger ale		0
DIET SOFT DRINKS* (12 oz. can)	Diet cola		0–60
	Diet Dr. Pepper		0–60
	Club soda, seltzer, sparkling water		0
CHOCOLATE	Cocoa beverage (5 oz.)	4	2–20
	Chocolate milk beverage (8 oz.)	5	2–7
	Milk chocolate (1 oz.)	6	1–15
	Dark chocolate, semisweet (1 oz.)	20	5–35
NONPRESCRIPTION DRUGS (1 tablet)	No Doz		100
	Vivarin		200
	Anacin		32
	Excedrin		65
	Aqua-Ban (diuretic)		100

* Other soft drinks, not listed here, also contain caffeine. Check the label or can for information on caffeine content.

Sources: U.S. Food and Drug Administration; National Soft Drink Association; *Tea and Coffee Trade Journal.*

Iced tea also originated in 1904, at the St. Louis World's Fair. Its creator, Richard Blechynden, an Englishman who had come to the fair to promote his teas, found few takers in the sweltering summer heat for his hot beverages—until he resorted to pouring the liquid over ice cubes. Iced tea, a refreshing drink ideally suited to America's hot summers, was an instant success. Its consumption has now far surpassed that of hot tea. Today, roughly four of five tea bags sold in the United States are used to make iced tea.

Contrary to the trend in Britain, tea consumption in the United States has increased slightly in recent years. In 1962, according to the International Coffee Organization in London, England, 75 percent of Americans drank coffee, while 25 percent drank tea. In 1987, 52 percent were coffee drinkers compared to 29 percent for tea. Plain black tea has, however, been losing ground to specialty teas—a category that includes herbal, decaffeinated, and flavored black teas—reflecting both increasing health concerns and the more sophisticated palates of the 1980s. Supermarket shelves are now likely to offer, in addition to standard national brands, a choice of decaffeinated teas, some herb teas with fancy names like Wild Forest Blackberry or Mint Medley, and perhaps some premium teas such as Darjeeling or Earl Grey. In recent years, consumption of herb teas, which may sound healthful but aren't necessarily, has increased at the rate of about 20 percent a year.

Iced tea is becoming a year-round favorite in the United States. Far more Americans drink their tea cold than hot.

Tea and Health

When first publicly sold in London in 1657 at Garway's Coffee House, tea was advertised as "that Excellent and by all Physitians approved China drink." What is the thinking about tea today? Is it good for us? Does it carry any health risks?

Tea contains caffeine, a substance that in large amounts has been shown to have some ill effects on some people. But a cup of tea contains, on average, half the caffeine in a cup of coffee, which is why some people drink it in preference to coffee. The table on the facing page compares the caffeine content of tea and coffee (as well as other products). The comparison is, however, inexact because of the wide variation in the amount of caffeine in a cup of coffee; for tea, too, the amount can vary greatly according to the type, the brand used, and the length of brewing time. Green teas generally have less caffeine than black; imported brands tend to have more than the standard U.S. brands. Decaffeinated teas have almost no caffeine. U.S. consumption of decaffeinated teas has shown a steady increase—in 1988 they accounted for some 8 percent of total tea bag sales.

Over the past ten years or so, much research has been done on the possible health hazards of caffeine. The substance was implicated as a possible factor in a number of diseases and conditions, including pancreatic cancer, birth defects, benign breast lumps, and heart disease—and in most cases exonerated for lack of conclusive evidence. After reviewing a number of caffeine studies, the U.S. Food and Drug Administration concluded in 1988 that most of the concern about caffeine—especially when the substance is consumed in moderation— was unwarranted. A problem general to all the studies was the difficulty in measuring the precise amount of caffeine the subjects consumed; a further problem was separating the role of caffeine from the role of other possible factors—for example, in the case of heart disease, the contribution of life-style factors such as diet and exercise.

The FDA did recommend in 1980 that pregnant women give up caffeine or consume it in very small amounts. The recommendation was based on results of a study in which one out of five pregnant rats fed high doses of caffeine gave birth to offspring with missing or incomplete toes or delayed bone development. Although there was no evidence that caffeine would have the same effect on human infants, the FDA has stuck to its recommendation, mainly because caffeine is a drug and the fetus is always more affected by drugs than the mother.

A more recent study, reported in late 1988, found some link between caffeine and infertility. In the case of 104 women who had been trying to become pregnant for three months, researchers found that, in subsequent months, the women who drank more than the equivalent of one cup of coffee (or two cups of tea) a day were half as likely to become pregnant as those who drank less than that. The sample was small, however, and the researchers warned that the results should be interpreted with caution.

What is beyond doubt is that caffeine is a stimulant to the central nervous system. Our morning cup of tea or coffee helps us get a start on the day, warding off drowsiness and increasing alertness. (Some people, once accustomed to consuming a certain amount of caffeine-containing drinks, find they must drink more and more to get the desired stimulation. Such people may eventually be drinking 10 to

Specialty teas—particularly colorfully packaged herb teas—now compete with plain black tea for space on supermarket shelves.

12 cups a day of coffee or tea.) Too much caffeine—and what constitutes too much varies with the individual and is affected by factors such as body weight, physical condition, and sensitivity to the drug—can produce a condition commonly referred to as caffeine jitters. Symptoms include irritability, nervousness, trembling, insomnia, and caffeine headaches. Nursing mothers are generally cautioned to avoid too much caffeine because the drug makes its way into the breast milk and may make infants irritable or sleepless.

An unquestionably beneficial substance in tea is fluoride, which protects against tooth decay. Although green tea has about twice as much as black, even a tea-bagful of black tea can provide 0.1 to 0.2 milligrams of fluoride. (In communities with fluoridated water, the average person's intake from the water is 1.2 to 1.5 milligrams a day.) It is true that children benefit most from fluoride protection and not many young children drink tea. But adults can benefit, too, especially those who have a history of tooth decay.

The chemicals in tea called tannins, which give the beverage its astringent taste, can be detrimental to the absorption of iron and other nutrients. This can be a problem in Third World countries where iron-deficiency anemia is prevalent and large amounts of tea are consumed. An advantage of tannins is that they can help stop bleeding; some dentists recommend that patients place a tea bag on the gums if bleeding occurs after surgery.

Herb Teas: An Alternative?

What about herb teas? Increasingly popular in the United States, they are promoted as healthful because they are generally caffeine-free and are made from natural ingredients. Actually, herb teas are not really teas at all because they are made not from the leaves of the tea plant but from the flowers, seeds, leaves, or roots of various plants, often in combination. Herb teas have been used as folk remedies for thousands of years, and a variety of medicinal properties have been claimed for them. Ginseng tea, for example, made from the ginseng root, is an ancient cure-all and is supposed to be an aphrodisiac. Rosehip tea is valued for its high vitamin C content. Mint tea is supposedly an aid to digestion, and chamomile tea is thought to soothe the stomach.

Today's herb teas bear little resemblance to the brews of the past, many of which had an unpleasant medicinal odor or taste. Modern herb teas are marketed as refreshing, exciting alternatives to plain black tea and are designed to appeal to the palate with exotic ingredients such as hibiscus flowers and lemon grass, as well as to satisfy health concerns. But few herb teas have been tested for any therapeutic qualities or even for safety when drunk in large quantities, and the FDA has warned that some may contain substances potentially more dangerous than anything in regular tea. Chamomile can cause allergic reactions, and sassafras, a dried root bark, is a known carcinogen. Such teas should therefore be drunk in moderation.

As for regular black tea, its health benefits lie as much in what isn't in it as what is. Drunk plain, it has practically no calories, no salt, and no sugar. And hot or cold, tea gives millions of us that small psychological lift that helps us get through the day. ☐

CHILDREN'S FEARS

Barbara G. Melamed, Ph.D.

All of us have experienced fear at one time or another, and children's fears are a normal and essential part of growing up. In fact, research suggests that such fears serve a purpose, marshaling energies in times of danger and impelling children to use caution and prudence. Many fears are transitory; very young children, for example, are often frightened by loud noises or sudden movements. Childhood fears change over time and should be seen as mileposts on the road toward independent functioning. The development of visual acuity changes children's reactions to the people around them. Children who did not object to strangers at the age of three months may scream

Barbara G. Melamed, a clinical psychologist, is dean and professor at the Ferkauf Graduate School of Psychology at the Albert Einstein College of Medicine campus of Yeshiva University in New York City. She has written widely on childhood fears.

Many Fears Are Age-Related

Above: Being left with a stranger can be an upsetting experience for a very young child, who may be afraid that the parent will never come back. Left: Babies are often afraid of going into the water, but if not forced most will get over this fear as they grow older. Right: A large dog can be scary to a preschool child, even if the animal is gentle and friendly.

with fear at seven months, having developed the capacity to recognize their own family members and to differentiate them from other people. (The table on page 111 lists some normal fears at various ages.)

Since overcoming fears is part of the process of self-mastery, parents should not attempt to protect a child from all danger and exclude the experience of fear. Unfortunately, many fearful adults transmit their own fears to their children or overreact when a child is actually showing a normal degree of fear. Studies have shown that children and their mothers tend to report similar fears, suggesting that children model their behavior on their mother's. If, however, fears continue for a long time and interfere with the normal social activities of the child and the family, this may be a signal that the child is overwhelmed and needs some professional help. Even so, since most fears *do* go away by themselves, before seeking therapy for the child, parents might first closely monitor the occurrence and severity of the fear and then discuss it with their pediatrician.

A recurrence of fears the child seemed to have already conquered may be a reaction to a particular situation. At times of great stress for the child, such as starting school, having an accident or injury requiring emergency treatment, or going into a hospital, children often regress to earlier emotional reactions. Children may also get upset for brief periods when a parent is under stress, perhaps because of illness, the death of a close relative, or a change in financial or marital status.

Fears Change as Children Grow

The Infant. The first experience of fear may be innate. Like many animals, infants typically show fear when faced with a change in the comfort of their bodies or a sudden intrusion into their environment. A loud noise or an abrupt change of body posture may be enough to make a baby cry. Newborns are especially fearful if they are not held securely since they are unable to hold up their heads or control their bodies themselves. The infant frequently responds to fear with grasping, thrusting movements and attempts to avoid or escape upsetting sounds or objects. Such spontaneous motor responses are likely to be accompanied by an increased heart rate, pallor, perspiration, dilation of the pupils, rapid breathing, and perhaps urination. The baby's reactions usually have the desired effect: they elicit comforting from the parent or other caretaker. The infant will be fed, changed, held or rocked, or removed from harm.

The fear of strangers, which typically occurs between 7 and 12 months of age, is a sign that normal social development has begun. The infant has become accustomed to its parents and depends on them for food, bodily care, and love. This interaction develops a sense of trust in the child, along with a fear of separation from the parents. (Fear of separation often persists through early school age.) Thus, the entrance of a stranger can trigger the fear of separation and distress the child, particularly if the child's experiences with nonparental adult figures have been discomforting. A pediatrician may be associated with painful inoculations, a barber with being restrained in a seat. And babysitters, given the difficulty a stranger has in understanding babies'

Pictures of missing children—and media coverage of kidnappings—may make children fearful that they too could be snatched away.

108

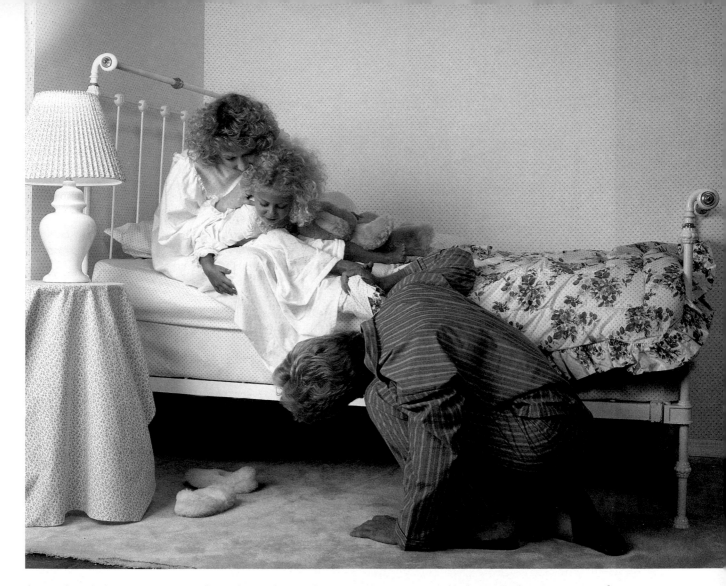

limited verbal repertoire, may have been slower than parents to comfort them when they cried.

It seems likely that there is an innate or genetic basis to some fears. However, the influences of learning and maturation soon come into play, and the development of normal fears—whether of loud noises, animals, the dark, or separation from the parent—can vary a great deal from one child to another. The intensity of the reaction also varies, as well as the persistence of the fear and the frequency with which it occurs. A single incident—such as the loud sound of balloons bursting—may trigger a long-term fear, particularly if the parent overreacts rather than downplaying the incident.

Toddlers. As children begin to move about by themselves and to discover the world beyond their bodies, new fears may develop. Bedtime may evoke fear of wetting the bed or of darkness, in addition to fear of separation from the parent. About half of all toddlers apparently suffer from nightmares, evidenced by their waking in fright during the night. Children may not be able to tell exactly what has frightened them, but it is likely that daytime stresses are carried over into nighttime dreams. Toilet training (usually after 18 months) sometimes leads to a special kind of fear. Since children often believe

The night brings terrors of its own, perhaps because a monster may be lurking under the bed. Parents should be reassuring and not make fun of their children's fears.

109

their bowel movements are part of their body, seeing them flushed down a toilet bowl distresses them and leads to fears that other parts of their body may be flushed away. Fear of animals—dogs in particular, but often insects, reptiles, and other creatures—is common in young children. They may also be terrified by the unexpected appearance of a strange object, say, a lifelike toy snake or fake bird suddenly produced by an older sibling; teasing the child by repeatedly showing the object will probably enhance the fear.

Preschool and School-age Children. Through the preschool and early school years, as children develop cognitive abilities and become more socially aware, their fears broaden and may include imaginary figures and objects and apprehension about future events. Supernatural beings such as ghosts, witches, monsters, or alien creatures that have been introduced through stories, movies, and television may arouse fears. Masks are often scary, and even clowns can be frightening.

As their moral development accompanies their increased sense of responsibility, children may add the fear of punishment to their roster of threatening events. Thunder and lightning, once feared because of their sudden loud noises and intense light flashes, may now be seen as punishment for bad behavior or unacceptable thoughts.

The fears and worries of children between the ages of 6 and 12 may include bodily injury and concerns over physical appearance and

A visit to a doctor can be frightening, especially if it involves pain or discomfort. Telling a child in advance what to expect is helpful.

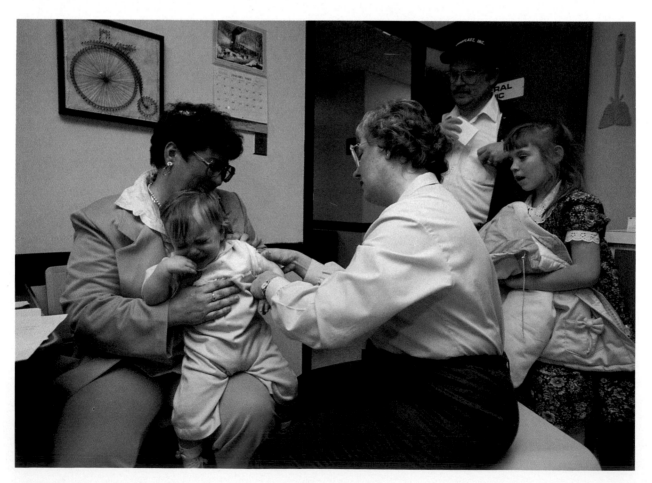

Some Normal Childhood Fears

0–6 months: Loss of support, loud noises.

7–12 months: Fear of strangers, fear of sudden, unexpected, and looming objects.

1 year: Separation from parent, toilet, injury, strangers.

2 years: A multitude of fears including loud noises (vacuum cleaners, sirens/alarms, trucks, and thunder), animals (for example, large dog), dark room, separation from parent, large objects/machines, change in personal environment.

3 years: Masks, dark, animals, separation from parent.

4 years: Parent separation, animals, dark, noises (including at night).

5 years: Animals, "bad" people, dark, separation from parent, bodily harm.

6 years: Supernatural beings (for example, ghosts, witches, Darth Vader), bodily injuries, thunder and lightning, dark, sleeping or staying alone, separation from parent.

7–8 years: Supernatural beings, dark, fears based on media events, staying alone, bodily injury.

9–12 years: Tests and examinations in school, school performance, bodily injury, physical appearance, thunder and lightning, death, dark (low percentage).

Reprinted with permission from Richard J. Morris and Thomas R. Kratochwill, *Treating Children's Fears and Phobias: A Behavioral Approach*, Copyright © 1983, Pergamon Press PLC.

acceptance by peers. At this stage girls seem to have more fears than boys. School phobias—fear of going to school—always are a cause for concern; in younger children, they may be a signal that something is preventing the child from separating from the parent. The illness of a family member or maternal overprotection may lead to school phobia and frequent absences from school. Children may also try to avoid going to school because they are afraid of examinations, of making mistakes, or of being criticized. Often, children will complain of ailments such as a headache or stomachache—whose existence cannot be disproved—so that their parents will allow them to stay home. When school phobia occurs, parents should seek help from a school guidance counselor or a health professional.

Fears About Medical and Dental Treatment

Visits to doctors and dentists are a necessary part of growing up. While they sometimes arouse fears—among them fear of injections, of human blood, and of being touched by strangers—these visits can also help the child develop the coping skills needed for dealing with uncomfortable or painful events. Children who have developed these skills in less serious situations may be better equipped to cope if they should be faced with hospitalization or a chronic illness that requires repeated uncomfortable or painful procedures.

If a child's fears are long-lasting and disrupt family life, it may be time to seek professional help.

Young children may have distorted ideas about pain and illness that heighten their apprehensions. Some children seem to believe that painful medical procedures, illness, and hospitalization are punishments for wrongdoing or the result of a deliberate desire on the part of the health practitioner to hurt them. Older children who are very upset or frightened about pain may regress to this more primitive level of reasoning. While preschool children appear to be most threatened by medical or dental instruments, school-age children are likely to be more upset by their dealings with health practitioners themselves. Adolescents, on the other hand, have fears about their health and bodily integrity. In preschool children, fears about separation from their parents and anxiety about strangers may be more significant than physical fears. Older children's fears are more likely to be the result of unpleasant memories of previous visits to the doctor or dentist. Anticipating pain, the child may build up anxiety when a new visit is impending.

To help children cope with a stressful medical or dental procedure it is important to prepare them ahead of time by giving them information appropriate to their age. They should be told why the particular treatment is necessary, what it specifically involves, and what discomfort or side effects there may be. Sometimes a parent's presence during the procedure can help the child remain calm. (However, current research suggests that children across a broad range of ages—

from five months to ten years—are likely to make a much bigger fuss when their mothers are present.)

Current Fears

Deep public concern about such problems as sexual or drug abuse, AIDS, kidnapping of children, and environmental contamination may add to children's fears about their own safety and well-being. If the dangers are overemphasized, children may become so scared that they are unable to absorb information about how to protect themselves. It is too soon to evaluate whether media emphasis on these risks will lead to phobias in normally healthy children; however, it is unlikely that children who have been encouraged in the home to approach new situations with courage as well as caution will be widely affected by these new risks.

Seeking Professional Help

Treatment is recommended only when fears cause significant disruption in the family's daily life, when they cannot be controlled or reasoned away, when they persist over an extended period of time, and when they seem inappropriate to the child's age or stage of development.

Professional intervention may involve tranquilizing drugs, traditional psychotherapy, behavior therapy, or a combination of any of these. The treatment chosen will depend upon the type of fear and the form it takes, as well as on the particular child and family. The effectiveness of long-term psychoanalytically oriented psychotherapy for specific phobias has been questioned because improvement generally takes place slowly and the problems created by the fear may get worse if they are not quickly dealt with. Behavior therapies, which do not focus on the origin or possible symbolic meaning of the fear but on eliminating the immediate problem, have been successful in treating children with specific phobias and have not led to other problems. However, it is recommended that any family problems—which may have indirectly manifested themselves in the child's behavior—also be addressed.

Behavioral Approaches. Behavior therapy uses four main approaches, called systematic desensitization, modeling, flooding, and operant reinforcement. Each involves presenting the fearful event in imagination or in reality with the goal of eliciting nonfearful responses.

Systematic desensitization involves gradually exposing the child to the feared event, either in fact or through conjuring up a mental picture of the event, while at the same time teaching relaxation techniques to help the child cope with the fear. In modeling, the child watches other children—either live or filmed—overcome fear, then tries to imitate their behavior in the presence of the therapist. Flooding involves a rapid rather than a gradual exposure to the dreaded situation, aimed at deliberately arousing the fear. The child remains in the situation (real or imagined) until the anxiety abates; the hope is that, with repeated exposure, the child will cease to feel fear when confronted with the situation. Operant reinforcement consists of rewarding the child—with praise, attention, or some kind of small gift—for reacting to the feared situation in a nonfearful manner. ☐

Behavior therapies have been used with success to treat children's phobias.

IS YOUR CHILD ON

George D. Comerci, M.D.

Most parents begin to worry about drug and alcohol abuse when their oldest child becomes an adolescent. Their concern intensifies as the adolescent gains more independence, especially when beginning to drive a car. But parents who wait until the teenage years to think about drug and alcohol abuse may be putting it off until too late. National surveys in the United States show that children are experimenting with drugs and alcohol at younger and younger ages. A

DRUGS OR ALCOHOL?

1987 survey found that 36 percent of fourth graders were under
pressure to drink. Researchers at the University of Michigan found
in a national survey of high school students in 1988 that by age 13,
about 30 percent of boys and 20 percent of girls have tried alcohol.
The number of students using drugs by the sixth grade has more than
tripled since 1975, from 1.1 percent to 4.3 percent. Graduating high
school seniors in 1986 reported that 22 percent of them had first used

alcohol, 11 percent had first used marijuana, and 0.6 percent had first used cocaine while in the seventh and eighth grades; 2 percent first tried cocaine in the ninth grade. In addition, other surveys show, almost 20 percent of high school seniors smoke cigarettes daily, with about 11 percent smoking half a pack or more a day. The use of smokeless tobacco (chewing tobacco and snuff) by boys and young men is alarmingly high. As tobacco use, along with marijuana and alcohol use, is a predictor of abuse of drugs such as heroin and cocaine and of future chemical dependency, it should not be taken lightly by parents.

To combat the threat to their children's well-being, parents need, long before adolescence, to begin looking for answers to some basic questions about substance abuse. What factors contribute to substance abuse? Are some children more at risk than others? Can parents do anything to decrease the risk for their child? How can parents tell if their child is developing—or already has—a problem with substance abuse?

Factors Contributing to Substance Abuse

Parents who frequently drink in front of their children may be setting the wrong example.

Understanding what may lead a child to abuse drugs or alcohol can help parents judge their child's degree of vulnerability. It may also provide a basis for preventive measures to be initiated early on.

There are both psychosocial and biological predictors of substance abuse. Many factors, including genetic influences, child-rearing practices, social and cultural values, and peer group pressures, may interact with each other and with individual temperament and personality traits to determine whether a child will never even try drugs, only briefly experiment with them, or become psychologically or physically dependent on them.

Parents and Family. Parents' child-rearing practices and the nature of parent-child interactions have a great influence on the behavior and attitudes of offspring and may contribute to the way in which an adolescent relates to drugs. Children who have poor relationships with their parents may use drugs as a means of coping with stress, of communicating feelings of anger and rebelliousness, or of satisfying a need for immediate gratification. Belittling and punitive parental attitudes, failure to give praise, neglect, and severe parental discipline including corporal punishment have been found in families in which the children abuse drugs. However, child-rearing practices that have been shown to be associated with increased alcohol and drug abuse in children and adolescents also include overpermissiveness, excessive indulgence, and inconsistent limit setting and discipline. The types of homes that tend to result in children who refrain from drug experimentation or abuse are those where good and close family relationships prevail, where parents set reasonable limits, where parents foster an attitude of respect for authority figures (including teachers), and where the family is involved in community or church activities.

Children of substance abusers are at very high risk of abusing alcohol or drugs themselves, for both genetic and environmental reasons. A growing body of data documents a biological predisposition to chemical dependency—especially alcohol dependency—in some individuals, and this predisposition appears to be passed from one generation to the next. For example, studies have found that adopted boys with one alcoholic biological parent are three to four times more likely to abuse alcohol than adoptees with biological parents who did not abuse alcohol. There is reason to believe that there are also biological vulnerabilities to heroin, cocaine, and other drugs.

When there is a family history of alcoholism or other substance abuse, it is extremely important that parents be aware of the increased risk for chemical dependency in their children. While parents can do nothing to change a child's genes or biological vulnerabilities, they can try to provide a supportive environment. When neither parent is a substance abuser, they can ensure that alcohol and other addicting substances are assiduously avoided in the household. They can also educate their children at an appropriate age regarding the likelihood that this biological vulnerability will be an ongoing problem for them.

Personality, peer pressure—even genes—can play a role in determining if a child will abuse drugs or alcohol.

George D. Comerci, a professor of pediatrics and family and community medicine at the University of Arizona Medical Center, is a frequent contributor to books and journals in the fields of pediatrics and adolescent medicine.

Another finding from addiction studies is the association of emotional disorders, such as depression, with alcoholism and other chemical dependencies. A family history of serious depression or of what psychiatrists now call bipolar disease (manic-depression) should also alert parents to the possibility of an increased susceptibility to substance abuse, especially alcohol dependency, in their offspring.

In all families, children learn by modeling their behavior on that of their parents. Children are more likely to abuse drugs or alcohol if they grow up in a home in which parents and other family members use illegal drugs, or abuse prescription drugs. Parents who ask their child to light their cigarette or fetch them a beer are, although unintentionally, conveying the message that smoking and drinking are acceptable. Parents need to evaluate their own habits and attitudes to be sure they are setting the example they wish to set.

The Community. Children from disadvantaged families who grow up in poor neighborhoods and whose families have no social connections such as church or club membership are at a higher risk of substance abuse than others. This may be true even if other factors, such as increased exposure to drug-using peers and increased availability of drugs, are discounted. If parents and older siblings are involved in antisocial activities or are at odds with the law, the likelihood of substance abuse in these children is even greater.

The movie Cocktail, *starring Tom Cruise, makes drinking seem like fun.*

When there exists little or no hope for the future, as is the case in so many impoverished communities, substance abuse becomes far more appealing as a way to forget, escape, and gain some pleasure and fulfillment from life, even if temporary and self-destructive. For children in such circumstances, whose problems may be compounded by emotional and learning disorders and who have experienced few successes, the pleasure and relief from psychological pain derived from substance abuse become attractive alternatives to repeated failure at school and at efforts toward personal achievement. Furthermore, immature youths yearn for peer acceptance and emulate their cultural heroes. When their peers are involved in delinquent and drug-related activities, or the local heroes are criminals and drug dealers driving expensive cars, it is difficult for young persons not to pattern their behavior after those who "succeed" in such an environment. (This is especially true when they are being offered drugs and large amounts of money to deliver drugs—thus leaving adult dealers safe from the police—as happens in some large metropolitan areas and even in some suburban neighborhoods.)

Peer Pressure. For youths in any community and any economic circumstances, one of the strongest predictors of substance abuse is abuse by siblings and friends. It is friends, not strangers, who usually introduce young people to drug or alcohol abuse. This does not necessarily mean that peer pressure always leads to drug abuse. It may, instead, reflect a peer selection process on the part of adolescents, who choose friends who are more like themselves and their families. The environment they grow up in, however, may limit their options with regard to a broad choice of friends, including those who abstain from substance abuse. The complexity of this increases when one considers the tendency of adolescents to believe that "everybody's doing

it" even when that is not the case. Unfortunately, the statements "everybody uses drugs" and "there's alcohol and drugs at all the parties" may be close to an accurate reflection of the situation in many schools and communities in the United States. The onus is on the parents to determine the validity of such statements. If they are true, parents must stand firm in setting limits on the adolescent's activities and must work with others to make community changes.

The child whose family must, for whatever reason, make frequent moves may be at increased risk. Entering a new school and making new friends is stressful, and usually the groups that tend to be most open to new arrivals are those on the fringe of mainstream academic activities and those who are more likely to be using drugs.

The Media. Television, movies, and other media present alcohol use in a very positive light. Alcohol is associated with having fun and being popular and successful and is promoted as a reward for hard work. Intoxication is joked about, and the use of alcohol is often presented as a means of coping under stress. Drug use is encouraged through glamorization of illicit drugs and promotion of self-medication. Popular music has increasingly glorified the use of drugs. Advertising, especially of alcohol and tobacco products, is particularly targeted to the young.

Young people are usually introduced to drugs by friends rather than by strangers.

119

Danger Signs

Teenagers whose schoolwork goes downhill (left), who start wearing clothing or jewelry with drug themes (below), or who become increasingly irritable or aggressive (right) may have, or be developing, a substance abuse problem.

The extent to which parents can regulate exposure to such messages is questionable, but some parental regulation of television watching by young children and control of other detrimental media exposure in the home is advisable.

Personal Characteristics. Research has shown that children with certain personality traits are more likely to abuse drugs. These traits include low self-esteem, poorly defined values, poor interpersonal relations, lack of attachment to family and community, high need for acceptance by others, low religiosity, inadequate coping and communication skills, inability to accept discipline, and unwillingness to accept the consequences of one's actions. Also more likely to abuse drugs are young persons who have difficulty delaying gratification, who have not had experience dealing with adversity, or who are impulsive. It follows that anything parents can do to counteract the development of these characteristics may have some preventive value.

Children who have no interest in school, or who fail for whatever reason, are more likely to become regular users of alcohol, tobacco, and other drugs. There are also strong correlations between substance abuse and childhood antisocial behavior, aggressiveness, rebelliousness, and introversion or loneliness. Finally, emotional problems, especially depression and anxiety, may lead a young person to use drugs as a form of self-medication. Parents who identify any of these characteristics in their children can arrange counseling for them as a preventive.

Less likely to abuse drugs are young people who are active in school and community activities, who are aware of and knowledgeable about the physical, psychological, and social dangers of substance abuse, and who care about their health and future. They may experiment, but they tend not to progress to the later stages of substance abuse. Having goals and aspirations and valuing the rewards of hard work and achievement seem to act as an immunization.

Spotting Substance Abuse in Your Child

The ultimate question is: How do you know if your child is on drugs or alcohol? The problem is that many of the signs of substance abuse are very much like those seen in normal adolescents. That is not to suggest that all adolescents exhibit terribly troublesome or problem behaviors, or that they all are "weird" and their actions bizarre. In fact, careful studies by psychologist Daniel Offer reveal that the vast majority of adolescents do not create chaos in their homes and misery for their parents and teachers, as the popular wisdom has it, but cope very well. Adolescence is a time of tremendous physical, psychological, and social changes in a young person's life, however, and some of those changes are reflected in adolescents' behavior. Young adolescent girls, for example, tend to become more introspective, while boys approaching or in early adolescence tend to regress (engaging in provocative activities and bathroom humor, among other things), become more physically

POSSIBLE INDICATORS OF SUBSTANCE ABUSE

Signs of Trouble

1. Does your child spend many hours alone in his or her room apparently doing nothing?

2. Does your child resist talking to you?

3. Has there been a definite change in your child's attitude at school? With friends? At home?

4. Has your child shown recent pronounced mood swings with increased irritability and angry outbursts?

5. Does your child always seem to be unhappy and less able to cope with frustration than previously?

6. Has there been a change in your child's appearance (that is, to sloppy dress and poor grooming and hygiene)?

7. Is there a paranoid flavor to all of your child's relationships with adults, siblings, and authority figures?

Strong Indicators of Problems

1. Does your child always seem to be confused or "spacey"?

2. Has there been a change in your child's friends from age-appropriate friends to older, "unacceptable" associates?

3. Has your child made excuses or lied in order to avoid confrontation or to get out of trouble?

4. Have there been episodes of skipping school? Has your child lied to cover up bad report cards?

5. Has your child recently quit a sport, dropped out of school clubs or social groups, stopped music lessons, quit the band or orchestra, or lost interest in a hobby?

6. Has your child been verbally abusive to you?

Very Strong Indicators of Problems

1. Has your child begun lying in order to cover up sources of money and possessions?

2. Has the child been stealing or shoplifting or had encounters with the police?

3. Have you noticed a marked increase in your child's interest in drugs, drug literature, and the drug "culture" (for example, wearing T-shirts, belt buckles, and jewelry with a drug theme)?

4. Has there been a deterioration of school performance, frequent truancy, or conflict with coaches or teachers?

5. Has your child been physically abusive to you?

6. Has your child talked about suicide or running away?

7. Have money or valuable articles recently disappeared from your home?

IF EVERYBODY SAYS IT CAN'T HAPPEN TO THEIR KIDS, THEN WHOSE KIDS IS IT HAPPENING TO?

Not yours, right?
Well, would you feel any differently if you knew 17% of all high school seniors have tried cocaine? And 40% of those are using it currently.
Not your kid? Well, how about his...54% of all high school seniors have smoked marijuana. And over half of them smoke it regularly.
Still not your kid? Or maybe you're not so sure anymore.
Well, the best way to know for sure is to talk with your child. Of course, speaking to your child like this

takes a lot of courage. And to do it effectively takes a lot of homework—like reading articles, attending meetings, and talking to other parents. This way, your child will see you as a well informed source.
Listen, we're not using these statistics about marijuana and cocaine to scare you.
Then again, that's exactly what we're trying to do.
If you're afraid your child may be included in some of these numbers, get help. Contact your local agency on drug abuse for more information.

© 1987, Smith/Greenland Inc.

PARTNERSHIP FOR A DRUG-FREE AMERICA

Parents should discuss drug use—and its consequences—with their children.

active, lose interest in academic work, and enjoy taking risks (both activities that put them in physical danger and those that violate school or parental rules). In the face of changes such as these, how can parents tell when their child's behavior has gone over the line between what is normal and what is a sign of trouble?

The best way to begin to understand the behavioral signs that indicate substance abuse is to look at them in the context of what some experts have identified as the five stages of adolescent drug abuse. These stages constitute a continuum, beginning with a stage of high vulnerability and proceeding through stages of experimentation and regular use to the final stage of dependency called burnout. They do not necessarily describe the experiences of every abuser but are fairly typical.

Stage 1: The Potential User. The adolescent has not yet used drugs but is curious about them, drugs or alcohol are available, and family members, friends, or acquaintances are abusers. The adolescent may act bored or rebellious, or seem especially concerned about peer acceptance.

Stage 2: Early Experimentation. The adolescent has tried tobacco, alcohol, or marijuana (usually obtained from friends), has experienced mild euphoria with a quick return to baseline mood, and may exhibit little change in behavior.

Stage 3: Early Regular Use. The adolescent regularly acquires drugs, expands usage to stimulants and sedatives, and may feel anxiety or guilt afterward. This stage is commonly accompanied by mood swings, lying, and changes in grooming, friends, and school performance.

Stage 4: Late Regular Use. The adolescent is now addicted to drugs and uses harder drugs, such as cocaine, opiates, and hallucinogens, every day, both alone and with others. When drug effects wear off, marked withdrawal symptoms (which often include nausea, vomiting, shaking chills, and muscle aches), depression, and suicidal thoughts are apparent. Family fights, lying, and school failure become the norm. To obtain money for drugs, the adolescent may resort to stealing, prostitution, and drug dealing. Overdosing begins.

Stage 5: Burnout. The addict needs drugs constantly and will use whatever is available. Physical and mental deterioration set in, with increased episodes of aggression, amnesia, overdosing, and withdrawal, along with self-destructive behavior and a suicidal attitude.

The earlier substance abuse can be identified, the better the outlook for effective treatment; however, parents and other adults rarely become suspicious until stages 3 and 4 because the outward signs are so

few. Even then, it is not always easy to tell if drug abuse is involved or if the child has another problem. It is especially difficult to judge whether the child is suffering from depression that led to drug abuse or whether drug abuse led to depression. For this and other reasons it is important that a psychiatrist or psychologist be involved in the evaluation and treatment of young people determined to be in stage 3 or a later stage of substance abuse.

Parents often ask for more specific help in trying to decide whether their child is developing or has a problem with substance abuse. One way to make this judgment is within the framework of a set of specific questions that parents can ask themselves as they observe their child's behavior. "Possible Indicators of Substance Abuse" on page 122 provides such a framework. It must be stressed that many of the behaviors questioned are frequently observed in adolescents who are not abusing drugs, although any adolescent exhibiting a number of them is in need of individual attention. Those listed under "Strong Indicators of Problems" should be considered to be more deviant, and those in the final section are definitely abnormal behaviors and warrant consultation with a physician or other specialist in adolescent behavior disorders or substance abuse.

Another way for parents to make a judgment about whether their child is developing or already has a drug problem is by discussing the subject with the child. Sample questions to use as a basis for discussion with adolescents include the following:

- I know that many schools have drug problems. Does your school have such a problem?
- Do most of your friends drink alcohol or smoke marijuana at parties?

Children of all ages can benefit from drug education. Left, high school students at a drug prevention fair. Right, cartoon characters from The Drug Avengers, *an award-winning anti-drug video parents or teachers can use with small children.*

• Do any of your friends use drugs other than alcohol or marijuana?

• Have you ever been ill as a result of using drugs or drinking? In what way?

• If you are using cigarettes, alcohol, or other drugs, do you think I am aware of it? If so, how do you think I feel about it?

• Do you ever worry about your alcohol or other drug use?

• Have you ever driven a car (or motorcycle) while drunk or stoned?

• What do you think I would do if you called and told me you were too drunk or "high" to drive?

Given the reluctance of many teenagers to participate in family discussions, the parent might give the list of questions to the teenager to think about beforehand, then plan a future quiet and relaxed time to discuss them. It is important that parents not present the questions in a threatening or accusatory manner, but express a genuine desire to learn more about the adolescent's feelings about drug abuse and related issues. It cannot be overemphasized that the time for discussion must be when the adolescent has no other distractions and the parents can devote their full attention to the discussion. It is critical that parents listen and not lecture or make pronouncements or ultimatums. This does not mean that parents should not express their beliefs and feelings about drug abuse, nor does it mean that parents should not set limits, establish rules, and inform the adolescent of their expectations regarding use of tobacco, alcohol, and other drugs.

For parents anxious to know how much their younger children have learned about drugs and to what degree they have acquired the skills necessary to avoid experimentation with or use of drugs, the following questions are appropriate:

• Do you understand the word "drugs"? What does it mean?

• Have your teachers ever talked about drugs?

• What have you learned about drugs at school?

• Have you and your friends ever talked about drugs?

• Have you ever wondered why some people use drugs?

• Why do you think grown-ups say that drugs are harmful?

• Has anyone ever tried to sell you drugs or tried to force you to take drugs?

Consulting a Physician

Physicians or other health professionals are often called in by parents to help determine whether a young person is using drugs. From the parent's point of view, a paradox exists in this situation, for in order to get the patient to admit to drug use, the physician often must assure the patient that such information will remain confidential. Physicians and others who face this problem always qualify the extent of confidentiality by informing the patient that it will be broken if there is a serious and relatively immediate threat to the patient's life, health, and welfare. Parents must have faith that the health professional will know when confidentiality must be broken. Many physicians will not necessarily disclose experimental use of drugs in the middle or older

Sometimes professional help is needed to determine if a child is a substance abuser.

126

adolescent but will always report to parents any use by a child or early adolescent. With the older adolescent or young adult, the physician may feel that maintenance of confidentiality is essential for successful intervention to take place. Furthermore, the timing of parental notification is important. Parents may not be told about substance abuse until the physician feels that a therapeutic "alliance" has been established between doctor and patient. This is a most delicate and sensitive area for the professional, the parents, and the patient.

Most physicians would rather determine drug use and its extent by interview and discussion with the patient and parents, but circumstances sometimes indicate that blood or urine tests would be helpful. Ideally, testing for drug use should be done with the knowledge and consent of the patient, regardless of age. But there are definite exceptions to this policy. A statement published by the American Academy of Pediatrics in 1989 reads: "Parental consent may be sufficient for the involuntary screening of the younger child who lacks the capacity to make informed judgments. Parental permission is not sufficient for involuntary screening of the older, competent adolescent, and the Academy opposes such involuntary screening. Consent from the older adolescent may be waived when there is reason to doubt competency or in those circumstances in which information gained by history or physical examination is strongly suggestive of a young person at high risk for substance abuse."

The identification of persons who are abusing drugs is necessary not only for the welfare of the individual, but also because of the harmful effects that substance abuse may directly or indirectly have on others. The dangers of substance abuse are now greatly increased because of the association of intravenous drug use with AIDS (acquired immune deficiency syndrome). Nevertheless, laboratory testing for drugs must be undertaken with the greatest discretion and with full awareness of its potential for error, the social and psychological problems it may cause, and how it may affect the relationships of the young people being tested, their parents, and their doctors.

Because of its association with AIDS, intravenous drug use is more dangerous than ever.

SOURCES OF FURTHER INFORMATION

Alcoholics Anonymous, Box 452, Grand Central Station, New York, NY 10017. (Also see telephone directory for local chapters.)
Do It Now Foundation, Box 27568, Tempe, AZ 85285.
National Clearinghouse/Alcohol Information, Box 2345, Rockville, MD 20852.
National Clearinghouse/Drug Abuse Information, Parklawn Building, Room 10 A-56, 5600 Fishers Lane, Rockville, MD 20852.
National Clearinghouse on Smoking and Health, Centers for Disease Control, 1600 Cliften Road, Building 14, Atlanta, GA 30333.

SUGGESTION FOR FURTHER READING

VAN OST, WILLIAM AND ELAINE. *Warning Signs: A Parent's Guide to In-Time Intervention in Drug and Alcohol Abuse.* New York, Warner Books, 1988.

PNEUMONIA

A. Martin Lerner, M.D.

Before the 1930s and 1940s, when modern anti-infective drugs came into widespread use, pneumonia was the most frequent cause of death in the civilized world. It was especially dangerous (as it still is today) in people over 50 years of age with such serious illnesses as chronic heart or lung disease, diabetes, or cancer. Even in people without ongoing debilitating conditions, pneumonia was always a long illness that required hospitalization.

Pneumonia today is far less often the killer it was earlier, but it still affects a vast number of people. Well over 3 million men, women, and children in the United States and Canada get the disease each year. A third of them become so ill that they need to be hospitalized, and tens of thousands of patients, most of them elderly, die from the disease.

Pneumonia, broadly defined, is an inflammation of the lower respiratory system, or the lungs. It can be caused by a wide variety of infectious microorganisms, including bacteria—the commonest cause—fungi, viruses, and parasites. (There are other causes, including damage to the lungs following inhalation of toxic chemicals, but these are rare.) Whatever the cause, the disease usually involves a number of symptoms, such as coughing, fever, the expectoration of blood-stained sputum, pain in the chest, and difficulty in breathing. The physician's first task, when confronted by such symptoms, is to determine if a patient actually has pneumonia, what is causing it, and whether the pneumonia is a minor illness that can be treated safely at home or a life-threatening one demanding prompt hospitalization.

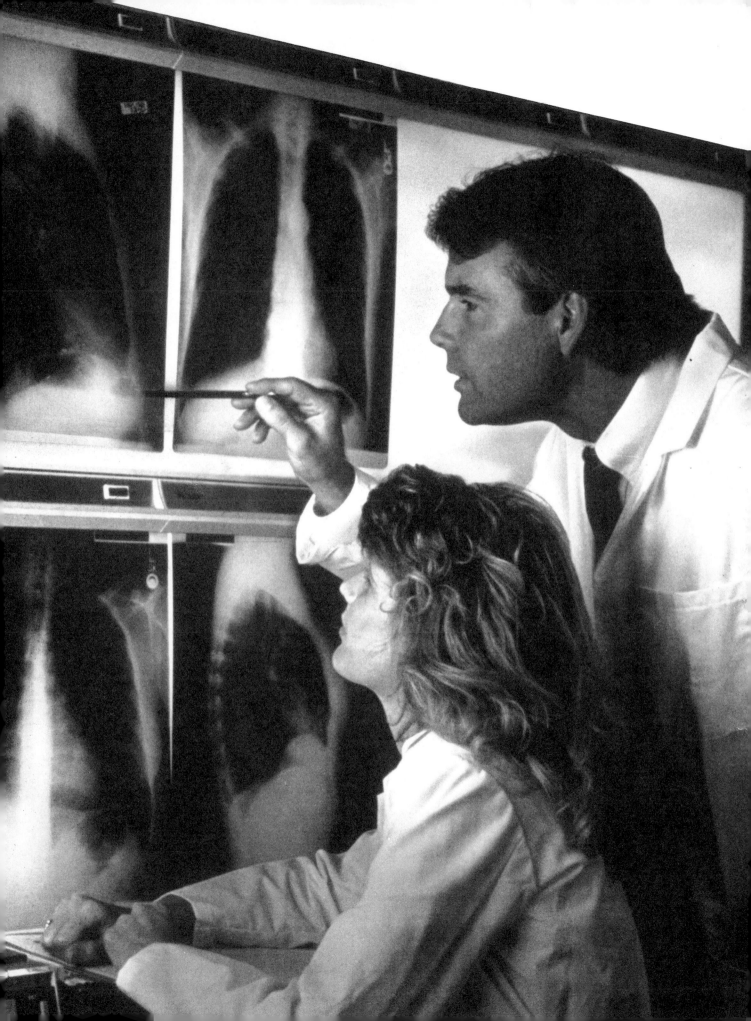

Anatomy of the Airways

The average adult breathes in and out about 22,000 times every day, with each inhaled breath taking about two-thirds of a second to travel along the roughly 16 inches of bone, muscle, and cartilage that form the linked airways known as the respiratory tract. The respiratory tract begins at the nose and mouth. Air taken in there goes through the pharynx (throat) and larynx (voice box) to the trachea (the windpipe), and then into the large tubes into which the trachea divides, the right and left bronchi. The bronchi carry the air into the lungs. The right lung has three lobes, or major divisions, while the left lung has two. These lobes are crisscrossed by a network of bronchioles, smaller tubes that lead from the bronchi to the alveoli, microscopic air cells. The alveoli, of which there are hundreds of millions, are fed by small blood vessels; here is where the purpose of the respiratory system is fulfilled—blood is enriched with oxygen from breathed-in air and carbon dioxide is released by the blood, to be exhaled.

How Infection Occurs

Every time air is breathed in, dirt, pollen, and a variety of infectious agents come with it. If any of these agents takes hold in the nose, throat, or bronchi, a person is said to have an upper respiratory tract infection. (Infection of the bronchi is more specifically known as bronchitis.) If infection develops in the lower part of the respiratory system, the lungs (which are usually sterile), the person is said to have pneumonia.

The respiratory system has many defenses against infection.

The body has many defense mechanisms to prevent infection from taking hold in the respiratory system. For example, the epiglottis—a flap of cartilage that covers the trachea and opens only to allow breathing—prevents the bacteria that normally live in the nose and throat of healthy people from getting down into the lower respiratory tract and causing infection. A layer of mucus throughout the respiratory tract traps invading organisms. Tiny hairlike cells, called cilia, project from the lining of the larger air passages and propel mucus, dust, and so on toward the back of the mouth and then into the digestive tract, where they are destroyed by digestive fluids. And coughing serves to expel large numbers of invading organisms.

A. Martin Lerner is governor of the Michigan chapter of the American College of Physicians and clinical professor of medicine at Wayne State University School of Medicine in Detroit.

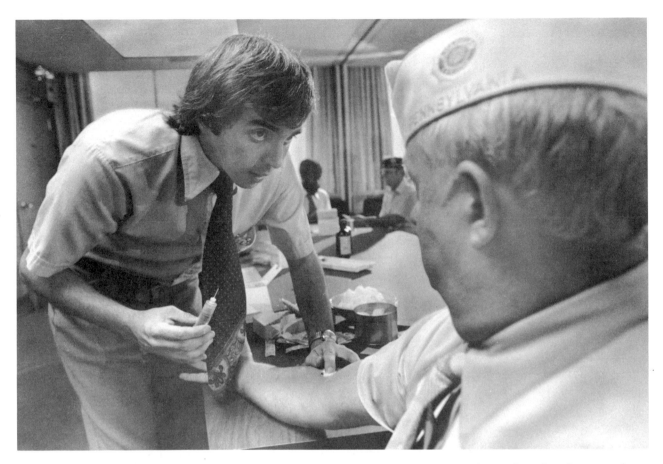

Furthermore, the body produces antibodies that play a protective role throughout the respiratory tract; in the lungs themselves, specialized cells of the immune system, known as T lymphocytes and macrophages, work to destroy agents of infection.

Sometimes, however, infectious agents evade the body's defenses. Perhaps the cilia are damaged by smoking or by a viral infection in the upper respiratory tract. Or perhaps the immune system is immature (in an infant) or is weakened by age or illness. Or the epiglottis fails to close normally due to weakness caused by loss of consciousness, general anesthesia, or a stroke or seizure. Whatever the reason, the outcome is pneumonia.

Blood samples taken from people attending an American Legion convention in 1976 helped scientists pin down the cause of the mysterious pneumonia that killed 34 Legionnaires.

Causes of Infection

In the early 1900s, when bacteriology as a science was first developing, physicians debated vigorously whether pneumonia was caused by the bacterium *Streptococcus pneumoniae*, which scientists called the pneumococcus, or by another organism, *Klebsiella pneumoniae*, also known as Friedländer's bacillus. Later, it became clear that the majority of cases then were caused by the pneumococcus. In the United States today, the pneumococcus is the largest single cause of pneumonia (about half of pneumonia cases are caused by any of dozens of pneumococcus strains).

The bacterium called *Legionella pneumophila* drew public attention in the 1970s for causing a type of pneumonia better known as Legionnaire's disease. This bacterium was unknown before it caused pneumonial infections at an American Legion convention in Philadelphia in 1976. A total of 221 people became ill, and 34 died, in that outbreak. Researchers at the U.S. Centers for Disease Control now suspect that the organism may account for between 25,000 and 50,000 cases of pneumonia in the United States each year. Scientists believe that the organism is transmitted by air and have found it in lakes, rivers, cooling towers, air-conditioning systems (the suspected means of transmission for the Philadelphia outbreak), drinking water taps, and whirlpool baths. Other bacteria that can cause serious pneumonias—especially during influenza epidemics, when people's defenses against infection are weakened—include *Staphylococcus aureus* and *Hemophilus influenzae*.

The symptoms of pneumonia include fever, chest pain, and a cough.

Another agent that can cause pneumonia is the bacteria-like organism *Mycoplasma pneumoniae*, which was recognized in the late 1940s as an important cause of pneumonia, one that most often occurs in children and young adults.

Newly recognized kinds of pneumonias occur in patients made more susceptible by chronic illness, cancer chemotherapy, or medications taken to prevent rejection of transplanted organs, all of which weaken patients' immune systems. Patients with AIDS, for instance, frequently get a type of pneumonia caused by the parasite *Pneumocystis carinii*.

Some patients with weakened immune systems get pneumonia caused by cytomegalovirus, and during a flu epidemic, influenza viruses themselves may produce pneumonia in some people. In general, however, viral pneumonias are relatively uncommon.

Lobar Pneumonia and Bronchopneumonia

Pneumonias are sometimes classified according to their extent. In lobar pneumonia, the entire area of one or more lobes of a lung is infected. In this type of pneumonia, the airy, fluffy, ordinarily marvelously efficient gas exchange tissues of the lungs are changed into a solid, nonfunctional, infected mass. The alveoli become plugged, so that oxygen and carbon dioxide can no longer be exchanged. Patients have difficulty breathing, in proportion to how much of the lungs are affected. Ultimately, if the disease progresses unchecked, tissues all over the body are underoxygenated, and the skin takes on a bluish or purplish color. Too frequently, death follows. Lobar pneumonia, which was once common, was nearly always caused by the pneumococcus. Most patients today are treated with antibiotics before the infection can spread so widely, and lobar pneumonia is now less common. The majority of pneumonias now involve patches of infection scattered throughout the lungs and are called bronchopneumonia.

Symptoms

The symptoms of pneumonia vary depending on what is causing it, how extensive the infection is, and the state of the patient's health. General symptoms that should alert a person to the possibility of pneumonia include a cough and the coughing up of sputum. This can be yellowish, greenish, or grayish and is sometimes tinged with blood. Patients usually have a fever, sometimes mild, sometimes severe. They often have chest pain.

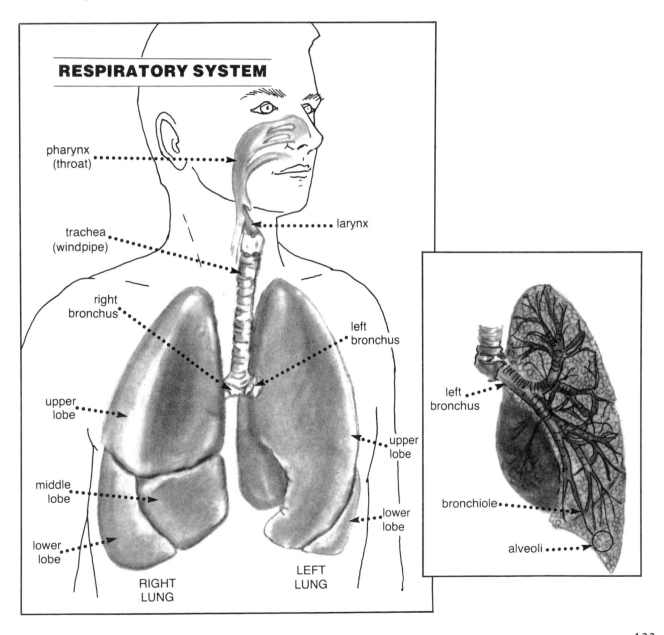

RESPIRATORY SYSTEM

pharynx (throat)

larynx

trachea (windpipe)

right bronchus

left bronchus

upper lobe

upper lobe

middle lobe

lower lobe

lower lobe

RIGHT LUNG

LEFT LUNG

left bronchus

bronchiole

alveoli

Complications

Complications of pneumonia include the spread of the infection to broader areas of the lung, the formation of abscesses (or pus-filled cavities) in the lung, and the spread of the infection outside the lungs to the chest (a condition called empyema) or to the covering of the heart (a condition called purulent pericarditis). Infection may spread to the blood (a complication known as bacteremia) and thereby to distant body sites, such as joints, where it causes septic arthritis, or the brain, where it causes meningitis.

Diagnosis

A patient who develops a cough, brings up sputum, and, in particular, has a fever, should promptly consult a physician. The physician will probably listen to the patient's chest through a stethoscope and note any sounds indicating abnormal breathing. Tapping the chest will help the doctor determine if there is fluid in the chest outside of the lung. A chest X ray will confirm the diagnosis of pneumonia and will show how much of the lung is affected. The doctor will probably take sputum and blood samples in order to determine which organism is causing the infection. If patients are severely ill or have chronic illnesses, they are usually admitted to a hospital, where oxygen can be given if necessary and where medications can be given intravenously. In other cases, patients may simply take medications at home.

Treatment

Before the advent of modern medicine, there was very little that could be done for someone suffering from pneumonia, beyond waiting and hoping. The 1881 discovery by the French scientist Louis Pasteur of the pneumococcal organism gave the medical community a handle on the disease. By the early decades of the 20th century doctors were treating pneumococcal pneumonia (the most prevalent kind then) with a serum developed by injecting the pneumococcus into horses, which then produced antibodies that helped fight the infection in patients' bodies. Unfortunately, the serum had to be injected into muscle tissue, which is very painful, because when it was injected directly into the bloodstream it sometimes caused blood clots. Some patients also developed adverse reactions to the serum, ranging from bloody urine and kidney damage to fever and arthritis. In spite of these serious complications, serum therapy continued to be used because pneumonia was such a threat to life. When serum typed to a specific strain of pneumococcal pneumonia became available, the mortality rate for pneumococcal pneumonia went from about 50 percent to about 30 percent. In the mid-1930s the sulfa drugs came into use and provided striking benefits in treating the disease. Then, in the mid-1940s, penicillin, for the discovery of which the British bacteriologist Sir Alexander Fleming shared the Nobel Prize in medicine, was put into general use, marking another major advance in treating pneumonia. With the advent of penicillin, the mortality rate from pneumococcal pneumonia fell to around 3 percent, where it remains today.

Sir Alexander Fleming's discovery of penicillin was a milestone in the battle against pneumococcal pneumonia—once a major killer.

134

Penicillin is still generally used for the treatment of pneumococcal pneumonias, but other drugs are available for other types of the illness. Erythromycin, for example, is used for pneumonias caused by mycoplasma or by the Legionella bacterium. Trimethoprim sulfa or pentamidine is used for *Pneumocystis carinii* pneumonia. Some physicians believe that antibiotics as a generalized treatment are so effective against pneumonia that identifying the specific bacterium, fungus, virus, or parasite causing the infection is not often necessary. However, pneumonia is best treated when the physician knows what specific organism is causing it and selects the appropriate medication. For really effective treatment, the right drug has to be in the right place in the body at the right time and be delivered safely, and each of the drugs mentioned can have significant side effects that must be considered.

Pneumonia is a life-threatening disease and must be treated as such.

How long treatment must be continued depends on the cause of the illness, its extent, and the patient's health in general. Anywhere from one to six weeks of treatment may be needed.

Despite the increasing effectiveness of available drugs and better supportive care, especially in intensive care units of hospitals, an informed, well-trained, and attentive physician is required to treat pneumonia successfully. Pneumonia remains a life-threatening disease, and effective care, promptly administered, saves lives and shortens the length of the illness and the extent of a patient's disability.

Vaccines

Today, there is an effective pneumococcal vaccine that can protect patients at increased risk of this severe infection. The vaccine protects against 23 prevalent strains of the pneumococcus that together are responsible for about 90 percent of cases of pneumococcal pneumonia. The vaccine is recommended for those who have other illnesses, such as chronic lung or heart disease or diabetes, people 65 or older, and people infected with the virus that causes AIDS. Until more long-term studies of it are completed, it is recommended that the vaccine, which is effective for at least five years, be given only once. This vaccine is not as effective in some patients with suppressed immune systems, such as those undergoing anticancer therapy.

Influenza vaccine should be given each year to the same people who are candidates for the pneumococcal vaccine, because they are at increased risk for pneumonia caused by influenza viruses and for secondary bacterial pneumonias should they get the flu. Because of frequent changes in the influenza viruses, the flu vaccine is changed annually to protect against the strains currently in circulation. □

The hormone adrenaline is secreted in response to physical danger—or a scary amusement park ride.

HORMONES

Merville C. Marshall, Jr., M.D.

What is a hormone? In the past, the answer to this question was a relatively simple one. Hormones were defined as substances secreted by specific glands and transported in the blood to other organs for the purpose of regulating metabolic processes. (Metabolism is a general term for the enormous variety of chemical processes constantly going on in the body to keep it functioning.) The classic example of a hormone is insulin, which is secreted by the pancreas and transported in the blood to fat and muscle tissues throughout the body, so that they can properly utilize glucose in the blood for energy.

But as more has been learned about endocrinology—the functioning of hormones and glands—the definition of what constitutes a hormone has broadened considerably. We now know there are hormones that act upon nearby tissues and are not transported to distant sites in the body. There are hormones that are secreted by many different tissues

in the body, not just by a single gland. The gastrointestinal tract and the central nervous system are known to produce a large number of different hormones. Some substances, considered neurotransmitters because they transmit "messages" from one nerve cell to another, also have been found to have important effects upon metabolic functions, and thus act like hormones. In turn, many hormones act like neurotransmitters. Finally, there are hormones that have no known physiological function, since a deficiency or an excess of them in the body does not appear to alter metabolic functions. As medical technology becomes more sophisticated, and knowledge of normal and abnormal physiology grows, the realm of the endocrine system will continue to expand.

What Hormones Do for Us

Simply put, the job of hormones is to keep things in balance, or maintain homeostasis. In a normally healthy person, the blood sugar level is constantly kept within a narrow range, regardless of whether the person has just eaten or has fasted overnight. The balance is maintained by the combined actions of insulin, which lowers blood sugar, and several other hormones that raise blood sugar. Another way of describing the role of the endocrine system is that it keeps metabolic function constant, even when external factors (such as eating or drinking) are not constant.

To maintain homeostasis, hormone secretion must be regulated—the body needs to know how much of various hormones to produce and when. Most glands produce hormones in response to specific stimuli, such as changes in blood chemistry, and are able to answer the call for more hormone production when necessary. The pattern of hormone production varies, however. Some hormones are secreted at a constant rate, while others (notably the hormones affecting sexual function) are produced at irregular intervals. Blood levels of the latter hormones vary throughout the day, reflecting random surges of hormone secretion. Production of still other hormones follows a regular daily cycle, with predictable peaks at the same time every day. This is known as a circadian or diurnal rhythm. Usually the peak secretion is during sleep or in the early morning. When people travel from one time zone to another and change their sleep schedule, the body's "biological clock," which regulates these hormone secretions, has to be reset. This resetting probably contributes to the phenomenon known as jet lag.

Not only must hormone production be turned on at the appropriate time; it must also be turned off—often through a process called feedback inhibition. For example, parathyroid hormone (PTH) acts to raise blood calcium levels, and a drop in blood calcium levels provides the stimulus for increased secretion of PTH. Then, higher calcium

Merville C. Marshall, Jr., is staff physician in the Department of Medicine, Long Island Jewish Medical Center, and assistant professor of medicine at the Albert Einstein College of Medicine in New York.

levels in response to the PTH "feed back" to the parathyroid glands a signal to stop secreting the hormone. In this manner, calcium levels in the blood are kept fairly constant.

Once a hormone is secreted and transported to its site of action, it must have a mechanism for telling the body what to do. That function is performed by receptors. All body cells have receptors that permit communication between hormones and cells. Some receptors are on the cell's outer membrane, others are in the cell's nucleus. Cells have different receptors for different hormones. The receptors can be compared to doors that have different locks, while hormones are like different keys. If the key fits the lock, the door opens. When a hormone interacts with a receptor, a series of molecular events ensue that lead to the final action of the hormone.

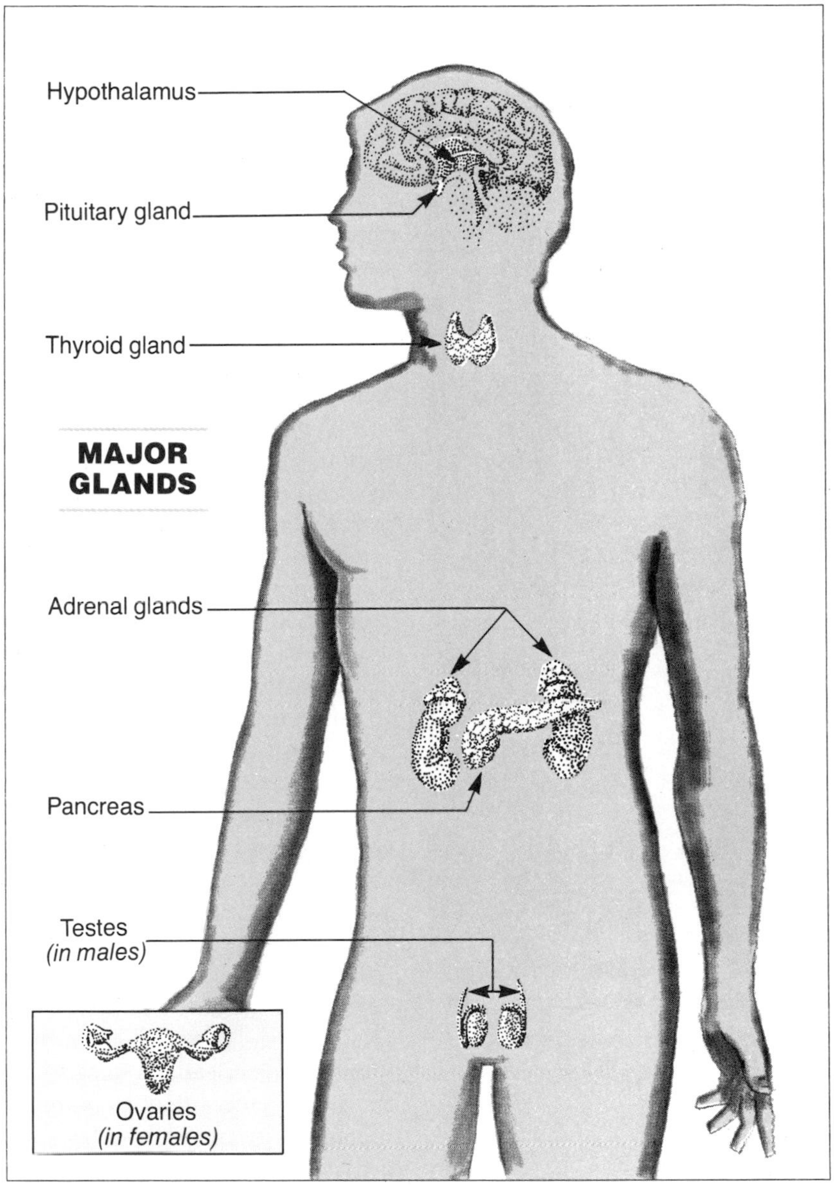

Endocrine Disorders

Endocrine disorders usually result from an excess or deficiency of a particular hormone or from an inability of the body to utilize the hormone. Tumors and a variety of other conditions can cause too much of a hormone to be produced. A hormone deficiency can be caused by the absence of the gland that secretes the hormone or by a disease of the gland that prevents it from secreting adequate amounts. Even if sufficient quantities of a hormone are produced, an endocrine disorder may develop because of an inability of the hormone to interact with its receptor. This inability can result from two conditions. The first is the rare case of a hormone that has an abnormal structure and thus cannot perform its biological function (it is as if the key has been altered and no longer fits the lock). The second and more common condition is a decrease in the number of receptors or a change in receptor function, either of which prevents the receptor from responding to the hormone (the door is not available to be unlocked).

MAJOR GLANDS

Hypothalamus

Pituitary gland

Thyroid gland

Adrenal glands

Pancreas

Testes
(in males)

Ovaries
(in females)

The Pancreas, Insulin, and Diabetes

Diabetes is a disorder of carbohydrate metabolism that results in high levels of glucose (sugar) in the blood. The inability of the body to use this sugar for energy and the excessive glucose circulating in the blood can lead to a number of serious medical problems. Diabetes is the most common endocrine disorder in the United States, affecting approximately 3 percent of the population. There are two major categories of diabetes: insulin-dependent (Type I) and non-insulin-dependent (Type II). Type II accounts for 80 to 90 percent of all cases of diabetes. The majority of patients with Type II develop diabetes when they are over the age of 40, while the majority of patients with Type I develop it during childhood or the teen years.

In Type I diabetes the body fails to produce enough insulin, a hormone secreted by the beta cells of the pancreas gland, which is located in the abdomen. When insulin is absent, glucose cannot be used by body cells and accumulates in the blood.

Paradoxically, in Type II diabetes blood glucose levels are high despite normal or even higher-than-normal levels of insulin production. This is because the insulin is rendered ineffective by abnormal insulin receptors. (However, in many overweight patients receptor abnormalities can be reversed by weight loss.) Type II diabetes tends to run in families; Type I does not.

In Type I the deficiency of insulin results from destruction of the beta cells. A malfunction of the body's immune system, whose role is to defend the body against outside invaders such as bacteria and viruses, is responsible for this destruction. When the immune system is directed against the body itself, the result is what is known as an autoimmune disease.

A consequence of the lack of insulin in Type I diabetes is a tendency to develop an acute metabolic emergency known as diabetic ketoacidosis (DKA). In DKA the blood glucose level is very high. Unable to utilize the glucose, the body starts to burn its own fat and muscle, which leads to uncontrolled production of ketone bodies or keto acids, substances that profoundly affect metabolism. The patient becomes extremely ill, suffering nausea, vomiting, abdominal pain, dehydration, and alterations in mental status that can culminate in coma. DKA can be the initial manifestation of Type I diabetes or can be precipitated by acute physical stress, such as an infection. The patient must be treated with intravenous fluids and insulin.

Treating Diabetes. Diet is an important element in the treatment of diabetes, whether or not oral medication or insulin is prescribed. The patient must avoid the simple sugars found in sweets such as pastries, candies, ice cream, and the like, since these sugars cause the most rapid elevations in blood glucose levels. Other carbohydrates (starch and complex sugars, such as those found in fruits and vegetables) need not be avoided. The overweight patient should go on a weight-loss diet.

Oral medications are useful for Type II patients in whom the disease cannot be controlled by diet alone. These drugs initially stimulate the secretion of more insulin by the pancreas, but their major effect is to reverse the receptor abnormalities associated with the disease.

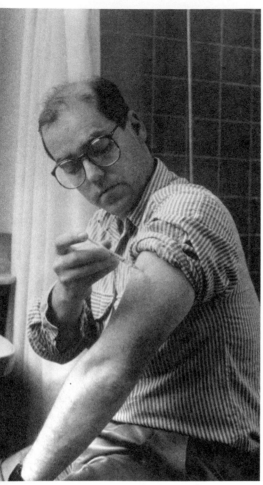

Many patients with diabetes give themselves daily injections of the hormone insulin.

Insulin is used to treat all Type I patients and those Type II patients who fail to respond to oral drugs. Insulin cannot be taken by mouth (since it is broken down by the digestive system). It must be administered by injection under the skin. The commercially available insulin preparations are pork insulin (drawn from the pancreas of pigs) and a more recent product of genetic engineering—human insulin, which is less likely to cause allergic reactions. Both insulins are available as long-acting, intermediate-acting, and short-acting preparations. These preparations can be given in combination, when necessary, to achieve optimal control of blood glucose levels.

An important potential side effect of insulin therapy is hypoglycemia, or low blood glucose levels. Hypoglycemia causes sweating, palpitations, hunger, and anxiety and can lead to coma. It is critical for patients taking insulin to recognize these symptoms, and when they occur, to eat or drink something quickly to reverse them. Hypoglycemia is less common among patients taking oral medication.

Two recent advances can be of great help to patients taking insulin. The first is the glycohemoglobin test, a blood test that can indicate the average blood glucose level for the preceding six weeks. This test is a better measure of how well the diabetes is being controlled than a single random blood glucose test done in the doctor's office. The second advance is home monitoring; kits are now available that make it possible for patients to monitor their own blood glucose levels at intervals throughout the day. A small, portable machine called a glucometer allows patients to draw a drop of blood from the fingertip and get an accurate glucose reading within minutes. In this way, patients can keep a record of how their glucose levels vary during the day, which is of great help to doctors in evaluating how effective their insulin program is.

Possible Complications. Diabetes can lead to many complications. People with diabetes are more susceptible to infections such as urinary tract infections, dental abscesses, and vaginal yeast infections. Other potential complications are kidney disease, eye problems (such as cataracts and disease of the retina), circulation problems, diseases of the peripheral nervous system (causing alterations in muscle strength, pain sensation, or sexual potency), and foot problems (such as infected skin ulcers). Complications often occur when diabetes has been present for 10 to 15 years or more, but not every patient is affected.

The Thyroid and Its Disorders

The thyroid gland lies in front of the windpipe, just below the Adam's apple. This gland secretes two hormones, thyroxine and triiodothyronine (abbreviated as T4 and T3, respectively), which affect the body's overall metabolism. An excess of these hormones is known as hyperthyroidism; a deficiency is called hypothyroidism. Each condition causes a distinct set of symptoms.

Hyperthyroidism (also known as thyrotoxicosis) is characterized by restlessness, nervousness, tremulousness, a fast heartbeat, increased bowel movements, weight loss, intolerance of warm weather, excessive perspiration, changes in skin and hair texture, and changes in

Overproduction of thyroid hormones can cause restlessness, nervousness, rapid weight loss, and a fast heartbeat.

menstrual cycles. These symptoms may appear in any combination. Hyperthyroidism is often accompanied by a goiter—an enlarged thyroid gland that can be detected by a physical examination. The most common cause of hyperthyroidism is Graves' disease, an autoimmune disorder in which antibodies are produced that stimulate the thyroid gland to secrete excess T4 and T3. Graves' disease often causes eye problems, such as a popeye stare, excessive tearing, eye inflammation, and even double vision.

Hyperthyroidism can be confirmed by simple blood tests. Usually, a 24-hour radioactive iodine uptake test is also performed, which gives doctors information on how the thyroid gland is functioning. Iodine is essential to the synthesis of thyroid hormones. In the test the patient drinks a very small amount (a diagnostic dose) of radioactive iodine, and the amount of iodine absorbed by the thyroid gland over the next 24 hours is measured by an instrument similar to a Geiger counter.

Gigantism can result from an excess of growth hormone in childhood, while dwarfism can be caused by a deficiency of that hormone. But not all very tall people are giants. Sudanese-born basketball player Manute Bol (left), at 7'6", is within normal range. Below, in a picture taken around 1880, are the legendary English dwarfs General and Mrs. Tom Thumb, dolled up in evening dress.

Hyperthyroidism is treated by one of three methods: antithyroid medication, surgery to remove part of the thyroid gland, or a therapeutic dose of radioactive iodine. (Barbara Bush, wife of U.S. President George Bush, was diagnosed with Graves' disease in the spring of 1989, after suffering eye irritation and a rapid weight loss; she was treated with radioactive iodine.)

All three methods of treating hyperthyroidism are equally effective, but each has advantages and drawbacks. Antithyroid medication inhibits the production of thyroid hormones; about 5 percent of patients, however, have an allergic reaction to the medication. Both surgery and radioactive iodine cause destruction of thyroid tissue and can ultimately result in hypothyroidism. For this reason patients who have had one of these therapies should have blood tests at regular intervals.

Hypothyroidism is characterized by lethargy, fatigue, a slow heartbeat, decreased bowel movements, weight gain, intolerance of cold weather, decreased perspiration, dry skin, and changes in menstrual cycles. Previous therapy for hyperthyroidism is the most common cause of hypothyroidism, followed by Hashimoto's thyroiditis, an autoimmune disorder in which the body produces antibodies that attack the thyroid gland. Both Hashimoto's thyroiditis and Graves' disease tend to run in families and, like most thyroid diseases, tend to affect women more often than men.

Hypothyroidism can be confirmed by simple blood tests. It can be readily treated with synthetic thyroid hormone preparations, which are available in tablet form. Most patients need take only one tablet a day, and the majority will require this thyroid hormone therapy indefinitely.

A goiter (enlarged thyroid gland) can occur in those with hyperthyroidism or hypothyroidism, as well as in people with normally functioning thyroid glands. For those with normally functioning glands, taking thyroid hormone will arrest further growth of the goiter and may even shrink it.

Sometimes, one or more lumps, or nodules, may develop on the thyroid. The presence of even a single nodule on an otherwise normal thyroid gland warrants further investigation, since approximately 20 percent of such nodules are malignant. The only definitive way to ascertain whether a nodule is benign or malignant is by removing it for laboratory examination. Other tests, however, will suggest a likelihood of malignancy with varying levels of accuracy—and therefore can help the physician decide which patients should undergo surgery.

Malignant thyroid nodules are more common in people who have previously had radiation of the head and neck area. Both radiation therapy for an enlarged thymus gland during infancy and radiation therapy for acne can lead to the development of thyroid nodules 20 to 30 years later. Diagnostic X rays such as chest X rays and dental X rays do not increase the risk of thyroid nodules.

Thyroid cancers are relatively slow-growing, and they can often be cured by surgery and radioactive iodine therapy. Chemotherapy is not necessary for papillary and follicular carcinomas, the two most common varieties of thyroid cancer. With proper treatment, survival rates for these two types are generally excellent.

In spring 1989, First Lady Barbara Bush was diagnosed as having Graves' disease and treated with radioactive iodine.

Regulating Calcium

Calcium, besides being the essential ingredient of bone, is an important constituent of blood. Calcium levels in the blood are regulated by parathyroid hormone (PTH) and vitamin D. PTH is secreted by the parathyroid glands, the very small glands (usually four in number) that lie behind the thyroid gland. As stated earlier, PTH production increases in response to low blood calcium levels and decreases when blood calcium levels are high. PTH increases blood calcium levels by several means. It stimulates the breakdown of bone to release calcium to the blood; it stimulates the kidneys to conserve calcium; and it stimulates the conversion of vitamin D in the body to its active form. In this active form, vitamin D stimulates absorption by the intestines of calcium in food.

The condition called hypercalcemia—high blood calcium levels—is a common endocrine disorder. Often, it is discovered when blood tests are done as part of a routine physical examination. Hypercalcemia is commonly caused by hyperparathyroidism. (In addition, the condition frequently results from cancer that has spread and affects the bones.)

Hyperparathyroidism is uncontrolled, excess PTH production by one or more parathyroid glands. It can lead to lethargy, muscle weakness, increased urination, nausea, constipation, and peptic ulcers. If the blood calcium level is high enough, calcium will spill over into the urine and may cause kidney stones. Because PTH causes removal of calcium from the bones, hyperparathyroidism can lead to loss of bone tissue.

When hyperparathyroidism is mild, it may not require any treatment. When it is more severe, the overactive parathyroid gland has to be removed by surgery. Hyperparathyroidism may be an inherited trait.

Estrogen and Osteoporosis

Osteoporosis—thinning of the bones—primarily affects women after menopause. A decline in estrogen levels is the probable cause.

Osteoporosis is thinning of the bones. The disease primarily affects older people, particularly women, and the most common variety is seen in postmenopausal women. Both sexes begin to lose bone mass after around age 35. But women have less bone mass than men to begin with, and in postmenopausal women the rate of loss is accelerated, apparently because of the decline in estrogen levels that accompanies menopause. Estrogen is one of the two female sex hormones (progesterone is the other) that are secreted by the ovaries and that are responsible for the normal development in girls that occurs at puberty and for maintaining the female sexual characteristics after puberty. Caucasian race, a lean body type, a small frame, premature menopause, and a family history of osteoporosis add to the risk of this disease in postmenopausal women. Another variety of osteoporosis, known as senile osteoporosis, is prevalent in both men and women over 70.

Because thin bones are brittle and easily fractured, the major consequence of osteoporosis is an increase in hip, spine, and wrist fractures. Spine fractures can cause loss of height and a stooped-over appearance, often referred to as dowager's hump when it occurs in women. Hip fractures can be particularly serious—in the United

States, 10 to 15 percent of people with osteoporosis who suffer hip fractures die of complications within a year.

The diagnosis of osteoporosis is generally based on recognition of the conditions in which it is likely to occur. There are no blood tests for osteoporosis, and X rays will show abnormalities only late in the course of the disease. There are procedures for specifically measuring bone density; however, they generally are not used for screening, but rather for monitoring the effect of therapy in some patients.

A long list of other conditions can lead to secondary osteoporosis, among them malnutrition, hyperthyroidism, and hyperparathyroidism. Physical exercise is good for bones, but very heavy exercise can halt menstruation and subsequently cause osteoporosis even in young women. Smoking, drinking alcohol, eating a diet poor in calcium, and taking certain medications, such as steroid drugs, will all cause thinning of the bones. Osteoporosis caused by any of these conditions or practices may be alleviated by treating the underlying condition or making appropriate life-style changes.

The only proven effective therapy for the osteoporosis that follows menopause is estrogen replacement, which works best if begun preventively as soon as menopause is evident. Estrogen is usually combined with progestin, a progesterone-like drug, and generally taken in pill form. Taking calcium supplements may also inhibit further loss of bone tissue. Several other medications have been tried, but none has proved to be consistently effective.

The best approach to treating osteoporosis is prevention. Women who are at risk can decrease their chances of getting the disease by getting enough exercise, giving up smoking or excessive use of alcohol, and keeping their calcium intake high (either through diet alone or with the aid of calcium supplements) throughout their adult lives. (*See also the Spotlight on Health article* MENOPAUSE.)

Exercising regularly, abstaining from smoking, and taking in enough calcium can help prevent osteoporosis in those at risk.

The Hypothalamus and the Pituitary

The hypothalamus is a small area at the base of the brain that secretes a number of hormones called releasing hormones. These hormones travel down a special system of blood vessels to the pituitary gland, which lies just below the hypothalamus. The pituitary gland itself secretes hormones that in turn travel to other glands. The area known as the hypothalamic-pituitary axis plays a major role in controlling the activity of these other glands.

For example, in a kind of chain reaction, the hypothalamus secretes a hormone known as TRH (for thyrotropin releasing hormone) that stimulates the pituitary to secrete a thyroid stimulating hormone (TSH). TSH in turn stimulates the thyroid gland to secrete thyroid hormones. The pituitary gland is very responsive to levels of thyroid hormones in the blood. If these levels are high, the pituitary will stop secreting TSH, and as a result the thyroid gland will secrete less of the thyroid hormones. If the thyroid hormone levels in the blood are low, the pituitary will secrete more TSH until the thyroid gland produces enough thyroid hormones to raise levels to normal. Much as a thermostat serves to maintain a constant temperature, the pituitary

How the Body Reacts to Danger

When we are faced with physical danger or psychological stress, our adrenal glands respond by secreting epinephrine (adrenaline). Epinephrine, a powerful heart stimulant, and norepinephrine, a related compound, enter the bloodstream and in seconds cause dramatic changes in body functions. The process is known as the fight-or-flight response, since it prepares one to either physically encounter or flee from an enemy.

● Heartbeat quickens and strengthens.

● Blood pressure rises.

● Blood sugar increases, so that more sugar for energy can be delivered to muscles and other body tissues.

● Surface blood vessels contract, which will lessen bleeding in case of injury.

● Pupils dilate, improving vision.

● Lungs take in more air, so that more oxygen can reach muscles and other body tissues.

● Digestion slows, freeing more blood to deliver sugar and oxygen to muscles.

● Perspiration increases, which keeps the body cool.

● Muscles tense, become ready for action.

acts to keep levels of thyroid hormones constant within a predetermined normal range.

Similarly, corticotropin releasing factor (CRF) secreted by the hypothalamus stimulates the pituitary to secrete adrenocorticotrophic hormone (ACTH), which then stimulates the adrenal glands to produce cortisol, a steroid hormone. To give still another example, growth hormone releasing hormone (GHRH) from the hypothalamus causes secretion of growth hormone (GH) by the pituitary gland; GH acts throughout the body to stimulate normal growth and development in children and adolescents.

One substance, dopamine, acts in opposite fashion to the releasing hormones—that is, it inhibits hormone production. Secreted by the hypothalamus, dopamine stops the pituitary gland from secreting prolactin. Prolactin acts to stimulate milk production by breast tissue.

Any disease that attacks the hypothalamus or the pituitary gland can cause a deficiency of one or more of the pituitary hormones. The effects depend upon which hormones are involved. A deficiency of growth hormone in a child could cause stunted growth, but in an adult such a deficiency would have no effect. Deficiency of thyroid stimulating hormone would cause hypothyroidism, and lack of ACTH would lead to atrophy of the adrenal glands.

Tumors of the pituitary gland can secrete excess hormones; usually, a single hormone is involved. The most common type of tumor is the prolactin-secreting tumor, or prolactinoma. Excess prolactin secretion in women can cause breast milk to flow spontaneously (a condition called galactorrhea), absence of menstruation, and infertility. In men, excess prolactin causes impotence. Prolactinomas are often small, and they can be easily treated with bromocriptine, a drug that stops prolactin secretion. The drug also causes the tumor to shrink.

Other hormone-secreting pituitary tumors include a tumor that secretes growth hormone. An excess of GH in a child causes abnormal growth of bone, cartilage, and other tissue, which leads to excessive height and a characteristic appearance known as gigantism. In an adult, the GH excess causes no change in height because fully matured bones will no longer grow; however, growth of cartilage and other tissue leads to the excessively large hands, feet, and jaw that characterize the condition known as acromegaly.

Cortisol is the major steroid hormone produced by the body. Among other functions, it helps protect against inflammation.

The Adrenal Glands

There are two adrenal glands, one atop each kidney. They consist of an inner portion, called the medulla, which secretes the hormone epinephrine (adrenaline) under the control of the nervous system, and an outer portion, called the cortex. Adrenaline is well known for its role in gearing up the body for action in times of physical danger or psychological stress. The hormone induces a variety of changes, including a faster heartbeat, a rise in blood pressure, and a general sharpening of the senses. (See the box on page 146.)

The adrenal cortex secretes cortisol, which is the major natural steroid hormone made in the body. Cortisol affects the metabolism of glucose, helps to protect against inflammation, and inhibits the body's immune response. (The synthetic drug cortisone is similar to cortisol.) The adrenal cortex also secretes small amounts of male sex hormones in both males and females, as well as a substance that affects salt and water balance in the body.

Cushing's Syndrome. An excess of cortisol causes Cushing's syndrome, a disorder characterized by obesity, high blood pressure, redness of the face, and muscle weakness, as well as menstrual abnormalities in women; it may lead to osteoporosis or diabetes. (It should be noted, however, that the vast majority of obese people and people with high blood pressure or diabetes do not have Cushing's syndrome.) Cushing's syndrome can result from long-term use of steroid medication, from an adrenal tumor that secretes cortisol, or from an excess of ACTH that continually stimulates the adrenal glands. Excess ACTH can come from a pituitary tumor or from an ectopic source (an organ that does not normally produce ACTH). Sophisticated blood tests can help determine the particular cause of a patient's Cushing's syndrome; depending on the cause, it may be treated by surgery or with radiation therapy or antiadrenal medication.

In adolescence the body begins to produce more of the sex hormones—estrogen and progesterone in females, testosterone in males.

Addison's Disease. Most cases of cortisol insufficiency result from Addison's disease, an autoimmune disease that destroys the adrenal glands. This deficiency causes weakness, fatigue, weight loss, loss of appetite, low blood pressure, and in some cases increased skin pigmentation. The condition can be treated by cortisol replacement; the hormone is available in tablet form.

The Ovaries

The hypothalamus secretes luteinizing hormone releasing hormone (LHRH), which stimulates the pituitary gland to produce two hormones—luteinizing hormone (LH) and follicle stimulating hormone (FSH)—that control the functioning of the ovaries and the menstrual cycle in women. LH and FSH stimulate the ovaries to secrete the female sex hormones estrogen and progesterone. A carefully orchestrated release of LHRH and a finely tuned feedback system involving the ovarian hormones and the pituitary gland are responsible for the normal sequence of hormonal changes that occur in the menstrual cycle.

The menstrual cycle can be thought of as having two functions: to condition an ovary to release a mature egg (a process called ovulation) capable of being fertilized, and to ready the uterus to accept and nurture a fertilized egg—in other words, prepare it for pregnancy. At the end of the cycle, if the egg is not fertilized, ovarian hormone production declines and the lining of the uterus breaks down and is shed, leading to menstrual bleeding. If a woman becomes pregnant, the presence of a fertilized egg acts to maintain production of hormones that keep the uterine lining from shedding.

The normal menstrual cycle is the most delicately balanced hormonal activity in the body, and therefore the most easily disrupted. Changes in diet, very vigorous exercise, medications, emotional stress, and virtually any acute illness can cause changes in menstrual patterns. Specific ovarian or other endocrine disorders also affect the menstrual cycle.

Amenorrhea—absence of menstruation—can result from, among other things, endocrine system abnormalities such as excessive levels of the hormone prolactin, adrenal gland disorders, and thyroid disorders. Some women suffer from chronic anovulation (lack of ovulation), which causes irregular menstrual periods. In this condition the normal cycling of ovarian hormones does not occur. It is often accompanied by obesity and excess facial and body hair. The condition can be treated with birth control pills, which stimulate the normal cycling of ovarian hormones.

The Testes

The testes produce testosterone and sperm, under the stimulus of LH and FSH, respectively. Testosterone, the male sex hormone, is responsible for male sexual characteristics. Inadequate testicular function, which may result in deficient testosterone production, deficient sperm production, or both, is known as hypogonadism.

Testosterone deficiency causes impotence (inability to have a normal erection), decreased sexual drive, weakness or fatigue, and sometimes decreased facial hair growth. Insufficient sperm production results in infertility. When hypogonadism is caused by a disease of the testes themselves, testosterone injections can be given to restore sexual drive and potency; infertility may, however, be permanent. When hypogonadism is caused by a disease of the hypothalamic-pituitary axis, synthetic LHRH or synthetic LH and FSH can be given to restore both testosterone production and sperm production. Hypogonadism that results from high prolactin levels may be reversed by drugs that reduce secretion of prolactin. (It should be pointed out that various factors other than hypogonadism can cause impotence.)

Hormone Therapy

When hormones are used as medications, they may be administered in what are called physiological or pharmacological doses. A physiological dose is one given solely to restore normal metabolism. It is used in hormone replacement therapy when the body's production of the hormone is too low. Since the dose is, ideally, no more and no less than what the body would normally produce, it should not cause side effects. In some cases (as in treating hypothyroidism) the effects of replacement therapy can be precisely monitored by blood tests—and dosage fine-tuned accordingly. In other cases, the exact dose of a hormone needed can only be estimated, and its effects monitored indirectly by less precise means.

A pharmacological dose of a hormone is any dose larger than the normal physiological requirement. When a pharmacological dose is given, it may produce effects that are quite different from, or an exaggeration of, the normal effects of the hormone. In treating various conditions, high doses of steroids are used for their anti-inflammatory effects and ability to suppress the activity of the immune system. But patients who take such high doses for prolonged periods may experience a wide range of side effects, including osteoporosis, high blood pressure, diabetes, increased susceptibility to infections, cataracts, and the physical characteristics of Cushing's syndrome (obesity, redness of face). An additional risk of long-term steroid therapy is that the patient may experience withdrawal symptoms if the steroids are tapered off too quickly. However, when doctors treat patients with high doses of steroids, they do so because the clinical evidence indicates that the benefits outweigh the risks.

Patients who take physiological doses of steroids to treat adrenal insufficiency do not suffer the side effects of pharmacological doses. In any case, steroid medication is an absolute necessity for such patients. Patients who take high doses of steroids for a short period of time (less than a month) are also unlikely to suffer side effects.

Some hormones are prescribed for purposes other than medical treatment. Examples are the use of thyroid hormones to induce weight loss or certain kinds of steroids to build muscles. Such nonmedical uses of hormones should be avoided because the risks of side effects are unacceptably high. ☐

Nonmedical use of hormones such as steroids should be avoided because of the risks of dangerous side effects.

Your Stay in the Hospital

Susan Carleton

Hospitalization can be frightening and stressful. Illness itself stirs up fears of pain and mortality. In the hospital, these anxieties can be compounded by unfamiliar surroundings, daunting high-tech equipment, and rigid routines that may seem cold and impersonal. Most difficult, perhaps, is the sense of helplessness many patients suffer. Not only are they ill, but their immediate comfort and ultimate recovery are in the hands of others, many of whom are strangers and not all of whom may seem compassionate or caring.

Small wonder, then, that depression is a frequent side effect of an extended hospital stay. But patients and their families can take steps to make hospitalization less stressful than it might be. For starters, they can become well informed, not only about the condition that necessitates hospitalization but also about the hospital itself—what its routines are, which staff members will be involved in the patient's care. Understanding what's happening will go a long way toward alleviating many of the fears that can be brought on by being in the hospital.

A Changing Scenario

Hospital care has changed dramatically in the past decade. Techniques such as laser surgery and endoscopic surgery have made it possible to treat many conditions, from cataracts to knee injuries, without conventional major surgery, thus lessening the need for inpatient hospitalization. Instead, these conditions may be dealt with in special same-day surgery units which, according to the American Hospital Association, now exist in 95 percent of U.S. hospitals (excluding institutions like psychiatric hospitals, rehabilitation centers, and nursing homes). In 1987, 44 percent of all surgery was done in outpatient settings, compared to 24 percent in 1983.

At the same time, hospitals have come under increasing financial pressure. In 1983 the U.S. government established a new payment system for all hospitalizations paid through Medicare, the federal health insurance program for the elderly. (Medicare at the time accounted for upward of 50 percent of hospital revenues.) Under the new system, called prospective payment, hospitals are paid not their actual charges, but rather a set rate for each patient according to diagnosis, regardless of how long the patient is hospitalized. Thus, hospitals have a financial incentive to send patients home as soon as possible. Insurance companies have also become more tightfisted, often paying for only a set number of hospital days for most types of surgery.

All of these developments, along with a growing trend among doctors and hospitals toward avoiding unnecessary hospitalizations, have shortened the typical hospital stay and made hospitalization much less common than it was in the 1970s. Between 1982 and 1985 the average length of a hospital stay fell 7.4 percent, to 7.1 days. From 1980 to 1987 the number of hospital admissions also fell, by a dramatic 19 percent. In practical terms, this means a hospital patient today is likely to have a more severe illness, but stay in the hospital a shorter time, than ten years ago.

Susan Carleton writes on a variety of healthcare topics.

Beginning a stay in the hospital— patient and admissions clerk take care of the initial paperwork.

151

Patient Rights

At the same time, hospitals have become more responsive to patients' social and emotional needs. Social workers now routinely meet with patients and families confronting life-threatening or debilitating illnesses and identify community resources that will help them cope after the patient leaves the hospital. In many specialized hospital units—AIDS services, for example—doctors, nurses, social workers, and other professionals work in teams to devise care plans that address the full range of patient needs.

Equally important, patients and families today are expected to participate in healthcare decisions that affect them. Although the physician outlines the options and makes recommendations, the patient ultimately chooses the course that care will take.

In 1973 the American Hospital Association spelled out the concept of patient rights in a document aptly entitled "A Patient's Bill of Rights." The 12 rights described in this document (see the box on page 154), which most hospitals have adopted as policy, say patients are entitled to consideration, respect, confidentiality, and full information about their conditions and treatment. Patients also generally have the right to refuse any treatment they do not wish to receive.

As of 1989, about half of all hospitals also had patient representatives (sometimes called patient advocates) to help patients handle any problems they may have with hospital policies, staff members, or procedures. Patient representatives know the ins and outs of hospital bureaucracy, so they can direct grievances through the proper channels. They also have access to department heads and administrators who have the power to solve problems. If patients are dissatisfied with their nursing care, feel they must make a room change, or feel their doctor is not explaining a diagnosis or treatment plan clearly, the patient representative can help. (From the hospital administration's point of view, the patient representatives, along with questionnaires distributed to most patients, are important sources of feedback, which is then passed on to the appropriate medical or hospital services staff.)

Even when a patient representative is available, most patients also need to have a relative or friend who will seek out answers to questions, keep track of tests and medications, and generally run interference when the patient isn't up to it. This kind of informal advocacy is particularly important now that hospital stays are shorter and patients are more likely to be critically ill.

Types of Hospitals

In most parts of the Unites States, finding a hospital is not a problem. There are nearly 7,000 hospitals in the nation, the bulk of which are private, not-for-profit institutions. Public hospitals, operated by county or municipal governments, make up the next largest group of hospitals. Some hospitals are run on a for-profit basis; these investor-owned hospitals are most common in the Southern and Western states.

The number of beds in a hospital may vary from as few as 6 beds in the smallest rural hospitals to over a thousand in some major urban

152

medical centers. Patients in rural areas may have to travel a considerable distance to obtain hospital care, but in most parts of the country every middle-sized town or county seat has its own community hospital.

Community hospitals exist mainly to provide care to patients in a given geographic area (although they may also train future doctors). They vary greatly in size and in the types of service they provide. A moderate-sized community hospital in an affluent suburb might have the full range of medical and surgical subspecialists on its staff, while a rural hospital of the same size might be forced to refer patients needing specialty care to the nearest medical center.

Medical centers are staffed by physicians in every specialty and are usually affiliated with universities and located on or near medical school campuses. In addition to providing patient care, they conduct research and train future doctors. They house the most advanced equipment and often serve as proving grounds for newly developed treatments. Sometimes medical centers include specialty hospitals that cater to certain types of patients— children, cancer patients, or patients with musculoskeletal problems. These kinds of hospitals may also be independent.

Which type of hospital is best for a particular patient depends on a number of factors. A major consideration, of course, is where your doctor can admit you; some doctors have admitting privileges at only one hospital, others at several. Equally important is the seriousness of

A patient in a same-day surgery unit talks to her doctor before surgery (above) and is later joined by her family in the recovery room (below).

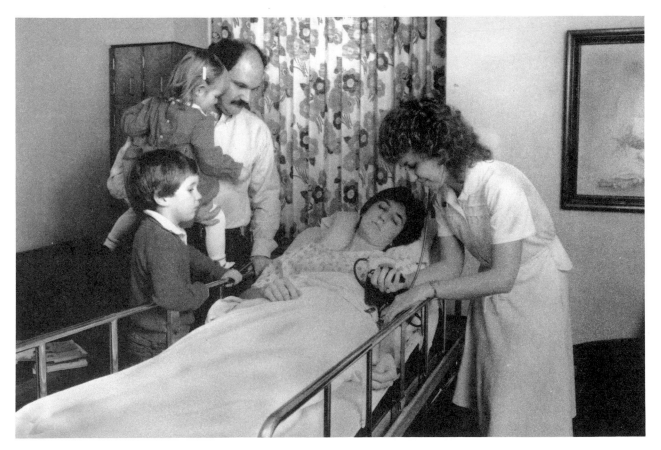

FROM "A PATIENT'S BILL OF RIGHTS"

1. The patient has the right to considerate and respectful care.

2. The patient has the right to obtain from his physician complete current information concerning his diagnosis, treatment, and prognosis in terms the patient can be reasonably expected to understand. When it is not medically advisable to give such information to the patient, the information should be made available to an appropriate person in his behalf. He has the right to know, by name, the physician responsible for coordinating his care.

3. The patient has the right to receive from his physician information necessary to give informed consent prior to the start of any procedure and/or treatment. Except in emergencies, such information for informed consent should include, but not necessarily be limited to, the specific procedure and/or treatment, the medically significant risks involved, and the probable duration of incapacitation. Where medically significant alternatives for care or treatment exist, or when the patient requests information concerning medical alternatives, the patient has the right to such information. The patient also has the right to know the name of the person responsible for the procedures and/or treatment.

4. The patient has the right to refuse treatment to the extent permitted by law and to be informed of the medical consequences of his action.

5. The patient has the right to every consideration of his privacy concerning his own medical care program. Case discussion, consultation, examination, and treatment are confidential and should be conducted discreetly. Those not directly involved in his care must have the permission of the patient to be present.

6. The patient has the right to expect that all communications and records pertaining to his care should be treated as confidential.

7. The patient has the right to expect that within its capacity a hospital must make reasonable response to the request of a patient for services. The hospital must provide evaluation, service, and/or referral as indicated by the urgency of the case. When medically permissible, a patient may be transferred to another facility only after he has received complete information and explanation concerning the needs for and alternatives to such a transfer. The institution to which the patient is to be transferred must first have accepted the patient for transfer.

8. The patient has the right to obtain information as to any relationship of his hospital to other healthcare and educational institutions insofar as his care is concerned. The patient has the right to obtain information as to the existence of any professional relationships among individuals, by name, who are treating him.

9. The patient has the right to be advised if the hospital proposes to engage in or perform human experimentation affecting his care or treatment. The patient has the right to refuse to participate in such research projects.

10. The patient has the right to expect reasonable continuity of care. He has the right to know in advance what appointment times and physicians are available and where. The patient has the right to expect that the hospital will provide a mechanism whereby he is informed by his physician or a delegate of the physician of the patient's continuing healthcare requirements following discharge.

11. The patient has the right to examine and receive an explanation of his bill, regardless of source of payment.

12. The patient has the right to know what hospital rules and regulations apply to his conduct as a patient.

the condition. Routine problems (minor infections or simple surgical procedures, for example) can be handled at small community hospitals. For more complicated illnesses (surgery necessitating general anesthesia, strokes, heart attacks, severe asthma), a larger community hospital staffed by physicians around the clock may be in order.

Serious conditions and complex procedures (heart surgery, brain surgery, invasive tests to diagnose heart disease) may require the specialized care of a medical center. Study after study has confirmed that survival rates following complex surgical procedures are best in hospitals where a large number of such procedures are performed.

For any but the most routine hospitalizations, patients should use hospitals where staff doctors are present 24 hours a day. Physicians Ronald E. Gots and Arthur Kaufman, in *The People's Hospital Book*, recount chilling stories about hospitalized heart patients suffering fatal heart attacks because emergency room physicians—the only doctors present in the hospital—were too busy to administer medications. "At [one] hospital, the outer trappings were impressive," write Gots and Kaufman. "The machinery was modern; the television monitors gave the appearance of 'the best of medical care.' But a hospital that has machines without doctors is like a fire department packed with new trucks but no firemen."

Kinds of Admissions

Under ideal circumstances, patients are admitted to hospitals where their private doctors are on staff. The doctor tells the admitting office when the patient will need a room and what the patient's condition is. Elective admissions (that is, admissions that are not urgent or emergencies), for procedures such as hysterectomies and knee operations, are scheduled a week or more in advance. A patient needing surgery usually enters the hospital on the day of the operation or the evening before. A few days earlier, most patients are requested to report to the outpatient department for preadmission testing, which usually consists of a blood test, a urine test, an electrocardiogram, and in some cases, a chest X ray. (Until recently, the hospitalization would have started earlier, with the basic tests being done during the first day or so of the hospital stay.) The preadmission tests help rule out unsuspected conditions that could make surgery particularly hazardous; they also provide a baseline to which tests performed during the hospitalization can be compared.

Patients with more serious conditions, such as heart disease, appendicitis, or dangerously elevated blood pressure, can be admitted on an urgent basis. These patients can usually go into the hospital as soon as their doctors have arranged their admission.

Emergency admissions are for patients who need immediate hospitalization—heart attack and accident victims, for example. Some hospitals allow emergency admissions to bypass the emergency room if their private physicians have called in advance; others require all emergency patients to be stabilized in the emergency room before they can be moved to a hospital room. In the direst emergencies, of course, patients should simply be taken to the nearest hospital with an empty bed. And in some areas, certain types of emergency admissions can be made only at designated hospitals—for instance, a medical center serving as a trauma center for an entire city or region. If at all possible, however, it's best to call your doctor and have the doctor admit you personally.

Every patient—whether admitted on an elective, urgent, or emergency basis—is entitled to respect, consideration, confidentiality, and full information concerning treatment.

Admission Procedures

When you enter the hospital, a clerk in the admissions office will request several kinds of information. You, or someone acting on your behalf, will need to produce your insurance cards (Medicare, Blue Cross, private insurance provided by your employer). If you are also covered by your spouse's employee insurance, that card should be brought as well; it is often possible to combine two employee health plans and get better benefits. You may also have to give the addresses and telephone numbers of your employer and your spouse's employer.

The admitting office will, in addition, want you to sign several releases, the most important of which allows the hospital to give your insurer information about your treatment. Another release, sometimes called a "conditions of admission" form, gives a kind of blanket consent for the hospital to treat you, and may in addition release the hospital from liability if any harm should befall you. Some patients object to

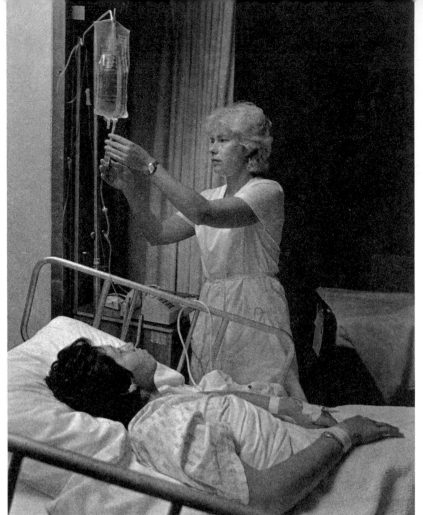

An Army of Specialists

Hospitals call on a variety of workers with specialized skills to care for patients. Left, a registered nurse checks a patient's intravenous drip; below, a staff physician at a teaching hospital reviews a patient's chart with interns and residents during rounds; right, a physical therapist applies a treatment to a disabled knee; far right, an anesthesiologist checks a patient's pulse during surgery.

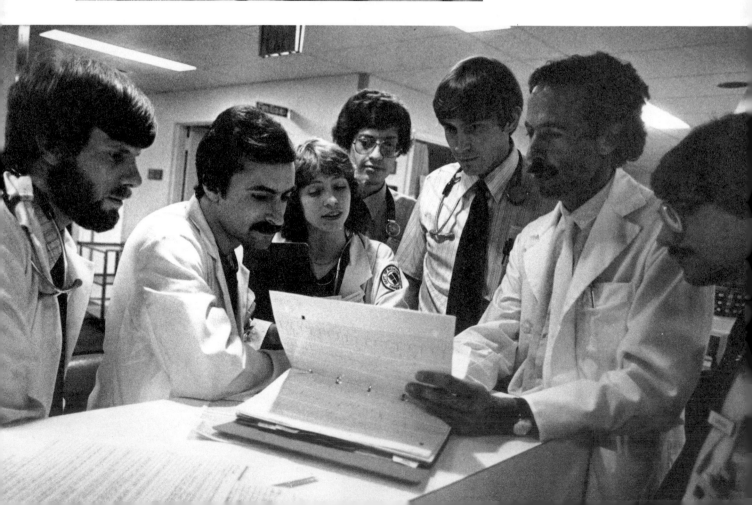

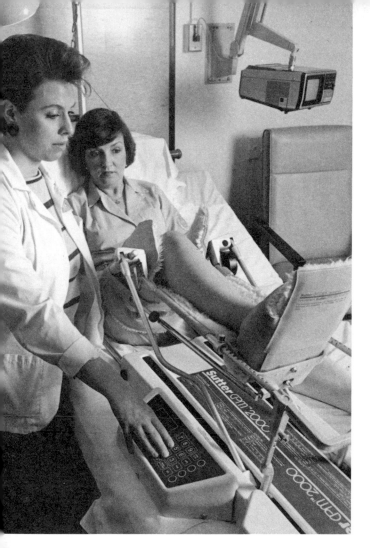
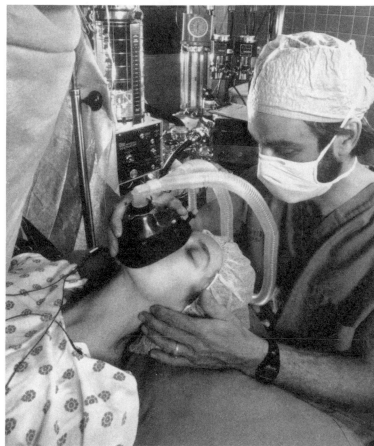

blanket consent/release from liability forms; however, such releases have not withstood legal challenges, so signing them does not really mean a patient is signing away any rights. Separate consent forms are provided later for surgery and major tests. These specific consent forms should be examined very carefully—and not signed until the doctor has explained the operation or test in detail. (In a life-threatening situation, the hospital will usually take whatever medical steps are called for, without the release or consent forms.)

Before admission, you should decide whether you want a private or semiprivate room. Hospitals charge higher rates for private rooms, but for patients who prefer solitude (particularly the seriously ill), they may be well worth the price. On the other hand, many patients find that semiprivate rooms, which hold two, three, or four beds, provide welcome companionship. If you do choose a private room, you may have to pay the additional charge when you are admitted, since most insurance plans cover only the cost of a semiprivate room.

The admitting office will also prepare an identification bracelet with your name, your doctor's name, and your room number on it, along with a separate wristband indicating any drug allergies you may have. These wristbands, usually put on in the admitting office, let hospital staff double-check your identity before giving you medication or taking you off to surgery.

What to Bring

If you get the chance to pack before going to the hospital, be sure to take a toothbrush, toothpaste, and any other toiletries you feel are necessary. Jewelry and other valuables should be left at home. Take no more than about $15 in cash, along with a few blank checks. Pajamas, slippers, and a robe can help you feel more comfortable, but you may have to give them up and wear a hospital gown—a loose cotton shift that ties at the neck and back—most of the time. Most hospitals will also let you bring pillows and blankets from home.

Hospitals usually do not allow patients to keep drugs—even aspirin or vitamins—in their rooms because of the risk that medicine patients take on their own may interfere with their hospital drug regimens. If you regularly take medication, ask your doctor whether it should be continued in the hospital; if it is supposed to be continued, check with the nurse to be sure the doctor has ordered it. Throughout your hospital stay, nurses will bring your regular medication, along with any additional drugs you might need, according to the schedule your doctor indicates on your chart.

A Typical Room

Hospital rooms are designed for maximum efficiency.

Hospital rooms do not possess the amenities of a luxury hotel, even though their price might suggest otherwise. What they lack in style, however, they make up for in efficiency. Each room (or patient unit in a semiprivate room) has a bed, a bedside table, and an across-the-lap table to hold meal trays. Hospital beds are high and narrow so that workers can reach, bathe, and turn patients with ease. Patients can raise and lower the head of the bed by pushing a button on a control panel that usually rests near the pillow. Buttons to control the television and summon nurses may be on the same panel as the bed control, or on separate devices that are also near the head of the bed. Each bed may also have its own blood pressure cuff and thermometer, and an oxygen outlet may be located on the wall right by the bed. Private rooms come with private bathrooms, but in semiprivate rooms roommates share a bathroom.

Soon after you reach your room, a nurse will interview you about your past hospitalizations, current medications, allergies, and family medical history. Since many such medical histories may be requested during the hospital stay, you might save time by bringing notes along for easy reference.

A Host of Doctors

If you are in a teaching hospital, one or more physicians in training, or residents, will examine you and take your medical history again. Residents are medical school graduates who are completing specialty training or undergoing the one year of hospital training most states require for physicians to be licensed.

A first-year resident, or intern, usually has primary responsibility for the day-to-day care of a certain number of patients. Interns are supervised closely by senior residents (in their second, third, and fourth years of training) and by the attending physicians (the fully trained practicing doctors who admit patients to the hospital). Teaching hospitals also have full-time staff physicians who oversee residents' work. The intern examines the patients each day, then writes orders on each patient's chart, which is the ongoing record of the hospital stay and contains all nursing notes, doctors' orders, and test results.

Some patients in teaching hospitals are overwhelmed by the sheer number of doctors who are in and out of their rooms in a day; others are uncomfortable with the notion of being cared for by anyone but their experienced personal physicians. Teaching hospitals do, however, offer several distinct advantages. For one thing, residents are usually quite accessible. Since they spend most of their working time on the hospital floors, if questions arise, they are on hand to give answers. And because residents work in teams, their patients get the advantage of several physicians' knowledge.

In a nonteaching hospital, your private doctor will see you every day and write or dictate orders that indicate what treatments, tests, or consultations with specialists are needed. Nonteaching hospitals may also have full time staff physicians or physician assistants (who have completed four years of undergraduate education plus a two-year postgraduate program) to handle emergencies and do much of the work performed by residents in teaching hospitals.

Patients who will be undergoing surgery are also visited by anesthesiology residents (in teaching hospitals) or anesthesiologists, who take medical histories and explain anesthesia procedures.

Nursing Staff

In any hospital, the people most directly responsible for patients' day-to-day comfort and well-being are the nurses. Around the clock, nurses monitor patients' conditions, minister to patients' needs, and generally troubleshoot for the hospital units they manage. If a patient complains of pain, for example, the nurse must see whether the doctor has ordered any pain medication and call the doctor to request such an order if it is not on the chart. Once the order is clarified, the nurse must see to it that the patient gets the medication promptly.

When a patient first enters the hospital, a floor or unit nurse, usually an R.N. (registered nurse), develops a nursing plan that outlines the patient's daily needs, including bathing, meals, and special services such as respiratory, physical, or occupational therapy. R.N.s have obtained a bachelor's or associate degree or completed a hospital training school program and have passed a state licensing examination. Nurses with less experience and training—L.P.N.s or L.V.N.s (licensed practical or vocational nurses), who have completed one-year training programs in community colleges or vocational schools, and nurse's aides—carry out the nursing plan from day to day.

Many hospitals have adopted a new style of nursing care called primary nursing, in which one nurse develops a patient's care plan and personally delivers most of the care throughout the patient's stay. Primary nursing allows nurses to become more involved in all aspects

Behind-the-scenes operations such as the medical charts department are essential to the smooth functioning of the hospital.

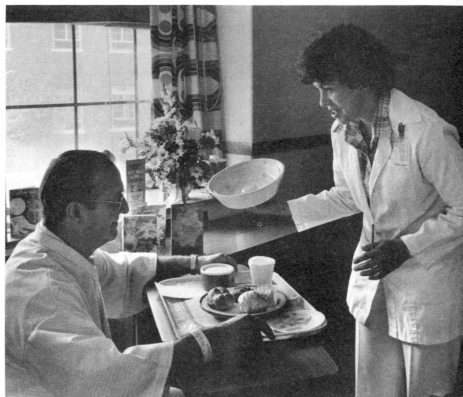

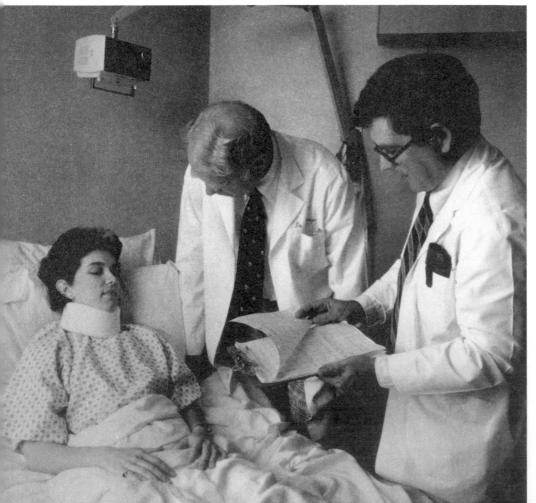

A Day in the Life

Among the routine signposts in a hospital day are (clockwise from above left) temperature and pulse checks, mealtimes, and bedside visits from doctors. Right: Visiting friends and relatives help to break up the day.

of patient care, increasing their responsibility and job satisfaction. Not surprisingly, patients also benefit from the continuity of care.

Other Hospital Staff

Besides doctors and nurses, a baffling array of technicians and other specialists have a hand in the typical patient's hospital stay. The larger the hospital, the greater the variety of ancillary staff. Phlebotomists start IVs (catheters inserted into veins to administer fluids and medications). Respiratory therapists administer oxygen, as well as performing other treatments to improve a patient's ability to breathe. Dietitians provide nutritional counseling and devise meal plans for patients with special nutritional needs. Physical therapists help patients increase or maintain their mobility, and occupational therapists show them how to dress, bathe, and feed themselves despite physical limitations.

In addition, a veritable army of orderlies, housekeeping and dietary staff, and volunteers keeps the hospital running smoothly. Orderlies do a variety of tasks, such as taking patients to surgery and specialty departments and bringing X-ray or laboratory results back to the nursing station. Housekeeping staff, by keeping patient rooms and common areas as clean as possible, help reduce patients' chances of picking up new infections in the hospital. Dietary staff prepare and deliver meal trays, and volunteers pitch in wherever help is needed— transporting patients around the hospital, bringing library and snack carts to rooms, and directing visitors and outpatients to the hospital areas they need. Finally, hospitals employ whole cadres of workers patients never see, including engineers, records clerks, and materials managers, who maintain supplies of the myriad articles, from surgical sponges to sutures to bedpans, used daily in the hospital.

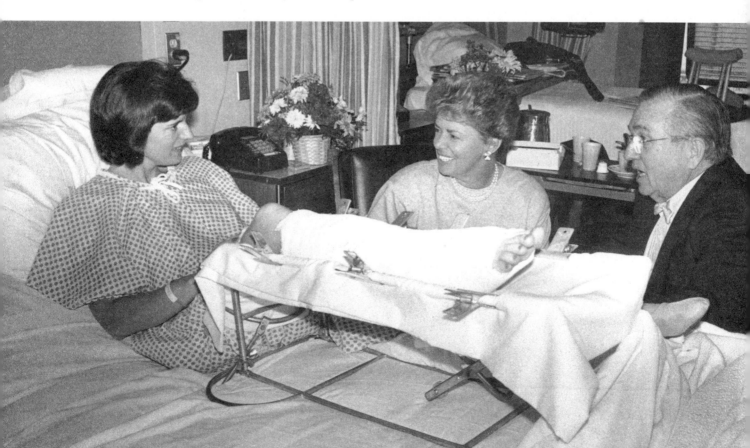

The Hospital Routine

The typical hospital day begins between 6 and 7 a.m., when night nurses make their final rounds to take temperatures, pulse rates, and blood pressure readings. Surgery patients are "prepped" (shaved, given enemas, or given medication, depending on the operation being performed), and patients scheduled for the first operations of the day are wheeled to operating rooms. Other patients may need to have blood or urine tests before breakfast; if so, technicians or nurses will come to collect the appropriate samples.

Between 7 and 8 a.m., the nursing day shift comes on duty and the night nurses report on the patients' conditions. This change of shift meeting, along with the scramble to bathe patients and distribute morning medications, makes the hours between 7:30 and 10:00 a.m. particularly hectic for nurses. Therefore, calls may not be answered as quickly as at other times of the day.

Breakfast arrives at about 8. Occasionally, a patient scheduled for surgery or for a test that requires fasting gets a breakfast tray by mistake. Patients not sure whether they are supposed to eat should check with a nurse before digging in.

During the morning, dietary aides distribute menus for the next day's meals. If none of the hospital's offerings is tempting and the patient has no dietary restrictions, visitors can bring in meals from home or from restaurants. A handful of hospitals have upgraded their food services to attract patients, but hospital fare, like most institutional food, is still largely uninspiring. If you miss a meal, nurses' stations usually stock fruit juice, crackers, cookies, Jello, and other snacks.

Physicians make rounds in the early morning as well. In teaching hospitals, this means the whole team of residents, with or without the attending physician, may stop by. In other hospitals, private doctors make brief visits on their own. Morning rounds are the best time for the patient to find out what tests and treatments are scheduled for the day and to ask any other pertinent questions.

Visiting hours often begin around 10:30 or 11. In some hospitals, visitors can come continuously from then until early evening; in others, visits are limited to a few two-hour periods each day. Certain units, such as pediatrics, obstetrics, and intensive care, usually have more restricted visiting hours. (Many pediatrics units allow parents to stay around the clock; some even have parents help with their children's nursing care. But visiting by friends and other family members may be limited.) Except in intensive care units, where visits are limited to a few minutes, close family members can usually stay with patients beyond visiting hours.

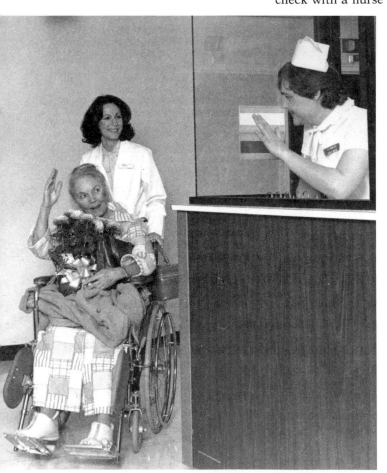

Nurse and patient say goodbye as a stay in the hospital comes to an end.

162

Lunch arrives at noon, and activity slows down somewhat in the afternoon, although patients may still be taken from their rooms for surgery, X rays, tests, and special therapies. Many tests and X rays must be done in hospital departments far removed from patient rooms. Generally, a nurse's aide or orderly escorts or transports the patient, in a wheelchair if necessary, to the appropriate department at an appointed time. Radiology (X-ray) and other specialty departments often fall behind schedule, however, forcing patients to bide their time in waiting areas. Many nurses advise their patients to take an extra blanket and wear slippers to make the waiting more comfortable.

Dinner is served between 5 and 6 P.M., and most hospital activity ceases by 9:30 or 10:00. Some doctors recommend, or even routinely order, sleeping pills for their patients, particularly those who are scheduled for surgery the following morning. People who have trouble sleeping in the hospital (and many do) often welcome this medication, but some patients do not. Discuss the matter with your doctor, who can order the medication on an "as needed" basis, so that it is available if you decide you want it.

As part of the routine in some hospitals, nurses must take patients' vital signs in the wee hours of the morning. Many patients also require medication every four or six hours, necessitating late night awakenings. If you have trouble getting back to sleep, ask your doctor if your medication schedule can be adjusted or if it is safe for you not to be checked until morning.

Going Home

In this era of shortened hospital stays, social service departments start planning each patient's discharge on the day of admission. Many hospitals run their own home care services, through which nurses, healthcare aides, or homemakers (aides who shop, cook, and perform other household tasks) can be hired. If you need this kind of help, find out how much coverage your insurance allows for it. Medicare and Medicaid (a state-by-state medical assistance program for the poor) pay for home care services, but only from agencies they have licensed. Private insurance policies vary greatly in their home care provisions.

Community agencies may provide other services, such as delivery of meals and free or low-cost wheelchairs, crutches, oxygen equipment, and similar items. The hospital's discharge planners (usually within the social services department) should arrange for patients to have these services as soon as they get home from the hospital. Discharge planners also make arrangements for patients who cannot return to their homes to go to long-term care facilities such as nursing homes or rehabilitation hospitals.

Before leaving the hospital, make sure you have written instructions from your doctor or nurse about what activities you can undertake, what medications you need, and when you should have a follow-up examination. Patients who must learn special procedures, such as caring for a colostomy (a surgically created opening in the bowel), should be trained thoroughly before leaving the hospital, as well as given follow-up education from visiting nurses. □

For Medicare Patients

Occasionally, Medicare patients feel they are being discharged before they have recovered sufficiently to be safe outside the hospital. Patients who believe this is the case can appeal to their state's Peer Review Organization (PRO). PROs are boards of physicians and other healthcare experts who, under contract with the federal government, monitor the hospital care of Medicare recipients. The American Association of Retired Persons in Washington, D.C., provides a listing of toll-free numbers for PROs in every state, as well as a booklet explaining the appeal process. The hospital's patient representative can also steer patients and their families through the proper channels to avoid a too-hasty discharge.

ELECTROMAGNETIC FIELDS: A DANGER?

Stephen F. Cleary, Ph.D.

Editor's Note: Growing controversy has developed over
whether electromagnetic fields from such sources as power
lines, video display terminals, and household appliances
can cause or promote cancer, reproductive problems, and
other adverse effects on human health. In the following
article a scientist active in this area reviews the evidence
and gives his recommendations.

In the wee hours of the morning a fisherman ventures forth to ply his trade on Chesapeake Bay as he and countless others before him have for the past few centuries. Aside from switching from sail power to internal combustion engines, commercial fishing in the bay had remained much the same until the past decade or so. But in recent years the typical fisherman has enlisted tens of thousands of dollars of space-age electronic equipment in his efforts to find the elusive quarry and to get safely to and from port. The array of technology includes ship-to-shore and citizens band radio transmitters, an AM/FM receiver, weather radio, marine navigational radar, a loran radio navigation system, and fish-finding and depth-finding sonar. The fisherman probably doesn't think or care much about how these devices work, as long as they do their job.

A lack of understanding of the basic principles of modern technology is not restricted to fishermen. In a recent newspaper account of a day in the life of such a fisherman, a reporter referred to a "seabed painted continuously by high-frequency radio signals beamed down from the bottom of the hull." In fact, the radar signals to which the reporter was apparently referring would be absorbed in a few inches of seawater; it is sonar, which employs sound waves and has an underwater range of hundreds of feet or more, that is used to find the fish.

Although we are all "painted continuously" with various forms of electromagnetic radiation and their associated electric and magnetic fields, most of us know little more about them and their sources than do the fisherman and the reporter, and this lack of knowledge extends to their effects on human health. True, exposure to extremely high-frequency "ionizing" radiation like gamma rays and X rays is generally known to be potentially quite dangerous. But what about radiation of lower frequencies? The microwave ovens in many people's kitchens show that microwaves can produce high heat. What about radio waves? Or what about our electric power system? It carries alternating current everywhere, constantly producing electric and magnetic fields that surge and collapse at a rate, in the United States, of 60 cycles per second. (In the parlance of scientists and engineers, the current has a frequency of 60 hertz.)

Hints of a Problem

Such electric and magnetic fields are so commonplace that they have been accepted as a totally benign, or at least harmless, part of our environment. Recently, however, evidence has surfaced indicating that such acceptance may be naive. Specifically, some scientists have suggested that the pulsing electric and/or magnetic fields produced by power lines, video display terminals, and various household appliances and radio equipment may be associated with adverse health effects, including cancer, birth defects, and changes in the body's central

Some scientists say the pulsing magnetic fields produced by power lines may expose those nearby to an increased risk of cancer.

Stephen F. Cleary is professor of physiology and biophysics at the Medical College of Virginia and coeditor of Charge and Field Effects in Biosystems.

nervous system. Concern among the general public over this possibility grew sharply in 1989 as a result of a flurry of press reports on the issue, most notably a three-part series, "The Hazards of Electromagnetic Fields," by Paul Brodeur, that appeared in the *New Yorker* magazine in June.

But the existence of a link between the reported health problems and exposure to lower-frequency electromagnetic fields has been questioned by some scientists. In addition to a cautious reluctance to accept the link as long as conclusive proof of it has not been found, the scientific doubt has been fed by the lack of a well-accepted or obvious explanation for how such electromagnetic radiation could affect biological systems. Since they cannot explain how it could, some scientists hold either that it does not or that the effects attributed to radiation are due to some other, unidentified causes. Some of the resistance to accepting the existence of the health effects reflects apprehension over the potential disruption that proven health effects could create in the economy and the military. The construction of power lines has already been delayed or abandoned in some areas because of citizen opposition.

Even though the health effects have not yet been definitely proved to be caused by electromagnetic radiation, the seriousness of the possible effects demands that the public be well-informed about the issue in order to direct future policy decisions that may affect their well-being.

Possible Ways of Affecting the Body

The pulsing electromagnetic fields that reportedly cause adverse health effects encompass a wide range of physical properties. Consequently, it is unlikely that the health effects are all due to a common cause.

At one end of the electromagnetic range are extemely-low-frequency (ELF) fields, with frequencies between 0 and about 100 hertz. By far the most common source of ELF exposure in the United States is 60-hertz electric and magnetic fields from high-voltage electric power transmission lines and secondary distribution lines, such as those found in residential neighborhoods. Secondary lines produce stronger magnetic fields because the strength of a magnetic field from a power line is directly related to the current flowing through it. Electric power transmission over long distances is most efficient at high voltages but relatively low current, and thus magnetic fields from primary high-voltage lines are typically relatively weak. Because household use requires low voltages, a series of transformers must reduce the voltage from 200,000-300,000 volts in transmission lines coming from generating plants to 240 volts for home distribution. The reduction in voltage yields a stronger current in the secondary distribution lines, producing stronger magnetic fields that may cause significant health problems.

The magnetic fields have created more concern than the 60-hertz electric fields because although ELF electric fields induce electric fields in a human body exposed to them, the induced fields exist primarily at the body's outer surface. They are not noticed unless the voltage is extremely high or a part of the body comes into direct contact with a

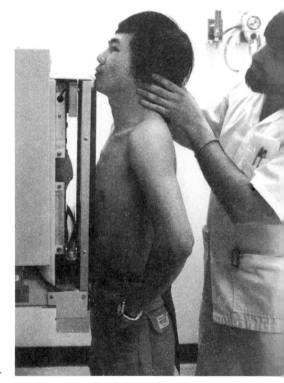

The amount of radiation this patient will receive in his X ray is considered safe. Too much exposure to X rays, however, is known to be dangerous.

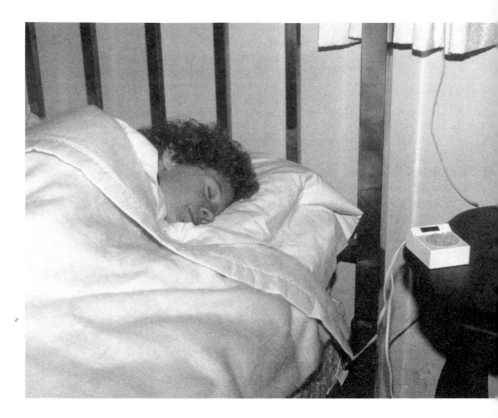

conductor (such as a metal fence), resulting in an electrical shock. Shocks from typical ELF electric fields at ground level near a transmission line, although annoying, are not thought to be dangerous, since current flow is relatively low. A shock from 120-volt household current can be significantly more dangerous because of the potentially high current flow. Electrical shock, however, can be easily prevented by proper insulation and safety practices.

Since magnetic fields interact differently from electric fields with materials that absorb them, essentially all of the human body rather than just the outer surface is exposed to 60-hertz magnetic fields. The magnetic fields interact with electric charges in the body to produce internal electric currents. Several types of substances in the body carry charges, but because of their central role in many physiological processes, perhaps the most important are positively charged atoms ("cations") of calcium, sodium, and potassium. Although magnetic field interactions with cations offer a possible explanation for reported health effects of ELF fields, the current understanding of the physics of the interactions indicates that they are too weak to cause the reported effects. Perhaps this dilemma will be resolved only when more is known about the intricacies of living systems.

Another ubiquitous and ever-increasing source of exposure to electromagnetic fields is radio-frequency and microwave radiation, ranging in frequency from thousands of hertz to billions. Such radiation causes different types of interactions with the human body. When the frequency of an electromagnetic field is greater than 1 million hertz (1 MHz), the body's surface charge literally does not have time to

Common appliances emit magnetic or electromagnetic fields. Some evidence links the strong magnetic field produced by an electric blanket (left) with an increased risk of miscarriage in pregnant women. A microwave oven (right) has built-in shielding to minimize exposure to its intense, heat-generating microwaves.

respond to the field. Consequently, fields with such high frequencies penetrate deeply into tissue. Radio-frequency and microwave radiation causes rapid movement of molecules and cations. At high intensity it heats tissue, which is why we use microwave radiation (at a frequency of 2,450 MHz) to cook food. Thus, high-intensity radio-frequency and microwave fields can cause tissue damage by heating. This damage has some rather unusual characteristics, however, since the heating can occur internally and quite nonuniformly. In particular, it may not be felt, since human sensitivity to heat is centered in or near the body surface, in the skin. Although perplexing to deal with, the heating effects can be controlled by limiting the intensity of the fields to which the body is exposed (with shielding and by staying away from radiation sources). Since except in certain occupations most radio-frequency and microwave exposure is at intensities far too low to cause body heating, it would appear to be no problem. However, researchers have found that such exposure also produces effects not due to heating, which have raised new questions about the consequences for health of electromagnetic fields at these frequencies. As with ELF magnetic field effects, how these "nonthermal" effects occur is not known, nor have many of the potential consequences been adequately defined.

A few things should be kept in mind about potentially health-compromising effects of exposure to "weak" electromagnetic fields. First, the term "weak" refers to intensities that are low compared with fields strong enough to cause immediate and painful effects such as burns or shocks. Relative to natural, or "background," intensities at these frequencies—intensities present in the environment during the evolution of life on earth—the fields produced by the development of electrical (and electronic) technology during the past century are quite high and ever increasing. Second, ELF fields possibly associated with harmful effects such as cancer have been estimated to be of the same approximate magnitude in intensity as those known to produce beneficial effects such as bone healing. They also have about the same frequency and intensity as normal electrical phenomena in the human body, such as brain waves. From this perspective it may not be appropriate to think of fields induced by ELF sources, such as 60-hertz power lines, as "weak" fields.

Magnetic Fields From Power Lines

In March 1979 a paper entitled "Electrical Wiring Configurations and Childhood Cancer" and written by Nancy Wertheimer, a psychologist, and Ed Leeper, a physicist, appeared in the *American Journal of Epidemiology*. In it Wertheimer and Leeper reported their finding that children in the Denver metropolitan area who had lived in homes near lines carrying high-current 60-hertz electric power had about twice the cancer death rate of children who lived near low-current lines. (They estimated that about 20 percent of all homes in the Denver area fell into the high-current category.) After ruling out the possibility that the increased cancer rate was due to such factors as noise, air pollution, or population density, they concluded it was caused by exposure to magnetic fields from the power lines. Although they were not able to explain the link, they suggested that continuous exposure to such fields may somehow strain the immune system, reducing the body's defense against cancer. Evidence that magnetic fields can in fact cause changes in cells in humans and experimental animals has been reported by other researchers.

In some localities concerned citizens have gone to court to block construction of high-voltage power lines through their communities.

Before Wertheimer and Leeper's article appeared, the possibility that cancer or other adverse health effects might result from exposure to the 60-hertz fields from electrical transmission or distribution lines would have been dismissed out of hand by almost everyone, including most scientists. Wertheimer and Leeper's findings and the dire, far-reaching implications were consequently met with disbelief and outright rejection. Many of their critics noted that they had categorized homes according to magnetic-field intensity mainly by observing the types, configuration, and location of power lines and transformers, rather than by making measurements. Their results were therefore claimed to be inaccurate and subject to bias.

But support for the association between ELF electromagnetic exposure and childhood cancer came from an independent study carried out by Dr. Lennart Tomenius in Stockholm, Sweden, and reported in 1986. Again, children who had developed cancer were twice as likely to have lived near high-current power lines as were those who had not. In contrast to Wertheimer and Leeper, Tomenius measured the intensity of the magnetic fields outside the study subjects' homes and found a correlation between the strength of the field and the incidence of cancer.

Additional evidence of a possible link with cancer is found in studies of occupational exposure to ELF fields in the United States and other technologically advanced countries. Results of these studies, which began to appear in the early 1980s, indicated a significantly increased risk of leukemia, brain tumors, and other cancers in people who routinely worked in electromagnetic fields.

Although most people were not aware of the possible association of 60-hertz electromagnetic exposure and cancer until relatively recently, concerned individuals have for years gone to court in attempts to block the construction of high-voltage transmission lines through their communities. One significant consequence of such actions was a series of hearings by the New York State Public Service Commission that ended in 1977 and led to an agreement by the Power Authority of the State of New York and seven utility companies to undertake a five-year, $5 million research program to determine the biological effects of power line fields. The final report on this program, issued in 1987, indicated that 12 of its 17 research projects detected statistically significant effects. One of the projects, a follow-up on the Wertheimer and Leeper childhood cancer study, used improved sampling and measurement techniques to corroborate the earlier findings. The Public Service Commission's scientific advisory panel concluded that if 60-hertz electric power distribution patterns throughout the United States were similar to those in the Denver area, and if, in fact, magnetic fields caused cancer, then 10-15 percent of all childhood cancer cases in the country could be due to magnetic fields from power lines.

Computer video display terminals, or VDTs, have become ubiquitous. Evidence is starting to accumulate that under certain conditions VDT use by a pregnant woman can raise the chances of an abnormal birth.

Since it has not yet been definitely established that magnetic fields do cause or promote cancer, the significance of this conclusion has not been determined. The overall weight of evidence, however, is such that the question of health effects of ELF electromagnetic fields cannot be ignored. In the near future ongoing research may provide a clearer picture of the true magnitude of the problem.

Video Display Terminals

Just as electric power lines had long been ignored as a possible source of health problems, video display terminals (VDTs) were at first accepted as totally safe additions to the workplace. Over 30 million VDTs are in use in the United States, and it has been estimated that almost all white-collar workers will be using them by the year 2000. Following a claim in 1976 by two newspaper copy editors that VDT use had caused them to develop cataracts, measurements revealed that VDTs emitted a variety of types of electromagnetic radiation, including pulsed fields with frequencies of 60 and 15,000 hertz generated by the terminal's cathode-ray tube. (The 15,000-hertz fields lie in the "very-low-frequency," or VLF, class of radiation.) At the time there was little or no data about biological effects of ELF or VLF radiation, but the possibility of adverse effects was generally dismissed because of the low intensities involved. Although the intensities from VDTs were indeed lower than those known to cause acute biological damage, they were comparable to or greater than those from ELF power lines.

Starting in the early 1980s there were a number of reports of unusually high rates of miscarriages, neonatal deaths, and fetal abnormalities among women working with VDTs at various places around the United States. Since the number of pregnant workers in any one workplace was usually small, the statistical significance of these reports was difficult to establish, and the high rates were widely attributed to a chance clustering of cases. However, the clusters typically involved a 50 percent or higher rate of abnormal outcomes of pregnancy, compared with an expected rate in the United States of 16 percent, and so the involvement of VDTs could not be easily dismissed.

Stronger evidence was provided in 1988 by the report of a study of 1,583 patients treated at Kaiser Permanente obstetrics and gynecology clinics in San Francisco during 1981 and 1982. The study found that women who worked with VDTs for 20 hours or longer a week had an 80 percent higher risk of early or late miscarriage than women who did similar work without using VDTs. The children of the VDT workers also had a higher rate of birth defects, but the difference was not large enough to be statistically significant. Meanwhile, researchers found that chick embryos, mice, and human cells could be affected by VLF magnetic fields with characteristics similar to those emitted by VDTs.

A consistent pattern emerges from the Kaiser Permanente study, the clusters of abnormal births at individual workplaces, and the experimental studies. The pattern suggests that under certain conditions VDT use may have adverse effects on pregnancy. In contrast, to date there has been no reported relationship of VDT use with cancer. Why should the effects of VDT radiation be different from

A study of amateur radio operators, like this ham radio buff, found a higher than expected rate of deaths from certain cancers of the blood.

those of power line fields? There are a number of possible reasons for this. But a simple explanation may be that electromagnetic fields of different frequencies and intensities have different biological effects.

Radio and Microwaves

Concern about the health effects of radio-frequency and microwave electromagnetic radiation dates back to the 1950s, when military and civilian personnel who worked with radar, which uses microwaves, began complaining about a variety of effects, including the development of cataracts. Aside from research on radar's effects on the eyes, no large-scale health effects studies were conducted in the United States.

Studies conducted in the Soviet Union and Eastern European nations, however, indicated that occupational exposure to microwave radiation had a variety of physiological effects, especially in the central nervous system. On the basis of these findings, the Soviet Union developed safety guidelines for microwave exposure that were a thousand times lower than U.S. guidelines, which were aimed at preventing tissue damage from microwave heating. In neither case was cancer considered as a factor in setting safety standards, since there were no data suggesting that exposure to radio-frequency or microwave radiation was associated with cancer. In retrospect this is not surprising, because most types of cancer take 15 to 20 years to develop, a period much longer than that of researchers' observations.

In the 1970s isolated reports of cancer alleged to have resulted from occupational exposure to the radiation began to surface in the United States, mostly through lawsuits against employers or equipment manufacturers. Because of the relatively small number of cases and the fact that most lawsuits were settled confidentially out of court, however, no scientific link between cancer and exposure was established. Clusters of cancer cases among people living near AM and FM broadcast towers have recently been reported in a number of locations around the United States, but their overall statistical significance has not been determined.

In 1988 the report of an epidemiological study of cancer among amateur radio operators, many of whom were also exposed to electromagnetic radiation at work, revealed a significantly higher than normal rate of deaths due to acute and chronic myeloid leukemia and multiple myeloma—cancers affecting the blood. Further evidence of a link between cancer and occupational exposure to radio-frequency and microwave radiation came from a study of Polish military personnel who worked with such radiation between 1971 and 1980. It found a 300 percent increase in overall cancer incidence and a 700 percent increase in cancer of the blood-forming organs and lymphatic tissue.

For the scientific community the association of radio-frequency and microwave exposure with cancer has come as a big surprise, which explains in part why there is a limited amount of pertinent experimental data. The only study ever conducted in the United States of long-term low-intensity microwave exposure found an approximately 400 percent increase in cancer in exposed rats. The results of a few other animal studies, as well as several cell studies, provide consistent

Some countries, like the Soviet Union, have issued especially cautious safety guidelines for microwave exposure.

support for the association of cancer in humans with occupational radio-frequency and microwave exposure.

Defining and Minimizing the Risks

Considering that we are continuously exposed to ever-increasing levels of electromagnetic radiation that has been associated with cancer and other adverse health effects, what can we do? First it is obvious that more information is needed to confirm that a danger exists, to adequately define its extent, and to determine what preventive measures are needed. Most public concern has arisen as a result of epidemiological research focusing on video display terminals and on ELF, radio-frequency, and microwave fields. These studies have identified an apparent problem, but because of the inherent limitations of epidemiological research (it may uncover factors associated with high incidence of a phenomenon—like cancer—but cannot prove causality), they have not adequately defined the problem. Additional research must specifically address such issues as how long one has to be exposed to electromagnetic fields to risk adverse health effects, how intense the fields have to be, and who is most at risk. Human studies must be supplemented with basic research to determine how electromagnetic radiation promotes cancer or other health effects. At present, U.S. research on possible health effects is very limited.

Finally, until the risks of electromagnetic exposure are better defined, what short-term and long-term measures can be adopted to minimize them? The most obvious is avoidance. Although in a technological society complete avoidance is generally impossible, certain types of exposure can be minimized. For example, electric blankets produce relatively intense 60-hertz magnetic fields in obvious close proximity to the body. Since there is evidence suggesting that such fields may cause abnormal births, it would appear prudent for pregnant women to avoid using electric blankets as well as electrically heated water beds. In general, since an electromagnetic field is most intense next to its source, everyone should stay as far away from field sources as practical. To be on the safe side, an electric alarm clock should not be put next to the bed, and one should avoid sitting too close to the television.

In the long term, electric power lines, VDTs, home appliances, and other electromagnetic emitters such as cordless and cellular telephones, walkie-talkies, and CB radios can be redesigned or reconfigured to significantly reduce exposure intensities. (In response to concern about possible health effects of radiation leakage, microwave ovens were in fact redesigned some time ago to dramatically reduce user exposure.) Commercial and military radar and broadcasting facilities as well as power lines can be located and operated to minimize occupational and public exposure. Obviously such long-term remedies will be expensive. However, the cost can be minimized by an investment in research to clearly determine what kinds of exposure to what kinds of fields can be hazardous. In view of the strong evidence that exposure to electromagnetic fields can have effects on health, the problems can no longer be denied or ignored. They must be faced and remedied. □

More research is needed on possible dangers; meanwhile, risks can be minimized.

SPOTLIGHT ON HEALTH

VOLUNTEERS
Their Key Role

Barbara Scherr Trenk

At Southside Hospital in Bay Shore, N.Y., volunteers arrange (non)wine and cheese parties for parents of newborns. At Providence-St. Margaret Health Center in Kansas City, Kan., volunteers give back rubs to patients—a "hands-on" service that nurses find difficult to provide in a time of staff shortages and mounting paperwork. And at State University of New York Medical Center in Brooklyn, N.Y., these unpaid workers read stories to youngsters who are recovering from surgery.

Every day, across the United States, volunteers in the healthcare system help in hundreds of small but important ways. In nursing homes they may mend clothes for the residents, make sure that all of them get Christmas presents, lead religious services, or organize recreational activities. In hospices—programs concerned with the care of terminally ill patients and their families—volunteers visit patients in their homes, sometimes help with care of the patient, and often provide psychological support for the family. So important are volunteers that hospices must include them in their programs in order to be eligible for federal Medicare reimbursement.

According to a 1988 Gallup survey, 45 percent of the U.S. adult population spends four hours a week or more volunteering in some way. While the polls did not determine the number of people whose time was spent in the health care field, the American Hospital Association reports that 5 million people help out in hospitals, and the National Hospice Organization says there are 75,000 volunteers in its programs.

Volunteers have become such an integral part of healthcare institutions that many hospitals and nursing homes hire a staff member whose job it is to recruit, train, and supervise volunteers. In fact, the Joint Commission on the Accreditation of Healthcare Organizations requires that any healthcare organization that has a volunteer program designate an individual to take charge of planning and supervising the program.

Who Volunteers and Why?

People volunteer for a variety of reasons. Connie Baird, director of volunteers at Southside Hospital, says that many of the volunteers at her hospital have friends or relatives who work there. "They keep hearing what a nice place this is, so they come in and volunteer their services," she says.

Some people volunteer to work in healthcare because they want to return something to an organization or institution that has helped them. Baird cites a man who came to volunteer after his successful recovery from neurological surgery. "I can't make a donation," he told her, "but I'd like to give you some of my time."

According to the National Hospice Organization, most hospice volunteers are surviving family members of patients who were part of a supportive hospice program. However, the NHO recommends that its member organizations not allow survivors to become volunteers until they have participated in a bereavement group for a year.

The growing number of early retirees—many of them men—who are looking for service opportunities have become an important source of volunteers. To some extent they have replaced the nonworking women who once provided most volunteer services. Betty L. Muder, director of volunteers at Providence-St. Margaret, says that over half her volunteers are now over age 55.

Some people with full-time jobs also find time to volunteer. For them it may be easier to work in healthcare facilities than in other kinds of institutions because hospitals can use help 24 hours a day, 7 days a week. This gives volunteers a choice of weekend or evening hours that fit into their schedules.

Junior Volunteers

Most hospitals have programs for Junior Volunteers, aged 14 to 18. Some students receive high school credit for their volunteer work; others are looking toward future careers in healthcare. Indeed, some teaching hospitals consider attracting teenage volunteers to be part of their educational mission. "Not only do we get help, we also teach them about career opportunities," says Phoebe Layne, director of volunteer services at State University of New York Medical Center in Brooklyn.

According to the American Health Care Association, many nursing homes also welcome young volunteers and bring children and teens into the facilities as part of an intergenerational program. Some schools bring whole classes of youngsters to nursing homes to visit with residents or to offer them holiday entertainment.

Helping AIDS Patients

Emergency situations sometimes create a particularly urgent need for volunteers. The AIDS crisis, which has had a devastating impact on the lives of the people suffering from the disease, is straining the resources of the healthcare system in some parts of the United States, and numerous organizations are recruiting volunteers to help people with AIDS both in the hospital and in the community. AIDS Project Los Angeles (APLA) trains volunteer "buddies" to provide companionship, emotional support, and practical assistance to AIDS patients. Volunteers with God's Love We Deliver, a program based in New York City, bring hot meals to homebound AIDS patients. Also in New York City, some 1,600 volunteers with the Gay Men's Health Crisis offer a wide array of services to people with AIDS, from preparing a meal to drawing up a will to taking calls on a hot line.

Making Home Care Possible

Some volunteer programs help to keep people out of healthcare facilities. Across the United States, 10,000 volunteers work through the National Federation of Interfaith Volunteer Caregivers to provide services such as transportation, friendly visits, shopping, and household chores. These services enable people who might otherwise need hospital or nursing home care to live at home. Often, programs to provide such services are set up under the auspices of church and synagogue coalitions in a community.

A Link With the Community

In addition to providing specific services at healthcare institutions, volunteers serve as a link between the facility and the community. A hospital volunteer impressed with the compassion of the facility's

staff may create goodwill for the hospital by telling friends and neighbors about the caring nurses and concerned physicians working there. Volunteers have more credibility than hospital personnel when they explain the reasons for the high cost of medical care to people in the community.

Nursing home volunteers serve as a link with the outside world for residents who would otherwise see the same few people day after day. In some cases they, too, may play a role in educating the community about the positive aspects of nursing homes and help dispel the sometimes unfairly tarnished image of these healthcare institutions.

Questions to Ask Before You Begin

The range of volunteer opportunities in the healthcare system is so broad that there is a place for nearly anyone who wants to help.

What Can I Get Out of It?
Before committing yourself to a specific program, think about the

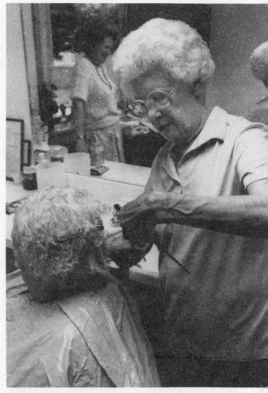

Hospital volunteering may take the form of fixing patients' hair or bringing round a book cart.

kind of service that would be both rewarding to you and useful to the community. Consider, too, the particular skills you have to offer. You won't be alone if you look for personal benefits: "Volunteers today are more choosy about what they will do," says Nancy Brown, who heads the Society of Directors of Volunteer Services, an affiliate of the American Hospital Association.

What kinds of benefits are there for volunteers in the healthcare system? For some people volunteering is a way to expand their social horizons. If you are hoping to make new friends, you may want to become part of a group of volunteers who work together on a project—perhaps preparing and serving refreshments for special occasions in a nursing home, or planning a fund-raising event for a hospital.

Volunteer work may provide experience that will help some people enter or reenter the workplace or make a career change. If that's your goal, let the director of volunteers know what kind of work you would like to do. If you are now working in sales but would like to get into an office job, you might be able to help at the reception desk, or with typing or filing. Or if you are considering applying for a job in a department store, working at a hospital gift shop may be a good way to find out if you like selling.

If you are looking for the personal satisfaction that comes from working with patients, consider the options that might be available. Would you enjoy playing board games with children who are in the hospital for a long stay? Would you prefer to read mail or magazine articles to nursing home residents whose eyesight is failing? Are you the special kind of person who can help terminally ill patients and their families through difficult times? If so, a hospice organization in your area might be able to use your services.

Is Training Provided? Ask about the training available before you begin your volunteer job, and be sure it is sufficient for you to feel comfortable. More training is usually needed for volunteers who will be working directly with patients than for those who will be helping out with such jobs as delivering mail or flowers, assisting with office work, or mending clothing for nursing home residents. Some people consider training a benefit of volunteer work; others prefer to help in ways that do not require learning new skills.

Will I Get Support? If your work is to involve patient contact, be sure there is someone to whom you can report problems and who will provide support for you if difficulties arise. At a hospital or nursing home, this person may be a nursing supervisor or the head of the institution's patient recreation programs.

Volunteering has its own personal rewards for some people and helps others to expand their social horizons.

Volunteers who work with AIDS patients at Goldwater Memorial Hospital in New York City exchange telephone numbers so that they can provide mutual support and relieve one another of some of the anxiety that comes from working with seriously ill patients. Would you welcome this intense kind of involvement—or would you prefer to limit your commitment to a regular schedule of patient visits?

Any Special Talents? Do you have special talents you would like to share? Many nursing homes welcome volunteers who can entertain residents by singing, playing an instrument, or doing a juggling act.

Can I Get There Easily? Before you promise to help, consider transportation. Is there convenient bus service between your home and the place you will be working? If you will be driving, is parking convenient?

How About the Hours? Find out how many hours each week you will be expected to work. If you need a flexible schedule, be sure the volunteer coordinator knows this before you start. Make it known before you begin working if frequent travel or working overtime during a busy period will limit your volunteer hours.

Is Child Care Available? Some hospitals and nursing homes have their own day care center for the children of employees. If you have youngsters who need supervision while you volunteer, ask whether this service is available to you. Be sure to find out in advance if there is a fee and also whether your child will need lunch or a snack.

What Costs Will I Have? The rewards of volunteer work are more psychological than financial, but there are ways to limit your out-of-pocket costs. Some hospitals reimburse volunteers for carfare and may provide a pass for a free lunch in the cafeteria. If a uniform is required, find out in advance if you are expected to pay for it yourself.

Keep a record of expenses related to your volunteer work. If you itemize deductions on your tax return, you may be entitled to charitable deductions for the cost of transportation, uniforms, and certain other expenses (not including child care) for which you are not reimbursed.

An Added Bonus?

In addition to the satisfaction gained from helping, volunteering may carry unexpected benefits. Research has suggested that people who volunteer at least once a week—particularly if they have personal contact with those they are helping—are likely to feel better and to live longer. □

MOTION SICKNESS

Ingrid J. Strauch

Even possessors of the strongest stomachs are probably familiar with the symptoms of motion sickness—nausea and vomiting that are often preceded by pallor, yawning, hyperventilation, cold sweats, restlessness that gives way to sleepiness or malaise, dizziness, and excessive salivation. As many as nine out of ten people have experienced or will experience motion sickness at some point in life. Dogs, cats, and horses are known to suffer similarly in transit. Even fish in a tank have been known to vomit when riding on a ship in rough waters.

Among humans, children between the ages of 2 and 12 are the most commonly afflicted. Infants are rarely affected, and most people eventually outgrow the tendency to become motion sick; it is less common after age 50. But some people, for reasons unknown, remain susceptible all their lives.

Any prolonged motion (or perceived motion) that upsets the normal sense of balance can bring on motion sickness. The movement of boats or cars is the most frequent cause, but some individuals feel sick on buses, trains, airplanes, swings, or carnival rides. Legend has it that Lawrence of Arabia became queasy from riding a camel and that Lord Nelson, the British naval hero, got seasick. More recently, many astronauts have reported nausea while adjusting to weightlessness—a lack of gravitational pull—in space. (Motion sickness caused by space travel is called space adaptation syndrome.) Watching movies filmed from aircraft and other fast-moving vehicles can provoke motion sickness, and even watching a too-rapid succession of microscope slides can make some viewers sick to their stomachs.

Possible Causes

Despite much study, no one knows for sure what causes someone to feel nauseous when exposed to motion. Because the symptoms involve the stomach, it was once believed that nausea was the digestive system's reaction to movement.

Today, however, most researchers believe that not the stomach but the vestibular portion of the inner ear, the part responsible for balance and equilibrium, more likely holds the clue to the cause of motion sickness. It is notable that the only persons immune to motion sickness are those whose inner ears are not functioning normally. Congenitally deaf individuals have been shown to be unaffected by motion sickness.

Within the vestibular portion of the inner ear are three fluid-filled, tubular structures called the semicircular canals, which lie in planes at right angles to one another and are responsible for the perception of motion and balance. When the head or entire body moves in any direction, the fluid pressure within the canals changes, and nerves carry information on these pressure changes from the canals to the brain. In addition, two other structures in the inner ear, called the utricle and saccule, sense any changes in the pull of gravity on the head and help determine which way is up. They likewise send information to the brain.

Several theories have been proposed to explain the onset of motion sickness, although none has been definitively proven. One, called the sensory conflict theory, is based on the idea that an area in the brain—called the vomiting center—reacts when contradictory signals are received from the eyes and the inner ears. For example, when a passenger is reading while on board a ship at sea, the inner ears perceive the motion of the rolling waves while the eyes see a

Any prolonged motion (or perceived motion) that upsets the normal sense of balance can bring on motion sickness.

stationary page. In a reverse situation, when a person is watching a movie filmed from a roller coaster, the eyes record movement while the inner ears report that the body is actually stable. The result in either case frequently is nausea.

Another possible cause of motion sickness is overstimulation of the inner ear. When a boat on the ocean moves fore and aft and from side to side simultaneously, the brain may simply be unable to sort out the multitude of signals it is receiving from the inner ears. When a boat is in a storm and its movements are faster and more violent, even people who normally don't experience seasickness sometimes feel ill.

Still another motion sickness theory, called the fluid accumulation theory, applies mainly to space travel, where weightless conditions cause body fluids to accumulate in the upper half of the body. It has been suggested that fluid shifted to the head may cause nausea by applying pressure on the brain or by changing the amount or composition of fluid in the inner ears.

Prevention

One obvious way of preventing motion sickness is to stay home or walk to all destinations. But for those who wish to venture farther and faster afield, there are various measures that may decrease the likelihood of feeling ill en route. It is important to institute these measures *before* discomfort begins; afterward may be too late.

Travelers should eat lightly and avoid alcoholic beverages before and during a trip. Reading in a moving vehicle is not advised, but many people find it helpful to concentrate on something other than how their stomachs feel. Conversation and word games are simple distractions, as are coloring books for children. If possible, the eyes should be focused on or slightly above the horizon rather than on the interior of the moving vehicle. In a car, children aged three or younger should ride in an elevated car seat that allows them to see out the windows. Older children and adults will find that riding in the front seat helps prevent carsickness. On a boat it helps to be on deck whenever possible. Reclining and closing the eyes may also prevent symptoms from occurring (or even bring relief).

Air travelers should ask for seats near the wing, where the plane is stablest, and boat passengers should ride midway between bow

Preventing Motion Sickness

Taking a few preventive steps can help stave off the ravages of motion sickness.

In a Car
- Don't read
- Focus your eyes on or slightly above the horizon
- Put young children in elevated car seats

On a Boat
- Stay on deck whenever possible
- Request a cabin at water level, midway between bow and stern

On an Airplane
- Request a seat near the wing
- Avoid the smoking section

In General
- Eat lightly before and during travel
- Avoid alcohol
- Dress comfortably
- Recline and close the eyes, if possible
- Take any anti-motion sickness drugs before travel begins

and stern. If boat travel entails spending a night or more on board, passengers should request a cabin near the water level in order to assure themselves of maximum stability.

Fresh air is a well-known remedy for seasickness and is also important during other types of travel. Tobacco fumes and food odors can be especially nauseating to a victim of motion sickness, so smoking sections and dining areas should be avoided. Car drivers should make sure their vehicles' exhaust systems are functioning properly and that gases are not leaking inside.

Wearing loose clothing may also help to make travel more comfortable and lower the chances of becoming sick. While vomiting may feel desirable and provide temporary relief, it should not be induced.

Many travelers report that taking two or three capsules of powdered gingerroot (available in health food stores) 15 minutes before departure and every four hours thereafter effectively reduces nausea with no unpleasant side effects.

Sometimes fear and anxiety can provoke an episode of motion sickness, especially for airplane passengers. The problem may disappear with more travel experience. Biofeedback, a technique that helps patients monitor and control their breathing, heartbeat, perspiration rate, and muscle tension, is being explored as a way to lower susceptibility when psychological factors are involved. It requires special training, and several weeks to several months of practice may be needed to achieve the desired results.

Scientists have found that people experiencing motion sickness have increased electrical activity in the stomach, a phenomenon often described as "butterflies in the stomach" and frequently felt during emotional stress. It has been suggested that training people to regulate the electrical activity could be useful in controlling motion sickness.

Drugs

If motion sickness is a persistent problem that doesn't respond to the sorts of preventive measures, that were mentioned above, there are two types of medications—classified as antihistamines and anticholinergics—that can be used as preventives. These drugs—some available over the counter, others by prescription—are usually most effective when taken at least an hour before exposure to motion; once nausea has set in, it is difficult to treat.

Antihistamines have a depressant effect on the functioning of the vestibular area of the ear. Over-the-counter antihistamines include Dramamine, Bonine, and Marezine. Dramamine is available in liquid, tablet, and chewable tablet form. Children as young as two can take Dramamine in accordance with dosage directions. Adults can take the drug every 4 to 6 hours, up to eight tablets or the liquid equivalent in 24 hours. Dramamine is not intended for prolonged use. Bonine, sold in chewable tablet form, is not recommended for children under 12. It should be taken only once a day and can be used for the duration of a journey. Mare-

---

Even fish in a tank have been known to vomit when riding on a ship in rough waters.

---

zine is sold in tablet form and can be used by children aged six and older. It can be taken every 4 to 6 hours by adults, up to four tablets in 24 hours.

A prescription is required for the antihistamine promethazine (brand name, Phenergan), which can be administered in syrup, tablet, or suppository form, or by injection. It can be prescribed for children (who usually take half the adult dose). An injection or suppository is used when oral administration cannot be tolerated.

Scopolamine, an anticholinergic frequently used for motion sickness, must also be prescribed by a physician. Scopolamine is most often used in the form of a small, disk-shaped patch—called the Transderm Scōp in the United States and Transderm-V in Canada—that adheres to the skin behind the ear. The drug, which reduces the activity of nerve fibers in the inner ear, is absorbed through the skin over a period of up to three days. If travel lasts for more than three days and the body does not become accustomed to motion, the disk should be discarded at the end of the third day and a fresh disk placed behind the other ear. Only one disk at a time should be worn.

After applying the disk it is crucial that users (or others who touch the disk) wash their hands thoroughly with soap and water. Scopolamine can cause temporary dilation of the pupils and blurred vision if it comes in contact with the eyes.

The most common side effect of the disk is dry mouth, but occasionally it causes drowsiness, blurred vision, memory loss, or disorientation. In addition, some people report dizziness, nausea, headaches, and trouble with balance after removing the disk. Elderly persons appear to be most susceptible to all of these side effects. Since it is not possible to predict which patients will experience the more serious side effects, scopolamine users should inform someone—a travel companion, crew member, or ship's doctor—that they have applied a disk. The disk should not be used by children.

In general, motion sickness remedies tend to cause drowsiness, so drivers and others who need to be alert or operate dangerous equipment should avoid them. The drugs should not be used, except when advised by a physician, by persons with asthma, glaucoma, certain pulmonary diseases, or enlargement of the prostate gland, as well as by pregnant women, nursing mothers, or people taking certain antibiotics, sedatives, or tranquilizers. As with all drugs, it is important to store motion sickness medications out of reach of children and to follow the package directions or doctor's orders when using them. As soon as travel is completed, any anti-motion sickness medication should be discontinued.

It is important to start preventive measures against motion sickness before the discomfort begins.

Serious but Not Immobilizing

Motion sickness, while rarely life-threatening, should be treated seriously. Excessive vomiting can lead to dehydration and loss of vigor, and motion sickness can be a serious complication in patients who are already ill. Nausea or vomiting that continues after travel has ended may indicate a problem other than motion sickness; in this case a doctor should be consulted.

Luckily, a predisposition to motion sickness need not preclude all travel. Even lifelong sufferers can usually tolerate some forms of transportation or respond well to some drugs or other preventive measures. A little experimentation and extra planning before a trip may be necessary, but, as anyone who has experienced motion sickness knows, it is better to expend the effort before a trip begins than to waste precious vacation time leaning over the ship's rail, making quick stops on the side of the highway, or groping for the air sickness bag while the rest of the party has fun. □

Teaching Good Health

Christine Martin Grove

Major diseases and disorders that lead to premature death in the United States, such as lung cancer and heart disease, are associated with personal behavior that can be changed. Yet anyone who has ever tried to make changes in health-related behavior—giving up smoking, for example, or cutting down on the amount of fat in the diet—knows what a struggle it can be. On the principle that it is easier to live a healthy life if bad habits aren't picked up in the first place, or if they are caught early, health educators are making a concerted effort to get comprehensive health education accepted as an important and continuing part of the school curriculum—if possible starting in the prekindergarten classroom and going all the way through 12th grade.

A second, but by no means secondary, concern is that the health and health-related behavior and attitudes of many American schoolchildren are, from very early on, not very good.

- As many as one-third of American schoolchildren over 12 have elevated cholesterol levels.
- About 10 percent of American children have high blood pressure.
- More schoolchildren of all ages are overweight today than 20 years ago.
- U.S. teenagers smoke marijuana and use other illicit drugs more than teenagers in any other industrialized nation.
- More high school students than adults smoke cigarettes.
- Nearly half of high school juniors and seniors admit to drinking and driving.
- Around 100,000 elementary schoolchildren get drunk at least once a week.
- Only one-third of students always use seat belts when riding in the front seat of a car.

- Only one-fifth give any thought to good nutrition when they buy food.
- More than one-fifth do not eat breakfast on schooldays.
- More than half sometimes give in to peer pressure and behave in ways that they know are not good for their health.
- Over one-third say they are very unhappy at least once a week; around one-quarter of these students will not talk about what is troubling them.
- Among junior high and high school students, one out of ten does not know that intravenous drug use is linked to AIDS.

And yet, of the 45 million students in U.S. schools, around 17 percent get little or no health education and less than a third get comprehensive health education.

Increasing health educators' concern is evidence that bad health habits that persist through childhood and adolescence can have long-term health effects even if they are corrected later in life. Poor eating habits in childhood, for example, can contribute to the later development of such serious conditions as atherosclerosis (hardening of the arteries) and osteoporosis.

An added incentive for teaching good health is financial. Health costs have skyrocketed in the United States in recent years, with the nation's bill now reaching almost $1.5 billion daily. Many of these dollars are being spent on treating disorders that could be avoided if people chose to behave differently.

What Is Being Taught?

Comprehensive health education programs tend to share some basic goals: to promote good physical health and safety practices; to foster emotional health, self-esteem, and a sense of personal responsibility; and to teach students about the functions and structures of major body systems and the effects on them of smoking, drugs, and alcohol.

An example of the kinds of topics that such programs deal with is provided by Growing Healthy, a widely used program for kindergarten through seventh grade. Originally funded by the U.S. government's Centers for Disease Control, it is now managed by a private, nonprofit organization, the National Center for Health Education. The NCHE markets the program, updates its content, and maintains a national network to train those who will teach the program and ensure that classroom teaching meets Growing Healthy's standards.

The Growing Healthy curriculum is divided into ten areas: human growth and development, including the structure and function of body systems—the respiratory system and nervous system, for example—and how they work together; disease prevention and control; mental-emotional health; safety and first aid; personal health (positive health habits, from grooming to the relationship between life-style and health); consumer health (how to choose health products and services wisely); family life and health, including an understanding of reproduction and of the changes accompanying adolescence; drug use and abuse; nutrition; and community and environmental health management (how the individual can contribute to the solution of community-wide health problems such as waste disposal and the spread of disease; what community health workers do).

Like other comprehensive programs, Growing Healthy sets specific objectives for each grade level in each content area, with the difficulty and sophistication of the material increasing with the grade level. For example, kindergartners who have studied Growing Healthy's nutrition materials should be able to list many kinds of food, differentiate between foods that are healthful and those that are not, and classify correctly foods that come from animals and foods that come from plants. Fifth graders should be able to explain why we need to eat a variety of foods daily and how a diet based on food fads may not provide adequate nourishment; they should also be able to interpret the labels on food packages. Seventh graders should be able to analyze whether a particular diet is nutritionally adequate for an adolescent, explain how body weight is related to calorie intake and level of activity, and describe safe ways of losing weight.

Getting the Message Across

In an effort to ensure that the health education message gets across, educators seek out creative ways to catch the students' attention and motivate them. To gain an understanding of the responsibilities of being a parent, high school students in a number of programs have had to take care of a "baby"—for example, a sack of flour or a fertilized chicken egg— 24 hours a day for a week or more. Participants in Know Your Body, a program of the nonprofit American Health Foundation, undergo an annual health screening, in which height, weight, blood pressure, and cholesterol levels are measured and a stress test given. Results are sent home to parents, and students are asked to enter the data in individual "health passports," to make them more aware of their own health and to motivate them to make changes.

The Growing Healthy program uses print materials, films, slides, records, tapes, demonstrations, and models. Students learn about the workings of the ear by examining a model of the ear, watch a portable smoke machine demonstrate what cigarettes do to the lungs, learn how the skeletal system works by playing a board game, and eat various types of food as they learn about the five senses.

Does It Work?

A number of surveys have shown that comprehensive health education programs have a positive effect on students' attitudes and behavior. According to a survey completed in 1988, third to twelfth graders with at least three years of health education were less likely than their peers to smoke cigarettes, take drugs, drink alcohol, or ride with a driver who had been drinking. They were more likely to clean their teeth every day, exercise on a regular basis, eat breakfast every morning, wear seat belts, and feel that they had a great deal of control over their own health. And the better the health program, the more marked the effects.

Comprehensive health education programs have not been in use long enough for there to be any research showing whether changes in behavior and attitudes are maintained into adulthood and have the positive long-term impact on health that is hoped for. There are studies, however, showing that such changes are having some impact on students' health right now. A study of over 3,000 fourth through eighth graders in the New York City area who had taken part in the Know Your Body program found that their cholesterol levels had decreased moderately over the five years of the study. The cholesterol levels of a comparable group of students who had not participated in Know Your Body remained virtually unchanged. Although the program's impact was not dramatic, the results suggest that health education does indeed have the potential to improve the health of the next generation. □

RAISING TWINS
Double Trouble?

Michael K. Meyerhoff, Ed.D.

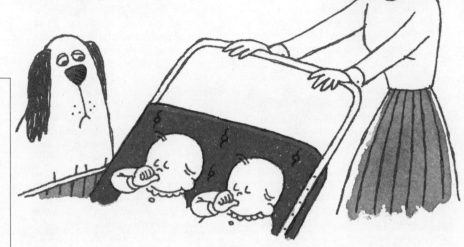

Because of improvements in prenatal care, the growing number of women delaying child-bearing, greater use of fertility drugs, and various other factors, multiple births are becoming increasingly common. Nevertheless, it is clear that twins, triplets, and other multiples are still considered quite special. And although modern medical technology allows most parents to receive ample warning that more than one baby is on the way, many still find themselves unprepared to handle the unusual challenges that come with raising simultaneously at least two children the same age.

There are no simple, universal rules for coping with multiples, as the makeup of each family is different and the personalities of all the people involved are unique. Experts on child development and experienced parents do, however, propose some general guidelines and specific suggestions. These, along with basic childrearing principles, can help mothers and fathers formulate strategies that will make raising multiples more pleasurable and less stressful for everyone involved.

The key to success seems to be to strike a balance between fostering a sense of individuality in each child and encouraging the mutually supportive relationship the children are naturally inclined to establish with each other. As the years go by, the particular problems that confront parents and their multiples change in form and content, and the degree of conflict often depends upon genetic makeup (for instance, whether the children are identical twins or different-sex fraternal twins). However, the importance of supporting both individuality and a special bond remains constant.

As the overwhelming majority of multiples are twins, most of the examples and recommendations given in this article will refer to twins. The principles behind the recommendations, however, apply not only to twins but also to all other multiples.

In the Beginning

As soon as the children are born, the factors of novelty and convenience often work together to diminish the individuality of each baby. Parents occasionally (and friends and relatives usually) fall into the habit of thinking of the twins as a matched set rather than as two distinct infants. While boy-girl fraternal pairs sometimes escape this trap, identical twins and same-sex fraternal twins tend to be given similar names and dressed in similar outfits, quickly becoming "the twins" in everyone's mind. They are expected to have growth and behavior patterns that are basically the same, and they are typically fed, diapered, bathed, and put to sleep in an assembly line manner.

But even genetically identical twins begin to show physical and temperamental differences as soon as they are born. Womb positions, prenatal incidents, events during delivery—all can imbue each child with distinctive characteristics. If the children are to develop optimally, it is important that the care they receive respect whatever dissimilarities they show. It is true that, at the outset, all babies, not only multiples, are a lot alike, and dissimilarities may be quite subtle; this being so, parents must make a special effort to detect and foster individuality right from the start.

It is strongly recommended that parents avoid the similar-name syndrome and not buy identical outfits (if these are received as gifts, the children can wear them on different days). It also is suggested that separate sleep areas be assigned and separate sets of bottles, bath towels, and other items kept to the extent that the family's living space and budget will allow. Furthermore, it is considered imperative that parents resist the temptation to simply go ahead and do the same for both children whenever one requires something; instead, parents should respond to each child as he or she has a specific need. While such practices cut down on efficiency and bring on added fatigue, they pay significant psychological dividends in the long run.

Infancy and Toddlerhood

As multiples begin to grow, their distinctive characteristics become more readily apparent to their parents, although not always to friends and relatives. It helps others to keep from lumping the twins together if the parents, in addition to following the practices mentioned earlier, always refer to each of the children by name (and do so often) and point out their dissimilarities more often than their similarities. Having separate portraits of the children is another good idea.

Indications of the special relationship between multiples also become evident during infancy and toddlerhood—cuddling together in the crib comes first, followed by mutual exploration and reciprocal babbling, and, eventually, interactive play. Interestingly, while one twin usually appears to be the leader or more aggressive at any moment, in roughly 50 percent of families the children regularly switch these roles back and forth, especially during the early years. In any event, since they have an almost ever-present playmate, multiples definitely have an advantage in finding entertaining and educational opportunities when parents do not have time to provide them.

Having a built-in buddy is nice for the twins but can create problems for other children in the family. An older sibling's natural resentment at the inevitably large loss of parental attention may be exacerbated by feelings of being "left out" by the twins too. The natural resentment of toddler twins toward a younger sibling, coupled with their tendency to "gang up" on their little brother or sister, may make them a physical threat to the younger child, although, fortunately, it is rare that real harm results. Because the twins have always had to share their mother and father with each other, the normal patterns of sibling rivalry usually are not as strong between the twins themselves, but parents need to watch for especially fierce rivalries between the twins and other siblings.

As might be expected, even though there are differences—sometimes subtle and sometimes substantial, with the extent of differences being greatest for different-sex fraternals and smallest for identicals—multiples tend to achieve most of the major milestones (including walking, talking, and toilet training) at approximately the same time. As might not be expected, however, multiples often achieve these milestones a bit later than their singleton peers. This may be due to prematurity, low birth weight, and other adverse physical factors associated with multiple births. The fact that parents have to divide their attention between two or more babies, the constant presence of poor role models (each other), and other environmental factors may play a part as well. In most cases this lagging behind does not last long, and the multiples ordinarily catch up to their peers by the preschool years. They will come through with their self-esteem intact if parents remember that all children differ in their rates of development and avoid making disparaging comparisons between the twins themselves and between the twins and other children.

The Preschool Years

As multiples move on and begin to engage in an increasing number of out-of-home activities, some problems may recur, and new considerations enter the picture. The children may once again find themselves being regularly referred to as "the twins" and treated as a single unit rather than as individuals—this time by preschool teachers. They may also get special treatment from classmates, from being shown off to visitors to being given leading roles in mischievous pranks or practical jokes (especially if they look very much alike). All of this can lead to the twins' developing a sense of power and privilege based not on their accomplishments or personalities, but merely on their twinship. To prevent this, parents may need to educate their children's educators and, if possible, should arrange that the twins be placed in different classrooms, or at least different areas within the same classroom.

Since they are accustomed to having the same constant com-

panion, multiples may find extended separation uncomfortable and even frightening at first. It is a good idea to introduce them to the concept gradually, starting in infancy and toddlerhood. If each parent routinely spends separate time with each twin and takes each twin on separate trips—initially, a brief visit to a neighbor, and later, a daylong outing to the zoo, for example—being apart in preschool won't be as scary. This practice also prepares the multiples for unforeseen and potentially traumatic separations, such as the hospitalization of one child.

Both in and out of the home, it is important that multiples learn to pursue activities according to their individual interests and abilities and to accept responsibility for their own actions. Whenever appropriate, each child should be encouraged to make independent decisions, and when it comes to household chores and other such routines, each child should be given different assignments. Furthermore, although multiples may tend to stick together when they are in trouble, and it may be difficult to determine "who did it," parents need to make an extra effort to figure out exactly who is at fault in each case and then customize any necessary punishment accordingly.

Later Childhood and Adolescence

With each passing year, multiples gradually grow farther apart in all areas, particularly if they continue to be placed in separate classrooms and especially if they are different-sex fraternals. They may develop not only distinctly different interests and abilities, but widely divergent personalities and priorities and different friends as well. While this does much to encourage and establish the individuality of each child, it also tends to threaten the mutual support system the twins have enjoyed since birth. As the constant companion of childhood becomes the ever-present competitor of the

teen years, the potential for problems between the twins increases.

To the extent that the twins already have learned to behave and be treated as individuals, these problems can be minimized. Inevitably, however, there are instances in which jealousy, resentment, and disappointment are almost impossible to avoid—if only one twin is invited to a party, only one wins a spot on an all-star team, only one makes the honor roll, only one can get a date for the prom. Even if the twins themselves remain essentially understanding and supportive of each

TYPES OF TWINS

About 1 in 90 births in the United States produces twins. (By comparison, triplets occur once in every 8,000 births, and quadruplets and other multiple births are even rarer.) Of every ten pairs of twins, seven are fraternal twins. Fraternal (or binovular) twins occur when two eggs are fertilized by two separate sperm. Fraternal twins may not look alike and may be of different sexes; genetically they are just ordinary siblings. Identical (or monovular) twins occur when a single egg is fertilized by a single sperm and the egg then splits into two halves. Identical twins, as their name suggests, look very much alike, are always of the same sex, and carry exactly the same genes.

other, the pressure of "equal expectations" placed on them by other people can become unbearable.

It is up to the parents to be compassionate and to try, whenever possible, to compensate for any inequities imposed by such circumstances. For example, they might set up an attractive alternative activity for the "excluded" twin or cherish and reward various unique qualities and separate accomplishments of the "unrecognized" twin. While reinforcing one, however, they must avoid denigrating the other. Promoting the concept that "different" does not automatically mean "better"

or "worse" and that "equal" does not necessarily mean "the same" is difficult and tricky business, but it is critical to the maintenance of each of the multiples' self-esteem and to the preservation of their close and caring relationship.

Neither Blessing nor Curse

Being a multiple is in itself neither a blessing nor a curse. Depending upon the degree of physical resemblance and the attitudes and expectations of the people around them, multiples may or may not enjoy advantages and may or may not suffer hardships. As long as parents keep in mind the notion that each child is a unique individual, they can help all their children cope with whatever circumstances arise in a manner that will tip the balance well toward the salutary side. □

Suggestions for Further Reading

ALEXANDER, TERRY PINK. *Make Room for Twins*. New York, Bantam Books, 1987.
NOBLE, ELIZABETH. *Having Twins*. Boston, Houghton Mifflin, 1980.
THEROUX, ROSEMARY, AND JOSEPHINE TINGLEY. *The Care of Twin Children*, 2nd ed. Chicago, The Center for Study of Multiple Birth, 1984.
Twins. A magazine for parents of multiples, published bimonthly by Twins Magazine, Inc., P.O. Box 12045, Overland Park, KS 66212.

Sources of Further Information

National Organization of Mothers of Twins Clubs, 12404 Princess Jeanne NE, Albuquerque, NM 87112-4640. Provides advice and information on bringing up multiples and referrals to local support groups throughout the United States.
Parents of Multiple Births Association of Canada, P.O. Box 2200, Lethbridge, Alberta T1J 4K7. Provides advice and information on raising multiples and referrals to local support groups throughout Canada.
Twin Services, P.O. Box 10066, Berkeley, CA 94709. Offers advice and information on the birth and development of multiples.

ORGAN DONATION
Why It's Important

Terrence Adolph

Advances over the past decade in the transplantation of body parts have resulted in more and more of such operations being performed in the United States. But the number still falls far short of meeting the need, largely because of a scarcity of suitable organs and tissues. Many people hesitate to pledge their organs for use after their death, being held back by misconceptions about what is involved. It takes very little on an individual's part to become a donor and costs nothing. The satisfaction to people is that their organs will be used to extend the life of others.

Transplantation Milestones

The first successful transplant of an organ, a kidney, was performed in Boston in 1954. For years afterward transplantation remained experimental, often marked by a lack of long-term success, as was seen in a well-publicized series of heart transplants in the 1960s. One problem was that people's bodies tend to reject implanted organs, and the drugs available to suppress that rejection response either were only moderately effective or had severe side effects.

A major step forward came in 1976 with the introduction of the drug cyclosporine. It was increasingly used experimentally through the early 1980s and won approval from the U.S. Food and Drug Administration in 1983. Cyclosporine proved more effective and less toxic than other antirejection drugs, encouraging surgeons to perform even more transplants. Possibly even safer and more effective than cyclosporine is the experimental antirejection agent FK-506, a Japanese drug derived from soil bacteria. If it gains FDA approval, its widespread use should further increase the demand for organs and tissues for transplantation.

Improved surgical procedures and better postoperative techniques also contributed to progress in transplantation. Today surgeons can successfully transplant over 25 different body parts, including such organs as the heart, liver, kidney, pancreas, and lungs and such tissues as the cornea, skin, blood vessels, bone and cartilage, and bone marrow. Since 1981 over 280,000 organ and tissue transplants have been performed in the United States.

National Organ Network

In the early 1980s the families of several individuals needing transplants made widely publicized appeals for organ donations. One such case in 1982 was a baby girl, Jamie Fiske, who was given only three weeks to live without a new liver, whereupon her family conducted a nationwide publicity campaign to find a donor; at the age of 11 months Jamie became the youngest liver transplant recipient up to that time. The following year President Ronald Reagan twice made national media appeals for liver donations for seriously ill infants. Along with the growing number of transplants being performed, these pleas focused public attention on the need for more donors and for a better organized system of procuring and allocating available organs. In 1984, Congress passed the National Organ Transplant Act, which called for the creation of a national system, the Organ Procurement and Transplantation Network, to match suitable donors with recipients.

A contract to run the national organ network was awarded by the government in 1986 to the United Network for Organ Sharing (UNOS), a nonprofit organization based in Richmond, Va., that had already been actively seeking to find and suitably place available organs. Under its congressional mandate UNOS formulated policies to ensure that donated organs are allocated fairly among patients waiting for them.

The United Network for Organ Sharing deals with major organs only—the kidneys, heart, liver, lungs, and pancreas, as well as heart-lung combinations. Its Organ Center—affectionately known among UNOS staffers as the "heart" of the organization—serves as a clearinghouse for all pertinent information on donors and recipients. Patients are placed on the UNOS waiting list by their physicians, who take into account their psychological, medical, and financial condition. When an organ becomes available, the center's computerized database is used to match it to the most suitable patient. The computer automatically lists waiting patients according to urgency of medical condition, geographical closeness to the donor, and the compatibility of the available organ. UNOS contacts the medical people associated with the patient at the top of the list and offers the available organ. Should that patient refuse it for any reason, UNOS goes down the list until a match is found.

When organs become available, fast action is critical for two reasons. First, the internal organs

ORGAN DONOR CARD

_____
Print or type name of donor

` In the hope that I may help others, I hereby make this anatomical gift, if medically accepta-
ble, to take effect upon my death. The words and marks below indicate my desires.

I give: (a) _____ any needed organs or parts

(b) _____ only the following organs or parts

_____
Specify the organ(s) or part(s)
for the purposes of transplantation, therapy, medical research or education;

(c) _____ my body for anatomical study if needed.

Limitations or special wishes, if any: _____

Signed by the donor and the following witnesses in the presence of each other:

_____   _____
Signature of Donor   Date of Birth of Donor

_____   _____
Date Signed   City & State

_____   _____
Witness   Witness

This is a legal document under the Uniform Anatomical Gift Act or similar laws.
For further information consult your physician or

UNOS P. O. Box 28010 Richmond, Virginia 23228

UNOS handles can with current technology be kept viable for transplantation for only short periods of time. The heart is most perishable, lasting only a few hours. The liver and pancreas, previously viable for only a few hours, can now be preserved up to 30 hours with a new solution, ViaSpan, approved by the FDA in 1989. Kidneys can be preserved up to 48 hours. Second, these organs most often come from people who have suddenly died in accidents. Surgeons and healthcare workers must decide quickly on appropriate placement for the victim's organs.

Other Sources of Tissues and Organs

Tissue Banks. Agencies that locate and preserve tissues function much like the national organ network. The American Red Cross has tissue banks throughout the United States that handle a broad array of tissues (not including corneas). The tissue banks work with hospitals to obtain family consent for tissue donations from dead or dying patients (also usually accident victims) and transport and store the tissue. Unlike organs, which deteriorate fairly quickly, some types of tissues can be stored for years. There is no national computer system to match donors with recipients; rather, tissues are simply taken to a tissue bank and stored there until a hospital or physician calls to see if they are available.

Corneas are handled by eye banks. The Eye Bank Association of America, operating like the American Red Cross, stores thousands of corneas a year, making them available to physicians for transplant. Corneas can be preserved for up to ten days.

Living Donors. Doctors have successfully transplanted kidneys and pancreas tissue from living donors; bone marrow can be transplanted only from living donors. Most such donations occur between family members. The first liver transplant from a living donor in the United States (such transplants had already been performed in Brazil, Australia, and Japan) took place in November 1989. Doctors at the University of Chicago Medical Center removed part of a mother's liver and transplanted it into her 21-month-old daughter. More experience with operations of this kind is required, but if they prove successful, they could save many lives. At present, half the infants in the United States awaiting liver transplants die before suitable matches are found.

Serious Shortages

As of early 1990, over 19,000 people were on UNOS's list waiting for organs to become available. This number reflects only a small portion of the individuals who need organ transplants, since many lack the financial means or other qualifications to be placed on the UNOS list. Just under 13,000 organ transplants were performed in the United States in 1988 (the latest year for which figures are available.) Similarly, even though 37,000 cornea transplants were performed in the United States in 1988, thousands more could have been done had more corneas been available.

Confronting Fears

More organs and tissues would be available were it not for the widespread existence of unfounded fears or misconceptions about donation. Some people worry that donating an organ may violate the teachings of their religion. The fact is, however, that organ donation is approved and supported by all major religious denominations in the United States.

Some people hesitate to pledge their organs and tissues for donation out of fear that they may receive a lower level of care when in the hospital. They seem to picture doctors hovering like vultures waiting for them to die in order to take their internal organs for the use of others. But the fact that a patient is an organ donor in no way affects the kind of care received while alive. The Hippocratic Oath taken by all doctors obligates them to do everything possible to preserve life. Also, a federal law prohibits transplant surgeons from being involved in the care of patients whose organs are to be donated or in determining brain death in these patients.

Another common concern is that donating organs might interfere with having an open-casket funeral. This fear, too is unwarranted (the face and hands, after all, are all that show in such a funeral).

Becoming a Donor

Perhaps the major reason for the scarcity of organs and tissues is that too few people are aware of the importance of donating them and concerned enough to take the steps to become donors. People do not like to think ahead to the time of their death or imagine themselves as victims of fatal accidents, and so they don't take to heart the suggestion that in such an event a decision they could have made long before could save other lives.

All you have to do to become a prospective organ or tissue donor is to fill out a donor card and carry it with you at all times. In the event of your death, the card will make healthcare workers aware of your wishes. A donor card can be obtained from various organizations, such as the United Network for Organ Sharing and the American Red Cross. It must be signed in the presence of two witnesses, one of whom should be a family member, and witnesses

also must sign. In many states driver's licenses have a space where people can indicate their wish to donate their body parts.

Prospective donors should be aware, however, that by itself a donor card or statement on a driver's license is not legally binding. At the time of death doctors must obtain permission from the next of kin to go ahead with the donation. (Even without prior indication of a desire to donate on the part of a deceased person, the next of kin can give doctors permission to use organs or tissues.) Therefore, it is important for those who want to donate their organs to tell their relatives of their wishes. Faced with the emotional trauma of the sudden death of someone close to them, some people balk at making such a decision. But if the matter has already been discussed, they may be more prepared to respect the deceased's wishes.

The federal and various state governments have taken steps to increase the probability of organ

Sources of Further Information

American Council on Transplantation, 700 North Fairfax Street, Suite 505, Alexandria, VA 22313. Tel. (800) ACT-GIVE.

American Red Cross, National Transplantation Services, 4050 Lindell Boulevard, St. Louis, MO 63108. Tel. (800) 2-TISSUE.

Eye Bank Association of America, 1725 Eye Street NW, Suite 308, Washington, DC 20006. Tel. (202) 775-4999.

Tissue Banks International, 815 Park Avenue, Baltimore, MD 21201. Tel. (301) 752-3800.

United Network for Organ Sharing, 3001 Hungary Spring Road, Richmond, VA 23228. Tel. (800) 24-DONOR.

Physicians, hospitals, local and state medical associations, and local liver, kidney, lung, and heart associations can also provide information on organ donation and how to become a donor.

and tissue donation. A federal law requires hospitals that accept Medicare and Medicaid reimbursements to set policies for making relatives aware that donation is an option; most states also have formulated policies on how hospital personnel should do this.

Who Can Donate?

People sometimes assume that once they reach a certain age no one would want their organs or tissues—often they themselves are pretty tired of them. While some organs—the heart, kidneys, liver, pancreas, and lungs—are generally not usable for transplantation from donors aged 65 or older, corneas, bone, and skin from older donors can often be used. In any event, doctors determine on a case-by-case basis which organs or tissues can be donated, regardless of the patient's age or medical condition.

Also, virtually all people can donate their whole bodies for medical research or education, even those (AIDS or cancer patients, for example) whose organs and tissues might not be acceptable for transplant. People who wish to make such donations should contact the specific medical school or teaching hospital they will leave their bodies to, since those institutions often require that a donation agreement be drawn up in advance of death. Doctors can arrange for donation (teaching and research institutions often request bodies from hospitals) without such an agreement if the next of kin consents.

People under the age of 18 require the consent of their parents or legal guardians to become donors. Both parents should witness the donor card.

If you fill out a donor card but later change your mind, just tear up the card and let your family know of your decision. If you have indicated on your driver's license that you wish to be a donor and then change your mind, cross out the appropriate portions of the license in red ink. □

What Are GROWING PAINS?

Ilona S. Szer, M.D.

There is nothing more frustrating for parents than being awakened from a deep sleep by a screaming child tucked successfully into bed a few hours earlier. The child looks normal, yet seems to have a deep pain somewhere in the thigh or the calf. The pain eases within an hour or less, and by morning the youngster (if not the parent) is fine, ready for a day of strenuous activity.

A child who wakes up at night complaining of limb pains but is entirely well during the day probably has growing pains. These may trouble as many as 20 out of every 100 children at one time or another. They usually begin between the ages of 3 and 12. The pains generally become less frequent and disappear completely after about one or two years. Girls may be affected more often than boys, and girls with growing pains often complain of headaches and belly aches as well.

Growing pains are intermittent, with painless intervals of days, weeks, or months. They tend to come at the end of the day or at night, when they are often severe enough to interrupt sleep. Children feel the pains most commonly in the muscles of calves or thighs, sometimes behind the knees or in the groin, and in rare cases in the arms. The pains may resemble cramps. With true growing pains a physical examination will reveal no indication of abnormality, such as redness, swelling, tenderness to touch, or difficulty in moving. Laboratory tests and X rays will be normal.

Despite their name, growing pains are not related to the process of growing. A French doctor first documented the condition in 1823; he attributed it to growth, and the name stuck. Doctors long believed that growing pains represented serious illness. Healthy children with such leg aches were put to bed for lengthy periods, sometimes even hospitalized, and were treated with available medicines. This unfortunate practice went on for about a century, until two English physicians in 1939 pointed out that the children suffering from the nighttime pains were otherwise healthy.

A number of theories have been proposed to explain the occurrence of limb pain in healthy, active children. The so-called emotional theory argues that the pains reflect a child's psychological difficulties.

Another common theory attributes growing pains to muscles, tendons, or ligaments being injured, stretched, or sprained during normal play. A recent study testing this "fatigue theory" found that children who did gentle muscle stretching exercises under parental supervision had significantly fewer growing pains than children who did not do the exercises. It is quite possible that the muscle conditioning helped prevent growing pains. It is of course possible that the attention the children received from their parents during the activity helped as well.

Although neither the fatigue theory nor the emotional theory has been proved conclusively, the process of growth has been ruled out as a possible cause. Children with growing pains do not grow faster than children without growing pains. In all children growth is actually slower during the years when growing pains are most frequent. Also, most growth occurs in the bones about the knee, and that area is not a common site for growing pains.

If your child complains of limb pains, you should let your pediatrician know. It's a good idea to keep a record for the pediatrician of when and how long each episode lasted. The pediatrician may want to do an examination, and perhaps tests, to make certain that there is no underlying illness.

While there is no cure for growing pains (assuming that is the diagnosis), you can take steps to ease the child's discomfort. Gentle massaging or warm soaks may help, and a dose of acetaminophen (such as Tylenol or Anacin-3 for children) can be tried. Emotional support is important, but don't forget that children love attention and are brilliant at figuring out how to get it. Try not to respond to painful episodes by rewarding your child for waking you up. Set a limit on how much time you spend with the child and decrease it by a few minutes each night, while increasing the time spent together during the day.

Remember, growing pains are common and benign and do eventually go away. □

VITAMIN PILLS AND OTHER SUPPLEMENTS

Eleanor R. Williams, Ph.D.

Most people get all the nutrients their bodies need simply by eating a balanced diet. Yet in recent years, Americans have been turning to diet supplements—products containing concentrated doses of vitamins, minerals, or other dietary components—in greater and greater numbers. Witness the staggering increase in sales of such products, which have gone from $500 million in 1972 to $3 billion in 1987. Supplements of multivitamins with some added minerals account for over 50 percent of sales. The most popular single-ingredient supplements are vitamin C, vitamin E, calcium, and iron. Also growing in popularity are fish oil, protein, amino acid, beta-carotene, and fiber supplements, as well as a host of more exotic products such as lecithin, choline, inositol, laetrile, bioflavonoids, pangamic acid, para-aminobenzoic acid (PABA), betaine, bee pollen, spirulina, and ginseng. Consumers are drawn to supplements by aggressive advertising, frequent media reports of studies suggesting possible relationships between nutrients and the prevention or treatment of common disorders, and the easy availability of supplements in drugstores, supermarkets, and health food stores.

Who Takes Supplements

Several surveys have shown that, overall, roughly 40 percent of Americans use diet supplements, but usage varies according to age, sex, race, income, and education. More adults than children and adolescents take supplements, and usage is highest among women, whites, and those of higher income and education levels. Studies indicate that anywhere between 35 and 70 percent of people 60 and over take supplements. And a fairly high percentage of health professionals, including dietitians, nurses, and physicians, take them occasionally if not regularly. Ironically, those who take supplements generally do not need them to correct dietary inadequacies—many studies show that the diets of supplement users are more nutritious than those of nonusers. But supplement users do appear to be more aware than nonusers of the relationship of nutrition to health.

When They Can Help

Supplements are necessary only when an individual is deficient in one or more nutrients, either because of a poor diet or as a result of a disease or a particular medical condition. A recent joint statement by the American Dietetic Association, the American Institute of Nutrition, the American Society for Clinical Nutrition, and the National Council Against Health Fraud pointed out that supplements may be needed in the following situations:

- Pregnant or breast-feeding women may need iron, folic acid, and, if their milk intake is low, calcium.
- People who remain for long periods on very-low-calorie diets may get insufficient amounts of some nutrients.
- Women who experience excessive menstrual bleeding may suffer from iron deficiency.
- Newborn infants often need a single dose of vitamin K to guard against abnormal bleeding.
- Some vegetarians' diets may be low in vitamin B_{12}, iron, zinc, or calcium.
- Some diseases and some medications may increase the need for certain nutrients by interfering with food intake or digestion or by hampering the absorption or metabolism of nutrients. In such cases supplements should be prescribed by the physician who is treating the disease or has prescribed the medication.

Registered dietitians and licensed nutritionists are trained to evaluate diets for nutrient adequacy and can advise about sensible supplementation.

Physicians sometimes use large doses of certain vitamins to treat particular diseases. For example, specific forms of vitamin A have been used to treat severe acne, nicotinic acid (a form of niacin) may be used to lower blood cholesterol, and vitamin E may be used in certain genetic disorders. When these vitamins are used as drugs, serious side effects may develop; therefore, they should be taken to treat disease only if prescribed by a physician.

Common Misconceptions

People give many reasons for taking supplements. Some want to "play it safe" in case their diet is inadequate; others hope for more "pep and energy" or enhanced athletic performance; still others believe diet supplements can prevent or treat colds, cancer, heart disease, osteoporosis, and other disorders; and some take supplements to counteract stress or heavy smoking or drinking. For most people, however, taking diet supplements is a waste of time and money.

All the above examples involve misconceptions. Vitamins and minerals do not give an energy boost—only carbohydrates, fats, and protein provide the body with energy. True, some vitamins and minerals are involved in the processes by which the body obtains energy from food, but only in tiny amounts; extra amounts from pills will not provide extra energy. Nor, contrary to the hopes and beliefs of many athletes, will protein, vitamin, or mineral supplements enhance athletic performance. As for stress, supplements are useful only in cases of severe trauma— for example, when large portions of the body's surface are burned. There is little evidence that they alleviate the kind of stress caused by daily frustrations such as fighting traffic.

Furthermore, claims that vitamin C prevents or cures colds or cancer are not supported by carefully controlled scientific studies. While very heavy smoking can increase the need for vitamin C, food sources can easily provide the extra amount needed. And additional research is needed to determine whether vitamin, mineral, fiber, or fish oil supplements play any role in preventing diseases such as cancer and heart disease. Because several studies have indicated that deep orange and dark green vegetables and yellow fruits (which contain beta-carotene) may reduce the chances of developing certain types of cancer, further studies are now in progress to determine whether beta-carotene supplements will have the same effect. At present, however, one is better off eating the fruits and vegetables themselves, since some factor other than beta-carotene may be the one involved.

Calcium tablets, taken by many women in hopes of preventing osteoporosis—thinning of the bones—have not been proven ef-fective against this disease. Estrogen therapy, not calcium supplementation, is generally the preferred method in preventing osteoporosis. Moreover, many commercially available calcium preparations fail to dissolve in the body; thus no calcium is absorbed into the bloodstream. Individuals concerned about osteoporosis should consult a doctor.

Among other common claims made for supplements are that large doses of niacin or other B-complex vitamins are valuable in treating mental illness, that vitamin E improves sexual performance, and that vitamin B_6 is beneficial in treating premenstrual tension or carpal tunnel syndrome (a condition in which compression of a large nerve causes numbness and pain in the hand). None of these claims is supported by reliable scientific evidence. Nor do the more exotic supplements referred to at the beginning of this article provide any known benefits.

Can Supplements Be Harmful?

Supplements can be harmful, particularly when used in very large doses. Large doses of some vitamins, particularly vitamins A, D, B_6, C, and niacin, can be toxic, and all trace minerals—iron, zinc, iodine, chromium, fluoride, copper, and selenium, to name a few—are toxic in high doses.

But how large a dose is too large? A good guide can be found in the U.S. Recommended Daily Allowances (USRDAs), which were developed by the Food and Drug Administration (FDA) as the legal standard for labeling the nutritional content of supplements and foods. (See the accompanying table.) These allowances are considered to be safe levels and are high enough to meet the needs of healthy adults and children over four years of age. Experts advise that, to be safe, vitamin and mineral supplements should contain no more than 50 to 100 percent of the USRDAs.

The FDA has, however, no authority to limit the amount of nutrients per supplement tablet or to prohibit the inclusion of ingredients that scientists deem to have no nutritional value. This lack of regulatory authority is the result of strong lobbying by supplement manufacturers and consumers. Thus, many supplements contain far more than ten times the USRDAs.

Vitamins A and D, like all fat-soluble vitamins, are stored in the body and not excreted. Toxicity results when dosages exceed the body's storage capacity. Symptoms of vitamin A toxicity include pain in the bones, dry, scaly skin, severe headaches, enlarged liver and spleen, and hemorrhaging. Large doses in early pregnancy can cause birth defects. Vitamin D toxicity can lead to loss of appetite, nausea, vomiting, high blood pressure, weakness, and kidney failure.

USRDAs

(U.S. Recommended Daily Allowances, set by the FDA for labeling purposes; recommendations are for adults and for children over four.)

Vitamin A	5,000 I.U.
Vitamin D	400 I.U.
Vitamin E	30 I.U.
Vitamin C	60 mg
Thiamin	1.5 mg
Riboflavin	1.7 mg
Niacin	20 mg
Vitamin B_6	2.0 mg
Folacin (folic acid)	0.4 mg
Vitamin B_{12}	6 mcg
Biotin	0.3 mg
Pantothenic acid	10 mg
Calcium	1,000 mg
Phosphorus	1,000 mg
Magnesium	400 mg
Iron	18 mg
Zinc	15 mg
Copper	2 mg
Iodine	0.15 mg

Note: The abbreviation I.U. stands for International Unit; mg = milligram; mcg = microgram (1 microgram = 1,000th of a milligram).

Large doses of niacin in the form of nicotinic acid cause severe itching and flushing of the face and neck, and both forms of niacin—nicotinic acid and nicotinamide—can cause liver damage. Excessive doses of vitamin B_6 damage the nervous system, resulting in numbness of the hands and feet and an abnormal gait. Taking more than 1,000 milligrams per day of vitamin C for long periods increases the risk for kidney stones in those who are susceptible and produces false-positive results for glucose in the urine (if one is tested for diabetes) and false-negative results for blood in the stool (in testing for colon cancer).

Excessive intakes of trace minerals also are damaging. For example, high zinc dosages impair the body's immune defenses and lower blood levels of high-density lipoproteins (HDL), the "good" cholesterol that helps remove excess cholesterol from the blood. Selenium toxicity causes loss of hair, extreme fatigue, gastrointestinal disturbances, jaundice, and brittle nails. High intakes of iodine produce goiter (as does a deficiency of that mineral). Fluoride toxicity results in mottled tooth enamel and, more seriously, crippling bone deformities and damage to the optic nerve.

Supplements can also be harmful because large intakes of some nutrients interfere with the absorption, metabolism, or excretion of others.

In the fall of 1989 the amino acid L-tryptophan, a supplement thought to help relieve insomnia, premenstrual syndrome, and depression among other conditions, was linked by the U.S. Centers for Disease Control to cases of a rare and serious blood disorder. However, it appears possible that a contaminant introduced during the manufacturing process, rather than the L-tryptophan itself, was responsible for the outbreak. The FDA warned consumers not to use the substance and asked stores to remove all products containing

L-tryptophan in dosages of 100 milligrams or more from their shelves. But illnesses and deaths associated with the blood disorder continued to be reported, and in March 1990 the FDA asked that nearly all supplies of L-tryptophan be removed from the market.

A Sensible Approach

If you have any chronic medical problems or regularly take any medications, you should consult a physician before deciding to take a diet supplement. If you have no medical problems, but think your diet needs improvement, have it evaluated by a registered dietitian or a licensed nutritionist. The chances are good that any deficiencies or imbalances can be remedied by changes in diet alone. This is the preferable way, since foods contain many substances as yet unidentified by scientists that may be important to health.

If you still wish to take a supplement (and for most people, taking a daily multivitamin pill that does not exceed recommended allowances may not do much good, but probably won't do any harm):

• Choose one that provides a variety of vitamins and minerals in amounts no greater than 100 percent of the USRDAs. Avoid "high-potency," "stress," or "therapeutic" supplements.

• Be aware that "natural" vitamin supplements are not superior to synthetic ones, and they are always more expensive.

• Do not take single vitamin or mineral supplements except on the advice of a physician, a registered dietitian, or a licensed nutritionist.

• Avoid supplements that contain the exotic substances listed earlier in this article.

• Avoid protein and amino acid supplements; they are a waste of money because these nutrients are easily obtained from food.

• Rather than taking fish oil and fiber supplements, eat fish and high-fiber foods such as whole grains, legumes (dried peas and beans), and fresh vegetables and fruits.

While the use of diet supplements in the United States has grown rapidly in recent years, little scientific research has been done on their effects, and it is likely that many cases of supplement overuse have gone unnoticed or unreported. In 1986 physicians across the United States were asked to report to the FDA on their patients' use of supplements and on any harmful effects observed. The results, when analyzed, will help determine the extent to which supplements, perhaps even in relatively low dosages, pose health risks. Meanwhile most nutritionists believe that we would be better off improving our diets than relying on supplements to bring us good health. □

Coping With Diabetes During Pregnancy

Lois Jovanovic-Peterson, M.D., and Charles M. Peterson, M.D.

When a women becomes pregnant, her body changes the way it uses and stores calories so that it can sustain the growing fetus. Calories are burned more slowly to ensure that nutrients will be available for the baby between meals. The amount of glucose in the woman's bloodstream increases. A simple form of sugar produced by the breakdown of carbohydrates from food, glucose is one of the body's chief sources of energy. In order to use it, the body's cells need insulin, a hormone made by the pancreas. Insulin acts like a key that unlocks the door to cells so that glucose can get in. When the body cannot produce insulin or use it effectively, or when, as with some women during pregnancy, the body cannot produce more insulin to compensate for higher glucose levels in the bloodstream, the result is diabetes.

If a pregnant woman's blood sugar levels get too high, the developing baby can be damaged. Women who already have diabetes before becoming pregnant must take special measures to compensate for the increased glucose in the bloodstream. Certain other women need to do so as well. These are women who during pregnancy develop what is called gestational diabetes. In this condition the pancreas fails to produce enough insulin to cope with the increased glucose levels. This might happen because the woman is overweight and her pancreas was already producing as much as it could before her pregnancy.

Screening

Gestational diabetes occurs in about 4 percent of pregnancies. It tends to develop most often in women who have a family history of diabetes and who are overweight and physically out of shape. Because it is the most common complication of pregnancy, doctors generally screen all women for this condition at about the sixth month, when it usually occurs.

In the past, women were commonly screened by checking for sugar in their urine, since it was thought that the presence of sugar indicated gestational diabetes. Urine tests, however, are inaccurate. Glucose can be present in the urine of women who do not have gestational diabetes and may occasionally be absent from the urine of those who do.

> **Gestational diabetes, usually developing at about the sixth month, is the most common complication of pregnancy.**

Now, as a first step, a blood sugar test is often used. The woman drinks a sugar solution, and an hour later blood is drawn from a vein so that the glucose level can be checked. If the level is below a certain amount, the woman does not have gestational diabetes. (The test may be repeated in the eighth month of pregnancy for women who are over 30 and overweight, since they sometimes develop the disorder in the last month.) If the level is found to be above the critical amount, then a glucose tolerance test is performed. It is similar to the screening test but is performed in the morning after an overnight fast. Again the patient drinks a sugar solution, but this time four blood samples are taken—one before and one hourly for three hours after. If two of the four samples have blood glucose levels above designated cutoff points, the woman is diagnosed as having gestational diabetes.

A woman may be asked to take a glucose tolerance test earlier than the sixth month if she had problems in previous pregnancies causing her doctor to suspect the presence of undiagnosed gestational diabetes. Also, as women age, their chances of developing gestational diabetes increase. That is why it is important for a woman each time she is pregnant to undergo a screening test and, if it is positive, a glucose tolerance test to ensure that she has not developed gestational diabetes.

Potential Problems for the Baby

If a pregnant woman with preexisting diabetes does not adjust her therapy to compensate for her increased energy needs, then her blood glucose levels will rise. High levels in the first weeks of pregnancy increase the chance of miscarriage by up to 20 percent.

High blood sugar levels increase the risk of miscarriage.

If a miscarriage does not occur, the high blood glucose levels may interfere with the baby's growth (the baby's organs are not fully formed until about the eighth week of pregnancy), and a birth defect may result. The prevalence of birth defects in infants of mothers with diabetes runs as high as 23 percent in cases where blood glucose levels are not kept normal at the beginning of pregnancy. The rate is lower for women with diabetes who maintain normal levels in their pregnancy's first weeks.

The only way to establish normal glucose levels is to achieve them before conception, through a prepregnancy program of strict glucose control with the help of stepped-up self-monitoring of blood glucose levels. Women who have been controlling their diabetes by dietary means can go ahead and try to become pregnant. Others must first take additional measures. Those normally taking insulin will divide their daily doses into three or four injections, which are adjusted until the blood glucose levels before and one hour after each meal are normal. Those using just oral drugs will stop and will start taking insulin.

Glucose control is also important for normal growth and development of the fetus after its organs are formed. If high glucose levels reach the fetus from the mother's bloodstream, the fetus will attempt to dispose of the glucose by making more insulin. Over time its pancreas becomes programmed to overproduce insulin. But insulin plus sugar leads to fat. The fetus will develop so much fat that delivery can be difficult for both the mother and the child. During a vaginal birth, the baby's arms or shoulders could be injured. If the baby is too large to be delivered vaginally, a cesarean delivery is necessary. Sonograms and other tests help the doctor estimate the baby's size and determine the safest method of delivery.

Gestational diabetes does not lead to a higher than normal risk of the baby having a birth defect, because the onset of the condition comes after the fetus's organs are fully formed. If women with gestational diabetes do not control their blood sugar levels, however, they, like women with preexisting diabetes, run a risk of having very large babies.

An overly fat baby is not the only potential problem as delivery approaches. If the blood sugar level is too high right before or during labor, the baby's pancreas will make extra insulin to balance the extra glucose it is getting from the mother. But after delivery the baby no longer receives glucose from the mother, and the extra insulin it produced can cause its own blood sugar level to fall below normal. Unless treated, this can cause serious difficulties for the newborn, such as damage to the nervous system. If necessary, the baby can be given sugar orally or intravenously to compensate for the low blood sugar. A baby at risk for low blood sugar must be watched carefully in the hospital intensive care nursery, with its blood sugar tested every hour after birth for six hours.

An early delivery may be necessary if the mother's blood sugar levels are too high, and babies born early are more likely to have jaundice, a yellowing of the skin from bilirubin, a waste product of the breakdown of red blood cells.

Before birth a baby requires a large stock of red blood cells; after birth it no longer needs an extra supply, and its liver works to break down and excrete the old red blood cells. If the liver is not mature enough, it may have trouble handling this burden, creating a buildup of old red blood cells and of bilirubin. Instead of being excreted, bilirubin is deposited in the baby's tissues, coloring the skin yellow. If enough remains in the body, it may cause brain damage.

It is common for babies to be born with a small amount of bilirubin in their systems. Some, however, are born with large amounts and may need to be exposed to special lights ("phototherapy"), which help the body break down and get rid of bilirubin. In most children born with jaundice, this treatment, which lasts only a few days, is successful. In cases of serious jaundice a special blood transfusion, called an exchange transfusion, may be required.

Women with diabetes risk developing high blood pressure.

Another possible complication of premature delivery is respiratory distress syndrome—a condition in which the infant's lungs have not developed enough for it to breathe on its own. This is the number one cause of death among premature babies. A baby born with the syndrome is provided with a respirator in an intensive care nursery until it can breathe on its own.

Problems for the Mother

Women with gestational or preexisting diabetes face an increased risk of high blood pressure and bladder and kidney infections. Pregnancy-induced high blood pressure, which is often accompanied by swelling in the feet and lower legs, can be life-threatening for the mother and baby. Treatments vary from limiting activity to hospitalization. The condition usually goes away shortly after the baby is born. Burning on urination and frequent urination are among the symptoms of bladder and kidney infections, which are treated with antibiotics. Since some antibiotics can interfere with the fetus's development, special ones are used, and they are given only after the fetus is fully formed (after the second month).

Dealing With Diabetes

Gestational. Even mild increases in blood glucose levels beyond the normal range can lead to complications during pregnancy, and so treatment for gestational diabetes should be started as soon as the woman's pancreas begins to fail. Normal levels can usually be maintained with changes in diet. Meals should be low in sugar and carbohydrates but high in protein. It is best to eat frequently—and in small amounts—so that an individual meal does not cause blood glucose to rise much.

The number of calories a pregnant woman with gestational diabetes needs to consume daily depends on her body weight. If she was at an ideal weight when she became pregnant, her daily caloric intake should equal her present weight in pounds multiplied by 14. For example, a woman who weighs 146 pounds should consume 2,044 calories a day. A woman who was overweight before pregnancy or rapidly gains excessive weight during it can determine her daily caloric intake by multiplying her present weight by 11. Total calories (with approximately 40 percent coming from

carbohydrates) should be distributed among three meals and three snacks. Breakfast should account for only about 10 percent of total calories. When the figure is higher, after-breakfast blood sugar rises too high, partly because the levels of hormones the body produces to limit the production of insulin vary during the day and are highest in the morning.

A diet is considered satisfactory only if there is no significant rise in blood sugar after meals. Many people who have diabetes monitor their blood sugar levels with test strips that change color when a drop of blood is placed on them; the shade of color indicates how much glucose is in the blood. Many persons use little devices called reflectance meters that can read the exact blood glucose level from a test strip. Each meal should be monitored with a blood test one hour after its start. In addition, a woman needs to measure her fasting, or "wake up," blood sugar levels. She should also check her blood sugar level after a snack if she fears she has overeaten.

A woman with gestational diabetes must start taking insulin if she still has, despite following a diet, high fasting blood sugar (the levels before breakfast) or high after-meal blood sugar (the levels one hour after meals). She should stay on the diet after beginning the insulin injections. Different types of insulin are available that vary in their intensity and in how long their effects last; they can be mixed in various proportions to satisfy individual needs. A pregnant woman should take insulin at least three times a day in short-acting and intermediate-acting doses based on six blood sugar tests she makes daily (before and one hour after each meal).

Preexisting. Women with Type I diabetes, which requires regular insulin injections, must increase their insulin doses during pregnancy and maintain a diet similar to the one described for a woman with gestational diabetes. Women

with Type II diabetes, a type that often does not require taking insulin, will begin taking insulin during pregnancy if they had not been taking it previously. The insulin is usually taken at least three times a day, with blood sugar levels monitored six times a day (again, before and one hour after each meal). For all women who normally took insulin before pregnancy, the total daily dose will increase, reaching by the time of delivery almost twice the usual amount.

Delivery and After

When the mother's blood sugar levels remain normal, the pregnancy is probably doing well, and an early delivery is generally not required. If blood sugar levels are less than satisfactory, then the fetus should be carefully monitored and delivered as soon as tests of the water surrounding the baby indicate that it is ready to breathe on its own.

All women with gestational diabetes should take a blood sugar tolerance test about six weeks after delivery. Almost all of them (97.5 percent) revert to normal blood sugar levels after giving birth, but the probability that gestational diabetes will recur with subsequent pregnancies is 90 percent. In addition, obese women who remain overweight have a 60 percent chance of developing nongestational Type II diabetes within 20 years. They can lower this risk by reducing their weight to the normal range and keeping it there. Fewer than 25 percent of women who have gestational diabetes and are at normal weight develop Type II diabetes later. Thus, gestational diabetes can serve as an early warning, helping to prevent obesity-induced diabetes. □

Choosing a PEDIATRICIAN

Christine Martin Grove

Choose a pediatrician" may not be an obvious entry on a list of things to do before your first child is born, or as soon as you move into a new community, but for many parents and parents-to-be it's a necessity. The decision about who will care for your child may be strongly influenced by circumstances—for example, if family finances dictate that the local clinic be used, or there is only one pediatrician you can realistically get to, or it is taken for granted in the community that the family doctor will care for young, old, and everyone in between. Many parents, however, do have the opportunity to select the doctor in their community they feel is the best one for their child.

You might be tempted simply to walk into the nearest pediatrician's office and sign up. Before doing so, consider these points. First, you and your child, especially in the early months and years, will be spending many hours with the pediatrician, more hours than people usually spend with their doctors. Second, people usually choose—and change, if necessary—their own doctors. Your child cannot do that but is dependent on your judgment. And third, think about what a pediatrician is. According to the American Board of Pediatrics, a pediatrician is a medical specialist who is trained to deal with "the diseases of and preservation and pro-

motion of health" in infants, children, and adolescents, to recognize normal and abnormal physical and mental development, and to diagnose and manage acute and chronic problems. Furthermore, the pediatrician, because a child's welfare is so dependent on the home and family, "supports efforts to create a nurturing environment."

In other words, the pediatrician's role goes beyond the obvious medical one of caring for your child's health as in "Johnny has an ear infection and this is what we have to do to make him well." The pediatrician is also responsible for monitoring the stages of your child's development and for taking action when that development is not proceeding normally. At the same time, the pediatrician must guide and advise

you, the parents, so that you will understand what to expect from your child, when to expect it, and what you can contribute to the child's well-being. Over the years you will have questions galore, on subjects as diverse as diarrhea, drug abuse, sexual development, teething, toilet training, and temper tantrums, and you must be confident you can ask them without being made to feel foolish. With all this in mind, it makes sense to ensure that the pediatrician, besides having the necessary medical qualifications, is someone you can trust and get along with.

Don't wait until the last minute to begin your search. Although you may decide not to follow all the steps in the scenario set out below, finding a pediatrician may be quite time-consuming. And there is no guarantee that the baby will wait its allotted nine months to be born or that your child will postpone getting sick until the family has had months to settle into a new community.

Collecting Names

The first step is to come up with names. There are several ways to do this, so that even newcomers to a community can get several leads. Ask friends, neighbors, and coworkers for the names of their children's pediatricians. (If they have any other information to offer—about the doctor's office hours and fees, for example, or how the doctor acts with the children—make notes for future use.) Check with your own doctors for recommendations, and if any of them are parents, ask who looks after their children. (If you're trying to do some groundwork before moving, speak to your own doctors anyway, plus your child's current pediatrician if you have one, because they can sometimes give you names in the new community.) Ask any other health professionals you know, socially or otherwise, whom they would recommend. Check with the neighborhood pharmacist, who is usually familiar with all the local doctors. Call the local hospital and ask for the names of pediatricians on the staff. Or ask the state or county medical board for names.

Checking Qualifications

Once you have your list, check the qualifications of those on it to make sure that they have special training in pediatrics. You may find that your sources gave you as much information on that question as you need. Or you may want to get more from the *American Medical Directory*, the U.S. *Directory of Medical Specialists*, the directories put out by U.S. state medical societies, or the *Canadian Medical Directory*. These publications, which should be available at local libraries, contain information about doctors' ages, where they trained, where they have worked, what hospitals they are affiliated with, and any teaching positions they hold. (Affiliation with a children's hospital, a teaching hospital, or a medical school means that a doctor's knowledge is especially likely to be very up-to-date.)

The directories will also indicate whether a doctor has passed the specialty examinations given in the United States by the American Board of Pediatrics and in Canada by the Royal College of Physicians and Surgeons. If so, the doctor is entitled to call himself or herself board-certified (in the United States) or certified by the Royal College (in Canada). Certification is an additional sign of competence. Some younger doctors may not have passed their specialty examinations yet, however, and some well-qualified older ones may never have undergone the process. If doctors you are considering are not certified, call their offices and ask if the doctors have all the qualifications that the American Board of Pediatrics or the Royal College require of anyone wanting to take the specialty examinations. In both the United States and Canada, these qualifications include an M.D. degree from an approved U.S. medical school or a recognized Canadian or foreign medical school and a license to practice in the United States or Canada; in the United States three years and in Canada four years of specialized pediatrics training after the M.D. degree are also required.

Other Considerations

Once you're satisfied about qualifications, there's a host of other factors you may want to consider.

Doctor's Age. Do you want an older doctor, with years of hands-on experience? Or do you feel that a younger doctor, with presumably more up-to-date training, would be better? (This choice is not as clear-cut as it may seem; many older pediatricians have kept up with all the latest developments.)

Location. Is it important that the doctor's office be nearby, or doesn't location matter? (Remember that a baby will be seen by the doctor at least half a dozen times during the first year.)

Kind of Practice. Is it very important to you that your child see the same doctor at every visit? If so, you need a doctor in individual practice or in the kind of group practice that maintains a separate list of patients for each

Suggested Pediatricians
Dr. Smith

doctor. Are long, flexible office hours more important? If they are, you probably need to consider the kind of group practice in which the child is seen by the next available doctor but there are extended evening and weekend hours.

Hospital Ties. Which hospital admits the doctor's patients? If there is more than one hospital in the community, it makes sense to look for a pediatrician associated with the one that has the superior reputation for treating children.

Special Interests. If there is a family history of a specific medical problem, it's a good idea to look for a pediatrician with a special interest in that area—for example, a doctor specializing in hematology if the problem is a blood disorder.

Doctor as Person. Last, but certainly not least, in view of the importance of the relationship between pediatrician and parent, what kind of person is each of the prospects on your list? Make some preliminary judgments if you can. Ask those sources whose opinions you trust to tell you something about the person they have recommended. Do they like and trust the doctor? Do they feel they can ask any question and be answered with respect and care? How do their children feel about the doctor—are they comfortable in the doctor's presence? If there was ever an emergency situation, was it handled to the parents' satisfaction? Do the doctor's ideas about medicine and about the role of the physician match your ideas—does the doctor, for example, prescribe medication for every cough or cold or prefer a more conservative approach; is the doctor directive or nondirective when discussing a child's care with parents?

The Final Round

Your list by now should be narrowed down to two or three names. The next step is to call the doctors on the list and find out

if they are accepting new patients. If so, make appointments with the doctors, explaining that you would like to come in for exploratory interviews. (Some doctors will charge for this appointment, while others will not.) Try to make the appointment for regular office hours so you can get a feel for the surroundings within which the doctor works. If possible, arrive a little early to check out the waiting room. It should be comfortable for parents and for children of all ages, with toys and activities to occupy children as they wait. (Some pediatricians have two waiting rooms—for well and sick children.) Office staff should be courteous and helpful. Note how long you have to wait to see the doctor, and ask any other waiting parents how long they usually have to wait.

Once you're talking to the doctor, try to get both answers to any practical questions you still have and, perhaps more important, an idea of whether this is someone you can get along with. Practical questions you might want to ask include the following: What are your office hours? Are you always able to see a sick child on the day a parent calls? On average, how long do you spend with each patient? Will you see the baby within hours of its birth to check for any problems? Do you have calling hours when I can telephone for advice? If I have questions, will you always answer them personally? (This is not al-

ways necessary. Sometimes it makes more sense for a nurse to answer routine baby care questions.) Are you usually on call evenings and weekends? When you are not reachable, who is on call in your place and what are their qualifications? Will the covering doctor or doctors be available only by phone or will they see the child as well? Will the treatments/diagnoses/recommendations they offer be added to the medical records you keep for the child? What are your fees? Do you accept payments directly from insurance companies or do parents pay you and then wait to be reimbursed?

If you have strong feelings about particular issues, now is the time to raise them. For example, if you do not want to breast-feed your child, will the doctor support this decision? If your child is a boy and you don't want him circumcised, how will the doctor react?

How the doctor responds during this interview will help you judge whether this is the pediatrician for you. Trust your instincts. If they tell you that you cannot feel comfortable with this doctor, it's time to move on to the next name on the list.

And remember. If, in spite of all your care, you end up feeling dissatisfied with your pediatrician, look for another one. It's your child, your money, your time. It makes sense to find a doctor who meets your needs. □

ELECTROLYSIS

Susan Carleton

Judging from the array of hair-removal products on the market, a sizable number of people must be troubled by excessive body hair. Drugstore shelves groan under the weight of bleaches (used to make hair less visible), depilatories (chemicals for removing hair), and assorted gadgets designed to take off hair. Many health clubs and salons offer waxing, in which melted wax is applied to the skin, allowed to dry, and stripped away along with embedded hair. All these techniques, however, provide only temporary solutions to the problem of unwanted hair. Hair roots are amazingly durable and have a way of surviving even the most persistent tweezing and relentless application of caustic chemicals. New hair—or, more accurately, fresh stubble—almost always replaces what was removed.

To get rid of hair for good, the structures within the hair follicles that produce and nourish hair cells must be destroyed. Each follicle is a pit in the skin out of which a hair grows. At the bottom of the follicle lies the papilla, a tiny, cone-shaped appendages that nourishes the growing hair. To date, the only hair-removal method that gets rid of hair permanently is thermolysis, the use of heat to burn away the papilla. This is the technique commonly called electrolysis.

Removing Hair for Good

Electrolysis is much more complicated than any of the handy hair-removal products available over the counter. It's a time-consuming process: because hairs must be removed one at a time, weekly treatments may be needed for as long as a year, depending on the body area involved and the amount of hair to be removed. In addition, hair passes through stages of growth and rest. At any given time some hairs are actively growing; others, no longer growing, will fall out within the next few months. Electrolysis is effective only during the active growing stage, so treatments must span many months to catch previously inactive follicles as they come to life.

The treatments must be performed by a skilled electrologist, someone with the experience and dexterity to insert an ultrafine needle, or "filament," into minuscule hair follicles at just the right angle and to the proper depth. Although some self-administered, electrically powered tweezer devices are advertised as permanent hair removers, this claim is false. The U.S. Food and Drug Administration has declared them ineffective for electrolysis purposes.

Electrologists usually charge about $15 per 15-minute session. But the treatments may be well worth the time and money for anyone whose unwanted hair causes extreme discomfort, embarrassment, or social isolation. Among those who can benefit most are women who have facial, chest, or abdominal hair, or thick, dark hair on their legs or arms.

Electrolysis can also be used to shape bushy eyebrows or an unruly hairline. Men bothered by excessive hair on the ears often seek electrolysis. (Because the nose is lined with fragile mucous membrane, electrologists do not remove hair within the nostrils.) Less common uses of electrolysis include removal of hair from grafted skin, which may be necessary when a graft taken from a hairy area such as the leg is placed in an area with little or no hair, and removal of normal body hair from men preparing to undergo sex change operations.

The Roots of Electrolysis

Electrolysis was developed in the mid-1870s as a treatment for ingrown eyelashes by Dr. Charles Michel, a St. Louis eye specialist. Michel used dry-cell batteries to create a direct, or "galvanic," current for delivery into the follicle. The current reacts with the moisture and salts in the body to form sodium hydroxide, or caustic soda, which destroys the papilla and the hair bulb at the base of the root and shrinks the follicle.

Several decades later a Parisian doctor named Henry Bordier developed an improved technique, using a high-frequency alternating electric current. In this technique, sometimes called electro-coagulation as well as thermolysis, the rapid oscillation of the current creates friction and heat that burn the follicle's vital structures.

Today the galvanic method has been largely replaced by thermolysis, which works faster than the galvanic method. The probe stays in the follicle only a split second, allowing the electrologist to remove more hair in each session. Up-to-date equipment employs an automatic timer to shut off the current, adding precision to the process.

The Treatment Session

In an initial consultation the electrologist finds out about the patient's medical history and examines the area to be treated. Many electrologists will shave the area and have the patient return in a week or so, by which time the growing hairs will be easily identifiable—only these will be treated, in weekly sessions. Other practitioners will begin treatment in the initial session.

In the first treatment the electrologist will proceed carefully to gauge the patient's skin reaction. Often no more than 15 to 20 hairs will be removed. Once the treatment is under way, however, more hair will be removed in each session. At the first treatment, the electrologist should be able to estimate how many additional treatments are needed and recommend a treatment schedule. A cost estimate should also be provided.

The patient lies on an examination table or in a reclining dental chair while the seated electrologist, often using a magnifying lens (perhaps supplemented by a special light), performs the treatment. Before inserting the filament into the follicles, the electrologist cleans the area to be treated with an antiseptic. The filament itself is sterilized.

Many electrologists use individually wrapped, disposable sterile instruments or assign a personal filament to each patient, to be used over the course of treatment. The best electrolysis system available uses a flexible insulated probe with a bulbous tip; this ensures totally accurate insertion into the follicle and concentrates and confines the current at the germinative portion of the hair.

Once the filament is inserted, the electrologist activates the current with a foot control, then removes the filament and gently tugs at the hair with sterile tweezers. If the hair comes out with no resistance, the follicle has been destroyed. If there is resistance, the electrologist reinserts the filament and applies the current again.

Following the treatment the electrologist may reapply antiseptic, in addition to a soothing solution such as witch hazel and a moisturizer. For the next few days the patient should avoid exposing the treated area to bright sunlight, and if the face has been treated, avoid putting makeup on the affected area. The treated area may be reddened and puffy for a few hours after treatment, and tiny scabs may appear a few days later. If scabs do develop, they normally fall off once healing is complete.

Most people who have had electrolysis say it causes less discomfort than tweezing, comparing the sensation to a pin prick. Others, however, find it more uncomfortable. The amount of pain depends partly on the area being treated. The upper lip, for instance, is quite sensitive, while forearms and legs are less so.

Because some hair follicles may be unusually shaped, particularly in individuals with curly hair, a few may continue to be active despite treatment.

Finding an Electrologist

Anyone considering electrolysis should choose a practitioner carefully, since improper treatments can lead to scarring and infection. The International Guild of Professional Electrologists (IGPE), an electrologists' trade group, estimates that about 6,500 electrologists are currently practicing in the United States. Most electrologists have private offices, although some work in beauty salons or dermatologists' offices.

At the end of 1989 only 26 states in the United States had licensure or other official requirements that electrologists had to meet before they could practice, and those requirements varied tremendously from state to state. There is a national board certification examination, but it is not mandatory in any state. Furthermore, the practice of electrolysis is not regulated by any federal law, nor do there exist any national guidelines for practicing electrolysis. It is therefore necessary to question an electrologist carefully about his or her training, as well as check references from prior patients. The guild recommends that all electrologists undergo 500-600 hours of training before practicing. An apprenticeship is also desirable. It should be kept in mind, however, that the quality of training programs, like that of electrolysis practitioners, can vary enormously.

Electrologists are usually listed in the phone book, or a dermatologist or endocrinologist (a doctor who specializes in hormonal disorders) may be able to make a referral. Also, the IGPE will supply names of its members in a given area. The guild can be contacted at IGPE Executive Offices, Professional Building, 202 Boulevard, Suite C, High Point, NC 27262. Its telephone number is (919) 841-6631. □

Causes of Unwanted Hair

Excessive hair growth may be due to a potentially serious medical condition. Therefore, anyone who is troubled by unwanted hair—particularly if the hair growth appears suddenly—should see a doctor before considering electrolysis. Common causes of unwanted hair include:

- Heredity; people of Mediterranean and Semitic ancestry tend to have more hair than Northern Europeans and blacks, while Asians and American Indians have the least hair.

- Hormonal imbalance; some women with excessive body hair have an imbalance of sex hormones, a problem often accompanied by infertility.

- Certain medications, including corticotropin (brand name, Acthar), for arthritis; the antibiotic streptomycin; oral contraceptives; hormonal drugs given to prevent bone deterioration after menopause; and the anticonvulsant phenytoin (brand name, Dilantin).

- Tumors of the adrenal glands.

TREATING HIGH CHOLESTEROL

Myron Winick, M.D.

Only a few years ago, it would have been difficult to find people who were aware of their own blood cholesterol levels. This is no longer true. There is now wide concern about the risk of heart disease associated with high levels. Cholesterol level is not, of course, the only risk to be considered. Other factors, such as high blood pressure, smoking, and obesity, can play an important role. But one recent study, based on 1986 data, estimated that approximately 36 percent of the U.S. population age 20 or older—or about 60 million adults—have cholesterol levels high enough to warrant their seeking medical advice. Many feel well and show no obvious signs of physical abnormalities. Why then is it important to treat their high cholesterol? To answer that question, it is necessary to understand the significance of elevated levels of cholesterol circulating in the blood.

Cholesterol is a waxy material, classified as a fat, which is manufactured by the body and also consumed in food. Some foods contain significant amounts of cholesterol itself; some contain, besides cholesterol, saturated fat— a type of fat mainly derived from animal sources, including dairy products and red meat—which the body converts to cholesterol.

Cholesterol is an essential compound in human metabolism; among other functions, it is involved in hormone production, it is used by the liver to form the bile acids needed for fat digestion, and it plays a role in the normal development of the brain. Cholesterol is manufactured primarily by the liver. Because it is so important, the body regulates the amount produced. Thus, if no cholesterol—or an insufficient amount— is consumed in the diet, the body makes more. If large amounts of cholesterol are consumed, the body makes less. The system is not perfect, however, and it can be overwhelmed if dietary intake is too high. Cholesterol is carried in the blood to various sites in the body; when the body cannot utilize all of its cholesterol, the excess remains in the blood—producing the high levels of blood, or serum, cholesterol found in some people.

Different Types of Cholesterol

Cholesterol, like any fat, is insoluble in water, and blood is a water-based liquid. Thus, like all fats in the blood, cholesterol attaches itself to molecules called lipoproteins, which act as boats, carrying the fats through the bloodstream. The type of boat—or lipoprotein— on which the cholesterol is riding plays an important part in determining its effects on the body.

There are several varieties of lipoproteins. Two important ones—differentiated by their size, or more precisely by their density—are low-density lipoproteins (LDLs) and high-density lipoproteins (HDLs). Between 70 and 75 percent of the total cholesterol in the blood is attached to LDLs, and 20 to 25 percent is attached to HDLs.

Since LDLs account for the highest proportion of total cholesterol, a high total cholesterol level usually reflects a high level of LDL cholesterol—often referred to as "bad" cholesterol. Dozens of scientific studies have shown that the higher the LDL cholesterol level, the higher the risk of coronary artery disease, the number one killer disease in the United States today. The reason for this is that much of the cholesterol bound to LDLs is deposited in the walls of arteries. This leads to the formation of raised, rough material called plaque, which can ultimately block the flow of blood and result in a heart attack or stroke.

By contrast, the cholesterol that is attached to HDL molecules— often referred to as "good" cholesterol—apparently helps remove excess cholesterol from the blood and thus protects against heart disease. Clearly then, in measuring cholesterol level, it is important to know not only the level of total blood cholesterol but also the proportions of LDL and HDL cholesterol represented in that measurement. Fortunately, there are ways to bring down high total cholesterol and LDL cholesterol to acceptable levels.

How High Is Too High?

To find out if you are at risk, the first step is to determine what your total cholesterol level is. In 1987 the U.S. National Heart, Lung, and Blood Institute recommended that all adults be tested at regular intervals for cholesterol levels.

Cholesterol is measured by a blood test, which can be done either through your physician or through the numerous screening programs now available. If your total cholesterol is below 200 (that is, 200 milligrams of cholesterol per deciliter of blood), you are at low risk and do not need to lower your cholesterol; however, you should repeat the test at yearly intervals. If your cholesterol is 200 or above, the test should be repeated, since results can often be unreliable. If the result is still in the same range, your levels of LDL cholesterol and HDL cholesterol, as well as your total cholesterol level, will determine whether you are at what is considered moderate or high risk.

It should be noted that the data on the risk of heart disease linked to high cholesterol levels—and on the benefits of lowering those levels—have come mostly from studies of middle-aged men. The data have then been extrapolated to the general population.

Treating Moderate Risk

If you are at moderate risk—total cholesterol between 200 and 240; LDL cholesterol between 170 and 200—your goal should be to reduce your cholesterol level sufficiently to put you in the low-risk category and to keep your cholesterol at the new, lower level *for the rest of your life*. Even if you do not reach your target level, any significant lowering of your total and LDL cholesterol levels will provide a benefit. For people in the moderate risk category a change in diet is usually all that is

needed—and the recommended changes in eating patterns are consistent with U.S. government recommendations for a healthful diet likely to decrease one's chances of developing a variety of chronic diseases.

From a practical standpoint the focus should be on reducing both the amount of fat and the kind of fat consumed. A relatively easy diet to follow is the so-called Step 1 diet drawn up by the American Heart Association. It involves reducing the intake of saturated fats by cutting down on fatty meats, limiting the number of egg yolks (including those in baked goods and other foods), increasing the consumption of foods with complex carbohydrates (vegetables, pasta, rice, potatoes), and increasing the intake of soluble fiber (as

in oat bran, beans, and lentils). Fiber is an indigestible organic material found in plant food, and its soluble variety has been shown to lower blood cholesterol, possibly by trapping cholesterol in the gastrointestinal tract and carrying it out of the body.

A good rule of thumb is to eat no more than two 8-ounce portions of red meat (beef, lamb, or pork) a week and no more than three egg yolks a week. All meat should be carefully trimmed and the least fatty cuts used. All types of fish can be eaten; those of marine origin may be particularly beneficial because of the kind of fat they contain. (Fish such as salmon, eel, and mackerel contain fatty acids of the omege-3 family, which have been found to decrease production by the liver of

SOME CHOLESTEROL COMPARISONS

Food	Serving Size	Fat (grams)	Saturated Fat (grams)	Cholesterol (milligrams)
DAIRY PRODUCTS				
Whole milk (3.3% fat)	8 oz.	8.1	5.1	33
Low-fat milk (1% fat)	8 oz.	2.4	1.5	10
Skim milk	8 oz.	0.6	0.4	5
Cottage cheese, creamed	½ cup	5.2	3.3	17
Cottage cheese, dry	½ cup	0.3	0.2	5
Cheddar cheese	1 oz.	9.4	6.0	30
Sour cream	1 Tbsp.	2.5	1.6	5
Yogurt, plain, low-fat	8 oz.	3.5	2.3	14
MEAT, POULTRY, AND EGGS				
Chicken, light meat, skin removed	4 oz.	5.2	1.4	96
Ground beef patty, lean	4 oz.	12.8	6.2	106
Pork loin, lean only	4 oz.	16.0	5.8	100
Liver (beef), cooked with added fat	4 oz.	12.0	3.4	496
Egg yolk	1	5.6	1.7	274
FISH AND SHELLFISH				
Cod, broiled	4 oz.	1.0	0.2	63
Tuna, light, oil-packed, drained	4 oz.	9.2	2.4	33
Shrimp, steamed	4 oz.	1.8	0.2	221
FATS, OILS, AND DRESSINGS				
Butter	1 Tbsp.	11.5	7.2	31
Margarine, stick	1 Tbsp.	11.4	2.1	0
Corn oil	1 Tbsp.	13.6	1.7	0
Mayonnaise	1 Tbsp.	11.0	1.6	8
French dressing	1 Tbsp.	6.4	1.5	0
SNACK FOODS AND DESSERTS				
Ice cream, vanilla	½ cup	7.2	4.4	30
Frozen yogurt	½ cup	1.5	1.0	6
Sherbet, orange	½ cup	1.9	1.2	7
Chocolate chip cookies	2	4.4	1.3	8
Cupcake, chocolate-frosted	1	4.5	1.8	17
Potato chips	10	8.0	2.0	0
French fries, salted, large	10	10.3	2.6	0
Peanuts, dry-roasted, salted	¼ cup	17.6	3.1	0

another lipoprotein from which LDLs are formed and to raise the levels of HDLs in the blood.)

Salads of all types can be consumed in almost unlimited amounts, but care should be taken with the dressing. If you buy commercially prepared dressings, choose those that use unsaturated fats. Foods such as potatoes (without sour cream), pasta, rice, and whole wheat bread should be emphasized. Vegetables can be eaten in large amounts, with peas, beans, and lentils providing soluble fiber. Poultry is also relatively low in fat if the skin is not eaten. Dairy products should be used in modified fat form (skim milk or milk with 1 or 2 percent fat, low-fat cottage cheese or yogurt).

The amount of food consumed is also very important. If you are obese (20 percent or more above your ideal weight), you should reduce your caloric intake because obesity by itself can result in elevated blood cholesterol levels. (*See the feature article* Diet Roundup *for ideal weight tables.*)

Over the past year or two, a great deal of attention has been paid to oat bran because it is a source of soluble fiber. Almost every major cereal company now markets its own version of both hot and cold oat bran cereals. But all oat bran cereals do not contain the same amount of soluble fiber. Read the package for fiber content and choose products with the highest amount of fiber, consistent with your particular taste. Another source of soluble fiber is psyllium, a grain grown in India, which can be found in some recently marketed breakfast cereals.

To summarize, a diet designed to lower cholesterol should:

• Include only enough calories to reach or maintain ideal body weight.

• Provide less than 30 percent of those calories as fat (each gram of fat equals about 9 calories).

• Provide no more than 10 percent of total calories (⅓ of fat calories) as saturated fat.

- Derive 7-10 percent of calories from polyunsaturated fat. (Vegetable oils such as safflower, sunflower, corn, and soybean oils are good sources of polyunsaturated fat, as are fish such as salmon, mackerel, and herring.)
- Derive 10-13 percent of calories from monounsaturated fat. (Canola, peanut, and olive oils are major sources of monounsaturated fat, as well as corn oil and soybean oil margarines.)
- Limit cholesterol intake to 300 milligrams a day or less.
- Include more foods containing soluble fiber.

If you keep to the American Heart Association Step 1 diet, your cholesterol level will probably be reduced by about 15 percent.

Treating High Risk

If your total cholesterol is above 240 or your LDL cholesterol is above 200, you are in the high-risk category. Initial treatment consists of diet alone, and the Step 1 diet described above may be all that is required to lower your cholesterol to an acceptable level. In many cases, however, a more rigorous diet (the American Heart Association Step 2 diet) may be required. The principles of the Step 2 diet are as follows:

- Include only enough calories to reach or maintain ideal body weight.
- Obtain less than 25 percent of these calories from fat.
- Obtain no more than 7 percent of total calories (less than $\frac{1}{3}$ of fat calories) from saturated fat.
- Derive 7 percent of calories from polyunsaturated fat and around 11 percent from monounsaturated fat.
- Limit cholesterol intake to 250 milligrams a day or less.
- Increase intake of soluble fiber.

The mix of foods in this diet is similar to the one described in the Step 1 diet. However, the emphasis on reducing fat intake is even more pronounced. The diet calls for no more than two 6-ounce portions of red meat (beef,

lamb, or pork) a week, two egg yolks or less a week, the use of skim milk and other low-fat dairy products, the substitution of soft margarines (to be used in moderation) for butter, and the elimination of creamy salad dressings.

For most people, adherence to the Step 2 diet should be enough to bring cholesterol levels into an acceptable range. If this does not happen, however, further treatment may be needed.

Treatment With Medication

Today there are medications that can be used to help lower cholesterol levels. They fall into two main categories: those that bind cholesterol in the gastrointestinal tract, preventing its absorption or reabsorption into the body, and those that inhibit the production of cholesterol by the liver. Medications in the first category are consumed as a powder taken in water

or in the form of a solid bar and are not absorbed by the body. Therefore they are tried first. Medications in the second category, which are taken in pill form, are used only if the binding agents do not achieve the desired result.

Cholesterol-lowering medications must be taken regularly and usually for life. Some side effects, such as flatulence and occasionally diarrhea, have been noted with the cholesterol-binding agents. The drugs that inhibit cholesterol synthesis also may have certain side effects in some people. These should be discussed with your physician. The vitamin niacin has been shown to lower cholesterol levels when taken in large doses. It too may have side effects, such as burning and flushing of the skin. The use of any of cholesterol-lowering medications should be undertaken only under a physician's supervision. □

CHLAMYDIA

The Most Common Venereal Disease

Robert C. Noble, M.D.

Most people have heard of gonorrhea or herpes or syphilis, but chlamydia is not exactly a household word. It is, however, the most common sexually transmitted disease in the United States. It is also one of the most difficult for the general public to understand. Often people with the infection have no symptoms, and when symptoms do appear—such as pain on urination or vaginal or urethral discharge—they may be similar to other sexually transmitted diseases.

A Bacterial Disease

The sexually transmitted disease commonly known as chlamydia is caused by a bacterium called *Chlamydia trachomatis*. The word "chlamydia," which comes from a Greek term for cloak, is appropriate. Although most other bacteria can grow in a wide variety of environments, *Chlamydia trachomatis* grows only inside human

---

Different strains of the chlamydia bacterium can infect different parts of the body.

---

or animal cells, where it cloaks itself, without detection and sometimes without causing any discomfort.

Different strains of the bacterium can infect different parts of the body, causing a variety of dis-

eases, not all of them sexually transmitted. Some strains cause trachoma, a chronic infection of the eye that is transmitted by direct personal contact or by contact with an infected item (such as a towel). Over time, it can lead to scarring of the eyelids and damage to the cornea, resulting in blindness. Trachoma is the greatest single cause of blindness in the world. Health experts estimate that 400 million people worldwide have the disease and that 6 million people are blind as a result of it. The disease occurs only occasionally in the United States but is common in many developing countries.

Other strains of *Chlamydia trachomatis*—those responsible for the sexually transmitted disease—can cause an infection in the eyes of newborn babies similar to that produced by the gonorrhea bacterium. If a pregnant woman has chlamydia, it can be transmitted to the baby's eyes during the infant's passage through the birth canal. Hospitals in the United States routinely place antibiotics in newborns' eyes to prevent infection. Infected pregnant women can also pass on to their babies a kind of pneumonia caused by chlamydia bacteria. About 30,000 cases of chlamydial pneumonia occur in newborns in the United States each year. Trachoma, chlamydial eye infections contracted at birth, and chlamydial pneumonia can all be treated with antibiotics.

The U.S. Centers for Disease Control estimates that 4 million people in the United States develop genital chlamydia infections

each year. Precise numbers are not available, since most laboratory tests to detect chlamydia are expensive and difficult to perform, and physicians are not required to report the disease.

Many people with chlamydia have no symptoms and so may unknowingly spread the disease to their sexual partners.

Who you are and what you do determines your risk of becoming infected with chlamydia. The more sexual partners you have, the greater the chance of infection. Age plays a role: Sexually active women under the age of 20 are infected at two to three times the rate of sexually active women over the age of 20, and women over 30 have lower infection rates than women in their 20s. Chlamydia is more common in teenage boys than in older men. Low socioeconomic status has also been linked with an increased risk of chlamydia infection.

Chlamydia involving urethral infection is three times more common in heterosexual than in homosexual men. However, between 4 and 8 percent of homosexual men visiting sexually transmitted disease clinics have been found to have rectal chlamydia infections.

> **Half the cases of pelvic inflammatory disease among U.S. women are caused by chlamydia.**

Damage Done

Many people who have genital chlamydia infection don't recognize that they have the disease because the infection may cause only minor symptoms or no symptoms at all. Up to a third of men with urethral chlamydia infections have no symptoms, and they may unknowingly spread the disease by having sex without taking proper precautions. Urethritis—or inflammation of the urethra, the most common form of genital chlamydial infection in men—often results in a burning sensation on urination and a discharge. (These are also symptoms of gonorrhea.) Men can also suffer infection of the epididymis—a tubelike structure attached to the testicle in which sperm mature.

Women with chlamydial infection most commonly develop infections of the cervix and may suffer vaginal discharge or bleeding, lower abdominal discomfort, or pain on urination. If undetected, the infection can progress to the lining of the uterus or to the fallopian tubes, where it can cause the chronic condition known as pelvic inflammatory disease (PID). Approximately 50 percent of PID cases in the United States are due to chlamydia infections. PID can result in chronic pain, sterility, and, if a woman becomes pregnant, an ectopic pregnancy, in which an egg is implanted outside the uterus. If not diagnosed and terminated, an ectopic pregnancy can threaten the mother's life.

Diagnosis

A cheap, convenient, and reliable method of diagnosing chlamydia is not yet available. One way to identify a bacterial infection is to take a sample from the site of the infection, put it in special nutrient substances, and see what kind of bacteria appear. This is usually done in plates containing agar, which is a substance from seaweed that supports the growth of bacteria. However, chlamydia bacteria cannot be grown in agar plates; they need living human cells, or tissue cultures that duplicate the conditions inside a cell where the bacteria normally grow. Tissue culture techniques are both difficult to use and expensive to carry out.

Other methods of diagnosis are less precise. A pathologist can sometimes look at a Pap smear and see evidence of chlamydia, but unfortunately, this test does not detect the bacteria in most women who are infected.

Diagnostic methods that make use of chlamydia antigens have been developed and are in use for both men and women who are infected. Antigens are distinctive small molecules on chlamydia bacteria, or other organisms invading the body, that provide a way of identifying the invader. Chlamydia antigens can be detected directly in samples of fluid or pus from the patient (the growth of bacteria in cultures, which takes several days, is not required).

Antigen detection tests, however, occasionally produce false positive results—that is, they indicate that a person is infected when he or she is not. For this reason, the usefulness of the antigen tests depends on the probability of infection among the people being tested. Among people who visit a sexually transmitted disease clinic, the frequency of the disease will naturally tend to be high; the number of false positives will be relatively low, and so use of the test might be justified. However, in groups less likely to have the disease, most positive results would be false, and the test would be less useful. The gold standard for chlamydia diagnosis remains the tissue culture test.

Prevention, Treatment

People can reduce the chance of contracting chlamydia during intercourse by using barrier forms of contraception, such as a condom

> **Use of a condom during intercourse reduces the risk of developing chlamydia.**

or diaphragm. Women who use birth control pills as their contraception method have a higher incidence of chlamydia. Because of the serious consequences of chlamydia infection, sexually active unmarried women should insist that their partners use condoms. (Condoms are one of the few ways of reducing, but not eliminating, the risks of other sexually transmitted diseases as well.)

Chlamydia can be treated with antibiotics taken in pill form. The most effective are tetracycline and doxycycline. People who cannot take these antibiotics can be treated with erythromycin. To prevent a recurrence of infection, the sexual partner of an infected person must be treated even if free of symptoms, since both partners are likely to be infected. □

The Numbers

Chlamydia is the most common sexually transmitted disease in the United States. According to the U.S. Centers for Disease Control, estimated new cases of common STDs in 1990 are as follows:

Chlamydia	4 million
Gonorrhea	1.5 million
Genital warts	500,000 to 1,000,000
Genital herpes	200,000 to 500,000
Hepatitis B	200,000
Syphilis	110,000

COSMETIC DENTISTRY

Alan R. Weinstein, D.D.S.

A smile that radiates health and self-confidence and makes us feel good about ourselves—this is something everyone wants. Today, because of dramatic changes in dental materials and techniques, cosmetic dentistry is making a beautiful smile available and affordable to more and more people.

Cosmetic dentistry refers to procedures such as enamel bonding, bleaching, veneering, and fitting crowns and bridges, procedures which are used to correct decayed, discolored, poorly positioned, or missing teeth.

In the past dentists have been primarily concerned with treating dental disease and providing proper restorative care for their patients. But in recent years, because of the widespread use of fluorides, better home care of teeth, and improved professional materials and methods, the incidence of dental decay—especially among younger patients—has dropped markedly. Moreover, many people are more health-conscious, and want attractive smiles to enhance their image of health and physical fitness. As a result, many dentists today devote less time to repairing teeth and treating dental disease and more to preventive and cosmetic work.

Enamel Bonding

Enamel bonding is a process in which tooth-colored filling materials are applied directly to specially prepared tooth surfaces. Its purpose is to improve both the appearance and the functioning of the teeth. The materials used—called composite resins because they are composed of epoxy-like materials and extremely fine glass-like particles (for strength and translucence)—are applied in layers to the teeth, shaped to the desired form, and hardened in seconds under intense (but harmless) blue light. These putty-like materials, which come in various shades of enamel and dentin (the bonelike material that makes up the bulk of a tooth), can be shaped and polished to look like a natural tooth surface. The materials actually bond to tooth enamel that has been microscopically roughened for a few seconds with a mild etching solution or to dentin or a root surface that has been chemically treated. Since many bonding procedures require minimal preparation of the teeth, patients feel little discomfort, and a local anesthetic is usually not needed.

Bonding materials are very versatile. They can be used to recontour front teeth (central incisors, lateral incisors, and canines), shortening, lengthening, or widening them; used to cover a small part of a single tooth, as in a filling; or used to cover an entire tooth surface. Gaps between front teeth can be repaired and filled in, broken fragments of natural teeth can occasionally be bonded back onto the original teeth, and the surfaces of stained teeth can be whitened. Teeth that overlap can be made to appear as if they have been realigned, and in some cases minor cross bites (a lower tooth overlapping an upper tooth) can be corrected by simply reshaping and realigning the teeth.

Bonding works best on front teeth that require minimal correction in their alignment and are not severely broken down or extremely discolored. If the teeth are excessively crowded or the bite is unfavorable, orthodontics (the repositioning of teeth with braces) should first be considered to ensure that gums and teeth remain healthy and that patients are not at risk from periodontal disease (the leading cause of tooth loss in adults). If many teeth need to be treated or if teeth are severely stained and worn, then other techniques such as porcelain veneers or crowns, which are stronger and cover more of the tooth surface, should be considered.

Back teeth (bicuspids and molars) can also be cosmetically restored with bonding. If the teeth are decayed or if old, worn silver fillings need to be replaced, tooth-colored composites can be used as fillings in place of silver amalgam. But if larger restorations are necessary or an entire bicuspid or molar needs to be rebuilt, an inlay or crown might be a better choice.

The composite resins used in bonding are relatively soft compared to gold, silver, porcelain, or tooth enamel. How long a resin restoration will last depends on its size, the biting stress placed on it, and its location in the mouth (generally the further back, the more wear it gets). It may be only five to eight years before the bonding has to be repaired or replaced, and in some cases even earlier. (For tips on how to care for bonded teeth, see the box on page 210.)

Not all teeth can be restored, nor is the use of resins a cure-all in modern dentistry. But if bonding cannot always take the place of crowns, bridges, or orthodontics, it can be a useful adjunct to more traditional treatments. It may also be less costly for the patient than those other methods because it involves no laboratory expenses and requires shorter appointments. In addition, virtually all dentists can perform bonding procedures, although some are likely to be more skilled than others.

Bleaching

Although it has been practiced for many years, bleaching has recently gained popularity because of advances in techniques, materials, and equipment. When properly done, bleaching is safe and noninvasive. It is the most conservative method available to lighten discolored teeth.

Teeth become discolored for various reasons. The most common discolorations include the darkening that occasionally follows root canal work, mottling from excessive fluoride, and the superficial stains frequently caused by aging, tobacco use, and excessive coffee and tea consumption. These superficial stains tend to be yellow to light brown and are the discolorations most easily treated by bleaching.

Stains can also be caused by exposure to certain antibiotics (such as tetracycline) during tooth for-

mation. These discolorations, which are intense and occur deep within the teeth, range from light yellow bands to a dark blue or gray color over the entire tooth. Bleaching alone may not completely remove these stains; it may have to be combined with bonding or veneering to solve the problem.

Fluorosis discoloration, or mottled enamel, is usually caused by excessive exposure to fluoride at a very young age, when the teeth are forming. Bleaching is usually not indicated because the stain does not uniformly cover the tooth.

In a typical bleaching session the teeth are isolated under a device called a rubber dam, a thin sheet of rubber stretched over the upper or lower front teeth with holes in it that allow the teeth being bleached to project. A peroxide solution is then applied to gauze placed over the teeth and activated with heat and light for 30 minutes. (This should not be tried at home; the peroxide solutions available in drugstores are not concentrated enough to bleach teeth.) The procedure is painless, the only side effect being occasional sensitivity in the teeth of some patients, which generally lasts less than a day. At least three bleaching sessions, and sometimes even six or more, are usually necessary. In the case of an individual tooth discolored from root canal work, the peroxide solution can be applied outside and inside the hollow crown of the tooth. Sometimes a bleach-containing paste can be sealed inside a tooth and left there for up to a week, then removed before a permanent filling is put in.

A new bleaching procedure is under study in which a plastic tray is formed to closely fit the patient's teeth. A special peroxide solution is placed in the tray, which is worn either day and night for three weeks or only at night for up to six weeks. The long-term effectiveness of this technique has not yet been established.

Laminate Veneers

The laminating process is an extension of the bonding technique. Veneers of porcelain or composite resin not much thicker than a fingernail are made in dental laboratories on models of the patient's teeth and then bonded to natural teeth with special resins.

Veneers are useful when many teeth—or even all the teeth in the mouth—require extensive color correction or repair, when front teeth are adequately spaced but need minor repositioning, or when the dentist concludes that a laboratory can produce better results than work done solely in the dentist's office.

Veneers made of porcelain, a furnace-fired ceramic, are stronger and more durable than composite resin veneers. Since porcelain

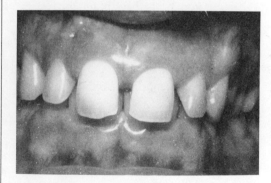

Composite resin bonding was used to reshape this patient's teeth and to close the spaces between them. Bonding can improve both the appearance and the functioning of teeth.

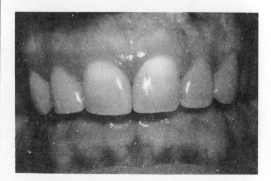

veneers are constructed in a laboratory, it is possible to restore several teeth in a shorter period of time than bonding would take. Unfortunately, because of laboratory expenses, fees for veneers are usually higher than for bonding.

Veneers are not indicated when teeth are severely stained or striated; when they are very crowded, broken down, or decayed; or when patients have periodontal disease.

Inlays

Inlays are very similar to veneers but are designed for back teeth. They are constructed in a laboratory of special wear-resistant composite resins or of porcelain, depending on potential stress from biting and on whether there are restorations in the opposing teeth. Inlays cover less tooth structure than full crowns and so require sound tooth structure (at least the front or the back of the tooth should be relatively intact) to support them.

Inlays are most effectively used to replace extensive faulty fillings that cannot be repaired by bonding and to restore teeth that are broken down but do not have to be covered completely. The main advantage of inlays is that they create a strong, aesthetically pleasing result without removing excessive tooth structure or going under the gum line.

Crowns and Bridges

The installation of a crown is the most extensive and costly cosmetic dental procedure. Generally used on teeth that are severely broken down (missing much tooth structure because of decay), very discolored, or treated with root canal, crowns cover a tooth completely, usually fit under the gum line, and require the removal of more tooth structure than inlays do. On the other hand, porcelain crowns are the most wear-resistant of all dental restorations and can often provide long-lasting, aesthetically pleasing results. It is not unusual for these restorations to

last from 5 to 12 years, and some porcelain crowns last for 20 years or even longer.

Crowns are made in a laboratory of porcelain or composite resins fused at high temperature to various metals, or else of all porcelain. All-porcelain crowns can be etched internally to roughen the surface and then bonded directly to a patient's teeth to provide a very natural appearance.

Multiple crowns that are constructed in one piece to replace missing teeth are called splints, or fixed bridges.

Costs

Dental insurance plans generally do not cover all expenses, particularly in the case of dentistry for aesthetic purposes. It is best to find out what procedures your insurance company covers before beginning cosmetic dentistry.

The costs of treatment can vary considerably. Bonding procedures can cost from $25 per tooth

Tooth Care After Bonding

- Brush and floss your teeth normally.

- Do not chew ice, bite your fingernails or thread, or chew on pencils, pens, eyeglasses, or pipe stems. Avoid biting directly into bones, hard candy, apples, carrots, nuts, or hard breads and rolls. These excessive forces can fracture bonding materials.

- To prevent staining, limit your intake of coffee, tea, grape juice, dark colas, soy sauce, blueberries, and fresh cherries. Avoid smoking. (Smoke can stain areas between the teeth as well as the bonding resin.)

- If you grind your teeth at night, a bite guard constructed by your dentist can help minimize wear on bonding materials.

- Have periodic dental checkups and cleanings. Be certain that the dental hygienist is aware of your restorations, so that cleaning techniques that can wear down bonding materials are avoided.

for very simple restorations to over $400 if a tooth has to be entirely rebuilt. Fees for porcelain veneers or porcelain and resin inlays can vary from around $350 to over $1,000 per tooth, and for porcelain crowns from $450 to over $1,500, depending on the amount of work involved. Bleaching fees range from $75 to $250 per session, depending on the number of teeth treated.

Good communication between dentist and patient regarding dental problems, treatment procedures, and fees is vital. Dentists and staff should provide enough information for patients to make logical decisions about what type of dental treatment is best for them. Patients, for their part, should not hesitate to ask questions about services or fees.

Finding the Right Dentist

Cosmetic dentistry is performed by most general and children's dentists, and your own dentist may be perfectly qualified to meet your needs. Nevertheless, you should be aware that the degree of success depends on the dexterity, artistic ability, and knowledge of dental anatomy of the practitioner, as well as on the level of commitment to improving these skills. That commitment means learning new techniques through continuing education and mastering them through practice.

Most dental schools have departments that specialize in various aspects of cosmetic dentistry, and local dental societies are usually familiar with their members' areas of expertise. A phone call will probably provide helpful information.

Local dental specialists, such as pediatric dentists, orthodontists, periodontists, and oral surgeons, often know the capabilities of other dentists in their communities and can offer recommendations. Plastic surgeons, cosmetologists, and patients who have had successful cosmetic dental care can be additional sources of information. □

New Problems of
POLIO VICTIMS

Richard R. Owen, M.D.

Poliomyelitis, sometimes called infantile paralysis, is a disease seldom encountered in developed countries today. But as recently as the 1940s and 1950s, a polio epidemic swept the United States; in its peak year, 1952, nearly 58,000 cases of the disease were diagnosed.

Unfortunately, many people who had paralytic polio decades ago are now experiencing new problems and disabilities associated with the disease—including progressive muscle weakness or atrophy, susceptibility to fatigue, unexplained pain, reduced mobility, breathing and sleeping difficulties, and poor tolerance of cold. Some individuals have had to go back to using the canes, crutches, or braces they had earlier discarded. Some who originally had weakness in the muscles used for breathing may now again need breathing assistance and have to use oxygen or respirators. In a number of patients the unexplained pain is chronic and debilitating. The causes of these new problems—which are referred to by doctors as postpolio syndrome—are not fully understood, but they are probably multiple and interacting.

Surveys indicate that anywhere from 25 to 80 percent of the 600,000 polio survivors in the United States suffer from postpolio syndrome. The troubling signs and symptoms occur 20 to 40 years after the onset of polio.

What Polio Is

Paralytic polio is a viral disease of the central nervous system that causes inflammation and damage to nerve cells and tissue in the lower brain and spinal cord. The virus enters the body through the nose or throat, then passes into the bloodstream. The first symptoms of polio are fever, headache, and stiff muscles. When the viral infection enters the central nervous system, patients develop severe tightness in the neck, back, and hamstring muscles as well as vary-

ing degrees of muscle weakness, as paralysis sets in. The primary targets of the infection are the motor nerve cells in the spinal cord. (Motor nerve cells control muscle functioning.) The virus is active for about two weeks, although the patient can be a carrier of the virus for 6 to 12 months after the acute attack. Initially, swelling and inflammation cause paralysis to spread. When these symptoms subside, improvement in muscle strength and control takes place. This improvement is due to physical therapy and to the fact that other nerve cells in the body compensate for the ones that were damaged. Physical therapy is important because in the first six months after paralysis begins unused muscles will tighten and scar in the absence of stretching and other activities designed to keep them flexible. Over a period of one to two years patients generally recover some of their lost muscle function. Some improve to the extent of having little leftover evidence of muscle weakness.

> **New symptoms of polio such as muscle weakness and difficulties with breathing are appearing in people who had the disease 20 to 40 years ago.**

Causes of Postpolio Syndrome

Controversy exists about the causes of postpolio syndrome, and a number of theories have been proposed. It is probable that there are several causes and that they interact. Premature aging of nerve tissue is one theory. Normally, there is a very gradual decline in nerve cells and in muscle strength after age 50. But because people who have had polio have already lost some motor nerve cells, they may suffer a decline in muscle strength earlier in life—perhaps in their 30s and 40s if they had polio during childhood. The decline is probably aggravated by the fact that those who have permanent weakness in some muscles use a larger percentage of other, unaffected muscles to carry out routine activities. This can be a particular problem in people whose muscles have not been conditioned by regular exercise. Overuse of unconditioned muscles can cause a sudden loss of strength, and the problem is compounded in many postpolio patients because their central nervous system monitors fatigue poorly—they don't know when their muscles have been overused. Other medical problems such as overweight, muscle and joint injuries, degenerative arthritis, and new neurologic diseases can all add to the loss of muscle strength in a person who had polio years ago.

The course of postpolio syndrome in some individuals had suggested the possibility of a resurgence of the old poliovirus or an infection with a new virus. However, research carried out at the U.S. National Institutes of Health has as yet found no evidence of a viral origin for postpolio syndrome.

Treatment

Although there is no cure for postpolio syndrome, there are ways to ease the symptoms. In planning treatment the doctor will make a careful assessment of the patient's medical history and of new symptoms, general health, and level of walking ability, hand mobility, flexibility, and muscle strength. Measuring lung function and cardiovascular fitness is also important in dealing with symptoms of new weakness, fatigue, and pain.

Sometimes a doctor can find a simple solution to new handicaps simply by reviewing any aids—braces, walker, wheelchair, envi-

---

Although there is no cure for post-polio syndrome, there are ways to ease its symptoms. Exercise programs provide the most effective relief.

---

ronmental aids such as grab bars in the bathtub—a patient may still be using. Any medical problems other than postpolio syndrome should be tackled before a rehabilitation program is begun. Treating problems such as overweight or poor posture may reduce the degree of disability.

People who have a renewed need for aids they had previously discarded may need counseling to help them adjust to these changes in their life-style. If decreased lung capacity is a problem, brought on by weakness in the muscles that control breathing, the person will require supplemental oxygen or the assistance of a respirator. People who are having

trouble sleeping or who wake up with morning headaches and fatigue—signs that they have taken in too little oxygen—may be helped by taking oxygen or using a respirator at night. Patients with sleep apnea—the sudden, tempo-

---

Specially adapted aerobic exercises can increase endurance and improve conditioning without further damaging weakened muscles.

---

rary stoppage of breathing at night—may require a small amount of oxygen to keep the nose and throat open during sleep.

Anti-inflammatory drugs such as aspirin can often relieve muscle and joint pain and stiffness. People whose sleep is disturbed by muscle cramps have been helped by short-acting muscle relaxants. For intolerance of cold temperatures, no treatment is available; all the patient can do is try to avoid the cold as much as possible.

Exercise

Exercise programs balanced with adequate rest provide the most effective relief of postpolio symptoms when used in conjunction with braces and other aids. Tight muscles should be carefully stretched to overcome pain, reduce mechanical imbalances (for example, the tendency of a knee to buckle), and prepare for other exercises that strengthen and condition. The large muscles of the trunk, shoulders and arms, and hips and thighs can be strengthened by exercises; these should not be of a strenuous type but should be geared to reeducating and stabilizing the muscles. Aerobic exercises adapted for postpolio patients that alternate activity and rest—for example, 2 to 3 minutes of exercise followed

by 1 minute of rest for a period of 15 to 30 minutes—have been shown to increase conditioning, muscle endurance, and oxygen intake without further damaging weakened muscles. Exercise programs must be individually designed to take account of the patient's muscle function and cardiac condition.

Help and Support

The problems of postpolio syndrome can be distressing, but help and support are available. It may be reassuring for sufferers to know that the syndrome is receiving wide attention. Some 60 rehabilitation hospitals and universities in the United States have established specialized postpolio clinics for the purposes of research and treatment. A number of national and regional conferences have been held under the leadership of the Gazette International Networking Institute of St. Louis, an organiza-

---

Polio survivors around the world have formed support groups to help one another cope with their problems.

---

tion that disseminates information on postpolio syndrome and other disabilities and helps create communications networks. Polio survivors around the world have also formed support groups that are helpful to the growing number of people suffering from postpolio syndrome. ☐

Sources of Further Information

Polio Society, 4200 Wisconsin Avenue, N.W., Suite 106273, Washington, DC 20016. Tel: (301) 897-8180.
International Polio Network, 4502 Maryland Avenue, St. Louis, MO 63108. Tel: (314) 361-0475.

MENOPAUSE
A Time of Transition

Wulf H. Utian, M.D., Ph.D.

Many people use the word "menopause" to mean the years immediately before and after a woman stops menstruating, years that doctors call the climacteric. Technically, "menopause" refers only to the final menstrual period.

The average age at which American women have their final period—51—has not changed for generations. Ideas about what menopause means, however, *have* changed. In earlier generations many people thought of the post-menopausal woman as someone whose meaningful life was over, since she had lost her ability to bear children.

These days, when a woman can expect to live 35 or more years after her final period, doctors and the general public tend to see menopause as marking a time of transition between two phases of life. More and more women are coming to realize that the post-menopausal years can be among the very best. At the same time the old attitude that women should simply put up with problems that might accompany menopause and the climacteric—problems that for some can disrupt life severely—has given way to a recognition that women should take full advantage of treatments available for troubling symptoms.

Key Hormones

Menopause and the body changes associated with the climacteric occur because ovulation, or the release of eggs from the ovaries, slows down and finally stops. A woman is born with a fixed number of eggs in her ovaries. Most of them die where they are. The rest make their way out of the ovaries into the fallopian tubes during successive menstrual cycles. In each cycle, in the expectation that an egg will be fertilized, the ovaries produce two hormones, estrogen and progesterone, that build up the lining of the uterus so that it will be ready to receive the fertilized egg. If the egg is not fertilized, the ovaries stop producing the hormones, and the built-up uterine lining is shed during the menstrual period.

As a woman reaches her 40s, ovulation slows down, and production of estrogen and progesterone decreases. When ovulation stops altogether, estrogen and progesterone production drops even further. Since virtually all tissues in the body are affected by estrogen, a number of changes are set in motion as the amount of the hormone in the body dwindles. Some of these changes, noticeable fairly soon, are relatively minor and may be termed nuisance disorders. Others, potentially fatal, may take years to develop.

Minor Symptoms

The two earliest symptoms of approaching menopause are changes in the menstrual pattern and hot flashes. The menstrual flow may be lighter than usual, or periods may be more widely spaced or may occur at irregular intervals. In some women the flow may be heavier than normal (since this may be due to a medical problem, rather than approaching menopause, a checkup should be done to exclude other possible causes). Eventually, when estrogen/progesterone levels fall below levels needed to stimulate the uterine lining, the periods cease altogether.

Before or after this happens, about two-thirds of women are troubled by hot flashes, in which a feeling of warmth spreads over the body, followed by perspiration and shivering. Hot flashes that occur at night are called night sweats. Some women never experience a hot flash. Others can be troubled for years by repeated hot flashes, both day and night. Although the occurrence of hot flashes is clearly connected with decreased estrogen production, their exact cause is not known.

Somewhat later, there may be symptoms or conditions related to tissue changes. For example, a vaginal infection or painful intercourse may reflect thinning of the vaginal lining. A similar thinning of tissues in the bladder may result in more frequent urination or in urinary stress incontinence—an inability to hold in the urine under the stress of exercise, laughing, or coughing. Vaginal or bladder symptoms may appear as early as 18 months after menopause. There might also be signs of changes within the brain and nervous system, such as lack of energy, decreased sexuality, and slight impairment of short-term memory.

Emotional Problems

It is frequently asked whether menopause is associated with psychological changes. There is no easy answer. Current research suggests that women at the time of menopause do not show an increase in psychiatric disorders. Research of my own in the early 1970s, later confirmed by other scientists, showed that postmenopausal women who took estrogen felt a "mental tonic," or mood-enhancing, effect. It is not clear, however, whether the opposite occurs—that is, whether the body's loss of estrogen around menopause has a direct negative effect on emotional state.

Certainly, frequent hot flashes—and especially night sweats that disturb sleep—can be upsetting and fatiguing. Beyond that, most doctors agree that if changes in mood occur, or if symptoms such as anxiety, depression, or irritability appear, they are probably due to psychological, social, or cultural factors. Women living in a youth-oriented society like the United States are less likely to tolerate menopause well than women living in a society that shows greater concern and respect for the aging. A woman's immediate environment is also important. Whether she is employed or unemployed, rich or poor, living alone or with supportive individuals will affect how or whether such symptoms develop. Finally, a woman's underlying psychological strength will also play a role. Someone who did not handle stress easily as a young person is less likely to readily tolerate a change in life's circumstances in her later years.

Bone Thinning and Heart Trouble

Two health problems are potentially fatal. One is osteoporosis, or thinning of the bones. Both men and women lose bone mass with age. But women have less bone mass than men to start with, and after menopause the rate of loss accelerates markedly, apparently because of the drop in the amount of estrogen. Of the 1 million people a year who have fractures among the 15–20 million Americans with osteoporosis, the great majority are women. The fractures usually involve the hip, the lower spine, or an extremity like the wrist. Hip fractures are particularly serious because in 10–15 percent of such cases the person will die within a year from complications related to the fracture or its treatment. Of the 300,000 hip fractures that occur each year in the United States, two-thirds are suffered by women. And women are ten times as likely as men to suffer spinal fractures. Osteoporosis costs the U.S. healthcare system, it has been estimated, as much as $8-10 billion a year.

The other major problem is coronary heart disease. While young women run a much lower risk of developing heart disease than do men of the same age, the gap narrows later. Among people in their early 40s, women account for only one in seven deaths from heart attack. But among people in their 60s, women account for one in three. Many researchers believe that estrogen plays a protective role for women. Women who lose their ovaries early (whether through surgery or because of radiation therapy or chemotherapy), and thus have early menopause, experience twice as many heart attacks as women going through a normal menopause at around age 51. In fact, a woman who loses her ovaries is at greater risk for all of the problems described here. In the past, hysterectomy, or surgical removal of the uterus, was often accompanied by removal of the ovaries. Today, in a woman of reproductive age the ovaries are removed only for specific medical reasons.

Hormone Replacement Therapy

Not all women suffer from the conditions associated with the climacteric years; some, in fact, are virtually symptom free. But for those who suffer from at least some of the conditions there are preventive or therapeutic measures.

Since many problems appear to be linked with estrogen deficiency, a logical form of treatment or preventive therapy would be to replace the estrogen. When hormone treatments were first offered, only estrogen was given. For several years now, however, it has usually been combined with progestin, a progesterone-like drug.

Such treatment is called hormone replacement therapy or HRT.

HRT has been found to alleviate hot flashes; reduce vaginal and bladder symptoms; enhance feelings of well-being; improve sleep, short-term memory, and skin quality; and decrease osteoporosis and bone fractures. There is evidence that taking estrogen may reduce the chances of having a heart attack or dying from coronary heart disease, probably because the estrogen lowers the level of total cholesterol in the blood and raises the level of "good" cholesterol. It is not yet clear, however, whether estrogen combined with progestin has the same effect.

The taking of estrogen by itself has been linked to an increased risk of cancer of the uterus, which is why it is now usually combined with progestin. In the United States each year, uterine cancer ordinarily occurs in about 1 of every 1,000 women over age 50. According to a number of studies in the mid-1970s, the rate for women taking estrogen alone can be as high as 4 to 8 cases per 1,000. A decade of research showed that giving a woman with an intact uterus both estrogen and progestin reduces the risk of uterine cancer to the level for the general population.

There is some evidence that taking estrogen may increase the risk of developing breast cancer. For example, a major Swedish study published in mid-1989 suggested that women on at least one form of estrogen replacement therapy run a slightly higher risk; the addition of progestin did not protect against this increase and possibly slightly raised the risk further. Women who already have breast cancer are ordinarily not offered estrogen therapy, as some breast tumors are stimulated by estrogen. Women suffering from certain other conditions that may be worsened by estrogen, such as blood clots, diabetes, and liver disease, may also be considered ineligible for HRT.

Many doctors have questioned whether a woman who has had a hysterectomy and cannot, therefore, get cancer of the uterus, should take progestin as well as estrogen. The consensus of experts seems to be that she should not, as overuse of progestin can cause unpleasant side effects (similar to premenstrual syndrome) and possibly increase the risk of heart attack and breast cancer.

Women who are eligible for HRT should discuss with their doctor the potential side effects as well as the possible benefits before deciding whether to undergo the therapy. The possible side effects include minor problems such as menstruation-like bleeding, nausea, breast tenderness, and, perhaps, slight bloating. Monthly bleeding, similar to the menstrual period, is probably the common side effect most disliked by patients on HRT. Up to 90 percent of women taking the estrogen/progestin combination experience this bleeding. Women often ask if the bleeding is a sign that they can become pregnant. The answer is no—hormone treatments do not make a woman ovulate again, and without an egg to be fertilized there can be no pregnancy.

The estrogen/progestin combination is usually taken in the form of pills. Since they pass though the digestive system, the hormones must go through the liver, where they may cause problems for some women, such as changes in various enzymes or proteins. This can be avoided by receiving estrogen from a skin patch (which is changed every three days or so) or in a skin cream. Estrogen taken in this way does not get into the digestive system and thus bypasses the liver.

Alternative Treatments

Because some women either should not take or cannot tolerate HRT, doctors have sought additional methods of treating such problems as hot flashes and of preventing osteoporosis and heart disease. Unfortunately, none of the methods developed so far are as effective as estrogen. Behavioral therapy, biofeedback, tranquilizers, and various sedatives have been used to deal with hot flashes. None have proved ideal.

Nor have calcium supplements proved adequate against osteoporosis. Although all women should be on a calcium-adequate diet, bone loss cannot be prevented by simply taking calcium. Exercise may help strengthen bones but is also not, by itself, a true preventive.

On the question of heart disease, women will benefit from losing excess weight, avoiding cholesterol-rich food, and not smoking. Early recognition and treatment of high blood pressure and diabetes can also significantly lower the risk of heart disease.

Looking Ahead

Marking as it does the loss of the ability to have children, menopause is a critical stage in the life cycle of the human female. Rather than dwelling on its negative aspects, the modern woman should regard menopause as a time to look ahead and take actions that can help ensure a healthy and fulfilled future. High on a list of such actions should be a full medical evaluation. Women identified as being in need of hormone replacement therapy would be well-advised to consider going ahead with this highly effective form of treatment. Those not needing it should still see menopause as a signal to reevaluate all their health habits. Women who may need some form of hormone treatment but are unable to undergo HRT should not despair. Other methods of treatment, though not generally as effective as HRT, are available, and researchers are continuing to seek new treatments, as well as improvements in hormone therapy and its alternatives.

A good source of further information about menopause is the North American Menopause Society, 29001 Cedar Road, Suite 600, Lyndhurst, OH 44124 ☐

Those Winter Blues

Michael Terman, Ph.D.
Jiuan Su Terman, Ph.D.

Depression is a psychiatric problem characterized by sadness, anxiety, irritability, difficulties with work and social relationships, decreases in energy and activity levels, and lowered sexual interest. It can occur briefly or chronically, and episodes can recur in clusters or be separated by many years.

Research during the past decade has revealed a striking pattern in the incidence of depression linked to the winter months in the temperate zones, where day length decreases significantly in the fall and winter. Furthermore, within these zones, the cases of winter depression increase in proportion to the shortness of the day. In the United States, which—except for part of Alaska—falls within the northern hemisphere's temperate zone, surveys indicate that the farther north one goes, the higher the incidence of winter depression. About 10 percent of the population in the subpolar region of Alaska, 8 percent in northern New England, and 5 percent in the Washington, D.C., to New York

City area suffer from winter depression. By contrast, in Southern California or Florida the rate drops to below 2 percent. These statistics refer to cases of severe depression, with marked and disturbing behavioral change. Much higher proportions of the population experience a milder, subclinical form of winter blues, in which the symptoms are described as personally bothersome but not overwhelmingly disruptive.

Special Symptoms

People suffering from winter depression, also known as seasonal affective disorder (SAD), have certain symptoms that are not typical of depression. They sleep longer than usual, often having difficulty waking up in the early morning, and they eat more, especially carbohydrates (sweets and starchy foods), and put on weight. Such problems contrast with other forms of depression, which are marked by insomnia and appetite loss.

With the advent of spring, most SAD patients show spontaneous remission of their symptoms and begin to naturally lose weight and

awaken earlier. Some, however, swing too far the other way—toward excessively high mood and hyperactivity (hypomania), which in itself can be troublesome.

Who Gets It?

In the authors' study of more than 200 cases in New York City, we found that 80 percent of SAD patients were female and that the average age at which winter depression was first experienced was 20 years. Some patients recalled seasonal swings extending back to childhood. The onset and remission of each patient's depressive symptoms followed a consistent pattern every year. (For the group as a whole onset ranged from September to February and most commonly occurred in November, and remission occurred between January and June, peaking in March.)

Half the patients in our study had at least one immediate family member who had experienced depression (although only one-quarter of the relatives suffered from seasonal depression). Most patients had never received antidepressant medications—perhaps because such drugs can be slow to take effect and it could be reliably anticipated that the symptoms would disappear at a certain time anyway—though a majority of patients had sought psychotherapy. Many females reported a worsening of symptoms during the week before menstruation.

Bright Light Therapy

Research has shown that SAD can be quickly and effectively treated with bright artificial light. Two important experiments in the early 1980s presaged this discovery. In one, Rutger Wever and colleagues, working in West Germany, found that people living in controlled isolation units whose only source of light was ordinary room light of a few hundred lux did not synchronize their sleep-wake and body temperature rhythms to a 24-hour cycle. (A lux is equivalent to the illumination from a candle 1 meter away.) When the level of light available was increased to match early morning outdoor light (3,000 lux and above), the rhythms *did* synchronize. Another experiment, performed by Alfred Lewy and colleagues at the U.S. National Institute of Mental Health (NIMH), analyzed the effect of light on the body's secretion of the hormone melatonin. Melatonin is released from a gland in the brain during the night. When participants in Lewy's experiment were exposed during the night to dim light, melatonin levels in the body were only somewhat reduced; when the light was increased to 2,000 lux, melatonin quickly dropped to daytime levels.

Because in some animals more melatonin is secreted during longer nights, less during shorter nights, it is believed to play a role in the timing of their seasonal rhythms, underlying annual cycles of reproduction and hibernation. Researchers therefore asked whether there was a parallel in human SAD—whether melatonin production, light, and human body rhythms were somehow linked. If so, perhaps artificial extension of the winter "photoperiod" (duration of daylight) would promote an antidepressant response in SAD patients.

The first case study exposed the patient to bright light of 2,000 lux in both the early morning and the evening, mimicking springtime conditions. Subsequently, more than 500 patients have participated in controlled clinical trials of light therapy, with a large majority showing significant benefits.

The treatment has generally involved daily exposure to full-spectrum fluorescent light—similar in color composition to outdoor daylight—of approximately 2,500 lux. An apparatus with a diffusing screen is set up at home on a tabletop, and the patient faces the light with eyes open but not necessarily looking directly into it. Recent studies have shown clinical improvement with both standard incandescent and cool-white fluorescent light, so it appears that the full-spectrum feature is unnecessary. Normal room light levels of 400 lux or below have been shown to be ineffective.

The required exposure time varies with the individual. With light of 2,500 lux, two hours or more per day is typically needed, although some patients benefit with as little as 30 minutes or one hour. The response usually occurs within three to four days, and if treatment is discontinued, symptoms often recur just as quickly.

Mimicking both springtime dawn and dusk is now thought to be unnecessary, although the time of day at which treatment takes place may be critical. A minority of patients respond well whenever the light is used, but most do best with exposure in the early morning. In a survey of patients at 14 research centers in the United States and Europe, we found no statistical difference between the proportion who improved after receiving light therapy in both the morning and the evening and the proportion who improved after receiving it in the morning alone. Significantly fewer patients responded to evening light alone.

How Does SAD Work?

The superior effect of morning light has been the primary basis for a hypothesis about SAD's underlying mechanism put forth by Lewy and his colleagues. They proposed that the body's internal biological clock, which regulates almost all physiological functions (including melatonin secretion) slows down in winter and that morning light resets it. The melatonin suppression brought about by light therapy is not in itself, however, responsible for the relief of symptoms. When Norman Rosenthal and colleagues at the NIMH, working with people not receiving light therapy, lowered patients' melatonin levels with a drug, there was no clear improvement in SAD symptoms. When the researchers gave melatonin to patients receiving light therapy, in an attempt to counteract the benefit of the light, patients remained well.

The physiological underpinnings of SAD are still under active investigation. One promising lead comes from a study of an experimental drug, d-fenfluramine, by Richard Wurtman and associates at the Massachusetts Institute of Technology. The drug increases the availability in the brain of serotonin, a substance produced by the body that transmits nerve impulses from one nerve cell to another. Patients receiving the drug without the use of light therapy showed a higher remission rate than those receiving a placebo, suggesting that serotonin levels are too low in people with winter depression.

Brighter Lights

A drawback of light treatment is the required daily time commitment—often several hours. In research we conducted at the New York State Psychiatric Institute, we increased the intensity of the light to 10,000 lux. Light was directed down toward the head in order to reduce glare. Given this increased dose, most patients required only 30 minutes of daily exposure to achieve the full effect. This brief, intense treatment has equaled or surpassed previous methods using lower levels of light for longer durations, and eye examinations have indicated no anatomical changes or abnormalities.

Winter depression may be only one manifestation of psychological and physical changes resulting from light deprivation. People with nonseasonal symptoms similar to those seen in winter depression may also be able to benefit from bright light therapy. □

HEARING AIDS

Brad A. Stach, Ph.D.

As many as 25 million people in the United States have some kind of hearing problem. People of all ages can have impaired hearing, although the elderly are most often afflicted, with an estimated 60 percent suffering some degree of hearing impairment.

Hearing impairment is generally a painless condition, but it can be devastating in its capacity to cut off a person from normal communication and social interaction. Fortunately, most hearing-impaired people can be helped. Depending on the kind of hearing loss involved, help can take the form of medical treatment or it can mean the use of a hearing aid. In the vast majority of cases (an estimated 90 percent), a hearing aid is required. To understand why this is so, it is helpful to have an understanding of how people hear and in what ways that capacity can be impaired.

How We Hear

The ear has three sections: the outer (or external) ear, the middle ear, and the inner ear. The outer ear consists of the auricle (the shell-like structure on the side of the head) and the outer ear canal. Together, they funnel sound waves so that they hit the tympanic membrane, or eardrum (which separates the outer and middle ears), and make it vibrate. The vibrations pass through the eardrum into three linked bones in the middle ear (the ossicles, or malleus, incus, and stapes—sometimes referred to as the hammer, the anvil, and the stirrup because of their shapes). In turn, the ossicles pass the vibrations into a delicate, snail-shaped organ in the inner ear called the cochlea. Tiny hairs lining the cochlea change the vibrations into electrical impulses, which are then transmitted to the brain along the auditory nerve.

Types of Hearing Loss

Two types of hearing loss can occur in this intricate system: conductive hearing loss and sensorineural hearing loss.

Conductive Hearing Loss. This happens when some kind of problem in the outer or middle ear prevents sounds from being transmitted (or conducted) properly to the cochlea. If, for example, the protective wax produced in the ear canal blocks the canal for some reason, sound waves will not be able to reach the eardrum as easily as they should. Or if there is an infection in the middle ear (otitis media), in which fluid or pus collects, the sound vibrations produced by the eardrum will be damped down. Or if a disease called otosclerosis causes the normal bone structure in the ear to be replaced by spongy tissue that hardens and immobilizes the ossicles, they will not be able to transmit sound vibrations. Disorders such as these can usually be treated medically. Only relatively few people with conductive hearing loss require hearing aids.

Sensorineural Hearing Loss. This kind of hearing loss occurs when sounds that have reached the inner ear successfully are not passed on to the brain, usually because of damage to the cochlea or the auditory nerve. Causes of such damage include excessive exposure to noise, heredity, large doses of certain antibiotics, or Ménière's disease. However, the most common cause of hearing impairment is presbycusis, an age-related degeneration of the cochlea.

In most instances, sensorineural hearing impairment cannot be treated medically—there are no drugs that can repair damage to the cochlea, and it is far too delicate for surgery. As a general rule, however, anyone whose sensorineural hearing impairment is causing a communication handicap can be helped by some form of hearing aid amplification, although there are a few limitations. Individuals with very mild hearing loss are less likely to benefit from hearing aid use than are those with greater hearing loss. Individuals with hearing impairment in one ear are less likely to benefit than those with hearing impairment in both ears. And individuals with too great a hearing impairment may not be able to benefit very much. Other problems that can interfere with hearing aid use include distortion of sound created by some inner ear disorders (Ménière's disease, for example) and difficulty processing sound, particularly background noise, because of changes in the auditory nervous system. While none of these conditions make hearing aid use absolutely inadvisable, they do worsen the prognosis for successful use.

One Ear or Two?

Since hearing impairment usually occurs in both ears, it seems reasonable that two hearing aids would be better than one, and in many instances this is true. Hearing through two ears helps people locate where sound is coming from and, quite importantly, helps to suppress background noise. In addition, many people prefer hearing "in stereo." Many people, however, benefit quite well from the use of a hearing aid on only one ear.

Conventional Hearing Aids

A hearing aid can be thought of as a sound amplifier that consists of a

Most people with impaired hearing can be helped, either by medical treatment or by the use of a hearing aid.

microphone, an electronic amplifier, a loudspeaker, and a battery (which must be changed every week or so) to provide electrical power. The microphone converts acoustical energy—the energy from sound waves—into electrical energy. This electrical energy is then amplified and filtered so that certain frequencies are emphasized more than others. (Speech, for example, is composed of many different frequencies. If a person has trouble hearing the higher frequencies of speech, the amplifier will be "tuned" to provide the highest volume in the higher frequencies and lower volume in the lower frequencies.) The amplified electrical energy is then converted back to amplified acoustical energy by the loudspeaker.

Most conventional hearing aids fall into one of three categories: behind-the-ear (BTE) hearing aids, in-the-ear (ITE) hearing aids, and in-the-canal (canal) hearing aids. The BTE hearing aid has all of its components, the microphone, amplifier, loudspeaker, and battery, in a case that fits over the ear. Sound is delivered to the ear through a tube that connects to an earmold, a soft plastic plug that sits in the ear canal and is custom-made for each patient. The ITE hearing aid has all of its components in an instrument that fits completely into the auricle. The canal hearing aid is a smaller version of the ITE and fits almost completely in the ear canal. Both canal and ITE aids are usually custom-made for each individual.

Canal and ITE hearing aids are the most popular types, mostly because they are thought to be less conspicuous than BTE hearing aids. But they are not without certain disadvantages. First, BTE hearing aids can be built with more and larger components, thereby permitting better sound quality, more potential for optional controls, and more flexibility in frequency response (that is, with a

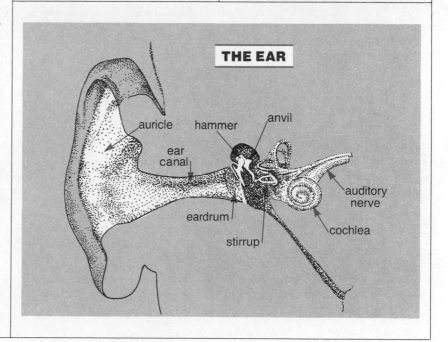

THE EAR

auricle

hammer

anvil

ear canal

auditory nerve

eardrum

stirrup

cochlea

wider range of frequencies that can be adjusted). Second, because the microphone and loudspeaker of an ITE or canal aid are so close together, the potential for "squeal," or feedback, is increased. As a result, the amount of power that an ITE or canal hearing aid can have is reduced. Third, because the electronic components are in the ear, problems due to earwax and perspiration increase the likelihood of hearing aid breakdown. Fortunately these problems are diminishing as technology advances, and many people now successfully wear ITE or canal aids.

Three lesser-used types of hearing aids include body-worn aids, in which the microphone and amplifier are contained in a pocket-sized case worn on the body, eyeglass aids, in which the hearing aid is attached to an eyeglass frame, and bone conduction aids, in which the loudspeaker is replaced with a device that vibrates the bones of the skull behind the ear. The bones conduct the vibrations to the cochlea, where they are converted to electrical impulses to be sent to the brain via the auditory nerve. Because of advancements in hearing aids, neither the body-worn nor eyeglass style of hearing aid is currently used except in unusual circumstances—the two styles constitute fewer than 1 percent of all hearing aids dispensed. Bone conduction hearing aids are used only in those rare instances when a patient has conductive hearing loss that cannot be dealt with medically and the patient cannot wear an earmold or hearing aid in the ear canal because of recurrent ear infections or a canal deformity.

Some hearing aids have options that enhance listening in certain environments. One such option is the telecoil, which can be switched on for better telephone listening. When the telecoil is engaged, the hearing aid's regular microphone is turned off, and the only sound being amplified is that coming from the telephone re-

ceiver. Another option is noise suppression circuitry. Noise suppression devices can be controlled either manually or automatically and are designed to reduce the amplification of background noises so that they are less distracting. Still another option that is becoming increasingly available is the use of remote control devices for adjusting volume, turning a telecoil on and off, changing the frequencies to be amplified, and switching the hearing aid itself on and off. Remote control of a hearing aid is particularly useful for individuals with conditions, such as arthritis, that limit the ability to manipulate small switches and dials.

Some hearing aids come with options that enhance the wearer's ability to hear in certain environments or that make the devices easier to adjust.

Digital Hearing Aids

One of the newest advances in hearing aids is the so-called digital hearing aid. A digital hearing aid can be thought of as a conventional hearing aid with a microcomputer that controls some or all aspects of the device's functions. (A completely digital hearing aid is not yet available commercially.) Some digital aids can be programmed to allow the amplifier setting to be changed depending on the listening environment. For example, one setting might provide optimum listening in a quiet environment, while another might provide optimum listening in a noisy environment. Other advantages include the potential to reduce amplification of background noise, to control loudness, and to

reduce feedback. But there are disadvantages too: digital systems consume greater amounts of power, which means that they use up batteries more quickly, they are larger in size, and they cost substantially more than conventional aids. It is not yet clear whether the advantages of today's digital hearing aids are significant enough to merit the increased cost.

Surgically Implanted Devices

At least three types of surgically implanted devices are currently being used or developed: cochlear implants, bone-anchored hearing aids, and implantable hearing aids.

Cochlear Implants. These are electrical devices with both external and internal parts. The external part can be considered a very sophisticated hearing aid, containing a microphone and some type of signal processor, and resembles, in appearance, a body-worn hearing aid. The microphone picks up sound, which the signal processor converts into electrical energy. This energy is delivered, via a receiver implanted under the skin behind and above the ear, to an electrode or electrodes implanted in or near the cochlea. The electrode stimulates auditory nerve endings within the cochlea, and the brain interprets this nerve activity as sound. Cochlear implants vary considerably in their complexity. In some devices, there is only one channel of information available. That is, electrical energy can be sent to only one site in the cochlea. In others, however, 21 channels are available, allowing energy to be sent to as many as 21 discrete points along the cochlea.

Cochlear implants have been used only in a relatively small number of individuals who have profound hearing impairment and who cannot be helped by conventional hearing aids. Many patients have benefited substantially from the implants, which allow them to hear environmental sounds and warning signals and even, in some cases, to understand some speech.

Bone-Anchored Implants. A relatively few individuals who have conductive hearing loss from an intractable middle ear disorder but who cannot use an earmold or a hearing aid in the ear canal are able to benefit from a bone-anchored implant. This device, which works on the same principle as the bone conduction hearing aid mentioned earlier, consists of an external microphone and amplifier and an implanted transducer. The external part of the device converts sound into electrical energy which is then passed to a transducer. The transducer converts the electrical energy back to acoustic energy, which vibrates the bones of the skull. The vibrations are then conducted by the bones to the cochlea.

Implantable Hearing Aids. These are now in a stage of rapid development. One type being studied is the middle-ear implant, in which a microphone is placed at the eardrum, and signals are sent to an amplifier that is implanted in the middle ear. The amplifier is connected to the bones of the middle ear and enhances their movements, thereby

> **People who cannot be helped by a conventional hearing aid can sometimes benefit from a device that is surgically implanted in the ear.**

increasing the amount of energy sent to the inner ear. Another type of implantable aid is the outer ear implant, which is set into the ear canal after the canal has been widened by surgery.

While implantable hearing aids

are desirable because of their invisibility, their general availability awaits improvements in reliability, longevity, and power supply constraints. Also, it is unclear as to whether the cosmetic and amplification advantages will be substantial enough to warrant the increased cost.

Assistive Listening Devices

Many people regard their hearing impairment as a real handicap only in very specific circumstances—for example, when they are speaking on the telephone, viewing television, or riding in a car with another person. In such cases the use of assistive listening devices (ALDs) may be an alternative to conventional amplification. ALDs may also be useful as a supplement to conventional hearing aid use, for individuals whose hearing aids are not sufficient in certain circumstances.

The term "assistive listening device" is used to denote a broad category of electronic instruments that are aids to hearing but that are not conventional hearing aids. ALDs include telephone amplifiers, television listeners, personal FM systems, infrared systems, and personal amplifiers. Telephone amplifiers include both volume-control telephone handsets and portable telephone adapters. The other types of ALDs differ from conventional hearing aids in that, in general, they make use of remote-microphone technology. A television listener, for example, has a microphone that is placed near the television speaker. Sound is transmitted from the microphone by means of infrared light waves or FM radio waves, and the signal is received by an infrared or FM receiver that is connected to the ear via earphones or a hearing aid. In like manner, a person who has difficulty hearing in church or while riding in the car because of background noise can ask the speaker to use the remote microphone of an ALD. This virtually places the

listener's ear no farther from the speaker's mouth than the speaker's mouth is from the remote microphone; thus, most background noise is eliminated. Theaters, movie houses, and concert halls have installed these kinds of devices for the convenience of their hearing-impaired patrons. Using rented headsets, the hearing-impaired receive signals from the sound source picked up by a microphone and sent by a transmitter.

> **Hearing aid amplification can help overcome speech and language disorders in hearing-impaired children and social isolation and job constraints in adults.**

What to Expect From a Hearing Aid

Hearing aids and ALDs can have a dramatic impact on the lives of people with hearing impairment. Use of hearing aid amplification has been shown to assist in overcoming such adverse effects of hearing impairment as speech and language disorders in children, occupational constraints in adults, and social isolation in the elderly. Hearing aids cannot make a damaged ear hear perfectly again, nor can they always differentiate speech from noise and amplify one more than the other. But if a person with a hearing impairment has reasonable expectations about the benefits and limitations of a hearing aid, and if hearing aids and ALDs are fitted and worn appropriately, then the prognosis for successful assistance in overcoming the communication handicap caused by hearing impairment is quite good. □

The Role of the
PHARMACIST

Barbara Scherr Trenk

The community pharmacist—the man or woman who fills your prescriptions—may be the only person in the healthcare business who can be seen without making an appointment; according to the National Association of Retail Druggists (NARD), pharmacists are the most accessible healthcare professionals in town.

Training and Licensing

Whether he or she works behind a pharmacy counter in a supermarket, in a chain store, or in a small independent pharmacy, the person who fills prescriptions is a specially trained and licensed professional. In the United States, to be allowed to practice their profession, pharmacists must complete a five-year college-level training program and serve a year's internship, as well as passing a state licensing examination. The pharmacy itself must be licensed by the state in which it is located and may be subject to periodic inspection by health department officials.

Pharmacists must be familiar with the composition of drugs, their chemical and physical properties, and the way they are manufactured and used. They must know about the effects of a drug on a healthy person as well as on one who is ill.

What Pharmacists Do

Checking Prescriptions. To the customer it may appear that the person filling a prescription simply counts pills and puts a label on the bottle. However, pharmacists do a lot more behind the scenes than most patients realize. According to NARD, pharmacists make changes in about 30 percent of all prescriptions they fill, most often substituting generic drugs for brand-name medications. Frequently a doctor will indicate when writing a prescription that the pharmacist may substitute the less-expensive generic equivalent if the patient so wishes. In fact, many insurance plans require that prescriptions be filled with generic equivalents when possible, and consumers who have no coverage for medications may prefer to buy generic drugs.

Pharmacists typically have about 25 telephone conversations each day with physicians, according to NARD. Many of these calls involve requesting permission to substitute generic products when a prescription indicates "dispense as written" (meaning the pharmacist cannot make a change without the doctor's consent). An alert pharmacist who knows the patient and what other medications that person is taking may contact the patient's doctor to discuss a possible drug interaction or a potential allergic reaction. The pharmacist may also call to double-check on the prescribed dosage of a medication if it appears inappropriate.

Some doctors consult with a patient's pharmacist before prescribing medications. According to Judy Shinogle of the American Pharmaceutical Association—herself a registered pharmacist—these tend to be younger doctors, who may have become used to talking to hospital pharmacists before prescribing for patients during their residency. Pharmacist Steve Pino,

Pharmacists can keep track of customers' medications by storing data in a computer.

who owns a Medicine Shoppe franchise pharmacy in St. James, N.Y., says that occasionally a doctor will call him to ask what drugs other physicians in the area are using to treat a particular condition.

Keeping a Patient's Profile.
Pharmacists often keep track of a patient's prescription "profile," recording all medications—prescription and over-the-counter—being taken on a regular basis and noting any history of allergic reactions to drugs. Increasingly, such records are stored in a computer, which automatically checks for drug interactions, as well as for a particular patient's adverse reactions to medication. Let us suppose that a physician gives a patient a prescription for a painkiller or muscle relaxant that contains aspirin. When the name of the prescribed medication is entered into the computer, a warning beep calls the pharmacist's attention to the fact that this patient should not be taking products containing aspirin. This may be because the patient is taking blood-thinning medication (aspirin also thins blood) for another condition or because the person has had an adverse reaction to aspirin. One computer-based prescription system claims to have 7,000 drug products and 14,000 possible interactions stored in its data base.

Specialized Services. Pharmacists buy most of their pills and potions in bulk, then dispense the amount called for in individual prescriptions. But a slowly growing segment of their business is specialized compounding, in particular the mixing of topical ointments and creams ordered by dermatologists and allergists. Patients with asthma may need specially blended cough and cold preparations, and some gynecologists are asking pharmacists to prepare custom progesterone suppositories for use by women who suffer from premenstrual syndrome.

Other Health-Related Services. Today many patients receive treatment at home—includ-

A good pharmacist will be able to answer questions about your medications (and help you avoid problems).

ing intravenous medications—that would previously have been provided only in hospitals. Pharmacists may be called upon to mix solutions such as antibiotics or cancer-fighting drugs that are designed to be administered with the help of a family member or visiting nurse. Some pharmacists work with visiting nurse agencies to provide at-home services; a few have added nurses to their own staff who will make home visits.

Some drugstores have expanded into other health-related services—for instance fitting patients who have had mastectomies with prostheses. Others offer rental of such equipment as wheelchairs, hospital beds, and commodes.

How to Choose a Pharmacist

It is a good idea to patronize only one pharmacist, who can get to know you and your family and build up a history of all your prescriptions. If you're seeing different medical specialists for heart

disease, arthritis, and an ear infection, your pharmacist may be the only person who has a record of all the drugs you take and is thus in a position to spot unhealthy combinations. In addition, your pharmacist can answer questions about your medications that may help you to avoid problems and to get the maximum benefit. (See the list of questions on the following page.)

Try to talk to the pharmacist before you decide on your prescription headquarters. Ask about the store's policies on billing, insurance acceptance, and other special services. If you use an insurance plan to pay for drugs, make sure the pharmacy participates in your plan. Ask yourself whether you would be comfortable talking to this pharmacist about your medications, or whether you might feel rushed or ignored. Some other criteria for choosing a pharmacist follow.

Record Keeping. Don't just assume that your pharmacist keeps prescription profiles—ask specifically whether this service is provided. Some pharmacists do not keep such records because they find the paperwork too time-consuming. Others keep records for customers who pay for their prescriptions themselves, but decline to do so for those who belong to a prescription plan under which the pharmacist has to wait for payment from an insurer. Having a record of prescriptions is especially important for the elderly, since older people are more likely to be taking several medications and may, in some cases, have difficulty keeping track of their various prescriptions.

Location, Hours, Delivery. Because it is sometimes important to have prescriptions filled quickly, the most knowledgeable pharmacist may not be the right one for you if the location is not convenient. People who commute a long distance may need a pharmacist whose store is open evenings or very early in the morning.

Some pharmacies will deliver prescriptions to the home. If this service is important to you, find out which stores in your area provide it.

Cost. In the United States, according to a recent survey by the American Association of Retired Persons, prices of prescription medications vary widely, not only from state to state but also within the same community. In choosing a pharmacist, cost should, however, be weighed against other factors; a large discount pharmacy may offer better prices than an independent neighborhood pharmacy, but not necessarily the same personal service and attention.

Other Factors. Another consideration is the type of store you'd like to patronize. There are about 25,000 chain store pharmacies in the United States, which typically offer a wide range of merchandise in addition to prescription and over-the-counter medications. Some customers

like the convenience of being able to shop for other items—from cosmetics to greeting cards to housewares—while they wait for their prescription to be filled. Over 5,000 supermarkets and general merchandise chain stores now have pharmacy counters.

Many of the 40,000 independent pharmacies in the United States also provide one-stop shopping, although they offer less variety than the chains. Many people find it easier to ask the pharmacist for information about over-the-counter products at smaller pharmacies than at large ones. Strictly health-oriented pharmacies may sell only pharmaceutical products—prescription drugs and over-the-counter medications plus health-related equipment such as items that are needed for glucose monitoring.

Some people who use over-the-counter birth control products—including condoms and contraceptive foams and jellies—prefer to select such items from self-help shelves rather than having to request them from a clerk or the pharmacist. Stores' policies on displaying these items vary; if you are uncomfortable asking for them, look for a pharmacy where you can find what you need by yourself.

Professional Responsibility

Occasionally it is the pharmacist's responsibility to refuse to fill a prescription. If a physician has called for what the pharmacist considers a dangerously high dose of a particular medication, the pharmacist may call the doctor and suggest the prescription be modified. According to pharmacist Steve Pino, doctors are usually happy to have the mistake caught. But occasionally, Pino says, a doctor will insist that the prescribed dosage is correct. To avoid liability, the pharmacist can then refuse to fill the prescription—and the patient must decide whether to find a new doctor or a new pharmacist. ☐

What to Ask About Medication

Pharmacists fill about 1.6 billion prescriptions each year, but nearly half of these drugs may be taken improperly, says the National Council on Patient Information and Education. To get the most benefit from your prescription medication, don't be afraid to ask your pharmacist the following questions:

- How often must I take this medication?

- How much should I take each time?

- Should it be taken at specific times of day?

- What if I miss a dose?

- Should it be taken with food? Before eating?

- Should certain foods be avoided?

- Can I take other medications (including antacids, aspirin, and allergy preparations) while using this one?

- Must I avoid alcohol?

- Will this medication affect my driving ability?

- What side effects, if any, can I expect?

- Where should this medication be stored? In the refrigerator? Away from sunlight?

- Will smoking interfere with the effectiveness of this medication?

Some of this information should be on the label, in particular how often the medication is to be taken and in what dosage. If it isn't there, ask.

HAND PROBLEMS

A. Lee Osterman, M.D., and Kant Y. Lin, M.D.

The hand is one of the most complex structures of the body. It is unique in its range of motion and in its capacity to perform a wide variety of functions, from delivering a boxer's knockout punch to executing a pianist's delicate fingering. The hand-wrist skeleton is made up of 29 bones, and over 50 muscles are involved in making these bones move. Adding their own contributions to the versatility of the hand are numerous nerves, joints, and ligaments.

Each year in the United States over 12 million people visit doctors because of problems with their hands that range from the mildly annoying to the totally disabling. This article discusses some of the more common hand problems and their treatments.

Ganglia

Ganglia are soft cysts of the hand and wrist which develop on joints or tendons. The most common hand tumors, they are never malignant. Ganglia are sacs filled with a jellylike material called mucin. The neck of the sac allows a one-way flow of joint fluid into the cyst, but occasionally pressure in the sac will push the fluid back into the joint, accounting for a fluctuation in the cyst's size. Many ganglia develop after some mild injury to the hand or wrist. They may develop gradually or occur suddenly, and most people complain either of a noticeable lump or of mild pain and weakness. Studies have shown that ganglia tend to occur singly and in very specific locations, most often on the back of the wrist beneath the index and middle fingers or on the palm side of the hand just beneath the thumb. But they have occurred in almost every location on the hand. They are most common in people in their 20s, 30s, and 40s.

Ganglia often spontaneously flatten out with rest only to recur with activity. Treatment in the past involved rupturing the cyst by pressing on it (the traditional home remedy was to hit it with a book). Puncturing the sac with a needle and draining the mucin is more effective, but all these methods have had only partial success in permanently shrinking the cyst. Sometimes the most effective treatment is reassuring patients that these are benign lesions.

Surgery to cut out a ganglion is recommended only when a cyst persistently interferes with an individual's daily functions. The outpatient procedure, done under local anesthesia, leaves a cosmetically acceptable scar and allows pain-free motion and a return to all activities. Following surgery, 5 percent of ganglia recur.

Carpal Tunnel Syndrome

Carpal tunnel syndrome (CTS) is the most common nerve disorder of the hand. The carpal tunnel is an area in the center of the wrist where a canal is formed by the wrist bones and a tough ligament on the underside of the wrist that binds the bones together. The tendons to the thumb and fingers and a major nerve, the median nerve, run through the canal. If the median nerve is compressed as it transverses the narrow tunnel (and this happens for a variety of reasons), carpal tunnel syndrome results.

Symptoms of CTS are weakness or clumsiness in the hand, a tingling feeling (pins and needles) in the thumb, index finger, and middle finger, aggravation of these symptoms when grasping with the hand, awakening from sleep with numbness in the fingers, and diffi-culty in holding the steering wheel of a car for prolonged periods. Forearm and upper arm pain is not uncommon, as the pain migrates up from the hand and wrist.

The most common cause of CTS is tendinitis (inflammation of the tendons). Swelling of the tendons from repetitive use makes them too large for the tunnel, causing them to press on the median nerve. However, any lesion (such as a cyst) that takes up room in the canal can cause CTS. The bony structures of the canal can also be narrowed by fractures or arthritis. Finally, CTS can result from certain medical conditions that cause swelling—rheumatoid arthritis, pregnancy, diabetes, im-

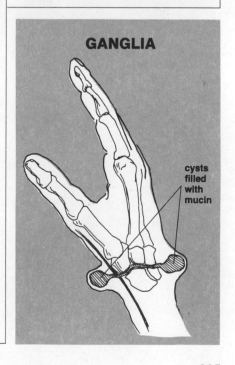

GANGLIA

cysts filled with mucin

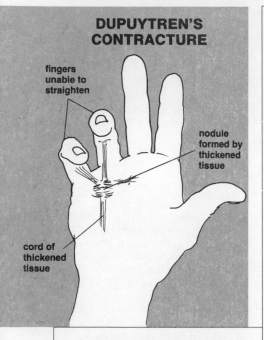

DUPUYTREN'S CONTRACTURE

fingers unable to straighten

nodule formed by thickened tissue

cord of thickened tissue

paired thyroid function, and other hormonal disorders.

CTS occurs most commonly in people between the ages of 30 and 70; women are affected more than men. Early diagnosis can lead to prompt treatment, but delay in treatment can lead to permanently impaired nerve function. CTS is

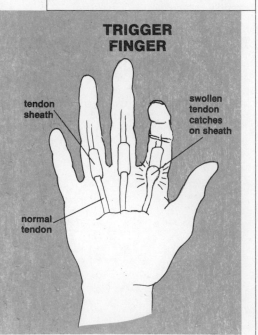

TRIGGER FINGER

tendon sheath

swollen tendon catches on sheath

normal tendon

diagnosed in a variety of ways. The physician will examine the patient to see if there is irritation of the nerve at the wrist. Simple nerve tests, in which the patient holds the wrist in a flexed position or the physician gently taps over the nerve, will often reproduce a patient's symptoms. To pinpoint the exact site of compression and determine how badly the nerve is damaged, other tests may be necessary. These include an X ray of the wrist to look for bony defects of the carpal tunnel, and two tests, an electromyogram and a nerve conduction velocity test, that trace nerve impulses.

Treatment of CTS begins with a lightweight, removable splint worn over the wrist, at night or at work, to support it and to prevent excessive bending and extension, both of which cause the carpal tunnel to narrow further. Patients are given nonsteroidal anti-inflammatory medications to reduce swelling and inflammation. When a physician believes that whatever is causing CTS will be only temporary, cortisone may be injected into the tunnel to reduce inflammation.

If the symptoms are very severe or nerve pressure is so severe that the nerve is in danger of being permanently damaged and the more conservative measures do not alleviate the syndrome, surgery is indicated. The objective of surgery is simple: to cut through the ligament that forms the "roof" of the carpal tunnel and thereby relieve the pressure on the nerve. The surgery can be done on an outpatient basis. Night discomfort will usually be relieved within a day of the surgery, and numbness may recede over time, depending on how much damage has already been done to the nerve.

Dupuytren's Contracture

Dupuytren's contracture is a disease of the thin layer of connective tissue located in the palm of the hand. The condition, named for the French surgeon (Baron Guillaume Dupuytren) who first

developed a surgical treatment for it in 1832, became widely known after President Ronald Reagan had surgery for the disorder.

The connective tissue anchors the skin on the palm to the interior of the hand so that it does not wrinkle with use like a glove. A thickening of this tissue—initially in the form of nodules, or lumps, and then in the form of ropelike cords—pulls some of the fingers down. Occasionally, tenderness will impair a patient's grasp, but by far the most common complaint is the awkwardness and frustration of not being able to fully extend the affected fingers. Patients have difficulty with such everyday activities as shaking hands, grasping objects, washing themselves, or getting their hands into pockets or gloves.

The cause of Dupuytren's contracture remains unknown. Genetic factors apparently play a major role: this is almost exclusively a disease of Caucasians of European ancestry. It occurs ten times more frequently in men than in women, and its onset is typically after the age of 40. The disease is more frequent and severe among alcoholics and in people with epilepsy or diabetes. In about half of all cases, the condition will affect both hands, usually starting in line with the ring finger and progressing to the little finger. These two fingers are involved more than all the other fingers combined. If untreated, the contractures lead to permanent deformity of the finger joints, especially of the second joint down from the fingernail.

Currently, the only treatment for Dupuytren's contracture is surgical. Whether surgery is done depends on an individual's needs and degree of disability. A nodule in the palm that does not affect movement of the fingers does not require surgery unless it is so large as to be very troublesome. Contractures of the fingers should be treated as soon as possible. The aim of surgery is to remove the diseased tissue and to release the contractured joint. While many patients will have some recurrence following surgery, only 15 percent will have it severely enough to require additional operations.

Trigger Finger

Stenosing tenosynovitis of a finger or thumb, a condition known as trigger finger, is another common cause of hand disability and pain. Patients typically complain of a clicking or snapping sensation in a finger when they move it. The finger locks painfully in midmotion, snaps, and releases; only then can it be fully extended.

Fingers move because of the pull of tendons attached to the forearm muscles. These tendons run through sheaths attached to the finger bones along their full length. Fluid within the synovial membranes lining the sheaths allows the tendons to glide without friction when fingers are moved. When there is a mismatch in the relative sizes of a tendon and its sheath, the tendon cannot move freely and triggering occurs. The most common cause is inflammation of the synovial membranes, or synovitis, which causes swelling around the sheath. Injury to the finger that causes swelling and accumulation of fluid in the tendon can also lead to triggering.

Nonsurgical treatment involves splinting the finger to prevent excessive motion and injecting steroids into the tendon sheath to decrease the inflammation. This may stop the triggering, but only if it has been of recent onset, the swelling is minor, and locking of the finger is infrequent. If one or two injections are unsuccessful, then surgery is needed, which involves cutting the sheath at the base of the finger where the tendon catches. The operation can be done under local anesthesia, as an outpatient procedure, and brings reliable permanent relief.

De Quervain's Disease

De Quervain's disease is synovitis involving the back of the wrist at the base of the thumb. First described in 1895 by Swiss surgeon Fritz De Quervain, it causes pain in the wrist that is aggravated by movement of the thumb. Normally, two tendons to the thumb pass through a tunnel formed by a ligament and the main wrist bone. As in the carpal tunnel, the space in this tunnel, or tendon compartment, is fixed; thus, any swelling of the tendon sheaths will cause pain. The condition occurs more commonly in women but can develop in anyone of any age with sufficient provocation from activities that require constant and repetitive thumb movement, combined with twisting of the wrist.

When the patient's wrist is examined, it will be swollen on the back at the base of the thumb and tender to the touch. A simple test confirms the diagnosis: the patient feels pain while holding the thumb in the palm of the hand and bending the wrist toward the little finger. De Quervain's disease is often associated with rheumatoid arthritis, pregnancy, or hormonal disorders and may also involve a small ganglion in the tendon compartment.

Treatment includes splinting and immobilization of the thumb and wrist, nonsteroidal anti-inflammatory medications, heat, and injection of steroids into the tendon compartment (generally two injections over a two-month period). This usually leads to temporary relief from symptoms, but as patients resume activity, the problem frequently recurs. If symptoms do recur, surgery is indicated. It involves cutting the ligaments overlying the tendons to relieve pressure within. This is done as an outpatient procedure. The thumb must then be immobilized for two or three days, after which the patient must wear a small wrist bandage. After another week of healing, the patient can resume all previous activities. The surgery is generally reliable and its effects permanent.

Osteoarthritis

Osteoarthritis of the hand is a common condition, estimated to affect up to 40 percent of people over age 50. The joints most often involved are the top and middle joints of the fingers and the joint at the base of the thumb. The wear and tear of daily use over time leads to the development and aggravation of this degenerative condition, although heredity also plays a role. It is especially common in postmenopausal women. Osteoarthritis can occur in a slow, relatively painless form, in which changes in the joints are noted only on an X ray, or in a rapid, more disabling form, in which pain, stiffness, and deformity of the joints causes considerable loss of hand functioning.

The disease begins as an inflammation of the lining of the joints, leads to the degeneration of cartilage, and progresses to the narrowing of joints and to the growth of new bone in the form of spurs, which show up as lumps in the fingers. The disease can also cause mucous cysts, fluid-filled sacs usually located on the backs of fingers over the topmost joints. These cysts may need to be surgically removed because of pain or because their location near the cuticle may lead them to rupture and infect the joint.

When the fingers are only mildly affected, treatment usually involves mild painkillers, oral anti-inflammatory medications, heat, and advice for judicious patterns of hand use. Persistent pain during activity and progressive deformity call for more aggressive treatment, namely arthrodesis, the fusing of the joint to prevent pain on motion, or arthroplasty, the replacement of the joint with either other tissue or an artificial joint.

Osteoarthritis involving the joint at the base of the thumb can be particularly disabling because the thumb is important in so many tasks. If moving the joint is painful, surgery may be required. Surgical options include repair of the joint's ligaments, joint fusion, or total joint replacement. Such treatments are effective in restoring a useful thumb. □

TESTICULAR CANCER

Robert J. Motzer, M.D., and George J. Bosl, M.D.

Testicular cancer—a cancer that affects the male reproductive organs, where sperm and the hormone testosterone are produced—is a relatively rare disease. Some 5,700 cases are diagnosed and 350 deaths occur annually in the United States. It accounts for only 1-2 percent of all malignant disease in American males. However, despite its low incidence, testicular cancer is extremely important for a number of reasons. First, it afflicts a young age group and is the most common cancer in American men between the ages of 15 and 35. (Beyond the age of 45, this type of cancer is extremely rare.) Second, it is a curable disease, even when the cancer has spread to areas of the body outside the testes.

To maximize the chances for cure, early diagnosis and proper therapy are necessary. If the disease is diagnosed before it has spread beyond the testicle, 97 percent of patients are cured; the figure drops to 60 percent if the cancer has spread to other parts of the body by the time of diagnosis. In the early stages, the disease is curable by surgery and, sometimes, radiation. In advanced stages chemotherapy is required. Because of the relative rarity of this cancer, it is advisable that patients be treated at medical centers with experience in its treatment.

Men at Risk

Although testicular cancer is more common in whites than in blacks or Hispanics, the only recognized risk factor is an undescended testi-cle. This condition (even if corrected surgically) increases the risk of developing testicular cancer up to 40-fold.

A frequently asked question is whether this cancer is inherited. The answer is generally no. There have been several reports of multiple cases of testicular cancer within families. However, aside from these occasional reports, evidence of a predisposition within families is lacking, and testicular cancer is not considered a hereditary condition.

Self-Examination

Men can and should take an active role in early detection of testicular cancer by practicing monthly self-examination, beginning in their teens. Such examinations should be done routinely, just as monthly breast self-examination should be practiced routinely by women to aid in the early detection of breast cancer.

The examination is best done after a warm bath or shower, when the skin of the scrotum (the sac in which each testicle is suspended) is relaxed. The testes are best examined while standing. Each testicle is held between the forefinger and thumb of both hands and gently rolled between the fingers, in a search for lumps. The size and consistency of the testicles should be compared. If any lump, swelling, or change in consistency is detected within a testicle, a physician should be consulted. (During the examination a rope-like structure, the epididimis, may be felt on the outside surface of the back of the testicle; this is a normal structure and no cause for concern.)

Signs and Symptoms

The first sign of testicular cancer may be either a painless lump in a testicle or acute pain or swelling of the testicle. Painless lumps, if not detected by self-examination, are often first noticed during a shower or during intercourse.

Not all patients with pain in a testicle or swelling have testicular cancer. Other conditions can cause the same symptoms, including testicular torsion (twisting of the testicle on the spermatic cord connecting it to the body), hydrocele (accumulation of fluid in the membrane surrounding the testicle), and various infections of the testes or surrounding structures. If the problem is an infection, patients can often be treated by a primary care physician, who will prescribe a short course of antibiotics.

Whenever the primary care physician considers testicular cancer a possibility or the patient has testicular discomfort that lasts longer than two weeks, the patient should be referred to a urologist for an examination and for a sonogram of the testicle. This noninvasive diagnostic test, which uses sound waves to produce an image of a part of the body, is highly reliable in detecting testicular tumors.

Occasionally, a patient may have other physical symptoms related to testicular cancer, since this type of cancer often spreads. These symptoms include back pain caused by cancer that has spread to lymph nodes located in the back of the abdomen, shortness of breath or a cough caused by spread to the lungs, and swollen lymph nodes at the base of the neck. There may also be swelling of the breasts, usually caused by an elevated level in the blood of certain chemicals associated with testicular cancer.

Confirming the Diagnosis

If the sonogram shows a tumor and the urologist suspects a testicular malignancy, the usual procedure to make a definite diagnosis is removal of the affected testicle, a procedure termed a radical inguinal orchiectomy. An incision is made in the groin, and the testicle and the spermatic cord are removed. As the patient's other testicle is not damaged, the man's sexual functioning and fertility should continue following surgery.

After the orchiectomy, the tissue removed is examined under a microscope to confirm that cancer is present and determine the type of malignancy. Almost all cancers—95 percent—originating within the testes are derived from the cells that make sperm and are referred to as germ cell tumors. From a practical standpoint there are two types of germ cell tumors, with different characteristics. One is called a seminoma. The other type, which has several subtypes, is called a nonseminoma. The distinction between a seminoma and a nonseminoma is important, as treatment varies depending on the cancer type.

Evaluation and Treatment

Following the diagnosis of testicular cancer, additional tests are needed to determine whether the cancer has spread, or metastasized, outside of the testicle. This process is known as staging. The evaluation includes a careful history and physical examination, a chest X ray, and a more sophisticated X ray of the abdomen—computerized tomography (CT scan). In addition, there should

be blood tests for two so-called tumor markers. These chemicals—human chorionic gonadotropin and alpha-fetoprotein—are produced by the tumor and can be detected in the blood. They are quite specific for testicular cancer, and when present in elevated amounts, they indicate active disease. (Blood tests for the tumor markers are also important during a patient's treatment and afterward, to evaluate the effectiveness of treatment.) Based on the results of all of these tests, a treatment plan is recommended.

Treatment depends on the type and extent of spread of the cancer. For patients with a seminoma confined to the testicle or with only limited spread to the lymph nodes in the abdomen, radiation therapy to the lymph nodes is indicated. This results in a cure rate of 85 to 95 percent. Patients with more advanced seminoma (wider spread of the cancer) are treated immediately after diagnosis with chemotherapy, which cures the majority of patients.

Patients with a nonseminoma apparently confined to the testicle have, until recently, all been treated with surgical removal of the abdominal lymph nodes. The reason for the surgery is that in some patients, although a minority, the cancer will have spread to the lymph nodes but this spread is not detectable. More recently, selected patients with cancer that seems to be confined to the testicle have simply been observed following orchiectomy. The decision on which treatment is best for the patient must be left to an experienced urologist or oncologist (cancer specialist), and patients who do not have the abdominal surgery must be tested periodically for any possible recurrence of the cancer. Patients with a nonseminoma and suspected spread to the abdominal lymph nodes generally undergo abdominal surgery. Patients with more advanced nonseminomas are best treated with chemotherapy, which, for the majority of patients, results in a cure.

The most disturbing side effect of the abdominal surgery to remove the lymph nodes is decreased fertility, which occurs because during the operation the nerves that initiate ejaculation are damaged. The nerves that are responsible for orgasm are left intact, and thus, patients are able to achieve orgasm even though they are unable to ejaculate semen. Recently, an effort has been made to do less extensive surgery, in order to preserve ejaculation and therefore fertility in selected circumstances.

For patients with advanced testicular cancer, combination chemotherapy (use of more than one drug) is the treatment of choice. More and more patients are cured with chemotherapy, largely because of the advent of a drug called cisplatin, first used in the early 1970s. Most chemotherapy regimens involve cisplatin plus one to four additional drugs. These are given by injection into a vein and act by killing dividing cells. Because cancer cells are dividing more rapidly than normal cells, the cancer cells are killed selectively, and the normal cells are spared. Treatment consists of three to four monthly cycles of chemotherapy, often followed by surgery to evaluate any areas suspected of containing persistent tumors and, if necessary, to remove those growths. For example, chemotherapy does not destroy the type of nonseminoma called a teratoma, which must be removed surgically after chemotherapy has been completed.

One of the troubling side effects of chemotherapy is infertility, caused by lowering of the sperm count. As most patients are young, may be considering having families in the future, and are destined to be cured of their cancer, patients are strongly encouraged to deposit semen samples (usually one to three) in a sperm bank prior to treatment. Sperm banking is also strongly encouraged prior to abdominal surgery to remove lymph nodes. □

Almost everyone has experienced brief episodes of ringing, buzzing, or other noises in the ears. Sometimes an episode of this kind follows exposure to loud sound: a rock concert, a gunshot, or the roar of a subway train. At other times it happens for no apparent reason.

In people who have a condition called tinnitus, these ear noises are persistent. For some, they are merely a nuisance. For others, tinnitus is distracting enough to interfere with work, sleep, relationships, and enjoyment of life. A few people are so disabled by the condition, they have even considered suicide.

According to the American Tinnitus Association, an organization dedicated to helping tinnitus patients and promoting research into this mysterious disorder, 50 million Americans have tinnitus and 12 million suffer severely enough that they have sought medical help. Yet when many patients first learn the name of their condition, the term is so unfamiliar that they wonder how to pronounce it. (It can be pronounced either tin-EYE-tus or TIN-ni-tus.)

The word is derived from a Latin term meaning "to tinkle or ring like a bell." The ear noises of tinnitus have been likened to the ringing of a telephone—by patients who actually answer their phone, to find that the ringing exists only in their ears. The noises have also been compared to other sounds, including the electrical hum of high tension wires, the hiss of escaping steam, the roar of the wind or of ocean waves, and the wail of a fire siren.

What Causes Tinnitus?

Although tinnitus was described over 2,000 years ago by Hippocrates, the "Father of Medicine," it is still poorly understood. In a few cases, known as "objective tinnitus," when the ear noises can be heard by others, they are usually found to have a specific cause, such as vascular problems

That Ringing in the Ears

Pat Costello Smith

or spasmodic opening and closing of the eustachian tubes. In most cases, however, in the condition called "subjective tinnitus," the noises are heard only by the patient. People suffering from subjective tinnitus are, not surprisingly, often reluctant to discuss their ear noises for fear they will be thought prone to flights of imagination or actually crazy.

The causes of subjective tinnitus can be difficult, if not impossible, to pin down. Sometimes the ear noises are found to be associated with an underlying disorder, but in the majority of cases, no underlying condition can be found.

Many researchers believe that in these unexplained cases the ear noises result from damage to the sensitive hair cells in the inner ear. Normally, the inner ear converts sound vibrations to electrical impulses that the auditory nerve then transmits to the brain. The researchers theorize that the damage may cause the hair cells to react in some way even when no sound stimulus is present. The damage to the cells may be a consequence of aging, of certain chronic diseases, such as diabetes, or of excessive noise. Indeed, many experts believe that excessive noise—which commonly makes the ears ring—is a leading cause of tinnitus and can worsen tinnitus arising from other sources.

Checking for Other Disorders

If an underlying disorder can be identified and treated, tinnitus can sometimes be alleviated. For this reason, and because some of the possible underlying disorders are serious, everyone who experiences persistent ear noises should be checked by a physician. Possible disorders include wax pressing on the eardrum, tumors of the auditory nerve, otosclerosis (a disease of the tiny, sound-conducting bones in the middle ear), Ménière's disease (which also causes deafness and dizziness), high blood pressure, and anemia. A blow to the head and certain medications, including aspirin in high doses, are among other underlying causes. So are problems with the joints in front of the ears that connect the upper and lower jaws, which call for consultation with a dentist, and hearing problems, which is why people with persistent ear noises should have their hearing evaluated by an ear specialist, or otolaryngologist. In fact, most people suffering from tinnitus have an associated hearing loss, although they may not be aware of it.

Treatments

Unless it is associated with a treatable underlying condition, there is no cure for tinnitus. In the majority of cases in which no underlying cause can be identified, treatment is aimed at alleviating the severity of the tinnitus and helping sufferers cope with its impact on their lives. Physicians have found that it is impossible to tell in advance what might help whom; thus, patient and physician need to work through the various possible treatments together in the hope that one of them will help.

One possible way to alleviate tinnitus is to avoid what is known to make it worse. Nicotine, marijuana, and excessive use of alcohol should be avoided. Some people find that cutting down on caffeine affects their tinnitus for the better. Above all else, people who have tinnitus should avoid loud noise. If they cannot stay clear of chain saws, motorcycles, and outboard motors, they should protect their ears with earplugs, earmuff-like "ear defenders," or both.

Once assured that their ear

noises do not mean they are losing their sanity or going deaf, people with mild tinnitus often manage to cope, as they would with other annoyances in their lives.

Others get along well during the daytime, when daily activities distract them and environmental sounds drown out their ear noises. But in a quiet bedroom, tinnitus may interfere with sleep. Adding a "masking" sound can help. Masking sounds—soft music, the hum of an air conditioner or fan, the "shh" sound of an FM radio tuned between stations, a recording of a waterfall or surf—may cover up the ear noises. Eventually, using the mind's ability to block out noises that are familiar or monotonous, some people learn to ignore the masking sound, too.

Some patients are helped by a more sophisticated variation of masking that is provided by a tiny electronic device called a tinnitus masker. The masker, which looks like a hearing aid and is worn in the ear, transmits a substitute sound directly into the ear. For patients with a low-pitch or medium-pitch hearing loss, a well-fitted hearing aid may be the answer. The environmental sounds amplified by a properly fitted hearing aid may be all that is needed to effectively mask the tinnitus (although a hearing aid does not work for all kinds of hearing problems or all kinds of tinnitus). Many times, a tinnitus instrument—a combination hearing aid and masker—is more effective than a masker or a hearing aid alone.

Not everyone is helped by masking aids, however. For some, the added noise simply compounds the problem. After being fitted with masking units, which can cost hundreds of dollars, patients should be permitted to wear them for a trial period before deciding whether to buy them.

No drugs have been approved specifically for the treatment of tinnitus. Several drugs approved for other purposes have been

found to reduce tinnitus in some people, but usually with unacceptable side effects. Drugs continue to be tried out on an experimental basis.

Also being tried experimentally is electrical stimulation of the cochlea, a part of the inner ear, which has shown promise in suppressing tinnitus in some patients. If this technique continues to show promise, tinnitus sufferers of the future may be able to get relief from surgically implanted stimulators.

A number of other treatments do not claim to reduce the noise level tinnitus sufferers have to live with, but try to teach them to cope with the stress the perpetual noise causes. Some patients feel they have been helped by biofeedback, which teaches people to monitor and control body reactions such as muscle tension. Others have turned to cognitive-behavioral therapy, which teaches tinnitus patients to focus on what can be changed—their reaction to tinnitus—rather than on the tinnitus itself. Hypnosis and acupuncture are also reported to have helped a few people, although no scientific studies of either have been done.

And finally, many people are helped by being able to share their experiences with other sufferers. The American Tinnitus Association sponsors a network of self-help groups whose members provide support for one another, trade information about treatments and coping strategies that seem to work, and listen to talks by experts on various aspects of tinnitus. □

Sources of Further Information

American Academy of Otolaryngology-Head and Neck Surgery, 1101 Vermont Avenue, NW, Suite 302, Washington, DC 20005.
American Speech-Language-Hearing Association, 10801 Rockville Pike, Rockville, MD 20852.
American Tinnitus Association, P.O. Box 5, Portland, OR 97207.
Tinnitus Association of Canada, 23 Ellis Park Road, Toronto, Ont. M6S 2V4.

HEAD LICE

Jan Stewart, R.N.

Mrs. Jones received a phone call from school requesting that she pick up her child as soon as possible because the child was found to have head lice. She reacted with a mixture of disbelief, panic, and embarrassment, thinking: "What will people say? This is not possible! We are a clean middle-class family! How did this happen? What do I do?"

Several million cases of head lice (the technical name for the condition is "pediculosis capitis") occur annually in the United States, and parental, community, and school reactions are all much the same. Misconceptions are common. Whether one gets head lice has no relationship to race, sex, socioeconomic level, length of hair, or personal hygiene. Contrary to popular belief, lice do not fly (they lack wings), are not transmitted by animals, and are not carriers of disease. Although they are more prevalent in school-

age and younger children, adults are not immune.

What Are Lice?

Lice are primarily a nuisance; people with severe cases may develop swollen lymph glands in the neck or under the arms because of infection from scratching too much.

A louse (the singular of "lice") is a small (approximately $\frac{1}{16}$ inch) grayish brown insect that needs a human "host" to survive. Lice feed several times a day on blood—causing severe itching. They deposit their grayish white eggs, or nits, usually at the base of the hair shaft, close to the scalp; six to ten eggs are laid every 24 hours, usually at night. The nits take from seven to ten days to hatch. The life cycle occurs over and over until treatment is begun.

Head lice are transmitted through direct or indirect contact with human hair. The problem is more common in children be-

cause they come into close proximity with each other as they study and play in school or play outside of school. In school, children sometimes share lockers where their clothing touches, and they work in group activities where their heads are in close contact. Small children enjoy playing "dress-up"—exchanging articles of clothing such as hats, scarves, and coats. Older children, becoming interested in their personal appearance, may share combs, brushes, or hair accessories.

Prevention

There is no sure way to prevent lice infestation, but parents, the school, and the community can take precautions. Children should be told not to exchange headgear or share combs and brushes. Children who hang their coats on hooks at school should place hat, scarf, and gloves in a coat sleeve (this also helps prevent lost or misplaced garments). Parents can help prevent head lice from spreading by checking their children's hair if anyone in the family has been exposed to head lice and by notifying the school if the condition occurs. In addition, parents should know the school's policy and procedure for head lice.

Detection

A primary symptom of lice is persistent itching, causing continual scratching of the head. In checking for the presence of lice and/or nits, a tongue depressor may be of use in separating the hair strands near the scalp. (Parents who do not have one at home can use a spoon handle, an ice cream or

Popsicle stick, or a cotton swab, such as a Q-tip.) Though lice and their nits are frequently found at the back of the head and around the ears, they can turn up anywhere near the scalp. It may not always be possible to see the lice, as they scurry rapidly throughout the hair, but the nits will be evident.

To distinguish the nits from dandruff or hair spray residue, try to brush out the white particles. Dandruff or hair spray residue will brush out easily, but because of a sticky substance secreted by lice, nits adhere to the hair shaft. Flakes of dandruff or hair spray residue are irregular in size and shape, while the nit is small and either oval or teardrop shaped. If there is any doubt, a school nurse or other healthcare professional can assist in the identification.

Treatment

Head lice can be dealt with effectively at home with medicated shampoos, provided that the directions are followed carefully. A variety of these shampoos are sold, with and without prescription, at pharmacies. Check with a healthcare professional or the pharmacist for recommendations.

The treatment usually includes wetting the hair, using the prescribed amount of medicated shampoo, and working up a good lather. The shampoo should be left on for the period of time stated in the product instructions. The hair is then rinsed and towel-dried. Most shampoo containers include a fine-toothed comb for combing the nits out of the hair.

Removal of the nits can be very time-consuming but is essential. Begin with one area and work slowly, section by section, over the entire head. Since young children tend to get restless, provide something for them to do during the combing. Watching television, reading, coloring, or drawing may help. Take a break when fatigued. Then begin again, making sure that all areas have been combed.

Some parents have found that the application of a vinegar rinse to the hair seems to loosen nits, which should then be combed out. Another suggestion is to use transparent tape for stubborn areas. Wrap the tape around your fingers and slide it down the hair shaft. The nit should adhere to the tape.

All members of the infested individual's family should be checked, and if found to have lice, treated. The whole process—the shampooing of the infested person and the checking of other family members—should be repeated in seven to ten days because any nits missed will hatch in that period.

Treatment of the hair alone is not enough. Anything that might have come in contact with lice could be contaminated and must be cleaned. Washable clothing and bedding should be washed in hot water and placed in a dryer (ironing is an alternative, since heat kills adult lice and nits), and articles that are not washable should be dry-cleaned. Any items that cannot be washed or dry-cleaned (such as stuffed animals or decorative pillows) can be placed in a plastic bag and sealed for a minimum of 10 to 14 days. Wash combs and brushes in medicated shampoo, or clean and soak them in boiling water. In addition, vacuum mattresses, upholstery, and carpeting. There are sprays available that may be used on these items; again, be sure to follow the package directions.

When lice are suspected, early treatment reduces the chances of their spreading. The transmission of this nuisance can be kept at a minimum with early identification and appropriate treatment. □

FEEDING YOUR BABY
The First Year

Eleanor R. Williams, Ph.D.

First-time parents often have many concerns about feeding their baby. Should they breast-feed or bottle-feed? When should they begin solid foods, and should those foods be store-bought or homemade? Do babies need vitamin supplements? The ins and outs of feeding during the first year may seem daunting, but they really aren't when a few basic concepts are understood.

Fortunately, given the chance, normal infants can regulate the amount of food they take in so as to achieve normal growth and development. They will demand to eat only when they are hungry and continue eating until they are full. This simplifies the task of parents, who need only provide the proper food at each stage of infant development and learn how to tell when the baby has had enough. Every baby is different and to some extent will feed differently, but all parents will know their baby is being well fed if their pediatrician finds that the child's growth rate is normal.

Breast-Feeding

The first decision is whether to breast-feed or bottle-feed. Most nutritionists recommend breast-feeding for many reasons.

There are a number of advantages of breast milk for the baby:
- It contains many immune factors and other substances that protect infants against infections.
- It contains no bacteria that can cause illness.
- It is less likely to produce allergic reactions than other infant foods.
- It is nutritionally designed specifically for human infants. The fat and protein in breast milk are particularly easy for a baby's digestive system to absorb, and infants absorb a higher percentage of iron and zinc from breast milk than from formula.

Breast-feeding also has many advantages for the mother:
- It aids in more rapid return of the mother's uterus toward its pre-pregnancy size, by stimulating the release of a hormone called oxytocin.
- It results in more rapid loss of the extra fat a woman accumulates during pregnancy because calories from the mother's fat stores are used to produce milk.
- It promotes close psychological bonding between mother and baby.
- It is generally more convenient than preparing formula, since the milk is naturally clean, safe, and at the right temperature.

The chief drawback of breast-feeding is that a working mother generally must use a breast pump to express milk, which is later fed to the baby by bottle. Women who are dedicated to breast-feeding simply take this in stride.

The nursing experience is most likely to be enjoyable for both mother and baby if the mother is relaxed and confident of her ability to breast-feed. She will gain confidence more readily if she has competent guidance from women who have successfully breast-fed, as well as the strong emotional support of those individuals closest to her.

Most babies need to be fed every two hours at first, since breast milk is so easily digested. As the baby grows older and the stomach enlarges, more milk can be taken in at each feeding, and the time between feedings lengthens. After the first weeks, most babies nurse seven to ten times a day, but infants differ in how often they get hungry.

To nurse successfully, it is important to feed only breast milk at first, until the milk supply is well established. After about four to six weeks, a bottle can be offered occasionally. If bottles are offered too frequently, though, the mother's milk supply will diminish, and the baby may begin to prefer the bottle because there is less work to nursing from a bottle than from the breast. It is possible to partially wean a baby from the breast by nursing only in the morning and evening and having a babysitter give bottles during the day.

Bottle-Feeding

If a woman is unable to breast-feed or chooses not to, she need not feel guilty. Today's commercial infant formulas are nutritionally adequate and, if properly used, support normal infant growth and development.

The most popular formulas are made from cow's milk. Some infants, however, cannot tolerate these formulas. If the intolerance is to lactose, the sugar in cow's milk (and human milk), formulas based on soybean protein may be appropriate since they contain the sugars glucose or sucrose. Contrary to popular belief, though, infants who are allergic to the protein (rather than intolerant to the lactose) in cow's milk are likely to be allergic to the protein in soy milk as well. Such infants should be fed either breast milk or special low-allergy-producing formulas.

Formula can be purchased in several forms: ready-to-feed (available in both large cans and single-portion disposable bottles), concentrated liquid, and powdered. The last two forms must be properly diluted with water before feeding (generally, regular tap water is fine). To bottle-feed successfully, one should dilute the formula (if necessary) according to

the instructions supplied by the manufacturer and use sanitary methods during preparation, storage, and feeding. Overconcentrated formula decreases the infant's ability to excrete urinary waste products and leads to dehydration; overly diluted formula retards growth. To ensure that the formula is clean and safe, either sterilize the nipples and bottles by boiling them or prepare one bottle at a time after first scrubbing hands, bottles, and nipples with hot, soapy water.

When bottle-feeding, support the baby's head, neck, and back along your arm to give a sense of security. Holding a baby while feeding helps to establish a close psychological bond between parent and child. A relaxed parent who enjoys the feeding experience communicates that feeling to the baby.

At first, most babies need seven to eight bottles a day (each bottle containing 3 to 4 ounces of formula), but small babies will take less than large ones. As the baby gets older, the number of bottles needed declines while their size increases. By 10 to 12 months, most babies are taking between two and four bottles, each containing 6 to 8 ounces. Many babies continue to prefer at least one bottle a day for a while after one year of age, just for the pleasure of sucking. But the amount of milk obtained from either bottle or breast at one year should be equal only to a snack and not to a meal.

Whole Milk

Whole cow's milk can be introduced—as either a partial or a total replacement for breast milk or formula—any time after the baby is six months old. Babies younger than six months should not be fed whole milk because it is too concentrated; it also can cause intestinal bleeding in young infants. Skim milk and low-fat milk (1 or 2 percent fat) are inappropriate during a child's first two years because their low calorie level is apt to result in poor growth.

Supplements

Infants fed adequate amounts of breast milk or formula have all their nutritional requirements met for the first four to six months, with the possible exception of vitamin D in those breast-fed babies who are rarely exposed to sunlight (which converts a substance in the skin to vitamin D). These babies should receive a supplement of no more than 400 I.U. of vitamin D daily (excessive amounts of vitamin D can be toxic). In addition, breast-fed babies and bottle-fed babies whose formulas are made with nonfluoridated water may be given 0.25 milligrams of fluoride daily to guard against tooth decay.

Solid Foods

Solid food should be introduced when it appears that breast milk or formula no longer satisfies hunger—as indicated by increased demand for feeding—but only if the infant is physiologically ready for it. Between four and six months, infants become able to swallow nonliquid foods, to open their mouths to indicate a desire for food, and to turn their heads away to show they have had enough.

Iron-fortified infant cereal is usually the first solid food given to babies. By four to six months, babies have used up the iron stores they had at birth, and because both breast milk and plain formula are low in iron, they need a reliable iron source. (Formula-fed babies can be given iron-fortified formulas, but they should become accustomed to an alternative iron source such as baby cereal by 10 to 12 months.)

The baby's teeth begin to come in at about five months, and by six months most babies begin chewing motions and can hold food in their hands and bring it to their mouths. This is the time to begin introducing babies to cooked, pureed fruits and vegetables and mashed bananas. Teething biscuits, crackers, and dry toast should be given to encourage chewing and finger feeding.

By eight to ten months, control of the tongue and lips and ability to chew and swallow have improved. Soft, mashed vegetables can be substituted for pureed ones, and babies can now begin to eat raw, peeled, seeded fruit and bread, rice, and pasta. They can also begin to eat high-protein foods like hard-cooked, mashed egg yolks, cottage cheese or cheddar cheese, mashed dried beans, and pureed meat, poultry, and fish. Egg whites usually are not given in the baby's first year because of the possibility of an allergic reaction.

Parents should encourage self-feeding of foods babies can hold in their hands. Milk and fruit juice can be given by cup beginning at eight to ten months. The baby can manage the cup alone at about one year, with an occasional spill.

As the amount of solid food increases as the baby gets older, the amount of milk in the diet should gradually decrease. By one year, the baby should drink no more than two to three cups of milk a day, to make room for other needed foods.

When introducing new foods, choose a single-ingredient food and feed it to the child for a week before starting another food. This way, any food intolerance a baby may have can be spotted, as indicated by skin rashes, wheezing, coughing, vomiting, or diarrhea.

After the teeth begin coming in, the child can start eating cooked, pureed fruits and vegetables.

There are a few precautions about solid foods. Avoid foods that can cause choking, such as whole grapes, chunks of frankfurter or raw carrot, raisins, nuts, seeds, popcorn, and hard candy. Don't give fruit juice and other sweet liquids by bottle because sugar can pool around the baby's teeth, inviting serious tooth decay. Instead, give fruit juice by cup during meals. During the first year, avoid honey, even in baked foods, because it may contain botulism spores that can produce a lethal toxin in a young infant's intestines. In older children and adults, conditions in the intestines have changed so as to prevent toxin production.

Homemade or Store-Bought?

Homemade baby foods may be more flavorful, although commercial products are satisfactory. When making baby food at home, use a scrupulously clean technique throughout preparation and storage. Cook the foods and puree them in a blender, food processor, or baby food mill; add water or milk to obtain the desired consistency. Avoid adding salt or using salty canned vegetables or soups because a diet high in sodium (found in salt and some foods) may be a factor in inducing high blood pressure in later life. Babies get enough sodium from milk and other foods. Add neither sugar nor fat to baby foods. Babies' calorie needs are low, but their nutrient needs are high. Fat and sugar furnish calories but few, if any, nutrients.

Commercial baby food manufacturers no longer add salt and sugar to most of their products. However, desserts and some fruit mixtures often contain added sugar and fat, so plain fruits are better choices. Some vegetables contain starch fillers and flour, which dilute the vitamin and mineral content; again, plain vegetables are preferable. Choose plain meats and poultry rather than combination dinners in which the meat is greatly diluted with other ingredients. The ingredient present in the largest amount appears first on the label.

A Varied Diet

By 12 months, a baby should drink less milk than at earlier stages (as noted, no more than two to three cups a day). The baby should continue to eat iron-fortified cereal and a variety of family foods without added salt, sugar, or fat.

Each day the baby should be offered four servings (about one-fourth the size of an adult serving) of breads and grain products like cereal, rice, and pasta. There should be four servings (1 to 2 tablespoons each) of fruits and vegetables, including citrus fruits and dark green and orange vegetables, and two servings (½ ounce each) of meat, poultry, fish, eggs, cheese, dried beans, or peanut butter. □

Varicose veins, which occur almost exclusively in the legs, are veins that have swelled, or dilated, and no longer function properly. One out of four Americans—and 50 percent of women over 40—have problems with leg veins, ranging from tiny, threadlike "spider" veins to large, ropelike "true" varicose veins. These conditions tend to be hereditary, and they are ten times more common in women than in men.

The symptoms of varicose veins are generally not incapacitating: early on, feelings of tiredness or heaviness in the legs, cramping pain, and mild swelling are common. In the more advanced stages, inflammation or infections of the skin, lower leg swelling, discoloration, and a type of infection beneath the skin called cellulitis are frequent. Because of constant increased venous pressure at the ankle, the skin and tissues there can break down and become ulcerated, and the veins themselves can break down and bleed.

What Causes Them?

Veins are an essential component of the circulatory system. As blood pumped out by the heart circulates through the body, it carries nutrients and oxygen through the arteries until all the cells of the body have been reached. Then the blood returns to the heart through the veins. The veins also regulate body temperature and store extra reserves of blood. Blood moves through the arteries by the force of the heart's pumping action. Then several forces work (against gravity in much of the body) to move it through the veins. The most important is the residual force of the heart's pumping; also at work are the negative pressures created in the chest during inhalation, which draw blood toward the heart, and the contraction of the muscles in the legs, or "muscle pump."

There are three groups of veins in the legs: superficial, which lie close to the leg surface; deep, which are embedded within the legs; and communicating, which connect the two. Each time the muscles in the legs contract, they squeeze the veins, making blood flow in the proper direction from the superficial through the connecting into the deep veins and then toward the heart.

Most veins in the lower body have one-way valves to keep the blood moving in the right direction. But if a valve fails to close completely, some of the blood on its way toward the heart spills backward. When this happens, the segment of vein now holding more than its share of blood swells, causing a subsequent failure of the valves below. This system of valves is extremely important. When it fails, whether in the deep, communicating, or superficial veins, or in all three, true varicose veins develop in the superficial veins.

Spider veins, which are sometimes mistakenly referred to as "broken blood vessels" or "broken capillaries," are smaller veins that have become dilated, usually because of hormonal imbalances. They range in color from blue to red and tend to appear in groups on the outsides of the thighs, the insides of the knees, or around the ankles. Spider veins—which have no valves—can appear alone or in conjunction with true varicose veins.

Who Gets Them?

Heredity plays an important role; if one parent had varicose veins, chances are ten to one that the children will have them as adults. Certain other factors can trigger or accelerate the appearance of varicose veins. Pregnancy is one

WHAT TO DO ABOUT VARICOSE VEINS

Luis Navarro, M.D.

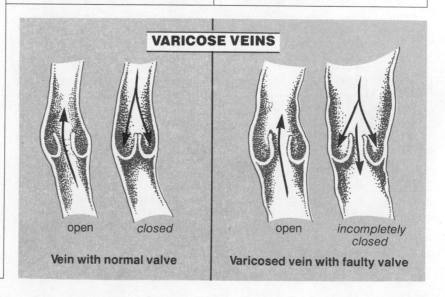

VARICOSE VEINS

open   closed

Vein with normal valve

open   incompletely closed

Varicosed vein with faulty valve

such factor. The weight of the uterus puts a great deal of pressure on the large veins. Also, pregnant women have more blood traveling through their veins and higher levels of female hormones in the blood. It is known that female hormones have an effect on the development of varicose veins—although how is not completely understood; varicose veins and spider veins often appear as early as the second week of pregnancy. Because birth control pills contain female hormones that literally trick the body into thinking it is pregnant, they, too, can trigger varicose veins.

Other factors implicated in varicose veins are tight-fitting garments such as girdles and garters, occupations that require standing or sitting in one spot for long periods of time, obesity, and chronic constipation.

Diagnosis and Treatment

Not only are varicose veins easy to see, but physicians can readily pinpoint the faulty valves by simple leg manipulations that allow them to observe the filling of the veins. Other tests and procedures involving ultrasound and X rays are available, but they are rarely found to be necessary.

For people in poor health, pregnant women, or those who prefer not to undertake more aggressive measures, conservative treatments exist. These include support stockings and elastic bandages, which alleviate some of the more bothersome symptoms, such as swelling, aching, and cramping, and also prevent worsening of the condition.

For people in good health who want a cure and good cosmetic results, more aggressive treatments are available that close up or remove the varicose veins in order to direct the blood flow to deeper veins. The treatments vary only in the method by which the veins are taken out of service. In many instances, treatment involves a combination of different methods.

To ensure optimum cosmetic re-sults with minimum discomfort, patients should seek out physicians with considerable expertise in treating varicose veins. Also, the earlier the treatment, the better the results.

Treatment will not prevent the future development of new varicose veins, particularly in people predisposed to the condition. However, treatment may eliminate all the visible varicose veins, and it takes years for new ones to develop.

Sclerotherapy. This nonsurgical method is effective for all spider veins and up to 90 percent of true varicose veins. It involves the injection of a chemical compound to irritate the inner lining of the veins so that the veins close down completely and eventually disappear. This 50-year-old procedure has been refined considerably in recent years. Hair-thin needles and milder chemicals are now used, as well as special lenses to magnify the area that is being worked on. Each office visit for sclerotherapy may involve multiple injections, depending on the severity of the condition. Immediately following injection, the affected area is wrapped with an elastic bandage for two to six hours in order to compress the injected veins.

There are few side effects associated with sclerotherapy. About 20 percent of those undergoing the procedure experience slight soreness or bruising in the injected areas. These symptoms disappear rapidly. In rare instances, allergic reactions may occur, which can be alleviated in minutes with an ordinary antihistamine.

Although sclerotherapy requires no special attention between office visits, walking (which activates the muscle pump and improves circulation) has been shown to improve its success. Support stockings may be recommended for one to three weeks. If the affected area is to be exposed to sunlight, a sunscreen that has a Sun Protection Factor (SPF) of 15 or higher should be used.

Surgery. In about 10 percent of cases of true varicose veins, when the long saphenous vein that runs along the middle of the leg from the groin to the ankle is affected, surgery is the treatment of choice. While sclerotherapy may afford good results, it will not prevent the saphenous vein from ultimately reopening in a process called recanalization. In European studies, 80 percent of patients treated with sclerotherapy alone for varicosities in their long saphenous veins experienced recanalization within five years.

The surgical procedure used is known as ligation and stripping. Developed at the turn of the century, it has been streamlined and simplified in recent years. Two incisions are made: a half-inch-long cut at the ankle, where the saphenous vein ends, and a one-inch-long cut above the bikini line at the groin, where the saphenous vein starts. An instrument called a stripper is inserted to remove the vein in its entirety. The two incisions are then closed without stitches.

The entire procedure usually takes no more than half an hour, and patients can usually return home just two hours after the surgery. While patients do experience some postsurgical bruising, they are advised to walk several miles on the day following surgery, to resume normal activities within 24 hours, and to return to work within one to three days. For the best cosmetic results, any leftover branches or any spider veins may be treated with sclerotherapy.

Laser Therapy. This nonsurgical method is effective but limited to the tiniest of spider veins—those 1/32nd of an inch, usually located on the ankles. (They may also occur on the face.) The laser, a light of uniform wavelength and great energy, is trained on the vein. The energy passes through the skin and is absorbed by the vein's red blood cells, which heat up quickly and cauterize the walls of the vein, thus sealing it off. □

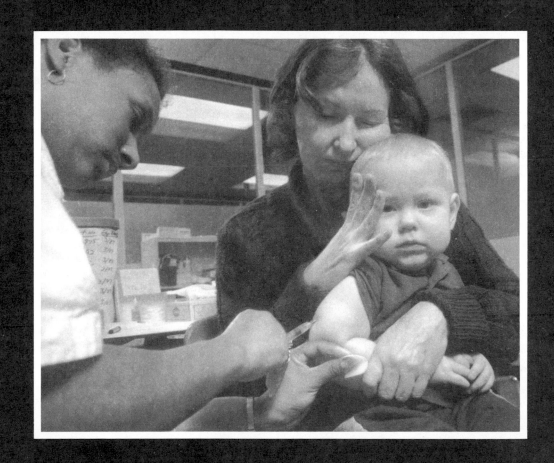

HEALTH AND
MEDICAL NEWS

AGING AND THE AGED

CPR Ineffective in the Elderly • Putting Sleep Problems in Perspective • New Drug for Parkinson's Disease

CPR and the Elderly

Cardiopulmonary resuscitation (CPR) has been found to be only rarely effective in older people—a discovery that may influence decisions made by the aged and their families about future medical care.

CPR was developed in the early 1960s as a way to attempt to revive someone who had either stopped breathing or suffered a heart malfunction that caused insufficient blood to be pumped to the body's vital organs, including the brain. It is an emergency treatment, until further medical help can be obtained and the patient hospitalized. Basic CPR consists of mouth-to-mouth breathing and compressing the chest to make the heart pump oxygen-rich blood to the rest of the body. Advanced cardiac life support (ACLS)—employed in hospitals and by paramedics—consists of basic CPR plus the use of drugs and other techniques to get the heart and/or lungs to function again.

Outcome in Older People. A 1989 study by doctors in Boston looked at the number of elderly people who survived at least long enough to leave the hospital after having required CPR. Specifically, the study looked at people aged 70 and over who suffered cardiopulmonary arrests, both witnessed and unwitnessed; in some cases the victims were already in a hospital, and in other cases they were not. The study found that of 244 patients who suffered a cardiopulmonary arrest while out of the hospital, 224 died immediately, 18 died after being brought to the hospital, and only 2 survived long enough to leave the hospital. Of the 259 people who suffered a cardiopulmonary arrest while in the hospital, 167 died immediately, 75 died later in the hospital, and 17 survived to hospital discharge. Of the total of 19 patients who ultimately left the hospital, only 8 returned home; 5 went to a rehabilitation hospital, and 6 went to either a nursing home or a chronic-care hospital.

The study showed that the type of person most likely to survive was one who was not suffering from dementia and was able to function in the community prior to the cardiopulmonary arrest and who had a witnessed arrest during which at least one vital sign (blood pressure or pulse or breathing) was maintained.

Computers can be a lifeline for older people, keeping them linked to the outside world. Here, a computer-literacy program designed for the elderly offers hands-on instruction.

Two other important factors were responding within five minutes to CPR and regaining consciousness promptly. The type of person witnessing the cardiopulmonary arrest—doctor, family member, friend—was not found to be significant.

These findings suggest that the maximum probability of surviving and leaving the hospital after an in-hospital cardiopulmonary arrest is less than 10 percent; the chances of leaving the hospital after an out-of-hospital arrest are less than 1 percent. These survival rates are considerably lower than those for younger people.

There may be several reasons for the low rates. First, as one ages, there is a greater likelihood of having chronic or acute diseases that can make the individual less able to withstand the extreme stress on the body from cardiopulmonary arrest. Most organ systems decline with age, also tending to make one less able to withstand such an attack. Last, CPR was initially developed for people who had witnessed arrests and a particular type of irregular heartbeat. Most elderly people who suffer a cardiopulmonary arrest do not have this particular set of circumstances.

Implications. The findings about CPR's relative ineffectiveness in the elderly have important implications for older people and their families as they ponder what are often referred to as advanced directives. These are a person's instructions, in the form of legal documents, about how medical care should be carried out in the event that the individual can no longer speak for himself or herself. The instructions can include whether the person should be resuscitated or not, whether the individual should be put on life-support systems or kidney dialysis, and even whether tube feeding should be used if the person can no longer take in adequate food and water. Knowing the facts about the poor outcome of CPR in the elderly may make a do-not-resuscitate decision less difficult.

Sleep and Aging

Sleep disturbances, a common complaint of older people, are now recognized as a natural and irreversible part of aging—and in most cases, do not represent a serious medical problem. Technological improvements have allowed researchers to better monitor and evaluate sleep patterns and enabled them to better understand some of the common complaints that older people have. Based on this new knowledge, physicians are able to relieve their patients' anxieties about their sleep problems.

A summary was recently published on the sleep disturbances and disorders of aging. Sleep was described using three different dimensions: sleep patterns, sleep structure, and evaluative responses about sleep. Sleep patterns refer to the amount and timing of sleep within a 24-hour period: total sleep time, when and where sleep episodes (including naps) occur, how long sleep episodes last, how long it takes to fall asleep. Sleep structure refers to the stages of sleep, or how deeply one is asleep. Evaluative responses are subjective comments people make about the quality of their sleep.

Sleep patterns were found to change with age. The total time spent sleeping and trying to sleep seems to remain about the same on the average; however, older people spend more time napping compared with younger people. Older people also tend to go to bed earlier and get up earlier than younger people. It takes more time for people over the age of 60 to fall asleep—on average, 30 minutes or more—with older women requiring more time than older men. And older people wake up more during the night. The majority of people over the age of 60 experience awakenings of 30 minutes or more, and these episodes may occur a number of times each night.

Sleep stages also undergo some change with age. There are various stages of sleep, from being awake to what is called REM (rapid eye movement) sleep, which is the deepest sleep. In older people there are marked reductions in the intermediate stages of sleep, and REM episodes are frequently shorter, with more interruptions. Older people's evaluative responses about sleep reflect these changes: they recognize that it takes them longer to fall asleep and that they awaken more often.

These sleep changes reflect an overall alteration in the body's biologic clock, or daily sleep-wake cycle—technically called the circadian rhythm. Sleep is less efficient with increasing age. However, recent research shows that there is no decline in people's overall functioning because of this inefficiency. Studies of older individuals who complain of sleep deprivation do not show the decrease in reaction time that younger people experience when they have been deprived of sleep. For most older people, the use of drugs that artificially induce sleep should be unnecessary.

It is important to understand that while sleep disturbances are common, true sleep disorders, which require specific medical treatment, are much less common. Sleep disorders are often characterized not simply by noticeable changes in sleep patterns. Patients with sleep disorders complain of feeling worse in the morning than in the evening and of almost never feeling rested, and their life-style and ability to perform routine activities are impaired.

New Drug for Neurologic Disorders

A drug called deprenyl has recently shown promise in the early treatment of both Parkinson's disease and Alzheimer's disease. Deprenyl (chemical name, selegiline; brand name, Eldepryl) was approved for general use in the United States in 1989 and in Canada in early 1990.

Parkinson's Disease. A team of investigators from medical centers around the United States and Canada reported in late 1989 that deprenyl could slow the progression of Parkinson's disease—something no other drug had ever been shown to do. Parkinson's disease is a progressively disabling illness in which a particular type of cell in the brain is destroyed. This results in shakiness, an inability to initiate movement (feeling frozen), and sometimes a deterioration of mental ability. In the past, treatment has consisted of administering the drug levodopa (commonly called L-dopa), which is converted in the body into dopamine. Dopamine is an important chemical secreted by the area of the brain affected in Parkinson's. However, L-dopa has side effects and should not be used until the disease progresses to the point of interfering significantly with the patient's ability to function.

In the recent study, deprenyl was used in the early stages of Parkinson's disease, before L-dopa was needed, in an attempt to see whether the progression of the disease could be slowed. The scientists found that deprenyl delayed the need for L-dopa by almost a year and enabled patients to continue full-time employment longer. The drug also alleviated some symptoms. The adverse effects of deprenyl were minimal, although as with any new drug, it is not yet known whether there might be long-term problems.

Alzheimer's Disease. Deprenyl has also been used experimentally in patients with Alzheimer's disease—in an attempt to improve memory and physical functioning, as well as to control some of the behavior problems associated with this devastating illness. This research is still in an early stage, and further studies are needed to establish the potential use of deprenyl in treating Alzheimer's.

PAUL R. KATZ, M.D.
IRIS F. BOETTCHER, M.D.

AIDS

Pace of Epidemic's Growth • New Drugs • Update on Preventive Measures • AIDS Orphans • Meeting Costs of Care and Research

Growing Numbers

In mid-1989 the United States passed the 100,000 mark for total cases of AIDS reported to the U.S. Centers for Disease Control. Although the number of new cases rose just 9 percent in 1989—the smallest annual increase since the CDC began reporting AIDS

in 1981—so far there is no convincing evidence that the epidemic is abating. New AIDS cases ascribed to heterosexual contact jumped 27 percent in 1989, to more than 1,500. While still found mainly in major urban areas, AIDS is fast making inroads elsewhere; the number of cases in U.S. towns of fewer than 500,000 inhabitants rose 33 percent in 1989, to over 6,500. By early 1990 the total number of cases exceeded 120,000, and the disease had killed over 72,000 people. Canada by then had well over 3,000 cases, with more than 2,000 deaths.

Some recent studies suggested that CDC figures for the present number of AIDS cases (and, hence, the projections of future numbers) may be too low. According to a University of Chicago study, CDC data reflect underreporting of the disease among groups who can afford private medical care. As with other socially unpopular diseases, reporting tends to be incomplete for people given only private care and fairly complete for those receiving public care. A U.S. General Accounting Office study blamed much of the presumed undercount on the rather narrow definition of AIDS used by the CDC. According to this study, the original CDC projections of between 185,000 and 320,000 cumulative cases through 1991 should be raised to between 300,000 and 480,000 cases, an increase of one-third or more. To complicate matters, the CDC in early 1990 was reportedly considering, on the basis of new data, decreasing its projections.

Also problematic are official estimates for the total number of people infected with the human immunodeficiency virus, or HIV, the virus that causes AIDS. A 1989 study from California indicated that standard tests missed HIV infection in about 20 percent of infected people for up to three years after their infection had been shown by a much more sensitive test. A previous study had found a patient who had had HIV infection for 42 months without making detectable antibodies to the virus. (The standard blood tests detect not the virus itself but antibodies that the body produces to fight the virus.) Other research, however, indicated that all or almost all patients who were studied produced antibodies to HIV within six months of acquiring the infection. Therefore, the incidence of "silent" HIV infection—an infection not detectable by standard tests—remains unclear.

Currently not only is the number of new cases of AIDS rising, but, because of advances in treatment, so is the length of time people survive with the disease. The proportion of AIDS patients who survive at least 18 months after being diagnosed has increased from approximately one-third several years ago to almost two-thirds. As a result, the total number of people alive who have AIDS, and need medical care, is growing rapidly.

Drug Treatment

The U.S. Food and Drug Administration authorized the marketing of new drugs for treating various diseases that afflict people with AIDS. Pentamidine, a drug that had been previously approved in injectable form for treatment of *Pneumocystis carinii* pneumonia, was approved for use as an inhaled aerosol medication, sold under the brand name NebuPent. Authorization for marketing came in June 1989, just a few months after the aerosol had been approved for wide distribution as an experimental drug. Also in June the FDA approved for marketing the drug ganciclovir (Cytovene) to treat a blinding eye infection that AIDS patients often develop from infection with cytomegalovirus; this medication also had been made widely available on an experimental basis earlier in the year. The FDA in January 1990 approved the drug fluconazole (Difluan) to treat serious fungal infections, including two that afflict many AIDS patients: candidiasis, which can cause sores in the mouth and throat, and cryptococcal meningitis, an inflammation of the brain and nervous system.

In August 1989 researchers reported that the drug zidovudine (sold as Retrovir and formerly known as AZT) could delay the onset of AIDS in people who had no symptoms but were infected with HIV. This prompted the FDA in March 1990 to approve the use of zidovudine in infected adults without symptoms. It had been approved only for those showing enough symptoms to be diagnosed with AIDS.

Among other developments, the FDA in September 1989 allowed wider distribution of the experimental medication dideoxyinosine (DDI), which, like zidovudine, attacks HIV directly. Considerable controversy was generated by unauthorized research on the effectiveness against AIDS of "compound Q" (trichosanthin), an experimental drug derived from a Chinese cucumber root. The FDA ordered a halt to the study in August 1989 but later, in March 1990, authorized the testing program to continue, in revised form.

HIV Research

Vaccine Progress. Some progress in vaccine development was noted in 1989. A vaccine from MicroGeneSys was found to be safe when tried in humans. Designed to prevent immunized individuals from becoming infected with HIV, it produced some antibodies of the desired type, but much more testing is required before its value will be known.

A group associated with Dr. Jonas Salk, of polio vaccine fame, has produced a vaccine to prevent the development of the disease in people already infected with HIV. Early tests in animals were encouraging, and preliminary testing in humans is under way.

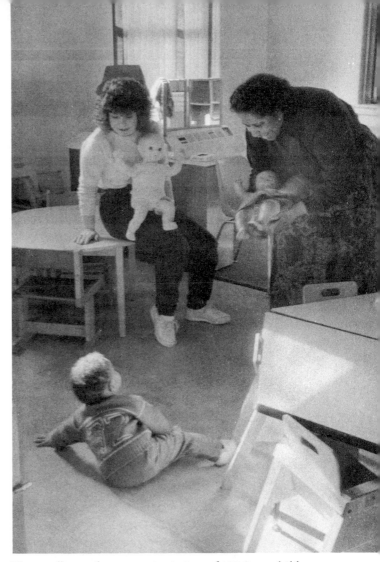

The smallest and most tragic victims of AIDS are children who not only suffer from the disease but often become orphaned as well. Here, a nurse and a social worker play with a stricken child whose mother passed on the virus during her pregnancy.

Infection of Cells. A recent study may have resolved a long-standing puzzle. If, as scientists believe, AIDS is due to infection by HIV, why did the virus appear to infect only 1 in 10,000 to 1 in 100,000 of the critical white blood cells called T4 lymphocytes? These cells, known to be a major target of the virus, play a key role in various immune system processes. Such a rate of infection did not seem to be enough to explain the magnitude of the effects of the disease. A new technique has now shown that more than 1 in 100 T4 cells is infected in a person with AIDS. In many of the cells the virus is inactive and is undetectable by the older techniques. An additional reason why older techniques found a relatively low proportion of cells infected may be that infected cells are destroyed soon after the virus becomes active.

Preventive Measures

Blood Safety. Despite the concern created by research suggesting that current standard tests may not detect HIV in all infected people, a 1989 study showed that the blood used in the United States for transfusions and other health-related purposes is 99.9 percent safe. This is a result of a two-step process. In the first and probably most important step, people likely to be infected are carefully screened out before they are allowed to donate blood. The second step consists in the screening of the donated blood in the laboratory.

Effectiveness of Condoms. A study by the FDA found that particles the size of the AIDS virus could leak through a significant proportion of off-the-shelf latex condoms that were tested. This meant that the protection provided by the condoms against HIV transmission was imperfect, although it was much better than not using condoms. If, as some researchers suspect, AIDS is transmitted mostly by HIV-infected cells rather than by the free virus (that is, the virus

not in cells), even the least adequate of the tested condoms would still be far better than none. The same general conclusions were drawn about the latex gloves used by researchers and healthcare workers: some leakage occurred during manipulation, but they still protected better than no gloves.

Needle-Exchange Programs. One of the most controversial approaches to fighting the spread of AIDS has been getting drug addicts to exchange their contaminated needles and syringes for clean ones. Intravenous drug users, who often share needles and syringes, account for about 25 percent of new AIDS cases.

Clean needles and syringes are not by themselves enough to block HIV transmission. Addicts need all of their paraphernalia ("works") to be clean, including the water, cottons, and cookers they use, and they need protection when they have sex. Therefore, in addition to needles and syringes, needle-exchange programs increasingly offer bleach to sterilize water and other works, along with clean cotton and condoms, as well as information about how to avoid spreading

Protesters demonstrate on Wall Street against the high price of the anti-AIDS drug zidovudine, also called AZT. Its manufacturer, Burroughs Wellcome, later announced a 20 percent cut in price.

the disease. Information alone, without assistance in the form of clean works, may not be well accepted or well used.

Opponents of needle-exchange programs voice concern that such programs will be interpreted as community support for illegal activity. Advocates of the programs argue that this is no more true than making condoms available in drug stores implies that society supports extramarital sexual relationships: it implies only a recognition that unhealthy behavior will occur and that making protection available is important for the public's health.

Are exchange programs effective? Most of the limited evidence available so far is positive. Where programs are in operation, sharing of works among the participants has declined somewhat, and there is even some suggestive preliminary evidence that transmission of HIV through needle sharing may have declined as well.

Children Orphaned by AIDS

The AIDS epidemic has left increasing numbers of children orphans, as AIDS or drugs take the lives of parents or render them unable to care for their sons and daughters. It has been estimated that in New York City alone between 50,000 and 100,000 of this generation's children have lost, or will lose, at least one parent to AIDS. The foster care system in the United States is unlikely to be able to handle the growing number of orphaned children, who are often from ethnic minorities and thus may be more difficult to find adoptive parents for. The situation is further complicated by the fact that many potential foster families do not want to care for babies infected with HIV by their mothers or babies damaged before birth by exposure to illegal drugs. If relatives cannot or will not take care of those children, their futures appear bleak.

The problem of orphaned babies is highest in areas of high illegal drug use, since women usually acquire HIV infection because of drugs. In many cases they are intravenous drug users themselves, or they have sex with men who have become infected with HIV through intravenous drug use. Many other women acquire the infection because they are addicted to drugs like crack (a smokable form of cocaine) that are not taken intravenously; in order to obtain the money to pay for their addiction, they take up prostitution and get infected through sex. Also, some people prefer to inject cocaine rather than use crack, and those who inject cocaine may be at especially high risk for acquiring AIDS. A study in California showed that blacks, many of whom preferred to inject cocaine rather than heroin or other intravenous drugs, had a much higher rate of HIV infection than did Hispanics

or whites. Apparently, cocaine addicts tended to shoot more frequently than heroin users and were more likely to share their needles and other drug paraphernalia.

Costs and Funding

Care. People with AIDS can be a significant financial burden to their families and to society, and the costs of caring for AIDS patients are rising rapidly. Zidovudine and pentamidine alone can cost thousands of dollars a year and must be taken for life. If people with AIDS or their families "spend down" their financial reserves enough to qualify for Medicaid, the cost of care is shared by federal and state governments. After being disabled for a year, AIDS patients generally qualify for federal Social Security disability payments and for Medicare. Thus, AIDS will potentially cost both major governmental medical care reimbursement programs an enormous amount, and it already has created a heavy load on medical services in areas with many AIDS cases. The manufacturer of zidovudine, Burroughs Wellcome, yielded to public pressure in September 1989 and reduced the price of the drug by 20 percent, claiming that it wanted to contribute to a reduction in the cost of treatment for AIDS.

Research and Prevention. In the United States, AIDS now receives more federal funds for research and prevention than any other disease. In the 1990 fiscal year (beginning October 1, 1989), federal funding for AIDS research and public health programs was set at about $1.6 billion, compared to $1.5 billion for cancer, with heart disease, which kills more people in the United States each year than either of the other two, well behind. No other disease or disease group is close. Despite these figures, some AIDS activists have remained critical of the federal government for not doing enough to fight AIDS. It is not clear, however, that more money could be spent wisely, because it takes time to develop the research and educational infrastructure needed to do good work, and in many areas progress depends on finding answers to prior problems that are as yet unresolved. Research takes time, and for the results of scientists' research to be published, they must go through the necessary, but somewhat time-consuming, process of review by other researchers.

Also, many doctors and scientists are concerned that the intense focus on AIDS is jeopardizing progress in research and prevention in other areas. Despite the importance of AIDS, it is not the only major health problem in the United States.

See also the Health and Medical News article WORLD HEALTH NEWS.

JAMES F. JEKEL, M.D., M.P.H.

One drink affects a woman more than a man, researchers in the United States and Italy reported. The reason: women produce smaller amounts of the protective stomach enzyme dehydrogenase, which breaks down alcohol.

ALCOHOLISM

Women Found Less Able to Digest Alcohol • New Doubts That Light Drinking Protects Against Heart Disease • Treatment Options for Alcoholics

Women's Stomachs Digest Less Alcohol

It is well known that women get drunk faster than men. A study published in early 1990 showed that a major reason may be that women's stomachs are less able to neutralize alcohol. A protective enzyme in the stomach called alcohol dehydrogenase generally metabolizes, or breaks down, some alcohol before it enters the bloodstream. But the researchers found that women produce less of this enzyme than men, allowing about 30 percent more alcohol to go directly into their blood and subsequently to their brains. As a result, one drink can have a greater effect on a woman than on a man of comparable size.

Heavy drinking among both men and women was found to reduce the amount of the enzyme produced in the stomach. Male alcoholics metabolized alcohol in the stomach much less efficiently than nonalcoholic men, and female alcoholics appeared to digest no alcohol at all in the stomach. Alcohol in the blood-stream is eventually broken down by the liver, but a constant flow of alcohol through the liver will damage it. Thus, the new findings on the role of the stomach enzyme may help explain why alcoholic women develop liver disease more quickly than alcoholic men.

Can Alcohol Help Prevent Heart Disease?

A recent British study suggested that having a drink or two a day may not—as was previously widely believed—add years to your life. Some research had indicated that people who consume one or two alcohol-containing drinks daily live longer than either teeto-talers or individuals having more than two drinks a day. It was thought that light drinking somehow offered protection against disease of the heart or of the arteries supplying it with blood. Alcohol, for example, was found to raise levels in the blood of so-called high-density lipoprotein (HDL) cholesterol, a "good" form of cholesterol that helps remove excess cholesterol from the blood. The picture was subsequently clouded, however, when it was discovered that alcohol actually increases the level of a type of HDL cholesterol that is not protective to the heart.

The British study, which dealt just with men, found that the relationship between light drinking and a longer life held true only for those who had a cardiac condition when the study began. The researchers suggested that the link between longer life and light drinking seen in previous studies for all people actually reflected a common tendency to reduce or give up drinking when one's health deteriorates. The previous research had not taken into account the prior drinking behavior of the individuals studied. Thus, teetotalers may have shown a higher death rate than light drinkers because many teetotalers were people with heart or other disease who had stopped drinking. The British study found little or no correspondence between the death rate of healthy men—those without underlying heart disease—and alcohol consumption.

AIDS and Alcohol

Some research has indicated that at least in some groups alcohol abuse and the drinking of alcohol during sexual activity may be associated with an increased risk of AIDS. A new study, published in late 1989, suggests that even a single bout of drinking may raise the body's susceptibility to infection with the AIDS virus. The researchers, who worked with blood samples taken from healthy humans, found that drinking 0.7 to 3.1 liters (between 24 ounces and a little over 3 quarts) of beer or its equivalent seemed to cause increased reproduction of the virus in certain types of blood cells. The researchers also found evidence that the alcohol interfered with the normal functions of both helper and suppressor T cells, white blood cells that play an important role in the immune system. The effects of alcohol on T cells lasted for several days after the drinking took place.

Drinking by Athletes

Carbohydrate loading—consuming large amounts of foods rich in complex carbohydrates before a sports event—has become fashionable among endurance athletes as a means to improve performance. However, some athletes mistakenly include beer as part of their pregame meal. Not only is alcohol a poor carbohydrate source (there are 13 grams of carbohydrates in 12 ounces of regular beer, compared to about 40 grams in 12 ounces of orange juice or of a soft drink like cola), it leads to dehydration and acts as a depressant. Because alcohol inhibits the production of a hormone that slows the body's elimination of water, it can cause water loss through urination even in dehydrated athletes. Significant fluid losses will most likely result in impaired athletic performance.

The depressant effects of alcohol can be downright hazardous for athletes. Consuming alcoholic beverages just before competing will slow reaction times and impair coordination, reflexes, and judgment, leaving the athlete susceptible to injury.

Use of alcoholic beverages during winter competi-

tions has a special danger. Because alcohol stimulates blood flow to the skin, considerable heat loss may occur, leading to a dangerously lowered body temperature. Such blood flow produces a deceptive feeling of warmth, which may prevent a person from trying to get warm. For all of the above reasons, athletes should avoid using alcohol for 24 hours prior to any athletic event and drink plenty of nonalcoholic beverages.

Older Alcoholics

It is estimated that in the United States approximately 5 percent of men and 1 percent of women over the age of 60 abuse alcohol. However, the magnitude of the problems faced by the older alcoholic is only now beginning to be recognized. Researchers at the Mayo Clinic in Rochester, Minn., recently reported on their experience in treating, over a 12-year period, more than 200 middle-class alcoholics of age 65 or above—approximately 10 percent of the admissions to their treatment center. These older alcoholics had more medical problems, particularly liver, lung, neurological, and ulcer disease, than would be expected in a comparable nonalcoholic group.

The researchers checked on the alcoholics' fate 2 to 11 years after treatment. It was found that 32 percent of the patients had died. Almost half of these deaths were attributable to alcoholism. The researchers divided the patients into two distinct groups: early-onset drinkers who developed degenerative medical complications (such individuals generally account for about two-thirds of older alcoholics) and late-onset drinkers who increased consumption in response to a significant life stress. The persons with late-onset alcoholism appeared to fare better after treatment. For the patients as a whole, in contrast to earlier studies, the treatment outcome was poor, with only 25 percent of the alcoholics remaining abstinent.

Inpatient Versus Outpatient Treatment

Researchers have been investigating the need for extended hospitalization in treating alcoholism. Traditionally, alcoholics have been hospitalized for up to several months in order to be rehabilitated after going through inpatient treatment for detoxification (the "drying out" period). But it has been observed that many alcoholics do just as well with shorter hospital stays for rehabilitation, especially when the disease is recognized at an early stage. Major studies of alternative treatment plans, such as keeping patients in the hospital for only a few weeks, are under way. In addition, intensive outpatient programs have been developed to rehabilitate alcoholics who are able to function in school or the workplace.

A recent study called into question the notion that inpatient detoxification is essential. Low-income, alcoholic male veterans living in the Philadelphia area who requested detoxification were randomly assigned to either inpatient or outpatient detoxification programs. Both the inpatient and outpatient groups were assessed six months after detoxification, and no measurable differences were found between them in outcome of treatment. The researchers concluded that outpatient detoxification was as safe and effective as inpatient treatment, which, they noted, had the disadvantage of costing ten times as much or more. The results of the study, however, need to be confirmed by studies of other groups of alcoholics before this treatment becomes the standard for detoxification.

The study participants who were detoxified as outpatients did not show severe withdrawal symptoms—such as seizures or delirium tremens, a condition characterized by tremors, anxiety, and mental confusion. The possibility that such problems requiring hospitalization may develop, however, remains a concern. Data from other research, on both rats and humans, suggest that the severity of the withdrawal symptoms may be related to the number of previous detoxifications, rather than to either the amount of alcohol consumed or the length of time a person has been actively drinking.

Legal Rights of Fetuses

Increasingly, public attention has focused on the consequences of alcohol and drug abuse by pregnant women and on the legal rights of pregnant women and their fetuses. In the United States the fetus is gaining more protection under the law, with rights to both health and welfare. The unborn child now has the right in some states to sue for personal injuries, inherit property, and be protected by criminal laws. Consequently, the number of monetary awards for prenatal injuries is increasing. Moreover, women who abuse drugs or alcohol during or after pregnancy have, in a growing number of cases, lost custody of their unborn or newborn children to the courts.

With greater awareness and knowledge on the part of doctors, infants with problems relating to alcohol and drug abuse are being identified earlier. In Los Angeles, the number of babies with such problems rose more than tenfold between 1982 and 1985. The cost of treating an affected infant is astounding, ranging from $28,000 in the case of a newborn with so-called narcotic withdrawal syndrome to $400,000 for lifetime care of a baby affected with fetal alcohol syndrome, infant abnormalities linked to maternal alcohol consumption.

See also the feature article Is Your Child on Drugs or Alcohol?
T. M. Worner, M.D.

BIOETHICS

Supreme Court Rules on Abortion • Right-to-Die Cases • Frozen Embryos—Children or Property?

Constraints on Abortion Rights

In a decision that will have a profound effect on the ongoing abortion debate in the United States, the U.S. Supreme Court in July 1989 narrowed the legal significance of *Roe* v. *Wade*, the landmark 1973 case that established a woman's right to abortion. In *Webster* v. *Reproductive Health Services*, a 5-4 majority upheld the constitutionality of a Missouri law that both restricts the availability of abortions funded with public money and requires doctors to test for fetal viability before performing abortions in the 20th week of pregnancy or later.

The *Webster* ruling could encourage state legislators to introduce new rules limiting access to abortion by denying state funds to public hospitals. Thus, in coming years the abortion battle might well be fought on many fronts, in numerous state legislatures. And the stakes will be high: the Missouri law, for example, prohibits doctors from using public funds when performing or assisting in abortions unless the life of the mother is in danger. Since it is virtually impossible for a healthcare facility to function without receiving some state money, nearly all of a state's medical institutions would be affected.

More difficult to assess are the implications of the Missouri requirement that doctors test for fetal viability. Currently there is no test that is both reliable and completely safe. By inserting a hollow tube into a pregnant woman's abdomen to withdraw amniotic fluid from the uterus—a procedure called amniocentesis—doctors can tell whether a fetus's lungs are mature enough to function outside the womb. But amniocentesis is invasive, carries about a 1 percent risk of miscarriage, and may not be conclusive until the 28th week of pregnancy. Ironically, the percentage of abortions performed after the 21st week of pregnancy in the United states is quite small: only about 1 percent in 1985.

In practical terms poor women are most likely to feel the results of state restrictions on abortion. In 1987, 62 percent of women who had abortions came from families with yearly incomes of less than $11,000. In the past ten years abortions have already become more difficult for women to obtain because many states reduced Medicaid funding for terminating pregnancies.

Abortion has long been controversial in medical ethics. The ancient Greek physicians who followed

A Matter of Life and Death

Agreeing for the first time to hear a right-to-die case, the U.S. Supreme Court will decide the fate of Nancy Cruzan (below), who has been in a vegetative state since a 1983 automobile accident. Nancy's parents, Joyce and Joe Cruzan (left), believe that removing her from life-support systems is what Nancy would have wanted, but the state of Missouri refused their request.

the teachings of the physician Hippocrates subscribed to the philosophy that all life is sacred (although the prohibition on abortion contained in their famous oath probably made them a small minority among physicians in the ancient world). Modern medical technology has made it possible to assess and even treat the diseases of fetuses before they are born, and to many, the new technology makes the fetus seem more and more like a patient entitled to the same consideration as all other patients—including the right not to be killed. Since medicine cannot settle philosophical questions about the moral status of the unborn, some legal scholars have preferred to put the issue in jurisprudential terms: should the fetus be considered a person entitled to constitutional protection?

With the viability standard in jeopardy the question is whether any other rationale for political compromise between the two bitterly divided sides of the

abortion issue can be found. Paradoxically, even as Chief Justice William Rehnquist agreed that Missouri could require doctors to assess fetal viability, he criticized the viability standard that was established in *Roe*—usually considered to be the 24th week of pregnancy—as the point at which state interest in abortion takes hold.

The Court will have ample opportunity to address this problem in its 1989-1990 term. When it announced its *Webster* decision in July 1989 it agreed to hear three more abortion cases (one case has since been settled out of court).

Right-to-Die Decisions

The clearest legal and ethical right that competent adults have in U.S. legal tradition is the right not to be touched without their consent, even if the touching is done by physicians who believe they are doing

Mary Sue Davis leaves a Tennessee courtroom after the dramatic ruling giving her custody of seven frozen embryos that were produced from her eggs and the sperm of her husband before the marriage broke up. In the ruling, the judge said that "human life begins at the moment of conception."

something beneficial. Three different cases recently tested this right in circumstances in which the result of exercising it would be certain death.

In November 1989 the Georgia Supreme Court unanimously ruled that Larry James McAfee could not be compelled to be kept alive by being attached to a machine that breathes for him, called a respirator. McAfee, who was in his mid-30s, had been injured in a 1985 motorcycle accident and paralyzed below the neck. But he remained alert and protested that he was fearful of facing each new day as a person with multiple and permanent handicaps. Since psychiatrists did not find him to be clinically depressed, the court ruled he was competent to express his wish not to be treated, as was his right.

The Supreme Court hearing took place as the result of an appeal of an earlier decision by a Georgia Superior Court, which had supported McAfee's request. The Superior Court had considered two other problems in connection with this case. First, because McAfee could not turn the respirator off himself, someone would have to do it for him. Since turning it off would be tantamount to causing McAfee's death, the judge could not order a doctor or anyone else to take such an action. Second, McAfee feared the distress and pain of death by suffocation following removal from the ventilator.

The Georgia decision found solutions to both of these issues. A friend of McAfee would be given permission to rig up a timing device to turn off the respirator, a device McAfee could operate with his mouth. And McAfee's physicians were given permission to give him sedatives to ease his death. To many this strategy seemed like nothing less than a plan for assisted suicide, which is contrary to the law. Advocates for the handicapped urged McAfee not to exercise his legal right to turn off his respirator. They and others pointed out that he was not dying and that what he needed was emotional support to realize his potential for a useful and satisfying life. After the case received a good deal of media attention, a number of individuals and organizations began searching for educational and employment opportunities for McAfee, as well as a means for him to live outside an institution.

In July 1989, in a similar case, a Michigan court allowed quadriplegic David Rivlin, 38, to have his respirator turned off and allowed him to be sedated before it was done, to ease the pain of death. Paralyzed 18 years earlier when his spine was severed in a surfing accident, Rivlin developed a spinal aneurysm in 1986, and the spinal surgery that followed left him able to move only his head. After three years on a respirator, he petitioned the court in May 1989 to authorize its disconnection. The court decided no authorization was needed, since competent adults have the right to refuse treatment. An unidentified physician disconnected the machine, and Rivlin died not long thereafter.

Another sad but very different story found its way to the U.S. Supreme Court as the first right-to-die case considered by the country's highest judicial body. Nancy Cruzan, in her early 30s, had lain in a persistent vegetative state since 1983, when she was injured in an automobile accident. In her condition, from which she was virtually certain never to recover, Nancy had no awareness of the world around her. Because the portions of her brain that are associated with consciousness had been destroyed, her brain could sustain only primitive vegetative functions, including respiration and digestion. But in order to digest she had to be fed, and this was accomplished by means of a surgically implanted tube leading to her stomach.

Medically, Nancy Cruzan's condition closely resembled that of Karen Ann Quinlan. In that famous case the New Jersey Supreme Court ruled in 1976 that Quinlan's respirator could be removed as her parents had requested; the parents had argued that their daughter would not want to live if God had meant her not to breathe. But Quinlan lived on in a coma for nearly ten years because her parents' interpretation of their Catholic faith did not permit them to ask that her feeding tube be removed as well. The Cruzan family, on the other hand, requested that Nancy's feeding tube be removed.

A number of state courts have ruled, in cases similar to the Cruzan's, that feeding tubes are therapeutic agents and therefore their use can be accepted or rejected in the same way as other devices, medications, or procedures. But in the Cruzan case the Missouri Supreme Court found that the state's interest in the continued life of its citizens outweighed the Cruzans' authority over Nancy's treatment, even though the family was the appropriate surrogate and in a position to report what her wishes would have been.

Whose Embryos Are They?

New biotechnologies continue to create astonishing dilemmas, and the field of human reproduction is no exception. When a Tennessee couple decided to resort to in vitro fertilization in an attempt to have a child, they did not consider the possibility that they might someday disagree about whether their embryos should be implanted and have a chance to become babies. But when Mary Sue Davis and Junior Davis decided to separate, that is precisely what happened: Mary Sue wanted the chance to have a baby using one of her (now-frozen) eggs, which had been fertilized in a laboratory dish using her husband's sperm, but Junior did not want to become a father with her.

The issue that faced Blount County Circuit Judge W. Dale Young is easy enough to state: Should the frozen embryos be considered children or property? If they are children, then the issue is which parent should be awarded custody, a decision that in such cases is based on the child's best interests. One might well argue that it is in the best interests of the embryos to have the chance, however remote, to develop into babies. If, however, they are property, then they must be awarded as part of an equitable negotiated divorce settlement along with the couple's other assets. The court's task would be to balance the equities. Mrs. Davis argued that she had undergone the physically uncomfortable and emotionally difficult process of harvesting her eggs and that this might be her last chance to have a child. Mr. Davis took the position that he should not be forced to shoulder the psychological and financial burdens of fatherhood.

Based on the proposition that human life begins at conception, Judge Young concluded that the embryos were children and ruled that temporary custody must go to their mother. The basis for this decision is sure to stimulate further debate when the ruling is appealed. For example, if this decision is taken as a precedent, some will claim that all frozen embryos must be implanted, a result that would make in vitro programs impractical on economic as well as medical grounds. Further, the ruling raises questions about the many forms of birth control that operate after conception, among them the intrauterine device (IUD). Once again the abortion debate casts its long shadow.

Fetal Tissue Research Ban Stands

Abortion affected yet another important decision, this one on research in biomedical science. A ban on federally funded research using fetal tissue that had been instituted in 1988 by the Reagan administration was extended by the U.S. Department of Health and Human Services (HHS) under President George Bush in November 1989. Under this rule no tissue recovered from fetuses in induced abortions can be used in experiments supported by public money; privately financed research remains unaffected. (Tissue from spontaneous abortions, or miscarriages, is unsuitable because it usually cannot be preserved.)

Proponents of the ban worry that research using fetal tissue would justify and even encourage abortion. Opponents have noted that very little tissue would be needed and that there is no evidence that there would be any effect on the frequency of abortion. In 1988 two special panels appointed by HHS found that the research was ethically acceptable so long as women were not paid for fetal tissues and scientists were informed of their source. Researchers have argued that numerous diseases could be better understood through fetal tissue research, including Parkinson's disease, Huntington's chorea, diabetes, and perhaps Alzheimer's, and that the potential relief of suffering justified the use of human fetal material. Such arguments were bolstered in early February 1990 when researchers reported the first well-documented evidence that a fetal tissue transplant had improved the condition of a man with Parkinson's disease. Critics of the HHS panels claimed that they did not take seriously enough the principle that certain types of research cannot be justified, regardless of their potential value.

JONATHAN D. MORENO, PH.D.

BLOOD AND LYMPHATIC SYSTEM

Regulating the Production of Blood Cells •
Understanding Genetic Blood Diseases •
Toward an Even Safer Blood Supply

Growth Factors

Great advances are being made in hematology thanks to the synthesis, for use in treating patients, of a group of naturally occurring substances that regulate the amounts of different types of cells that circulate in the blood. Clearly, in order to meet its changing needs, the body must have a way of controlling the numbers of red blood cells that carry oxygen throughout it, the various types of white blood cells that fight infection, and the platelets that help stop bleeding. Such regulation is carried out by chemical messengers known as hormones.

Knowledge that these substances—or growth factors—exist is not new. Claims that one substance—erythropoietin—had been detected date back nearly a century, and intensive study of the substances has been going on for over 30 years. But it is a long road from merely postulating that a substance exists or even demonstrating its activity in experimental animals to preparing a pure substance that can safely be administered to treat medical problems in human beings. Scientists must be able to develop accurate, reproducible, and sensitive methods for measuring such a substance and then find ways to produce a pure form of it. It was the development in the 1970s of methods of culturing bone marrow cells that made it possible to purify growth factors. And the techniques of gene splicing have made it possible to produce adequate amounts of such materials to allow them to be tested clinically and make them available to physicians for use in treating patients.

Erythropoietin. By 1989 enough trials of a genetically engineered form of erythropoietin had been carried out for it to become the first of these materials to be licensed for sale by the U.S. Food and Drug Administration (FDA). Erythropoietin is a hormone normally made in the kidney. When the kidneys are damaged by disease, the body is unable to make sufficient amounts of it to stimulate the bone marrow to make enough red blood cells. Thus, the condition in which erythropoietin has been tested most thoroughly is kidney failure. The drug was licensed specifically to treat the anemia that results from kidney failure. Many patients suffering from this condition previously had to undergo repeated blood transfusions to provide them with more red blood cells. The new drug will likely eliminate the need for such transfusions in some patients.

Erythropoietin may also be effective for other conditions. Because of concern about infections such as hepatitis and AIDS, patients are increasingly depositing their own blood in blood banks for later use in planned surgery. But the number of pints that they can donate is limited by the ability of their bone marrow to make red blood cells. If such patients are given erythropoietin, their marrow is stimulated to greater activity; they would therefore be able to deposit larger amounts of blood for their own use.

Erythropoietin may also prove to be useful in some

patients with the anemia that sometimes accompanies chronic inflammation or cancer; however, this application remains to be studied.

It is less likely that erythropoietin will be useful in the treatment of the anemia that accompanies leukemia or other bone marrow disorders, because the abnormal marrow cannot respond by producing more red blood cells.

Experimental Hormones. Erythropoietin is the first growth factor to come to market, but others are not far behind. GM-CSF (granulocyte monocyte colony stimulating factor) causes bone marrow to make two kinds of infection-fighting white blood cells, granulocytes and monocytes. It has already been shown that GM-CSF can raise the granulocyte count in patients with bone marrow disorders and in patients who have received cancer chemotherapy and radiation therapy, which destroy cancer cells but also kill the bone marrow that produces white blood cells. Other hormonal substances that are under active investigation include G-CSF (granulocyte colony stimulating factor), interleukin-2, and interleukin-3. G-CSF may be useful in treating low granulocyte counts, interleukin-2 in stimulating immunity, and interleukin-3 in causing growth of the stem cells that are needed for the bone marrow to produce all blood cells.

As with any powerful new substance, the use of these growth factors may involve dangers that researchers may not yet fully appreciate. These are potent substances that may increase the rate of growth not only of normal cells but also of cancer cells, and, indeed, there is some evidence that they can do so in the test tube. Nonetheless, it is clear that, when properly used, they will emerge as an important addition to the tools that physicians have at their disposal for fighting disease.

Understanding Genetic Blood Diseases

Only in the past few years has it become possible for scientists to analyze the material contained in DNA (deoxyribonucleic acid), from which genes are made. Now this knowledge is being applied to advance understanding of blood diseases.

The thalassemias are genetic diseases in which not enough hemoglobin, the red oxygen-carrying pigment of red blood cells, is produced. This results in a form of anemia in which the red cells are small and poorly filled with hemoglobin. Study of the DNA sequence of the hemoglobin genes has shown just how heterogeneous this type of disease is and has highlighted several different genetic mechanisms as possible causes.

Now such studies are being extended to other blood diseases. In the bleeding disorder hemophilia, for example, numerous abnormalities have been found in

DNA. These include frank deletions—abnormalities in which parts of genes are missing—and point mutations—changes in the individual chemicals that make up genes. In glucose-6-phosphate dehydrogenase deficiency, which is another hereditary cause of anemia, the genes responsible have also been identified, and many different mutations involving chemical changes have been found.

Gaucher's disease is a rare hereditary fat storage disorder that results when an enzyme called glucocerebrosidase is lacking. This enzyme is required by macrophages—the scavenger cells of the body—in order for them to break down certain types of fat. The gene that makes the missing enzyme has now been cloned, and several different mutations of it have been identified in this disorder.

Identifying disease-causing genes is important for two reasons. First, it greatly facilitates diagnosis, particularly prenatal diagnosis. Almost every cell in the body has a full complement of DNA, and the amount of DNA that can be obtained from a very small blood sample, a few hair roots, or a small number of cells from a developing embryo is sufficient to make an exact diagnosis when the molecular defect is known on the DNA level. This makes possible prenatal diagnosis using small amounts of the amniotic fluid that surrounds the fetus or small samples of chorionic villi, the small hairlike projections lining the membranes surrounding the fetus, and eliminates the need for the much more difficult and hazardous procedure of obtaining blood from the unborn fetus. Second, it raises the hope that it may be possible in the future to treat genetic blood diseases by placing healthy DNA into immature bone marrow cells that have been harvested from patients with a given disease. Reintroducing the corrected cells into the body may then effect a cure. Progress has already been made toward this goal.

Hepatitis

With the enormous public concern about the possible transmission of AIDS by blood transfusion, many people have lost sight of a much greater danger: the transmission of hepatitis. This disease remains the most common complication following blood transfusions in the United States. A test to detect one of the major forms of blood-borne hepatitis, hepatitis B, has been available since 1970, and the vigilance of blood banks has made the U.S. blood supply virtually free of this infectious hazard. But another form of hepatitis—non-A non-B hepatitis, or hepatitis C—is quite common. It has been estimated that 1 percent of blood donations are contaminated with this dangerous virus; about 5 percent of those who receive transfusions in the United States get hepatitis C.

Now a group at Chiron Corporation, a California biotechnology company, has successfully used molecular techniques to identify the hepatitis C virus and has developed a test to detect it. In trials conducted at the National Institutes of Health, the U.S. Centers for Disease Control, and in foreign laboratories, the Chiron screening test was found to be highly effective in detecting the hepatitis C virus. The test, which is in use in Japan and Europe, has been submitted to the FDA for approval. If it goes into general use in the United States, it should serve to make the blood supply even safer than it is now.

ERNEST BEUTLER, M.D.

BRAIN AND NERVOUS SYSTEM

*Prenatal Screening for Muscular Dystrophy •
Cancer's Effects on the Nervous System •
Progress in Treating Parkinson's Disease*

Muscular Dystrophy

Recent research has yielded considerable new information about the genetic and biochemical defects that underlie many of the fatal genetic disorders collectively known as muscular dystrophy. This new information has, in turn, led to progress in prenatal screening. Muscular dystrophy causes progressive weakness in muscles and nearly always leads to death. It can affect individuals of virtually any age but most commonly occurs in children, adolescents, and young adults. Boys and men are affected far more often than girls and women.

The most common form of the disease, affecting young boys, is called Duchenne's muscular dystrophy; a similar but milder condition in adolescents and young men is called Becker's muscular dystrophy. Scientists have known for over a century that both types are transmitted by the mother, through some genetic defect on the X chromosome—although until the late 1980s, the nature of that defect was not known. Duchenne's occurs in about 1 out of every 3,500 male babies and is found throughout the world in nearly all populations. About two-thirds of all families have more than one affected member, usually in different generations, while about one-third have no family history of the disease.

The symptoms and progression of the disease vary, but usually in Duchenne's dystrophy weakness of the legs or abdominal muscles becomes evident within a year or two of the time when the boy begins to walk. Eventually the child begins to waddle because of weakness of the hips, and the muscle weakness be-

comes more serious over a period of years, usually requiring braces or a wheelchair by age 10 or 12. The heart muscle is also affected by the disease, leading to disturbances of cardiac rhythm or to heart failure. Weakness of the muscles involved in breathing leads to respiratory abnormalities and pneumonia. The heart and respiratory problems are often the cause of death. Mental retardation can also occur, although this is usually mild.

Until recently, the diagnosis of Duchenne's muscular dystrophy was possible only after birth, at the time weakness first appeared. Physical examination, measuring the amount of the chemical creatine phosphokinase (CK) in the child's blood, electromyography (which provides a record of electrical activity in a muscle), and sometimes muscle biopsy were routinely used for diagnosis. However, in 1986 researchers at

Harvard Medical School discovered that a specific abnormal gene underlies Duchenne's muscular dystrophy and that a protein they called dystrophin, which is produced by the gene, is also abnormal in the disease. The researchers further determined that both Duchenne's and Becker's dystrophy are caused by abnormalities of the same gene. In the more severe Duchenne's dystrophy, dystrophin was found to be nearly completely absent; in Becker's dystrophy, dystrophin was abnormal and defective, although not entirely absent. Researchers were able to show that variations in the abnormality of the gene and in dystrophin accounted for variations in patients' symptoms.

Since the genetic abnormalities of Duchenne's dystrophy have been unraveled, it has become possible to reliably identify prospective mothers who are likely carriers of the genetic defect that causes the disease—

Disabilities Made Heroic

Two recent films celebrated people with neurological disabilities. In My Left Foot, *Daniel Day-Lewis (far left) portrays Christy Brown (inset left), an Irishman born with cerebral palsy who became a writer and painter. In* Born on the Fourth of July, *Tom Cruise (right) plays Ron Kovic (below), who was paralyzed from the chest down in the Vietnam War.*

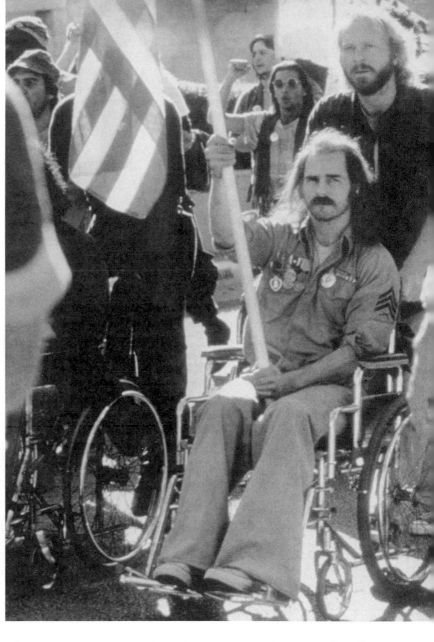

by measuring dystrophin levels in these women. Also, it is possible to measure dystrophin levels in the muscles of unborn children through a muscle biopsy. Fortunately, DNA obtained from amniotic fluid (a simpler and safer procedure) can also be used to measure dystrophin levels in the fetus, which over the coming years will lead to a safe and routinely available method of prenatal testing.

Effects of Cancer

Cancers originating in all parts of the body can cause neurological complications. Most often, these complications occur when the cancer spreads and a new tumor develops on the brain, spinal cord, or peripheral nerves, causing pressure or damage. Sometimes, however, neurological symptoms occur when no new tumor is evident to explain them. Since the 1950s such conditions have been known as "remote effects" of cancer on the nervous system. Abnormal immune system proteins have recently been found to cause these relatively rare neurological curiosities.

The two most common remote effects of cancer on the nervous system involve the muscles and the cerebellum (the part of the brain important for maintaining balance). The first, involving muscles, is known as Eaton-Lambert syndrome and is similar to the more common condition called myasthenia gravis. The patient is weak and becomes weaker with exercise or activity; other symptoms include a dry mouth and variable blood pressure. The second remote effect, cerebellar degeneration, causes instability of gait, impaired coordination of limbs, and sometimes impaired movement of the eyes and an abnormal, wobbly voice. Both conditions typically become worse over

255

a period of months or years and in some patients can be quite severe.

Many types of cancer can produce these conditions. The most common causes are the kind of lung cancer called small-cell lung cancer, ovarian cancer, and Hodgkin's disease. However, cancer of the breast, uterus, colon, or other organs can also cause them. In more than half the cases of Eaton-Lambert syndrome or cerebellar degeneration, the remote effects on the nervous system actually precede—by a year or longer—evidence of a primary tumor anywhere in the body.

Recent research has identified the immune system abnormalities that underlie these conditions. A number of researchers have found specific abnormal proteins called immunoglobulins that bind with certain cells in the cerebellum or, in the case of Eaton-Lambert syndrome, to the junctions between nerves and muscles. Patients with small-cell cancer of the lung or ovarian cancer most frequently have these abnormal proteins, but they have also been found in patients with other types of cancer. Just how these proteins do their mischief is not known, but in the case of Eaton-Lambert syndrome, it is widely believed that the abnormal proteins impair the ability of nerve cells to transfer calcium across their membranes, thereby inhibiting muscle contraction. In the case of the cerebellum, the proteins appear to kill cells by binding to certain elements in their nuclei.

Recent progress has also been made in the treatment of these disorders, particularly Eaton-Lambert syndrome. Researchers at the Mayo Clinic in Rochester, Minn., reported that the drug 3,4 diaminopyridine temporarily improves muscle power and relieves other symptoms in individuals with small-cell lung cancer and this syndrome. This drug and others similar to it seem to allow nerve cells to release acetylcholine, a chemical that transmits nerve impulses, partially reversing the blockage of calcium channels. Researchers are now attempting to discover other approaches to treating both Eaton-Lambert syndrome and cerebellar degeneration.

Drug for Parkinson's Disease

Clinical trials of the drug deprenyl, conducted in 28 U.S. and Canadian medical centers, have shown that progression of Parkinson's disease can be partially forestalled by early use of the drug. This was the first time any drug had been shown to halt the progression of a neurological disorder. Deprenyl, approved for use in the United States in June 1989 and in Canada in January 1990, is the commonly used name for a drug whose chemical name is selegiline and whose brand name is Eldepryl.

The researchers published their preliminary findings on deprenyl in late 1989. The study began in 1987 and was originally expected to last five years, but the success of the drug led the investigators to end the initial phases of the study early.

Parkinson's disease, which affects over 400,000 people in the United States and 70,000 in Canada, is characterized by shakiness, by an inability to initiate movement (feeling frozen), and in some patients by mental deterioration. It results from a deficiency of a chemical called dopamine that carries messages between nerve cells in the brain. Deprenyl inhibits the activity of an enzyme in the brain that breaks down dopamine, thereby leaving more dopamine in the brain. Deprenyl also inhibits the toxic effects of certain other chemicals that may play a role in the development of Parkinson's disease.

In the study begun in 1987, half of the 800 patients enrolled received deprenyl, while the other half did not. The progression of all patients' disease was closely monitored, so that levodopa (commonly known as L-dopa), the standard therapy for Parkinson's, could be promptly begun if the need arose. (Levodopa relieves the symptoms of the disease but does not affect the disease's progression; it also has serious side effects and in some patients loses its effectiveness after it is taken for a few years, so doctors wait as long as possible after diagnosing Parkinson's to prescribe it.) After an average of 12 months of follow-up, only 97 patients who received deprenyl, compared with 176 who did not, required treatment with levodopa. The risk of their condition progressing to the point where they required levodopa was reduced by 57 percent for those who received deprenyl. Also, individuals who received deprenyl were less likely to have to give up full-time employment. Because of these positive results, all 800 patients in the study were given the opportunity to switch to deprenyl as soon as the results became available. The researchers are continuing to monitor those individuals on deprenyl to ascertain whether the benefit is temporary or whether it will be maintained for more than just a year or two. (The same study was also examining the effects of another drug—alpha tocopherol, a form of vitamin E. To date this drug has not been found to have any significant effect in forestalling the progression of Parkinson's disease.)

Further studies will be required to determine whether deprenyl should be given to all individuals with Parkinson's. Although the drug appears to be safe and seems to be useful in early stages of the disease, as well as in selected individuals in advanced stages, it is by no means clear that all individuals should receive it. Further work is under way to clarify that question.　　　　Hamilton Moses III, M.D.

CANCER

Changing Cancer Rates • New Drug Combinations for Colon Cancer and Bladder Cancer • Vaccines Against Cancer • Using Light-Sensitive Drugs

Cancer Rates Today

Four out of ten Americans diagnosed with cancer today will survive for at least five years, compared with one in three in the 1960s. When the cancer death rate is adjusted for deaths from other causes, today's cancer survival rate is 49 percent. Cancer death rates have leveled off or declined over time for the major types of cancer, except for lung cancer, the leading U.S. cancer killer. There was a steep rise in lung cancer deaths among women in the 1980s because of higher smoking rates among women in the 1960s.

Blacks and the poor die from cancer at disproportionately high rates. Blacks have an 11 percent greater risk of developing cancer than whites, and blacks with cancer have a 30 percent higher mortality rate than whites. The major reasons for these disparities appear to be lack of access to medical facilities, lack of understanding about cancer prevention (blacks are more likely than whites to smoke cigarettes, drink alcohol, and eat high-fat diets), lack of understanding of the importance of early detection, and possibly discrimination in the application of appropriate treatments. The U.S. National Cancer Institute and the National Medical Association recently signed agreements to work together to improve cancer prevention and control among blacks.

Prevention and Detection

If advice about life-style and screening tests, based on what is already known about prevention and early detection, were universally followed—and if the latest treatment methods were universally applied—cancer deaths could be reduced by 50 percent. New efforts are under way both to educate the public and to further advance knowledge about cancer prevention and detection.

Cancer Control Programs. National Cancer Institute grants to seven state health departments and the District of Columbia will allow them to develop plans for cancer prevention, early detection, and treatment. The plans will be made in cooperation with individuals and organizations living in regions with

Pioneering a new treatment for cancer, Dr. Thomas Dougherty works on the technique known as "photodynamic therapy." A light-sensitive, cancer-destroying drug is injected into the patient and then activated by a laser beam sent through optical fibers.

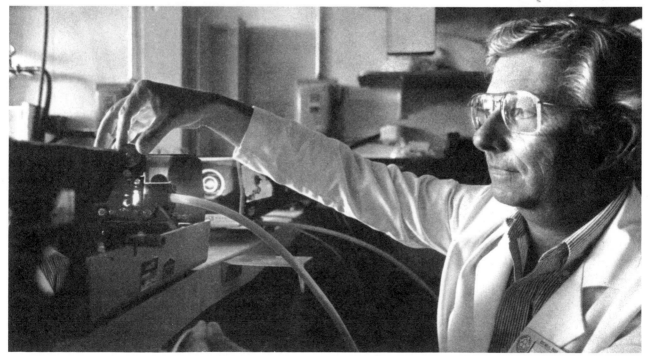

cancer risk and are expected to result in
___g campaigns and improved access to cancer
diagnosis and treatment.

Diet and Nutrition. There seems to be some truth
to the saying "You are what you eat." The U.S.
National Research Council, the National Cancer Institute, and the American Cancer Society have developed dietary guidelines to help reduce the incidence
of cancer. All recommend a low-fat, high-fiber diet
including a number of servings of fruits and vegetables
each day—at least five servings, according to the the
National Research Council. The National Cancer
Institute estimates that 35 percent of cancer deaths
are related to diet. However, scientists acknowledge
that heredity is also a major factor.

Eating vegetables was found by a study in Hawaii
to protect against lung cancer. Earlier work had
indicated that the risk of lung cancer could be reduced
by consumption of beta-carotene, a compound found
in carrots, squash, and other vegetables that is converted into vitamin A in the body. The Hawaii study
confirmed this but also showed a role for other compounds in vegetables. Eating a variety of vegetables
offered stronger protection than consumption of any
one kind. A study in England found that low intake
of fruit and salad vegetables and high intake of salt
were clearly associated with stomach cancer.

High-fat diets and high cholesterol levels in the
blood have been linked to colon and rectal cancer. A
group of California scientists reported in 1989 that a
chemical involved in synthesizing cholesterol is needed
for a certain gene to function as a trigger of tumor
formation in the pancreas, colon, and rectum. This
research underscores the importance of eating a diet
that is low in fat and high in fiber to reduce cholesterol
levels.

A study of breast cancer patients found that larger
tumors were associated with lower dietary fiber intake.
Eating more foods high in beta-carotene correlated
with having a type of breast cancer with a better
prognosis.

Chemoprevention. Using chemical agents to prevent cancer or to reverse early precancerous changes
in cells is called chemoprevention. In a pilot study
of patients with leukoplakia, taking beta-carotene
supplements for six months reversed the condition in
more than 75 percent of the patients without toxic
side effects. The leukoplakia returned when patients
quit taking the supplement—which suggested that it
must be taken on a lifetime basis. Leukoplakia appears as precancerous white spots in the mouth and
can lead to head and neck cancers that are difficult
to treat without disfiguring surgery. Smoking, drinking alcohol, and chewing tobacco are linked with its
development.

Genetics. In 1989 the U.S. National Institutes of
Health established the Office of Human Genome Research, which will supervise an ambitious effort to
map, identify, and define all human genes. Among
those hoping to benefit from this effort are cancer
researchers trying to locate genes believed responsible
for specific types of cancer. Eventually, they hope
not only to discover the precise genetic changes that
must occur to make a normal cell cancerous, but also
to be able to identify people who are vulnerable to
cancer and to develop ways to determine whether a
tumor is likely to spread. Such information and
capabilities could enable physicians to warn susceptible people to practice prevention and could offer
clues to early treatment. Genetic analysis is already
being used as an aid in diagnosing, classifying, and
detecting the recurrence of lymphomas and leukemias.

Geneticists recently located a gene they think could
be responsible for all the inherited cases of malignant
melanoma, a deadly form of skin cancer. Inherited
melanoma accounts for about 10 percent of all cases
of malignant melanoma. Researchers located the
gene by studying genetic material from blood or skin
cells from 125 members of six melanoma-prone families. Once the gene's functioning is understood, the
researchers hope to explain the cause of inherited
melanoma and to understand how sun exposure can
cause noninherited melanomas. Families with two
or more living melanoma patients can become involved in the research by calling 1-800-4-CANCER.

Treating Major Cancers

Although no "magic bullet" has yet been found to
cure all types of cancer, progress has been made in
understanding and treating major cancer killers. These
advances will result in increased survival for patients
and a better quality of life.

Colon and Rectal Cancer. Over 30,000 rectal
cancers are diagnosed each year in the United States.
New surgical techniques have enabled many rectal
cancer patients to keep normal bowel function. The
main difficulty physicians have had is in identifying
which rectal tumors can be completely removed or
destroyed, curing the patient, and which tumors have
already spread to other parts of the body. X rays and
magnetic resonance imaging help to determine how
far the cancer has spread but can be misleading.
Intrarectal ultrasound, using minute sound vibrations
inside the rectum, appears to be more accurate in
identifying patients who can be cured with local
surgery. Another new method for detecting colon and
rectal cancer that has spread involves a hand-held
radiation detector and laboratory-produced antibodies that tend to stick to colon and rectal tumor cells.
The antibodies have radioactive tags attached to them

258

and are administered to the patient before surgery. The surgeon then uses the detector to track the tagged antibodies so that cancer cells that might otherwise be missed can be removed. If any cancer cells discovered in this way cannot be removed surgically, chemotherapy is called for.

The National Cancer Institute announced in October 1989 that two drugs given together after surgery could substantially reduce the death rate for patients with advanced colon cancer that has not yet spread to distant parts of the body. In a study of over 1,200 colon cancer patients, almost half of those who received the experimental drug levamisole in combination with the established anticancer drug 5-fluorouracil after surgery were alive five years later, compared to only 37 percent of those who received no further treatment after surgery. The U.S. Food and Drug Administration was asked by levamisole's manufacturer to approve the drug for general use.

Breast Cancer. A new experimental therapy may make modified radical mastectomy, in which the breast and some underarm lymph nodes are removed, unnecessary in most women with tumors that used to be considered too large to treat more conservatively. Italian scientists who treated women with large tumors by giving them standard anticancer drugs for three months found that the chemotherapy shrank the majority of tumors, allowing more limited surgery. However, larger-scale, longer-term studies are needed to find out if patients receiving this treatment survive longer than patients who have a mastectomy.

Scientists have found an enzyme that seems to predict which patients have breast cancer that is likely to spread. Tests for this enzyme could help doctors decide which women need further therapy and which can be cured with surgery alone.

Controversy continued over the impact on breast cancer risk of replacement hormones taken to alleviate symptoms of menopause. Studies by the U.S. Centers for Disease Control had found that women taking the hormone estrogen were not more likely to get breast cancer. In 1989, however, Swedish scientists reported they had found about 10 percent more breast cancers than expected in a group of 23,244 women who used replacement hormones for menopausal symptoms. Using the medications for nine years or more increased the risk of getting breast cancer to 70 percent above expected levels, the Swedish researchers reported. Short-term use for severe menopausal symptoms such as hot flashes and night sweats did not seem to be associated with any increase in breast cancer risk.

Regular mammograms (breast X rays) play an important role in preventing deaths from breast cancer—by detecting the disease in its early stages when it is easier to cure. New studies have found that breast cancer risk goes up with breast density. The number of dense regions in the breast, which are thought to be composed of epithelial (skinlike) and connective tissue, can be detected only through mammograms. Many U.S. states now require insurance companies to pay for screening mammograms.

See also the feature article BREAST CANCER: DETECTION AND TREATMENT.

Bladder Cancer. Bladder cancer is not as common as lung, colon, or breast cancer, but there were about 47,000 new cases in the United States in 1989. Smoking and exposure to workplace chemicals increase the risk of getting this cancer. Surgery is the usual treatment for early stages of bladder cancer but is not effective once the cancer has spread to other parts of the body. A new anticancer drug combination called M-VAC made all evidence of the cancer disappear in over a third of patients with widespread bladder cancer, and the chemotherapy reduced the size of the tumor by more than half in another third. This new treatment is expected to help more people survive longer.

Leukemia. Chronic lymphocytic leukemia is the most common type of leukemia in the Western world, and it strikes more than 27,000 people in the United States each year. It develops mostly in elderly people, and its incidence is expected to increase as the U.S. population ages. Many different anticancer drugs have been tried in the past but with little success. In a study reported in 1989, a new experimental drug called fludarabine helped over half of patients who had not benefited from other treatments. In a second study fludarabine made the disease disappear in a third of patients who had not been previously treated.

New Treatment Methods

Research advances have been made using substances called biological response modifiers and using light-sensitive anticancer drugs. For new cancer treatments to be developed, patients are needed to take part in investigational studies, called clinical trials. As a result of efforts begun by the National Cancer Institute in 1988, more patients are now enrolling in clinical trials. Patients and doctors interested in finding out about these trials can call the NCI's Cancer Information Service at 1-800-4-CANCER.

Biological Response Modifiers. Biological response modifiers are substances that the body's immune system produces naturally to fight infection or abnormal cells. They can be produced outside the body in large quantities through genetic engineering. Researchers at the NCI have been removing from patients tumor-infiltrating lymphocytes—white blood cells that are particularly effective at penetrating and killing cancer cells—and culturing them with the biological response modifier interleukin-2 to increase their numbers by billions. These cells are then injected back into the patient. The therapy is very effective for some but not for others.

In May 1989 researchers began the first-ever study with human patients using cells that had been altered by inserting foreign genes. The genes, which are transplanted into the cultured tumor-infiltrating lymphocytes before they are reinjected into the patient, act like homing devices, making it possible for the researchers to track the reinjected cells as they move through the body. So far, the researchers have found that it is practical, feasible, and safe to use the genetically altered cells in humans and that they can identify the cells in patients' blood and tumors. The next step will be to introduce genes that will make the cells better cancer fighters.

Research is also continuing on developing vaccines that are designed to stimulate immune responses to patients' tumors. After discouraging results with such vaccines over the past 20 years, scientists are seeing signs of success. The old vaccines were not tailored to a particular type of cancer, but the new ones are different. They use tumor cells, often taken from the patient's own cancer, to encourage specific immune responses against that tumor. Tests so far have shown that the vaccines are safe and may be effective in some circumstances with minimal side effects. Eventually, researchers hope to use the vaccines when a cancer is first treated, to prevent it from spreading.

Light-Sensitive Drugs. In the treatment called photodynamic therapy, a light-sensitive drug called a photosensitizer is injected into the patient. The drug tends to concentrate in the cancer cells. It is activated to kill the cells by light from a laser beam sent through a fiber-optic probe inserted into the body through the mouth, the nose, or the urethra (the tiny tube through which the bladder empties). Research has been going on for over ten years using photodynamic therapy, but only recently have advances in photosensitizers, fiber-optic light delivery systems, and lasers created a resurgence of interest in it. Studies comparing photodynamic therapy with conventional treatments are under way to see which is most effective. Photodynamic therapy appears to be most useful for cancers that the fiber-optic probes can more easily reach, including lung, esophageal, and bladder cancers.

Basic Research

Important basic research is focusing on such questions as how cancer cells become resistant to anticancer drugs, why cancer is able to metastasize, or spread to different parts of the body, and why anticancer drugs are unable to penetrate some tumors.

Multidrug Resistance. Progress has been made in understanding one of the ways cancer cells can become resistant to several different anticancer drugs after exposure to only one drug. P-glycoprotein, a protein produced by tumor cells, seems to act as a pump to push the drugs out of the cells. Scientists are now able to make copies of the gene that produces P-glycoprotein and have found antibodies that can detect the protein. They are attempting to discover exactly how it works to create multidrug resistance, so that its effect may possibly be counteracted.

Researchers are also working to develop agents that will make cancer cells more sensitive to anticancer drugs, to get around the problem of multidrug resistance. Verapamil, a drug used for heart problems, seems to reverse multidrug resistance in some types of cancer and may eventually be used before anticancer drugs are given to prevent multidrug resistance. Docosahexaenoic acid, found in fish oil, has also been found to reduce resistance to a common anticancer drug used for small-cell lung cancer.

Metastasis. Cancers ignore the normal biochemical commands that limit cell growth. Most also develop the ability to metastasize. These secondary growths are usually the reason cancers kill. Researchers are working to understand the changes that cancer cells go through that enable them to travel—and working to find ways to stop metastasis. One promising approach is to find compounds that keep the cancer cells from penetrating or binding to the basement membranes that cover and separate different tissues in and around organs. Several of these compounds successfully prevented metastases in mice. The compounds' effects are reversible. Therefore, any treatment developed might have to be lifelong.

Impenetrable Tumors. Solid tumors develop barriers to anticancer agents delivered through the blood. While many cancer treatments affect the tumors, often shrinking them significantly, most treatments fail to get rid of them completely. The tumors develop high pressure zones and collapsed blood vessels that make it difficult for blood-borne cancer treatments to reach a tumor's innermost core. This helps to explain the disappointing results of some of the newest biological therapies, since the immune system cells and molecules that are the basis for these therapies are larger than drug molecules and have even more difficulty penetrating tumor barriers. Researchers are studying animal tumors to better understand how they are organized and develop ways of defeating the barriers.

See also the Spotlight on Health article TESTICULAR CANCER.

PAUL F. ENGSTROM, M.D.
SHARON WATKINS DAVIS

Strenuous exercise may be great for your heart and lungs, but researchers have found that it can be rough on your gastrointestinal system. Studies have shown that long-distance running may be associated with a range of complaints, including heartburn, nausea, cramps, and internal bleeding.

DIGESTIVE SYSTEM

*Running and Digestive Complaints •
Heartburn Drug Approved • New Findings
on Gallstones in Overweight People*

Runners' Digestive Disorders

The beneficial effects of long-distance running on the heart and lungs are well-known, but it has been associated with a variety of digestive complaints, including heartburn, nausea, vomiting, abdominal cramps, loose stools, and gastrointestinal bleeding. Researchers are now beginning to understand what brings about such adverse effects and are working to assess their seriousness.

Heartburn, an uncomfortable burning sensation over the front of the chest that may radiate up to the throat, occurs in one out of ten long-distance runners. A similar proportion may experience nausea and vomiting following prolonged running. Although the explanation for these complaints is unclear, some researchers believe that strenuous activity may slow the rate at which the stomach empties, with the result that its acid contents back up into the esophagus, causing the above symptoms. To prevent this problem, some runners avoid eating large meals or drinking highly concentrated beverages prior to running.

A recent study focused on bleeding in the digestive system of runners. (Gastrointestinal bleeding may occur during or following any strenuous exercise, such as running, bicycling, and swimming.) Researchers tested the stools of 41 runners prior to and after the 1988 Chicago Marathon. Eight runners had "occult" blood—that is, not visible to the naked eye—in their stools following the race. These individuals were more likely than the others to have had symptoms of cramping and diarrhea while running or soon thereafter.

Seeking to locate the site of bleeding in the eight runners, the researchers viewed the lining of the stomach, upper small intestine, and large intestine with endoscopes, flexible fiber-optic tubes inserted through the mouth or anus. Places where the stomach lining had been worn away were found in two runners, and similar "erosions" of the colon were seen in a third. In all three cases the tests were performed within 48 hours following the race. No site of bleeding was found in the remaining five runners, in whom the tests were performed more than 48 hours after the finish of the race.

The researchers concluded that the erosions—and associated bleeding—lasted only a short time and cleared up soon after the period of exertion ended. They believed that the erosions were caused by the diversion of blood (and consequently oxygen) away from the digestive tract to supply energy to the large muscles used in running.

Runners who notice the presence of blood in their stools should not automatically attribute it to strenuous exercise, since they can develop intestinal bleeding for the same reasons that nonrunners do. The causes can include ulcers, gastritis (inflammation of the stomach), and cancer, as well as the usually benign growths called polyps. If intestinal bleeding occurs, runners should consult a physician so that appropriate tests can be performed in order to make sure one of these more serious conditions is not responsible for the problem.

New Drug for Heartburn

The U.S. Food and Drug Administration (FDA) in 1989 approved for marketing a new prescription drug, omeprazole (brand name, Losec), for the short-term (four to eight weeks) treatment of severe heartburn in people who respond poorly to other drugs. It is not intended for cases of simple heartburn. The FDA in addition authorized the marketing of the drug for the treatment of severe erosive esophagitis (inflammation of the esophagus). Omeprazole was also approved in 1989 in Canada for these uses and for treatment of stomach and duodenal ulcers.

Heartburn occurs when acid contents of the stomach back up into the esophagus; it affects a considerable number of Americans daily. In addition to causing heartburn, this acid "reflux" into the esophagus may result in the regurgitation of acid into the mouth, pain or difficulty in swallowing, or unexplained coughing. Chronic reflux may lead to the development of erosions and sores (ulcers) in the esophagus, which may become narrower. Occasional heartburn should not be of concern, but frequent occurrences may cause complications and should be brought to a physician's attention.

Omeprazole is the first of a new class of drugs called acid pump inhibitors to gain FDA approval. These drugs have the ability to suppress the action of an enzyme system called the acid pump, which is located in the cells in the stomach lining that produce acid. Inhibition of the acid pump results in a marked decrease in stomach acid.

In comparison tests the medication, taken orally once a day, produced relief of symptoms and healing faster than other currently available drugs. The drugs called histamine H_2-receptor antagonists also inhibit acid production in the stomach, but they do it in a different way from the acid pump inhibitors and result in less acid suppression. Ranitidine (Zantac) is the only H_2 antagonist approved so far by the FDA for the treatment of disorders of the esophagus. When omeprazole and ranitidine were compared in a study of 144 people with severe inflammation and erosions or ulcers of the esophagus, 85 percent of those treated with omeprazole healed within eight weeks, compared with 50 percent of those given ranitidine. In addition, the omeprazole group reported earlier relief of heartburn symptoms.

The FDA also approved omeprazole for use in the treatment of Zollinger-Ellison, or ZE, syndrome, a rare condition involving excessive stomach acid leading to persistent ulcers of the stomach or duodenum (the top section of the small intestine). ZE syndrome causes severe abdominal pain and diarrhea. The condition is difficult to control with other currently available medications but has responded well to omeprazole.

The drug has been shown to be effective against stomach and duodenal ulcers and is used for such treatment in about 20 countries. However, the FDA did not approve omeprazole for this use, apparently because of studies indicating that some rats receiving large doses of the drug for over two years developed stomach tumors. No such tumors have been reported in people taking it for four to eight weeks for esophagitis. Moreover, individuals with ZE syndrome have been treated with large doses for over five years without developing stomach tumors.

Gallstones, Obesity, and Dieting

Doctors have long known that a person who is markedly obese runs a higher-than-normal risk of developing gallstones. A recent major study indicated that being even slightly overweight can increase the risk. Gallstones are solid particles that form in the gallbladder. They are most commonly composed of cholesterol (70 to 80 percent of cases in the United States) but may also be made primarily of bilirubin, a pigment in bile, which is a liquid secreted by the liver that aids in the digestion of fats.

The new study, which sought to assess risk factors for developing painful gallstones, involved over 88,000 female nurses between 35 and 59 years of age. To measure obesity, the researchers used the concept of relative weight, defined as the weight in kilograms divided by the square of the height in meters. They found that women whose relative weights were more than 32 kilograms per square meter (about 6½ pounds per square foot) were six times more likely to have gallstones than those whose relative weights were below 20, while slightly overweight women (about 24 kilograms per square meter) were about two times more likely. A woman of average height, 5'4", and weighing about 190 pounds was six times more likely to develop gallstones than a 5'4" woman weighing about 120 pounds. A slightly overweight 5'4" woman at about 140 pounds was twice as likely to develop gallstones as the 120-pound woman.

The study also revealed that the chances of developing painful gallstones increase for middle-aged women who gain weight during their middle years or who have been obese since their teens.

Another recent study suggested that overweight individuals who go on a diet to rapidly reduce their weight run an increased risk of gallstones. The researchers had 51 obese men and women, who showed no signs of gallbladder disease, follow a diet of 500 calories a day for eight weeks. A quarter of the group developed gallstones. By contrast, no gallstones were seen in a comparison group of overweight people who did not go on a diet.

Obesity can have significant adverse effects of health, and so dieting to reduce weight may certainly be appropriate for many people. Individuals on such diets, however, should be aware that they may be increasing their risk of developing gallstones.

DANIEL PELOT, M.D.

DRUG ABUSE

War on Drugs • Debate Over Legalization • Emergence of "Ice"

The War on Drugs

In September 1989, U.S. President George Bush presented to Congress a $7.9 billion antidrug plan for fiscal year 1990. The plan, drafted by "drug czar" William Bennett, emphasized law enforcement over treatment and prevention programs and was criticized by some for doing so. Congress increased the funding by $900 million, most of it for education, prevention, and treatment, and by the end of 1989 appropriations bills that included a total of $8.8 billion in antidrug financing had been signed into law. Separate legis-

lation requiring schools to adopt drug education programs became law in December.

The seizures of large stores of illicit drugs provided dramatic evidence that the drug war was underway. In September 1989 one such raid by federal drug agents on a warehouse near Los Angeles uncovered 19 tons of cocaine. A federal initiative to identify and confiscate money obtained in drug sales called for increased cooperation between investigative agencies and the banking system, both national and international. On the local level, some municipal governments set up operations in which the cars of people caught purchasing drugs were confiscated. This is fairly simple to accomplish because many people obtain cocaine by driving into an area where vendors sell it to passing motorists. The police can record such transactions with a hand-held video recorder and—if all goes as planned—arrest the purchaser within several blocks. In New York City as many as 3,000 autos were confiscated in this way. The ultimate effect of this technique is yet to be shown; however, it could result in additional funds for the drug war.

Fighting the Cocaine Producers

In conjunction with domestic efforts to reduce the demand for drugs, the U.S. government increasingly focused on stopping cocaine production in South American countries, especially Colombia, Bolivia, and Peru. The Bush administration poured millions of dollars into Colombia in 1989 to assist the government in its military efforts against the Colombian drug cartels and pledged some $2 billion more, to be shared by the three countries. In addition, U.S. Secretary of Defense Richard Cheney ordered the Joint Chiefs of Staff to prepare plans to use military resources, such as ships, planes, and electronic surveillance equipment, to intercept drug traffickers.

The citizens of Colombia and President Virgilio Barco Vargas, already staging an offensive against the drug cartels in their country, redoubled their efforts when a popular presidential candidate, campaigning on an antidrug platform, was murdered by hired assassins in August 1989. The killing provoked military raids against clandestine laboratories in which cocaine was being produced, confiscation of property owned by drug cartel members, and serious attempts to capture the leaders of drug cartels. It also led to the signing of a treaty that permits extradition of Colombian nationals indicted for drug crimes in the United States. The drug barons responded to these actions with threats, bombings, more assassinations, and attempts to bribe the government (for example, they offered to pay off the national debt), but the pressure on the drug cartels did not let up. On December 15, 1989, a major drug trafficker, José

Increased efforts to seize illegal substances played a major role in the war on drugs. In two seizures on one day in February 1989, Los Angeles police captured nearly half a ton of cocaine and arrested five people.

Rodríguez Gacha, was shot to death by law enforcement agents, and attempts to capture Pablo Escobar, one of the most notorious drug kingpins, continued.

Debate Over Legalizing Drugs

The prominence of the drug problem in the news media reopened an old debate about how best to respond. Some observers drew an analogy between attempts to reduce drug use and the United States' unsuccessful experiment in prohibiting alcohol in the 1920s and 1930s. Others drew an analogy between the increase in U.S. military support for the fight against drugs in Colombia and the first steps of U.S. involvement in the war in Vietnam in the 1960s.

In support of legalizing drugs, some critics have maintained that law enforcement efforts alone will never be successful in curbing drug use. Others use arguments based on economics. Nobel Prize-winning economist Milton Friedman, for example, asserted that the U.S. government could earn money if drugs were sold and taxed like alcohol; these funds could be used for treatment and for social programs to address some of the possible underlying causes of drug use. He also said that legalization would markedly reduce crime, violence, and the associated costs.

Proponents of keeping drugs illegal claim that U.S. drug laws have never been enforced to the extent possible. Most treatment providers feel legalization would make the problem even worse. Public opinion appears to support a legal approach to reducing the drug supply and punishing drug offenders, as demonstrated by opinion polls and citizens' approval in many states of municipal bonds to raise money for more prisons. Many states are experiencing severe overcrowding of prisons because of the influx of drug offenders who are serving longer sentences.

Expanding Drug Treatment

Additional funding became available in 1989 to increase the number of people served by drug abuse programs. The National Institute on Drug Abuse (NIDA) established several treatment research units, intended to make help available to more people and to evaluate the outcome of different types of therapies.

The research units were also designed to test new treatments, with special emphasis on drug therapies that may be helpful for cocaine abuse and dependency. Many drug abuse researchers feel that the existing psychosocial treatments—such as psychotherapy and behavior modification—could be improved by the addition of therapeutic drugs, but very few have been found effective against drug dependency. Only one drug, desipramine, an antidepressant sold under the brand names Norpramin and Pertofrane, has been shown to be useful for helping cocaine addicts remain abstinent, but its effects are not always powerful. NIDA intends to spend approximately $100 million over a period of two to three years in search of effective medications.

NIDA has also established a close liaison with the U.S. Food and Drug Administration, which has created a new committee to develop standards that can be used to assess the safety and efficacy of drug therapies for drug abuse treatment.

Another important area of drug abuse research involves identifying the effective ingredients of drug treatment, identifying which patients do best with which therapies, and matching patients to the most effective treatments. Such studies can not only improve the immediate outcome for specific patients but may also help develop cost-effective treatment programs. One ongoing project is assessing different levels of services in two methadone programs. (Methadone is a drug given to heroin addicts to ease withdrawal symptoms and to keep them off heroin.) Some patients are given only methadone, while others have access to drug and social counseling and to physicians' services. Data from this project should help establish what level of staffing is most beneficial for methadone treatment centers.

"Ice"

An old drug has reportedly reappeared in the United States under a new name, "ice." Ice is a crystalline form of methamphetamine, a drug with a long history of abuse in the United States and elsewhere. It is allegedly being manufactured in parts of Asia and in Hawaii and on the West Coast of the United States. It is being sold, primarily in Hawaii and on the West Coast, in a very pure form, to be smoked.

This drug could become a significant public health problem. The effects of methamphetamine are similar to those of cocaine, but the drug is longer-acting and thus the euphoria lasts much longer and the psychological crash afterward is worse. One of the most common adverse reactions to methamphetamine is paranoia or a psychotic reaction resembling paranoid schizophrenia. In Hawaii there has been a substantial increase in the number of people admitted to hospital emergency rooms because they have been abusing ice. It is too early to know how serious this form of drug abuse will become.

AIDS and Drug Abuse

AIDS remains a major issue in drug treatment programs as the disease continues to spread among drug abusers. Though prevention efforts continue to be the backbone of AIDS activities in drug treatment programs, attempts have been made to integrate medical services into existing programs for drug abusers who are infected with the human immunodeficiency virus (HIV) but have not yet developed AIDS. Some methadone programs have established close working relationships with AIDS clinics, while others have hired physicians to provide on-site care for HIV-infected patients. Recent studies indicate that HIV infection progresses at about the same rate in drug abusers as in non-drug abusing populations—the average time from infection to the development of AIDS is about eight years. It is thus expected that there will be a tremendous increase in demand for medical treatment by drug abusers within the next decade.

GEORGE E. WOODY, M.D.
A. THOMAS MCLELLAN, PH.D.
CHARLES P. O'BRIEN, M.D., PH.D.

ENVIRONMENT AND HEALTH

New Look at the Risks of Low-level Radiation • Radiation Hazards During Flight • Legionnaire's Disease From Mist Machine

Hazards of Moderate Radiation

Exposure to small amounts of certain kinds of radiation increases the risk of cancer and mental retardation more than formerly believed, but the risk of genetic damage in children of those exposed is less than had been thought. These findings were presented in a report made public in December 1989 by the National Research Council, an arm of the U.S. National Academy of Sciences. The report, called *Health Effects of Exposure to Low Levels of Ionizing Radiation*, dealt with various types of penetrating radiation, such as gamma rays and X rays, that can break apart, or ionize, molecules. The National Research Council has been issuing a series of reports on the biological effects of ionizing radiation, and the new study (the fifth to appear and so dubbed BEIR V) revised risk assessments published by the council in 1980.

During the 1980s scientists recalculated the radiation produced by the atomic bombs dropped by the United States on Hiroshima and Nagasaki, Japan, in 1945. These reassessments, based on studies of survivors of the bomb blasts and their children, showed that survivors received lower doses of radiation than had been thought; the cases of cancer, genetic damage, and mental retardation found among them and their children were actually caused by less radiation than previously believed. The new report affirmed those findings, as well as the corollary that the health risks per dose of radiation are greater than formerly thought.It also affirmed the finding that the mixture of radiation at Hiroshima and Nagasaki was different from what had been assumed: the dose from neutrons was smaller, and that from beta particles (electrons) and gamma radiation was greater.

Cancer Risk. The report said that in general the risk of cancer from radiation increases in direct proportion to the radiation dose. The 1980 study had concluded that this "linear" pattern holds only at low doses and that the risk increases with the square of the dose at higher doses. The new data on the Japanese survivors, however, revealed a linear pattern for all forms of cancer except leukemia, which seemed to follow the pattern used in the 1980 report. This finding, together with the fact that survivors were not exposed to doses as high as had been thought, means that low doses of X rays and gamma rays are about three times more likely to cause cancer than had been estimated.

According to the new report, the risk of radiation-induced cancer is similar for men and women. However, it varies greatly with age, being at least twice as great for children as for adults. This can be seen by dividing the population into groups of 100,000 people of all ages and assuming that each person receives a single dose of 10 rem. (The rem, for "roentgen equivalent man," measures radiation absorbed by the average man; current U.S. regulations set a limit of 5 rem per year on the amount of radiation to which nuclear workers may be exposed on the job.) In such a group of 100,000 people of all ages, this 10-rem dose would cause about 800 people to die from cancer in addition to the 20,000 deaths expected normally. But if a group consisting solely of 100,000 5-year-old girls received that dose, there would be about 1,500 excess cancer deaths; for 15-year-old girls there would be about 1,550. For boys the comparable figures are approximately 1,275 and 1,150 excess deaths. And even for 25-year-olds, there would be about 1,180 excess female deaths and 920 male deaths. The risk of cancer from an accumulated dose of 0.1 rem per year over a lifetime is at most half as great as that from a single 10-rem dose.

Retardation. Perhaps the report's most surprising finding concerned radiation's effects on the brains of people irradiated before birth. Among individuals who were still fetuses in their mothers' wombs at the time of the Hiroshima and Nagasaki explosions, the prevalence of mental retardation and small head size increased in proportion to dose in those exposed during the 8th to 25th weeks of pregnancy. The performance of these people in their early school years and on intelligence tests given at ages 10 or 11 showed a direct relationship between dose and lower performance. The greatest rate of severe mental retardation was found among those exposed during the 8th to 15th weeks of pregnancy. This is a period of fetal development when the number of brain cells increases rapidly and the cells move to the sites where they will develop. The chance of retardation occurring is calculated at 4 percent for each 10 rem received during this period, a risk at least four times greater than that for people irradiated between the 16th and 25th weeks of pregnancy. During the latter period, the brain cells take on specialized characteristics, and the overall brain architecture is defined.

No increased risk of retardation was found in people exposed to low levels of radiation during other stages of pregnancy. Before the eighth week, brain cells that are destroyed are replaced, or else the fetus dies. At 26 weeks and beyond, the brain cells are mature, and large amounts of radiation are needed to cause measurable damage.

The report warned that the risk of retardation must be included among the hazards of low-radiation doses in women of childbearing age. Retardation and developmental, behavioral, and emotional problems have also been seen in some people who received low therapeutic doses of radiation as children.

Genetic Effects. At present, scientists find it difficult to relate genetic damage in offspring to parental exposure to specific substances that cause mutations, or inheritable changes in genes. Most estimates for humans are based on laboratory studies that have been conducted with animals. Currently, between 37,000 and 47,000 mutations occur in the United States for each 10 million children born in a generation. The report estimated that an additional 1-rem dose of radiation would cause a maximum of 53 additional mutations. This is a smaller increase than those found in laboratory animal studies, in which each additional 100-rem exposure in a generation doubles the mutation rate in the next generation.

Practical Implications. The report's findings will be studied by regulatory agencies to see if changes in permissible radiation exposure levels are called for. Some experts said that the maximum allowed levels would probably be lowered for workers in fields where radiation exposure is more common, such as the nuclear power and nuclear weapons industries and radiological medicine. For the average person with negligible exposure to radiation, the slight changes in known risk levels may not carry any practical significance. According to one scientist who helped write the report, standards for use of simple diagnostic procedures involving radiation—like chest or dental X rays—will probably not be altered, "because the doses to patients are so small." The report's findings do, of course, strengthen the importance of performing only diagnostic procedures that are needed, especially in the case of children and pregnant women.

Radiation Dangers Aloft

The potential hazards of long-term exposure to radiation from the sun and stars during extensive air travel drew public attention in February 1990 when the U.S. Department of Transportation released the results of a new study. The report estimated that pilots or other crew members who make, for example, about 100 round-trip flights annually between New York and Seattle for 20 years run about a 1 percent risk of dying from cancer caused by in-flight radiation. The risk figures used in the report, however, were based on extrapolations from the known risks of higher doses of radiation rather than on studies of people actually exposed to in-flight doses, and so the accuracy and significance of the risk estimates were unclear. Late in February, however, it was reported that the first actual measurements of radiation in airline cockpits showed that some crew members received higher doses than the maximum allowed for pregnant women.

The solar and stellar radiation of concern consists largely of neutrons and gamma rays of such high energy that blocking them would require using shielding material too heavy to be practical on aircraft. Scientific concern about such exposure has grown in recent years, partly because planes now fly for longer periods at higher altitudes, where the earth's atmosphere provides less protection from the radiation. In addition, an increasing number of international flights take routes over the north pole, where the radiation is more intense because it is concentrated by the earth's magnetic field. At an altitude of 40,000 feet the average radiation dose over the north pole is more than twice that over the northern United States and four times that over the equator. The Transportation Department report predicted that if 100,000 crew members flew the polar route between New York and Tokyo 37 times a year for 10 years, 1,200 of them would die of cancer caused by in-flight radiation exposure.

The report warned that passengers who make very frequent long flights also run an increased risk of

U.S. industry is putting hazardous substances into the environment at a rate of over 20 billion pounds a year, according to a national survey of industrial release of toxic chemicals.

developing radiation-induced cancer and that women in the early stages of pregnancy who fly during periods of especially intense radiation caused by solar storms are slightly more likely to have children with birth defects, mental retardation, and childhood cancer. Some scientists suggested that pregnant women avoid long flights during the period when the risk is greatest or, if they are airline workers, take leaves of absence. A possible way to reduce exposure for all on board a plane would be to install monitoring devices that would alert pilots to fly at lower altitudes during periods of higher than normal radiation.

The Federal Aviation Administration is considering whether to require the introduction of new precautions for airline workers.

Electromagnetic Fields

Can electric and magnetic fields from power lines and electrical equipment cause or promote cancer and other health problems? This question was for decades usually answered "probably not" by scientists, because the fields were considered too weak. However, recent reassessments and new research have caused the skepticism to wane, changing the answer to "possibly yes." This development is significant because the fields affect virtually everyone in industrialized countries, both out of doors and in the home and workplace.

The question was the subject of a study released in mid-1989 by the Office of Technology Assessment, which evaluates scientific and technological issues for the U.S. Congress. The OTA report, *Biological Effects of Power Frequency Electric and Magnetic Fields*, reviewed research on fields produced by power lines and electrical equipment, including home appliances, and concluded that they may pose health risks. Further research is necessary to clarify the nature and extent of these health effects, according to the report.

Strong new evidence that such fields may increase the risk of cancer was presented late in 1989 in a preliminary report of results from an ongoing study of 50,000 New York State telephone workers. The study found more cases of leukemia, male breast cancer, and other cancers among the workers than expected in the general population. Line workers, who experience the greatest exposure to electric and magnetic fields, had the highest overall cancer rate among the telephone workers; the three cases of leukemia found among the 4,500 line workers represented an incidence seven times that in the other workers. There were two cases of breast cancer among the almost 10,000 men who work on central office switching equipment—compared with one case per 1,000,000 men in the general population.

The United States contains over 300,000 miles of high-voltage electrical transmission lines and 2 million miles of lower-voltage distribution lines, and virtually every household has a wide array of electrical appliances. Should any or all of these be regulated, moved, changed, or forbidden? At present, too little information is available to make a rational decision. The OTA report concluded that scientists are just beginning to know enough to form specific hypotheses that they can test experimentally.

Some protection against fields from power lines already exists. Ordinary buildings, fences, and even trees shield against as much as 90 percent of an electric field. However, only structures containing large amounts of iron or a few other special metals protect against magnetic fields. Although some states have begun to limit the strengths of fields permitted within transmission line rights-of-way, certain potential health effects are apparently not directly proportional to the intensity of the fields—a fact that may diminish the value of such regulation. At this point, most scientists recommend that possible risks be avoided where prudent and that a major research effort be undertaken to discover precisely what health effects do exist and to determine their importance.

See also the feature article ELECTROMAGNETIC FIELDS: A DANGER?

Pollution Surveys: Bad News

Several government surveys of toxic materials released into the environment in the United States were made public during 1989, and they showed that the air, water, and land are being polluted to a far greater extent than had previously been thought. The hazardous pollutants involved are known or strongly suspected to cause cancer, birth defects, central nervous system damage, or other harmful health effects. However, the effects are hard to determine exactly, because many of the materials have never been studied thoroughly. Also, little is known about possible additional harm from combinations of substances.

Air Pollutants. According to industry estimates compiled by the U.S. Environmental Protection Agency (EPA), 2.7 billion pounds of more than 300 toxic chemicals were released into the air during 1987 (the latest year for which data were available). This total excludes emissions from motor vehicles, discharges on land and in water that evaporate into the air, and pollution by small sources, such as dry cleaners and gas stations. Some of the toxic substances released are used in manufacturing processes, while others are by-products. Of the 320 chemicals reported, 60 are listed as carcinogens (cancer-causing substances) by the U.S. Public Health Service.

Toluene (a carcinogen) and ammonia were the leading chemicals discharged. Also released in substantial amounts were acetone, methanol, carbon disulfide, 1,1,1-trichloroethane, methyl ethyl ketone (a neurotoxin, which affects the central nervous system), xylene (also a neurotoxin), dichloromethane (or methylene chloride, a carcinogen), and chlorine. Other substances released in large quantities included the carcinogen benzene, sulfuric acid, and lead and lead compounds.

The chemical industry accounted for about a third of the total discharge. The rubber and plastics industry and the fabricated metals industry each discharged over 100 million pounds. Other major industrial sources included electric and electronic equipment and petroleum and coal products. By state, the largest total was from Texas, at well over

200 million pounds. Other states with substantial releases of air pollutants included Louisiana, Tennessee, Virginia, Ohio, Michigan, Indiana, and Illinois.

Water Pollutants. In 1989 the EPA compiled its first comprehensive list of toxic pollutant releases into waterways. On the basis of data from 55 states and territories, the agency said that 495 lakes, river segments, and other waterways were contaminated by one or more of the most harmful substances, called priority pollutants. Many of the substances also appear on the list of pollutants discharged into the air; these include benzene, toluene, vinyl chloride, cyanide, and several heavy metals. Polluted waterways were found in all states except Arizona, Hawaii, Nebraska, North and South Dakota, and Vermont and also in the District of Columbia and Puerto Rico.

The sites affected by the priority pollutants were among more than 17,000 waterways found to be contaminated by some type of pollutant, including sewage and other forms of pollution not classified as toxic. Among the hundreds of identified sources of toxic pollution were 240 municipal sewerage and storm drain systems. Other sources included metal-finishing and manufacturing plants, pulp and paper mills, oil refineries, organics and plastics manufacturing plants, and federal facilities such as military bases and nuclear plants.

States with large numbers of polluted waterways included Pennsylvania, with 181 (primarily metals and organic chemicals); Washington, with 70 (dioxin, metals, organics, and polychlorinated biphenyls, or PCBs); and Wyoming, with 56 (metals).

Although contamination from specific discharges (so-called point sources) is widespread, diffuse or nonpoint sources, such as agricultural fertilizers and septic systems, may produce even more pollution and constitute an even greater health threat. They not only affect waterways but also seep into the underground drinking-water supply. A 1989 report by the California Water Resources Control Board found widespread pollution of California's water supply by organic chemicals, including nitrates, which impair the body's ability to carry oxygen and have been associated with cancer and birth defects.

The Great Lakes in 1989 were linked once again to harmful health effects. For almost 20 years, people had been warned to limit the amount of Great Lakes fish that they eat because the fish contain pesticides, PCBs, and other toxic substances. A new study by toxicologists in Michigan, however, suggested that even the permitted amount may cause cancer.

Overall Pollution. The EPA was startled in 1989 by the amount of toxic substances that it found was being put into the air, water, and land by industry. An EPA survey showed the release of a total of over 22 billion pounds of toxic pollutants during 1987. This first comprehensive national compilation of pollution data, based on reports from the industrial dischargers themselves, was important chiefly because it defined the approximate magnitude of the problem. The results did not indicate the extent of the associated health risks—the release of substances is not the same as exposure to them. In addition, it is often very hard to link patterns of illness to specific chemicals or discharges. But the new information provided for the first time a factual basis for evaluating the environmental and health threats posed by industrial production and other human activities. This evaluation may in turn stimulate increased efforts toward cleanup and prevention of future contamination.

Legionnaire's Disease Outbreak

One of the largest outbreaks of Legionnaire's disease since the ailment was identified in 1976 was traced to an automatic misting machine in the produce section of a supermarket. The outbreak, which occurred in mid-autumn 1989 in Bogalusa, La., resulted in 33 confirmed cases of the disease and 2 deaths.

Legionnaire's disease is a bacterial infection of the respiratory system. Contracted by inhaling water vapor containing the bacteria, it can be treated with antibiotics. It is often not diagnosed, however, because its flulike symptoms are similar to those of a number of other diseases. Its incidence in the United States is generally believed to be far higher than the 500 to 1,000 cases recorded each year by the federal Centers for Disease Control. The elderly, smokers, and people with chronic heart and lung disease are most vulnerable to the disease, which has a fatality rate of, on the average, about 15 percent.

The Louisiana outbreak was the first to be traced to misting machines, which produce a fine spray that helps to keep produce fresh. Most previous outbreaks had been spread through the cooling towers of large air-conditioning systems. A report by the Centers for Disease Control linked the Bogalusa outbreak to the specific type of misting machine used. It featured a reservoir of standing water, where bacteria could grow more easily than in the tap water used by most other misting machines. Also, the machine, like "ultrasonic" home humidifiers, sprayed a fine mist that was more likely to be inhaled than the larger droplets created by most other systems. The Centers for Disease Control said, however, that even this kind of machine was safe if maintained properly, and it recommended that all misting machines and home humidifiers be drained and cleaned regularly according to the manufacturers' instructions.

ELLEN THRO
JOHN P. ELLIOTT

EYES

*Limits on Extended-Wear Contact Lenses •
Scarring From Ultraviolet Rays • New Drugs*

Contact Lens Risks

The U.S. Food and Drug Administration (FDA) recommended in 1989 that so-called extended-wear contact lenses not be used continuously for periods longer than a week. Nearly 4 million people in the United States currently use extended-wear lenses, which are soft lenses originally designed to be worn continuously, both day and night, for up to 30 days. Over the years there have been occasional reports of the lenses causing adverse effects on the cornea, the transparent tissue that covers the front of the eye. These have included abrasions, mild scarring, and vascularization (the formation of tiny blood vessels). The most serious problem has been a bacterial infection known as ulcerative keratitis, which can lead in

hours to severe destruction of the cornea and total loss of vision, necessitating a corneal transplant. Until recently, however, the scope of the problem was unknown.

Researchers reported in 1989 that users of extended-wear contact lenses are 10 to 15 times more likely than users of daily-wear lenses to develop bacterial infection of the cornea. It was found that the longer people wear lenses without removing and cleaning them, the greater the risk of developing an infection. This is because proteins from tear fluid are deposited on the surface of the lenses, making it easier for bacteria to begin growing there. Contributing to the problem in some cases are people's ignorance about the proper care of the lenses and the use of poor cleaning or sterilization techniques.

The findings on the risk of developing a corneal bacterial infection led the FDA to recommend that extended-wear lenses be used for a maximum of seven days before they are removed. Lens manufacturers were asked to revise the labeling on their products accordingly, and eye-care professionals were re-

Touching is allowed in this art exhibit, part of a new program at New York's Museum of American Folk Art dedicated to helping people with visual and other disabilities experience works of art. "Bringing Folk Art Closer," the first touring exhibit sponsored by the program, was scheduled to travel to 13 cities.

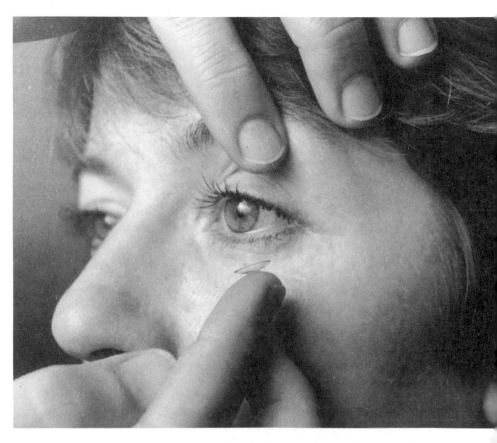

To reduce the risk of infection of the cornea, the U.S. Food and Drug Administration has recommended that extended-wear contact lenses be used for at most a week before they are removed for cleaning.

quested to help educate patients in how to use and care for the lenses. For example, users need to know that if an eye becomes red, the lens should be removed at once, and a physician's care should be sought immediately.

An earlier attempt to eliminate the problem of corneal infections led to the marketing in 1988 of disposable contact lenses, which are worn for one week and then discarded. It was hoped that a week would not be long enough for deposits to build up and cause a bacterial infection. However, some patients have developed infections even when the lenses are used properly. Research is now under way to assess the risks associated with disposable lenses.

Laser Treatment for Corneas

Researchers continue to experiment with ways to use lasers to correct vision problems. Promising results have been reported from preliminary tests on humans of the use of the excimer laser, a high-power source of ultraviolet light, to remodel, or sculpt, the front surface of the cornea. The laser corrects what is known as refractive error—an inability of the eye to focus rays of light on the retina. The procedure takes only seconds and could potentially help millions of people. However, its widespread use—if it is ulti-

mately proved effective and safe—remains years away.

Meanwhile, research has proceeded on applying the smaller, simpler "solid-state" laser to the correction of refractive errors. In this technique, which is at a far earlier stage of development than the excimer approach, the laser changes the cornea's shape by vaporizing cells within the cornea, rather than at its delicate surface (as in the excimer technique).

The Dangers of Sunlight

Doctors know that extensive exposure to ultraviolet light—a component of sunlight—not only can cause sunburn and skin cancers but can promote the development of cataracts, the clouding of the lenses of the eyes. Exposure to short-wavelength ultraviolet light (ultraviolet beta, or UVB) was recently shown to be responsible for yet another visually disabling condition.

Researchers studying the effect of sunlight exposure on men who work on Chesapeake Bay found that ultraviolet light caused scarring to develop on the surface of the eye, a condition known as a pterygium. Generally benign, a pterygium can be a cause of refractive errors (creating a condition such as astigmatism), and eyeglasses may be needed if it becomes advanced. Occasionally the scar tissue may require surgical removal.

It has long been suspected that sunlight, focused by the lens of the eye on the retina, causes retinal deterioration, but surprisingly no linkage between exposure to light and retinal degeneration was detected in the Chesapeake Bay research. This finding was especially welcome since macular degeneration—a disease in which a part of the retina responsible for central vision deteriorates—is the most common cause of irreparable visual loss among adults in the United States.

In view of the damage that ultraviolet light can cause, it is prudent to protect the eyes from unnecessary sunlight exposure by wearing sunglasses and a hat with a brim. Ideally sunglasses should absorb at least 90 percent of ultraviolet light. The FDA announced in May 1989 a new voluntary labeling program to let consumers know how much protection from ultraviolet light a given pair of nonprescription sunglasses provides. The new labels give information on both short-wavelenth (UVB) ultraviolet rays and the more penetrating longer-wavelength (UVA) ones and suggest appropriate uses for the sunglasses. Those classified as "cosmetic" block at least 70 percent of UVB, 20 percent of UVA, and less than 60 percent of visible light and should be used only when sunlight is not harsh. "General purpose" sunglasses—recommended for outdoor activities such as boating or hiking—block at least 95 percent of UVB, 60 percent of UVA, and from 60 to 90 percent of visible light. And "special purpose" sunglasses—intended for very bright environments, such as ski slopes—block at least 99 percent of UVB, 60 percent of UVA, and 97 percent of visible light. The FDA cautioned that none of these types of sunglasses offer enough protection for use in tanning booths; special goggles are needed for that.

Damage caused by light is cumulative, and its effects will last for an entire lifetime. Therefore it is crucial that protection begin in childhood. Children should wear hats that shade the eyes and should not be unduly exposed when ultraviolet rays are at their peak, between 10 A.M. and 2 P.M.

Drugs for Visual Loss

In 1989 the FDA approved for marketing the drug ganciclovir (trade name, Cytovene), which had been found to halt and in some cases prevent a virus-caused infection of the retina that leads to total blindness in AIDS victims. The drug was also approved in Canada in 1989. As many as 38 percent of people with AIDS may develop the infection, produced by the cytomegalovirus. Normally the infection is harmless, but for individuals with AIDS, it can be devastating. Once they begin taking ganciclovir, people need to continue with "maintenance" doses for the remainder of their lives. The FDA urged that the eyes of AIDS patients be regularly checked so treatment can be started as soon as possible after infection appears.

In January 1990 the FDA approved the drug botulinum toxin type A (Oculinum) to treat two eye muscle disorders, blepharospasm and strabismus, in patients aged 12 or older. In strabismus, or squint, the eyes fail to align; cross-eye or walleye may result. In blepharospasm constant spasms of the muscles surrounding the eyes cause the eyelids to remain closed. These conditions have often been treated with surgery. The new drug offers an alternative. It is injected near, but not in, the eye to weaken muscles that are pulling the eye too far in or out or to reduce muscle spasms that are causing the eyelids to close. The drug, produced by a bacterium, is a toxin that can appear in improperly handled food, causing severe food poisoning. However, no serious adverse effects have resulted from the toxin's use as an eye drug. The most commonly reported side effects have been drooping eyelids and a feeling of irritation in the eyes. The drug was approved in Canada in March 1990.

MICHAEL X. REPKA, M.D.

GENETICS AND GENETIC ENGINEERING

Progress and Setbacks in Genetic Clues to Disease • New Treatments With Genetically Engineered Proteins • Cheaper Ways to Make Monoclonal Antibodies

Genetic Diseases

Scientists recently found key genetic defects responsible for two major diseases. The discoveries may make prenatal screening for the diseases possible and may lead to the development of new forms of therapy. Unfortunately, researchers also suffered disappointments concerning two mental illness genes that some thought had previously been identified.

Cystic Fibrosis. Canadian and American researchers announced in August 1989 that they had identified a gene that, when defective, can cause cystic fibrosis, the most common lethal genetic disease in the United States. In cystic fibrosis, mucus builds up in the lungs and impairs breathing, leaving the victim susceptible to respiratory infections. The disease also hampers the digestion of fats by blocking the secretion of digestive enzymes by the pancreas. Most people with the disease do not live past their 20s.

A person will develop cystic fibrosis only if he or she inherits two copies of a defective gene, that is, one from each parent. Many people carry single copies of the defective gene—in the United States about 1 in every 20 whites and smaller proportions of other groups, for a total of some 12 million people. Approximately 1 in every 2,000 children actually suffers from the disease.

Researchers had previously found that cystic fibrosis seems to involve a defect in the movement of chloride ions, a component of salt, into and out of cells—which is why the sweat of people with the disease is unusually salty. This defect reduces the amount of water inside cells and thus leads to the production of unusually thick mucus, which clogs the lungs. The researchers who identified the cystic fibrosis gene believe that it is the blueprint for a protein that pumps chloride ions

into and out of cells; when the gene is defective, the protein is also.

In November 1989, Integrated Genetics of Framingham, Mass., began marketing a screening test for cystic fibrosis based on the new discovery. The test should be useful in most families with a history of the disease. Cystic fibrosis in other families is thought to be caused by one or more other genetic defects.

Eye Disease. American and Irish researchers identified the locations of three different genes that may, when defective, cause retinitis pigmentosa (RP), a condition that leads to degeneration of the retina of the eye and afflicts 100,000 Americans and 1.5 million people around the world. The first symptom, the decreased ability to see in faint light known as night

After years of arduous research, Canadian and American scientists announced the identification of the gene defect that causes most cases of cystic fibrosis, a breakthrough that may someday lead to new forms of treatment. Dr. Lap-chee Tsui (left) and Dr. Jack Riordan (right) of Toronto and Dr. Francis Collins of Michigan celebrate with four-year-old Ashley Dryer, a victim of the hereditary disease.

blindness, usually occurs in childhood; many victims eventually become completely blind. The new discoveries brought to five the total number of RP genes with known locations, and scientists now believe they have found most of the important ones.

RP shows three different family inheritance patterns, called X-linked, dominant, and recessive. In the X-linked form, which accounts for a small percentage of cases and strikes only males, the defective gene is located on the X chromosome, one of the two chromosomes that determine sex. The existence of two X-linked RP genes had been discovered in the past.

In the dominant form a child who receives the defective gene from either parent will develop the disease; if one parent carries the defective gene, a child has a 50 percent chance of inheriting it. In July 1989 researchers from the University of Texas Health Sciences Center and Trinity College in Dublin announced that they had found the location of a gene that caused a type of dominant RP in a large Irish family. Massachusetts scientists in January 1990 reported finding at this location an actual gene defect responsible for the disease. This was the first time such a defect had been identified for RP. Researchers are now studying a large family in Kentucky and Virginia that may have a different dominant gene.

In the recessive form of RP a child will develop the disease only if the defective gene is received from both parents. In March 1989, University of Texas scientists found a recessive RP gene in mice, and in December a University of California at Los Angeles group discovered a second one. Both groups believed that the locations of the human counterparts of these mouse genes would soon be identified.

There are also cases of RP where a family has only one victim and researchers do not see an inheritance pattern. Most likely, however, the disease in these individuals is due to the same genetic defects that cause the other forms of RP.

Disappointments. Researchers were unable to confirm previous studies that seemed to reveal genetic defects that cause schizophrenia and manic-depressive illness, two of the most common forms of mental illness. Scientists are not yet certain, however, whether the original results were mistaken or whether each of the diseases can be caused by more than one genetic defect, which would confound the original findings.

In 1987 researchers had reported that they had found the location of a defective gene linked to manic-depressive illness, as a result of a study of 81 members of an Amish family in Pennsylvania. Manic-depressive illness, which causes sharp mood swings between depression and elation, affects about 2 million Americans. The Amish do not have an unusually high incidence of the disease, but they are ideal for tracing genetic links because of their large family size and tradition of intermarrying, as well as their religious prohibitions against drug and alcohol use, which is a complicating factor in mental health studies. A second team of geneticists reported in November 1989 that a reexamination of the Amish family, including dozens of additional family members, considerably weakened the evidence that a gene in the previously announced location caused the illness.

In 1988 research had been reported that located on a specific chromosome a gene linked with schizophrenia, which causes hallucinations, delusions, and inappropriate emotional responses in about 1 out of every 100 people. At a meeting in the fall of 1989, however, different researchers reported that they could not find a similar gene in other families. Scientists have not had access to the families studied for the original report and have thus not been able to confirm it. An editorial in a November 1989 issue of the British scientific journal *Nature* concluded, "This leaves us with no persuasive evidence linking any psychiatric disease to a single [gene]."

Proteins Through Genetic Engineering

Wound Healing. In July 1989 researchers from Georgia, Kentucky, and Tennessee reported that the healing of human wounds could be speeded up by the application of a protein called human epidermal growth factor. The supply of the protein used in their study was made by genetic engineering techniques. The substance may prove especially valuable for treating severe burns and chronic wounds, such as bedsores and foot ulcers, as well as for promoting the regrowth of skin removed for grafting onto burn areas.

Epidermal growth factor is normally produced by the body to promote wound healing. Researchers had speculated, on the basis of studies with animals, that application of additional amounts would accelerate the process. In the study, wound healing was speeded by an average of 1.5 days—not a huge amount, but enough to show that the approach is viable.

Saving Infants' Lungs. Tests in humans were begun in 1989 to determine the effectiveness of a genetically engineered form of a protein that may be able to safeguard the lungs of premature infants. Of the 250,000 premature babies born in the United States each year, 1 out of every 7 has poorly developed lungs and experiences a gradually worsening difficulty with breathing known as respiratory distress syndrome. This condition is commonly treated by raising the proportion of oxygen in the air the infants breathe, sometimes to as much as double the usual level. With such high oxygen concentrations, however, as many as 30 percent of the infants develop a condition called bronchopulmonary dysplasia, which can scar and permanently damage the lungs. The damage is produced by oxygen "free radicals," which are highly reactive chemicals that form in the presence of high oxygen levels.

The new tests, begun in March by researchers from Bio-Technology General Corporation of New York City, involve an enzyme, called superoxide dismutase, that destroys the free radicals before they can damage the lungs. Previous studies with superoxide dismutase obtained from cows had shown it to be effective for this purpose, although it frequently provoked a reaction by the immune system. It is hoped the new form will be as effective and produce no reaction.

Food Ingredient Approved. In March 1990 the U.S. Food and Drug Administration approved for marketing the first genetically engineered food product for human consumption. The product, made, by Pfizer Inc., is a bioengineered form of the enzyme rennin (or chymosin), which is used by cheese makers to curdle milk into curds and whey and has traditionally been extracted from calves' stomachs.

Prenatal Screening

Researchers believe that an extremely safe means of testing for genetic diseases may someday develop out of a highly experimental technique for studying the fetal red blood cells that appear, in small numbers, in a pregnant woman's bloodstream. The technique does not disturb the fetus and creates no risk of a miscarriage. It thus would be safer than the two "invasive" procedures now often used—amniocentesis and chorionic villus sampling.

Boston researchers reported in July 1989 that they used special antibodies to mark, or "tag," the fetal cells, which were then separated from the mother's blood. A special enzyme called DNA polymerase was used to increase the small amount of DNA present so that it could be analyzed by conventional techniques. In November other scientists revealed that they had used a similar technique in 19 pregnancies. All the researchers cautioned, however, that several years may elapse before the extremely complicated test could be used for routine screening.

Test for Diabetes

In June 1989 researchers in Pittsburgh reported that they had developed a test to predict genetic susceptibility to Type I (insulin-dependent) diabetes, the most serious form of the disease. Experts believe that the onset of Type I diabetes in susceptible individuals is triggered by some outside factor, such as a virus-caused infection.

At present, physicians have no way to prevent the development of diabetes in susceptible individuals, but research in animals suggests that prevention may eventually be possible. For now, however, the test could allow parents to monitor their children's health in order to detect the onset of diabetes, whose initial symptoms are similar to those of influenza. In many cases the disease is now detected in the emergency room after a child has entered a diabetic coma.

Making Monoclonal Antibodies

Scientists at the Research Institute of Scripps Clinic in La Jolla, Calif., have devised two powerful new ways to isolate and manufacture monoclonal antibodies. These specialized proteins, similar to the antibodies normally produced by the body's immune system, are now widely used for measuring small quantities of drugs, hormones, vitamins, and other substances in the bloodstream and show immense promise for the treatment of a wide variety of human diseases. They are already employed, for instance, to help prevent the body's rejection of transplants and to kill tumor cells. The new techniques should reduce the price of the monoclonal antibodies used in such therapy from thousands of dollars a gram to only a few dollars.

Antibodies are ordinarily made by white blood cells to target foreign substances—including bacteria, viruses, parasites, and chemicals—for destruction by the immune system. Their principal characteristic is an ability to bind selectively to only one substance, be it a foreign chemical or a protein on the surface of a bacterium. At any given time the human body has more than 100,000 different antibody-producing cells circulating in the bloodstream, and it can generate literally billions of them.

In the mid-1970s researchers developed a technique for producing monoclonal antibodies. They injected mice with a virus or other material for which an antibody was desired and later removed the animals' spleens, the organ that makes white blood cells. The white cells from the spleens were then fused with mouse tumor cells to create hybrid cells called hybridomas, each of which inherited the reproductive ability of the cancer cell and the antibody-producing ability of the white cell. A hybridoma making the desired antibody could then be selected and grown in quantity to yield large amounts of the antibody. This hybridoma approach, however, is expensive. Also, the technique does not work well with human cells. Antibodies produced in mouse cells can be used in therapy, but humans quickly develop an allergic reaction to them.

In December 1989, Scripps researchers announced that they could perform the selection process in bacteria. They inserted the antibody-producing genes into special viruses, called bacteriophages, that infect bacteria. As the bacteriophages reproduced, the genes continually mutated, so that a virtually infinite number of different antibodies were produced. The researchers also developed a simple screening process to select the bacteriophages that produce a desired antibody. Overall, this process is much cheaper and quicker than making hybridomas and will work equally well with animal or human genes.

Independently, a separate research group at Scripps reported in November 1989 that they had devised a way to produce monoclonal antibodies in plants. When the gene for an antibody was introduced into tobacco plant cells, for example, the antibodies that were made could be readily separated from other proteins produced by the plant. The researchers said that the antibodies could be produced on plantations much more cheaply than they could be made with hybridomas.

THOMAS H. MAUGH II, PH.D.

GOVERNMENT POLICIES AND PROGRAMS

UNITED STATES

Scandal Strikes Approvals of Generic Drugs • Federal AIDS Funding Surges • New Abortion Developments

Generic Drug Scandal

In 1989 a major scandal erupted involving the procedures used by the U.S. Food and Drug Administration to approve generic drugs for sale to the public. Generic drugs are chemical equivalents of name-brand drugs whose patents have expired. Generally less expensive than their name-brand counterparts, they account for about a third of all prescriptions written in the United States.

Charges of corruption in generic drug approval first emerged in 1988, in the course of an extensive congressional investigation into the FDA. The investigation, by the oversight subcommittee of the House Energy and Commerce Committee, resulted from a complaint brought against the FDA by Mylan Laboratories Inc. of Pittsburgh. Mylan, convinced that it was being discriminated against when its applications to manufacture generics were subjected to repeated delays by the FDA, had begun its own private investigation of the agency in 1987.

Mylan also eventually filed suit against two former FDA employees and four drug-manufacturing companies, charging that corruption within the federal agency resulted in racketeering and in violations of antitrust law. Mylan officials contended that the order in which new generic drugs were approved was set by FDA employees even before drug manufacturers submitted applications. This illegal procedure, the suit alleged, was followed in order to give preferential treatment to certain companies.

During the summer of 1989 three FDA officials pleaded guilty to criminal charges of accepting bribes from generic drug makers, and two companies pleaded guilty to having given bribes. In addition, it was discovered that several manufacturers had falsified data submitted in seeking FDA authorization to market certain generic drugs. Vitarine Pharmaceuticals of New York, which sought approval for a generic version of the drug Dyazide, a popular medication for high blood pressure, submitted Dyazide, rather than its generic version, for FDA equivalence tests.

In April the FDA began investigating 11 generic manufacturers suspected of irregularities; the number was later increased to 13. Manufacturing and record-keeping problems were found at nearly all of them. It was announced in August that the FDA would increase surveillance of generic drug firms. The agency undertook comprehensive inspections of the 20 leading manufacturers, tested numerous generics, including the 30 most frequently prescribed ones, and moved to withdraw its approval of certain drugs. In addition, dozens of drugs were suspended or recalled by manufacturers. Federal officials said, however, that no significant problems in safety or effectiveness of generic drugs were discovered.

Developments continued to unfold in early 1990. The U.S. Securities and Exchange Commission filed securities fraud charges against the Bolar Pharmaceutical Company, a major generic manufacturer based on Long Island, N.Y. Bolar was cited for failing to inform investors promptly when it decided to suspend delivery of over 70 products (including its version of Dyazide) as a result of reports that it had submitted falsified documents to the FDA. In March federal prosecutors charged another former FDA official with accepting a payoff from a generic drug company.

AIDS News

Funding. Spending by the federal government on research and public health programs focusing on AIDS was set at $1.6 billion for the 1990 fiscal year, which began on October 1, 1989. For the first time, AIDS funding topped the figure for cancer.

In June 1989 an article published in the prestigious *New England Journal of Medicine* raised provocative questions about the level of federal spending on AIDS. Between fiscal years 1982 and 1989 total AIDS spending by the federal government, including funding for treatment, rose from $6 million to $2.2 billion. The article warned that further growth might raise questions about whether federal funds were being used in an effective way. The authors compared AIDS with other major life-threatening diseases in terms of funding and number of deaths. In fiscal 1989 the federal government spent $1.31 billion on AIDS in the areas of research, education, and prevention. This was nearly as much as it spent on cancer ($1.45 billion) and substantially exceeded funding for heart disease ($1.01 billion). Cancer, however, was expected to kill almost 15 times as many Americans as AIDS in 1989, and heart disease more than 20 times as many. The authors did not take a position on the adequacy of funding for AIDS in comparison with funding for other diseases. They did, however, note several possible justifications for increased AIDS funding; these included the fact that AIDS is infectious and continues to spread and that it strikes a high proportion of relatively young adults in comparison with other major diseases.

Passport Curbs Eased. In response to protests by various organizations, including the World Health Organization, the federal government announced in early 1990 that it would relax restrictions on people with AIDS seeking to enter the United States. Persons with AIDS would still be required to declare their condition when applying for a visa, and they would have to request a waiver of regulations that prohibit people infected with the disease from entering the country. But the requests would now be processed quickly, and the government would no longer stamp passports to indicate that the holder has AIDS. The changes, however, did not satisfy opponents of the U.S. restrictions, and several organizations threatened to boycott major scientific meetings on AIDS scheduled to take place in the United States in 1990.

Restrictions on Abortion

In July the U.S. Supreme Court by a vote of 5 to 4 handed down a historic ruling expanding states' powers to limit the right to abortion, which had been established in the celebrated case of *Roe* v. *Wade* in 1973. In the new case, *Webster* v. *Reproductive Health Services*, the Court upheld three provisions of a Missouri law. One barred public employees from performing or assisting in abortions unless the mother's life was in danger. A second prohibited the use of public facilities for abortions except for those necessary to save the life of the mother. And the third required doctors performing an abortion after the 19th week of pregnancy to first test the fetus for viability (a separate Missouri law forbids the abortion of a viable fetus). The Court's decision guaranteed

that the abortion controversy would intensify in two arenas: in state legislatures, which could approve restrictions on abortion at least as stringent as those upheld in the Missouri law, and in the courts. The Supreme Court agreed to hear three more abortion cases in the fall of 1989; one was settled out of court, and decisions in the other two were to be handed down in 1990.

While initially the decision in *Webster* v. *Reproductive Health Services* was viewed as a major victory for right-to-life advocates, the ultimate political fallout from the ruling was unclear as of early 1990. Many observers believed that the Democratic victories in the New Jersey and Virginia gubernatorial elections in November 1989 were in part due to strong opposition to abortion by the Republican candidates. The governor of Florida called a special session of his state's legislature to impose restrictions on abortions, but the legislature voted down the proposals.

On the other hand, Pennsylvania enacted a particularly restrictive abortion law in late 1989. In January 1990, shortly before the law was to take effect, a federal district judge issued a preliminary injunction against some of its major provisions. Two months later, Guam, a U.S. territory in the Pacific, enacted the most restrictive law in any American jurisdiction. The statute outlawed abortion except when the pregnancy endangered the mother's life; performing or helping in an abortion was made a felony, and it became a misdemeanor to have or solicit an abortion or to solicit a woman to have one. Enforcement of the law was temporarily blocked by a federal district judge. Meanwhile, Idaho's governor vetoed a bill that would have been the most restrictive state abortion law in the nation. The bill would have prohibited abortions except in cases of severe fetal deformity or threat to the mother's physical health or in cases of rape reported to police within seven days or of incest where the victim was under 18 years of age.

Following the Supreme Court decision, the pro-choice bloc in the U.S. Congress demonstrated more political clout than it had shown for a decade. The House of Representatives pushed for a reversal of long-standing antiabortion provisions in three annual appropriations bills, but the pro-choice forces lacked sufficient strength to override President George Bush's vetoes of the resulting bills.

See also the Health and Medical News article BIO-ETHICS.

Medicare and Medicaid

The Medicare Catastrophic Coverage Act, passed in 1988, proved to be short-lived. By the end of 1989, Congress had repealed its major provisions, largely in response to extensive lobbying by the elderly, many

Demonstrators on both sides of the abortion controversy turned out in force when the U.S. Supreme Court considered a restrictive Missouri abortion law. The Court's ruling, which narrowed abortion rights established by the Roe v. Wade *decision of 1973, seemed certain to provoke many more demonstrations, as the future of abortion legislation was largely returned to the state legislatures.*

of whom objected to the increased costs they were required to pay for the expanded protection. (*See the Health and Medical News article* HEALTHCARE COSTS AND INSURANCE.)

Congressional tinkering with Medicaid, which provides medical help to welfare recipients and other low-income Americans, slowed markedly in 1989. In previous years Congress, despite the deficits dogging the federal budget, had enacted major expansions in eligibility. These annual liberalizations caused budget problems for the states. (The states share in the cost of the program, paying on average roughly 45 percent of the total expense.) As a result, the National Governors' Association in August called for a two-year moratorium on federally mandated increases in Medicaid benefits that would mean further costs for the states. That move, as well as a prolonged impasse between the Bush administration and Congress over the 1990 budget, caused the liberalization of the Medicaid program to be more modest than in previous years. Just before adjournment late in 1989, Congress approved a requirement for states to extend Medicaid eligibility for certain services to pregnant women and children up to age six in families with incomes under 133 percent of the federal poverty threshold ($10,060 for a family of three).

New Federal Health Appointments

In March 1989, Dr. Louis W. Sullivan won overwhelming confirmation by the Senate as secretary of health and human services in the new Bush administration, despite some controversy over his position on abortion. Sullivan had been quoted in an Atlanta newspaper as apparently supporting the right to abortion, but in the face of opposition to his nomination from anti-abortionists he indicated that his position was actually close to that of Bush. Sullivan had previously been president of the Morehouse School of Medicine in Atlanta, a primarily black institution, which he helped found.

The new administration did not reappoint Dr. C. Everett Koop as surgeon general. Koop had used that previously obscure federal post to become the nation's family doctor. Voicing strong and controversial opinions on health issues, he vigorously supported anti-smoking measures and did not shy from blunt talk about how AIDS is spread. The U.S. National Academy of Sciences in 1989 awarded Koop its highest honor, the Public Welfare Medal. Late in the year the administration nominated as surgeon general Dr. Antonia Coello Novello, who had been deputy director of the National Institute of Child Health and Human

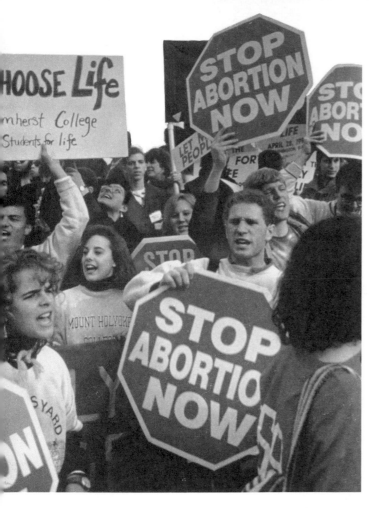

CANADA

*New Antismoking Moves • AIDS Update •
Federal Abortion Law • Nurse Walkouts*

Smoking Regulations

Smoking is addictive, the Canadian government learned in October 1989. In June, Health and Welfare Canada had paid $30,000 (Canadian dollars used throughout) to a team of leading Canadian scientists to study the issue, despite the fact that the U.S. surgeon general had already declared smoking to be addictive. On October 31, government regulations took effect requiring that all tobacco products carry one of four warnings, covering 20 percent of each of the front and back of product packages. The warnings include "Smoking decreases life expectancy" and "Smoking is the major cause of lung cancer." Packages must also carry information on toxic substance content. Intense lobbying by the tobacco industry, with vague threats of court action, had prevented the inclusion of a warning that tobacco is addictive. In January 1990, however, Health and Welfare Minister Perrin Beatty announced plans to increase the number of warnings to eight, among them one on the addictiveness of tobacco use, and to require that cigarette packages contain a warning leaflet.

Meanwhile, three of Canada's leading tobacco manufacturers fought court battles against laws banning, as of January 1989, tobacco advertising from publications, radio, and television, as well as from billboards and other signs. The companies maintained that the laws violated their freedom of expression as guaranteed in the Canadian constitution's Charter of Rights and Freedoms.

The federal government announced that at the end of 1989 it would extend its airline smoking ban to cover international flights of Canadian airlines. Smokers who had bought tickets before the new rule was made public voiced loud protests, and the effective date of the regulation was postponed to July 1, 1990. The ban, affecting all flights except charters by special groups, would be the first of its kind in the world.

AIDS Policies

The federal government announced in mid-December 1989 that it would give $120,000 over four years to each of 1,250 Canadians who were infected with the AIDS virus through tainted blood transfusions or blood products in the early 1980s. (Contaminated blood was virtually eliminated from Canadian blood banks in later years as a result of new screening measures.) The money would be given as "a form of disaster relief," beginning in April 1990, said Health and

Development. Like Koop, Novello, who is originally from Puerto Rico, is a pediatrician. Her nomination was confirmed by the Senate in March 1990.

Early in 1989, Dr. James O. Mason, the director of the Centers for Disease Control, was named assistant secretary of health. Dr. William L. Roper, a White House adviser, became the CDC's new head in March 1990. The CDC, which tracks the spread of infectious diseases, has been in the forefront of the war against AIDS. Roper, a pediatrician and public health administrator, previously headed the Health Care Financing Administration, which manages the Medicare and Medicaid programs. In that job he started the practice of publishing the death rates for individual hospitals and releasing information to the public about health and safety violations in nursing homes. Not long before Roper took up the CDC post, Gail Wilensky was confirmed by the Senate as the HCFA chief; she was formerly a vice president of Project HOPE, an international medical education foundation.

In November, Dr. Frank E. Young was transferred from his post as commissioner of the FDA to that of deputy assistant secretary of health for health science and environment. He had headed the FDA during one of the most controversial periods of its history.

JAMES ROTHERHAM

Welfare Minister Beatty. Most of the recipients would be hemophiliacs.

The federal government in July 1989 asked the provinces to help finance a national program to combat the spread of AIDS by giving clean needles to drug addicts. Many users of intravenous drugs have been getting AIDS from contaminated needles. Touting the free needle program as highly successful in other countries, Beatty said he did not believe distributing needles would encourage people to start using drugs. As of early 1990, only Quebec and Ontario had agreed to join the federal initiative.

Beatty announced in September that AIDS victims in Canada could now get the experimental drug dideoxyinosine (DDI) free, under an emergency drug program. AIDS lobbyists had been pushing for release of the drug since July, when U.S. researchers reported it was a promising new treatment.

The Supreme Court of Canada upheld Chantal Daigle's right to have an abortion despite the objections of her former fiancé. The closely watched case was heard while Canadians awaited new national legislation on abortion rights.

Abortion Legislation

The House of Commons approved a new abortion law in principle in late November 1989, by a vote of 164 to 114. The bill was expected to be returned to the Commons for a final vote in the spring of 1990.

Prime Minister Brian Mulroney said the legislation reflected an attempt to balance the rights of both women and the unborn. Still, the bill faced several obstacles on the road to enactment. Some antiabortion members of Parliament who supported the proposal in November said they would not do so the next time around unless it were amended to protect the rights of the unborn. Pro-choice critics of the bill—including at least one cabinet minister—were angry because it did nothing to increase, let alone guarantee, access to abortion. Moreover, under the bill an abortion would be legal only if a doctor says a woman's physical or mental health is endangered—a provision denying women the right to make decisions on their own about their bodies.

Canada had been without abortion legislation since the federal Supreme Court ruled in January 1988 that an existing law—which required that the operation be performed only in accredited hospitals and only after approval by a committee of doctors—was unconstitutional because it interfered with a woman's right to control her body and thus violated the Charter of Rights and Freedoms.

In July two men obtained court injunctions preventing their former girlfriends from having abortions. One injunction was quickly overturned by the Ontario Supreme Court, but the other was upheld by the Quebec Court of Appeal, which declared the fetus to be protected under the Quebec Charter of Rights and Freedoms. However, the Supreme Court of Canada overturned that injunction in mid-August, after the Quebec woman had already undergone the operation, in the United States. The Supreme Court judgment in the case, made public in November, stated that a fetus is not a person under the province's civil law or charter of rights, nor is it a person under the common law of other provinces. The court also ruled that a potential father has no legal right to prevent a woman from having an abortion.

Nurses Strike

Nurses flexed their collective striking muscle in 1989, briefly crippling the medical systems of British Columbia and Quebec.

Irate members of the B.C. Nurses Union picketed some 80 hospitals for 17 days in June. Because of a law requiring the union to maintain essential services, an average of 70 percent of the nursing staff stayed on the job at any one time. But during the strike the working nurses refused to do overtime and nonnursing chores, including moving patients. Hospitals were forced to cancel elective surgery and sent patients home early.

The dispute between the 17,500-member union and the Health Labor Relations Board—the bargaining unit for British Columbia's 144 hospitals—was finally settled by binding arbitration in mid-August, after threats of government intervention by provincial Premier William Vander Zalm. Under the resulting retroactive contract—the old agreement had expired on March 31—the nurses received a 20.9 percent wage increase over two years.

In September, Quebec's 40,000 nurses staged an illegal walkout after months of failed negotiations with the province over wages and other issues. The strike lasted a week, and the nurses went back to work without a contract on September 12, the same day 95,000 hospital support staff walked off the job to begin a six-day strike. A wave of other public service strikes followed.

Within days of returning to work, the Quebec nurses agreed to accept a retroactive 4 percent increase for 1989. By 1991, the year the new contract expires, starting nurses would earn more than $28,000 a year (up from $24,325), and top salaried nurses would make $41,000 (up from $33,139). The contract also brought increased compensation for night shift work and a reduced work week for preretirement nurses. In October the union and two of its leaders were found guilty of contempt of court for ignoring a government order and staging the illegal strike. They were fined a total of $5,000. Sanctions, including pay cuts and loss of seniority, were applied against the nurses who participated in the strike.

LYNNE COHEN

HEALTHCARE COSTS AND INSURANCE

Costs Continue to Surge • New System for Medicare Payments to Doctors • Medicare Catastrophic Care Repeal

Rising Costs

At the end of a decade marked by moves to control health costs, the total U.S. healthcare bill exceeded $600 billion. Costs, which in 1965 accounted for only 6 percent of the gross national product, consumed more than 11 percent in 1989, with no relief in sight. The increases occurred despite the best efforts of the government, private insurers, and employers to contain the damage. The government managed to reduce the rate of growth in the Medicare program for the elderly and in Medicaid for the poor. The private sector was able to redesign health plans to favor cost-conscious providers of care. But these successes were more than countered by the steady growth of the elderly population, with its need for more and more sophisticated care, by the development of expensive new drugs and technologies, and by the increasing tendency of malpractice-wary physicians to practice defensive medicine.

That grim fact—as well as the existence of more than 30 million Americans with no health insurance and growing pressure to provide some type of long-term care coverage for the chronically ill—triggered renewed interest in replacing patchwork fixes with a restructuring of the U.S. healthcare system. As commissions met and experts debated, the underlying message was clear: healthcare is a benefit everyone wants, but no one wants to pay for.

Reform in Physician Payments

After the government cracked down on Medicare charges by hospitals in 1983, pegging reimbursement rates to a system of "diagnosis-related groups," doctors were the next obvious target. It was only a question of when and how. In the waning hours of its 1989 session, Congress added to the Budget Reconciliation Act for the 1990 fiscal year a complete overhaul in the way Medicare pays physicians. To be phased in gradually beginning in 1992, the new system will reimburse physicians according to a nationwide fee schedule based on a number of factors, including the time, training, and skill required to care for patients.

By adopting the so-called resource-based relative value scale, a program designed by William Hsio of Harvard University, Congress attempted to correct inequities in physician payments that tended to over-reward the technicians—surgeons, radiologists, and anesthesiologists, in particular—and undervalue family practitioners and internists, who perform few "procedures" but spend time examining and talking to patients. The change is expected to redirect the way medicine is practiced away from diagnostic and surgical procedures to a new emphasis on primary and preventive care.

In theory the new program merely redistributes payments more equitably among physicians and will not affect overall spending. To prevent physicians who will lose revenue from making up the difference by shifting costs to other patients or performing more procedures, the new law limits the amount doctors are permitted to bill their patients above the Medicare reimbursement and contains a mechanism for controlling volume.

Gray power shows its muscle as angry senior citizens in Chicago block the car of U.S. Representative Dan Rostenkowski in a demonstration denouncing the Medicare Catastrophic Coverage Act. The bill, which was later repealed, would have been financed in part by an income tax surcharge on the elderly with incomes over a certain level.

Catastrophic Care Repeal

In the final hours of the 1989 session, Congress bowed to the will of angry senior citizens and repealed key portions of the Medicare Catastrophic Coverage Act, which had been designed to provide protection against prolonged healthcare expenses resulting from a serious illness or injury. Hailed as the first major expansion of Medicare since the program began in 1965, the act had been passed overwhelmingly only 16 months earlier. It had not even gone into effect when seniors began objecting to financing the new program through an income surtax on the wealthiest elderly. Only 40 percent would have paid any of the tax in 1989, and about 5 percent would have paid the maximum $800, but that group turned out to be extremely vocal.

The demise of the act followed months of angry controversy in which supporters struggled unsuccessfully to find less objectionable ways to fund at least part of the program. In the end Congress repealed all the new Medicare benefits: unlimited hospital coverage after payment of a single annual deductible, a cap on out-of-pocket physician and outpatient med-

ical expenses, coverage for outpatient drugs, expanded coverage for home, hospice, and nursing-home care, coverage for mammography to detect breast cancer, and some coverage of healthcare for homebound Medicare patients.

In other Medicare developments, the government managed to trim $1.3 billion in Medicare spending during 1989 by shifting the prime responsibility for hospital and doctor bills for elderly workers and their spouses to private employers. The saving came through a requirement that private plans fulfill their obligations for doctor and hospital bills before Medicare kicks in. Plans to identify covered workers over age 65 by computer checking of Internal Revenue Service and Social Security records were expected to shift as much as $900 million more to private payers in the following year.

Medicaid Expansion Retained

Although it repealed Medicare catastrophic coverage, Congress left intact the expansion of coverage through Medicaid, the joint federal-state program for the poor, that was part of the same bill. This expansion included a requirement that Medicaid pay all Medicare premiums, deductibles, and copayments for elderly patients with incomes below 100 percent of the federally defined poverty level ($10,060 for a family of three) who do not qualify for Medicaid. Another provision required states to increase the amount of income and assets that can be kept by the spouse of a nursing-home patient whose care is covered by Medicaid. Congress in late 1989 also expanded mandated Medicaid coverage for pregnant women and infants to include children up to to the age of six and families with incomes under 133 percent of the federal poverty level.

The Health Care Financing Administration estimated that the new coverage would add more than $1 billion to the federal-state Medicaid bill. Although expanded coverage for the poor has had a high priority for Congress and many states, the prospect of higher expenditures put a number of states in a financial bind. States pay, on average, about 45 percent of Medicaid's $60 billion cost, with the federal government supplying the rest. In 1984 about 8 percent of state revenues went to Medicaid; in 1989 states spent about 15 percent of their total revenues on the program. The growth in Medicaid costs (about 12-13 percent a year) is outpacing the growth in state revenues (about 5-6 percent). Many states, required by law to balance their budgets, have tried to find ways to hold the line on Medicaid spending. One way has been to limit Medicaid eligibility. In the late 1970s, Medicaid covered 75 percent of those below the federal poverty line. In 1989 the program covered only 38 percent.

Employers' Costs Soar

Workers at four regional phone companies went on strike in August, focusing national attention on the struggle of employers to control the cost of providing healthcare coverage for workers. Unable to slow spiraling costs, three of the four "Baby Bells" wanted their employees to pay part of the bill. (The fourth, Ameritech, had in 1986 moved to stem the costs surge by instituting a "preferred provider" network of hospitals and doctors agreeing to charge the company lower fees). Angry workers countered they were not responsible for the increases and walked off the job. At two of the Baby Bells, Pacific Telesis and Bell Atlantic, contract settlements reached in the following weeks called for the establishment of preferred provider networks. At the third, Nynex, the strike lasted much longer, and in the end labor and management agreed to form a joint cost-containment committee.

The Baby Bells were only the most visible of the many companies experiencing health cost shock.

Overall, corporate health costs rose 20 to 40 percent in 1989. Experts expected the upward trend to continue and predicted average increases of at least 20 percent for 1990, with far greater increases for small firms. Providing healthcare cost firms an average of almost $2,750 per employee in 1989, with the figure expected to reach $3,000 in 1990. To insure 160 million workers, dependents, and retirees, U.S. business spent an estimated $140 billion in 1989.

Striking telephone workers in New York City stage a mock funeral for their health benefits as they protest a new company plan requiring employees to bear a part of the cost of health coverage. With health insurance costs soaring, many corporations began seeking to shift some of the expense to their workers.

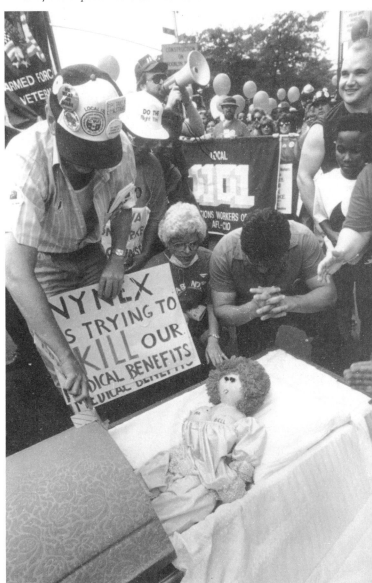

The increases reflected, in part, the insurance industry's response to 1988 pretax loses of $4.7 billion, which it sought to pass on to companies. Businesses were also hit with higher rates from doctors and hospitals trying to make up for cutbacks in payments from Medicare and Medicaid, as well as for the costs of providing care for the uninsured.

The overall increases occurred despite Herculean efforts by many firms to control costs. Surveys showed more than 70 percent of employees with employer-sponsored coverage were enrolled in some form of managed-care plan. In addition, many employers had switched to cheaper plans or introduced flexible benefits to shift part of the burden for expensive coverage to employees. In numerous instances employees were paying more of their ordinary health bills, through higher copayments and deductibles, in return for better catastrophic coverage. Certain companies were refusing to hire workers with known health risks, like smoking. And some firms were employing their own medical staff.

Despite union efforts to maintain "first dollar" coverage—no deductibles, no premiums, no copayments—for workers, a recent survey by the Employee Benefit Research Institute confirmed that workers are now paying more of the bill. Nearly half of those polled said monthly premiums had increased in the past two years; moreover, one-quarter of those surveyed reported that they were paying part of the premium for the first time.

The jury was still out on the overall impact of cost-control measures. The notion of creating "prudent buyers" of care by having employees share the cost could be undermined if workers delay seeking needed care, and it is still not clear whether managed care will produce long-term savings. Older and larger health maintenance organizations, which provide total care for a fixed annual fee, did better financially than the newer and smaller groups and were less likely to increase fees. A study by the Institute of Medicine, based in Washington, D.C., found that reviews of care by a third party, a popular cost-containment strategy, produced some savings for employers but seemed to have little impact on the long-term rate of increase in costs.

Access and Quality

Renewed interest in establishing a national health plan was sparked by frustrations about the inability to control the growth in costs, coupled with the challenge of caring for people without insurance and of finding some way to help families bear the financial burden of providing long-term care for those with severe chronic illness. In the wake of studies suggesting that at least one-third of care may be unnec-

essary or inappropriate, the need to find ways to assess and assure quality of care added to the debate.

The idea of restructuring the U.S. system along the lines of the Canadian program gained momentum in 1989. A group called Physicians for a National Health Program outlined in the *New England Journal of Medicine* a plan, much like Canada's, that would provide universal coverage for all Americans, with free choice of physicians and no out-of-pocket expenditures. Eventually the plan could be funded by the income tax or some other form of progressive tax. During a transition period, in which the plan would be tested in state demonstration projects, it would be paid for by money now going to Medicare, Medicaid, and state and local health programs, along with money from a tax on employers and individuals and from private health insurance revenues.

Ideas for reform that fell short of a national health plan were also debated. Proposals were put forth aimed at a public and private mix that would guarantee that all Americans were covered for at least basic, minimum healthcare.

Oregon Experiment

With surveys showing that two-thirds of Americans favor some form of universal health coverage, states have seemed to move in that direction more quickly than the federal government. Hawaii has had mandatory employer-based programs since the 1970s, and a new state insurance plan for the uninsured was enacted in 1989. The fate of the highly publicized Massachusetts program is in doubt because of the state's budget problems; but California is contemplating a statewide insurance plan for 1992, and other states, including Washington and New York, as well as the District of Columbia, are looking at similar proposals.

Perhaps none of these approaches is as far reaching or controversial as Oregon's plan to experiment with new ways of providing care for the poor. The state legislature approved three laws designed to ensure that all state residents have access to healthcare. One requires employers to offer a minimum package of benefits, the second creates a state risk pool for those with medically uninsurable conditions, and the third would expand Medicaid to include everyone below the federal poverty line. The plan would add at least 77,000 new beneficiaries to the 135,000 already in the Medicaid program.

In return for the expansion, Oregon wants to be able to choose what medical services Medicaid beneficiaries will receive, cutting lowest priority services first in order to free the funds needed for the expanded coverage. Since federal law requires that Medicaid provide all "necessary medical services," the Oregon proposal would require a congressional waiver. The Oregon legislature began its reform effort in 1987 by voting to stop spending Medicaid funds on certain expensive, and often unsuccessful, transplant procedures, choosing instead to use the funds for lower-cost basic services like prenatal care. While opponents argue that Oregon's approach amounts to rationing medical care, its backers say that care is already being rationed for poor people who do not qualify for Medicaid or whose doctors decline to provide care because of low reimbursement payments. Although the notion of rationing is probably unacceptable to most Americans, the Oregon debate could well be a forerunner of what the future holds in store for the entire nation. MARY HAGER

HEART AND CIRCULATORY SYSTEM

Death Rates Decline • Jarvik Heart Withdrawn • Cholesterol-lowering Debated • Fish and a Healthy Diet

Declining Death Rates

Does healthier living make a difference? Epidemiologists analyzing heart disease death rates in the United States, which have steadily declined since the mid-1960s, now believe it does. A recently published study gave a detailed account of coronary deaths among white men aged 35 to 44 years old in Allegheny County, Pennsylvania. Heart disease death rates for 1985 to 1986 were 55.5 percent lower than for 1970 to 1972. Another study, using less precise data pooled from 40 states between 1980 and 1985, showed an 18 to 19 percent decline in heart disease death in men between 35 and 74 years of age.

In both of these studies, a reduction in the rate of deaths outside the hospital, usually sudden deaths, accounted for nearly two-thirds of the total decline in deaths from heart disease. The researchers speculated that preventive medicine measures, such as treatment of high blood pressure, an end to cigarette smoking, better long-term therapy for cardiac chest pain (angina), better emergency paramedic services, and perhaps diets lower in fat have played a part. In-hospital cardiac death rates also decreased, probably because of better treatment of heart attacks and more sophisticated and safer surgery.

Preventing Sudden Cardiac Death

Despite declining death rates from heart disease, sudden cardiac death remains the leading cause of mortality in the United States. Sudden death often results from a type of arrhythmia called ventricular fibrillation, a disorganization of the electrical impulses of the heart that causes normal blood pumping to cease. Defibrillation, or electric shocks applied immediately to the heart, can correct this problem. Until recently defibrillation could be administered only by relatively large devices stationed in hospitals or carried by paramedics. Now, patients at high risk for ventricular fibrillation and other dangerous heart rhythms have a new option: automatic implantable defibrillators.

These devices, which are implanted like pacemakers, detect potentially lethal heart rhythms and administer electric current to correct abnormalities. Recent advances in miniaturization and battery life have made implantable defibrillators practical for many heart patients. But they are costly, they produce a very uncomfortable feeling when they discharge electric shocks in an awake patient, and they require battery replacement every three to five years. Therefore, they are usually reserved for individuals who have lost consciousness from an abnormal heart rhythm or who have required emergency defibrillation.

Patients with less severe arrhythmias may be better off without specific treatment. Two powerful drugs that reduce extra heartbeats, given to patients with arrhythmia after heart attacks, were found to increase death rates. The U.S. Food and Drug Administration in 1989 advised that the drugs—encainide (brand name, Enkaid) and flecainide (Tambocor)—be used only in cases of life-threatening arrhythmia.

Jarvik Heart Recalled

In January 1990 the FDA withdrew its approval of continued experimental use of the Jarvik-7 artificial heart—the first ever to be implanted in humans—because of serious manufacturing problems. The Jarvik was used both as a permanent replacement and as a temporary organ for patients awaiting a human transplant. An FDA inspection of the Symbion Inc. plant where the hearts are manufactured revealed poor quality control, inadequacies in personnel training and equipment servicing, and a failure to report adverse reactions in patients.

Cholesterol Debate Continues

Medical experts generally agree that there is a link between elevated levels of cholesterol in the blood and heart disease. But they do not agree on the benefits of and approaches to lowering cholesterol in individual patients. In 1987 the U.S. National Heart, Lung, and Blood Institute issued guidelines recommending dietary and drug therapy for elevated blood cholesterol, a problem that potentially affects over 30 percent of American adults. The guidelines have sparked lively debate about the effectiveness of cholesterol-lowering programs in reducing heart disease and cardiac death.

Critics of the recommendations make several points. First, many people with high total blood cholesterol levels do not develop heart disease, and many others with "safe" levels still develop coronary obstruction. Second, the measurement of cholesterol in many laboratories is not as accurate as it could be and may lead to misdiagnosis. Third, the effectiveness of cholesterol-lowering drugs in reducing heart attacks has been shown only in middle-aged men, whereas the institute's guidelines cover all adults. A study published early in 1990 reported a relationship between

Inventor Robert Jarvik displays the Jarvik-7 artificial heart, which gained worldwide acclaim when it was first used in a human patient in 1982. In January 1990, however, the U.S. Food and Drug Administration announced it was withdrawing its approval of experimental use of the Jarvik-7, citing "serious deficiencies" in the procedures followed by the device's manufacturer.

total blood cholesterol and heart disease among men aged 65 and older, but the relationship remains questionable among women. The benefits of cholesterol lowering have not been studied in women, the elderly, or young men.

Critics also argue that, in all but one study of cholesterol reduction, overall death rates were not reduced, even when significant reductions in heart attacks were documented. This finding suggests that cholesterol lowering may be associated with the development of other health problems. For example, violent accidents occurred more commonly in patients on cholesterol-lowering drugs in two separate studies, and intestinal cancers have been associated with lower total cholesterol levels, although it is not generally believed that reducing blood cholesterol causes cancer.

Supporters of cholesterol reduction feel that it will have long-term benefits. Such long-lasting effects were seen in a 15-year study of the cholesterol-modifying vitamin niacin. In this study the overall death rate decreased by about 10 percent, but the decrease was not seen until 7 to 10 years after the study began. Supporters also contend that there is little risk in a national awareness program advocating low-fat, low-cholesterol diets with drug therapy in selected patients. As the program already may have contributed to declining national cardiac death rates, supporters believe it should not be withheld from individuals who might benefit.

Because the potential benefit of cholesterol-lowering treatment is greater for those at highest risk of cardiac deaths, some physicians prescribe it only for patients with multiple other cardiac risk factors such as high blood pressure, cigarette smoking, diabetes, obesity, and family history of cardiac death. In these people, the risk of heart disease is greater than the sum of the risks from individual factors. Physicians also rely on measurements of high density lipoprotein (HDL) cholesterol, often referred to as "good cholesterol," to assess cardiovascular risk. High levels of HDL seem to protect against coronary artery disease and seem to be a better predictor of cardiac risk than cholesterol alone, especially in women.

Advances in research and laboratory techniques offer physicians new ways to identify patients at high risk for heart disease. Many clinical labs can now measure another type of lipoprotein, called Lp(a), which is strongly associated with heart attacks. Breakthroughs in the analysis of this substance show that it has structural similarities to low-density lipoprotein cholesterol (LDL or "bad cholesterol") and a protein called plasminogen that limits blood clotting. These findings may help scientists understand the link between the gradual formation of coronary artery obstructions and the sudden development of blood clots at the site of such obstructions, the cause of most heart attacks.

It is unknown whether lowering Lp(a) lipoprotein reduces heart disease. Medications that reduce total cholesterol do not necessarily reduce Lp(a). The drug lovastatin (Mevacor), for example, which can dramatically reduce total cholesterol, tends to increase Lp(a) lipoprotein.

Diet and Heart Attacks

In an era when the medical profession increasingly relies on sophisticated technology and medication, it is ironic that perhaps the most important new finding concerning the treatment of heart attack is the simple advice, "Eat fish." Another recommendation is to stay away from coffee.

In a British study of more than 2,000 men who had had a heart attack, subjects were randomly selected to receive advice about reducing dietary fat, increasing cereal fiber, or eating fish. Those advised to eat fish (such as mackerel, herring, sardines, and salmon) at least twice a week had a 29 percent reduction in death from all causes after two years. Subjects advised to reduce fat managed only a 3 to 4 percent reduction in cholesterol levels and experienced no difference in death rates. The fiber advice resulted in a slight, probably insignificant, increase in mortality.

Coffee did not fare as well as fish in the medical literature. A study of over 100,000 people revealed that drinking four or more cups of coffee a day was associated with a 36 to 45 percent increase in heart attacks. Drinkers of three cups a day or less had slightly more heart attacks than nondrinkers, but the increase was not statistically significant. One possible explanation for the increased risk of heart attacks among heavy coffee drinkers came from another study comparing 181 men who drank caffeinated coffee, decaffeinated coffee, or no coffee at all. Decaffeinated coffee was found to be associated with higher levels of harmful LDL cholesterol.

Food Rating Program

In February 1990 the American Heart Association (AHA) began a food endorsement program called HeartGuide. For a fee, manufacturers of products meeting certain standards for being relatively low in total fat, saturated fat, cholesterol, and sodium could put the distinctive HeartGuide emblem on the product's label or packaging. The program was engulfed in controversy from the start, in particular because of fears that it would appear to endorse specific foods rather than encourage a more healthful diet. In early April, under strong pressure from the FDA, the AHA canceled the HeartGuide program.

Exercise and the Heart

Evidence is growing that exercise and fitness confer longevity. In an eight-year study of over 13,000 initially healthy men and women, fitness was determined by a treadmill exercise test. During the follow-up period, overall death rates in the least physically fit 20 percent exceeded those in the most fit 20 percent by more than three times for men and four times for women. These results held up after statistical adjustments for age, cholesterol level, blood pressure, and parental history of heart disease.

In another study, which followed over 3,000 white male U.S. railroad workers for 20 years, a correlation was shown between increased physical activity during leisure time and decreased heart disease death. After adjustments for other cardiac risk factors, sedentary men had rates of heart disease about 30 percent greater than men who expended about 1,000 or more calories per week in a variety of recreational activities.

Both studies found that levels of fitness resulting from even moderate amounts of activity, the equivalent of brisk walking 30 minutes each day, resulted in greater life expectancy. This finding should make beginning an exercise program less intimidating to those who cannot (or feel they cannot) exercise vigorously.

Testing for Heart Disease

The intravenous form of a drug called dipyridamole (Persantine), currently administered in an oral form to help prevent strokes or clotting of coronary artery bypass grafts, may make it possible to identify people at risk of heart disease who cannot undertake the traditional stress test. Cardiologists routinely use exercise testing with electrocardiogram monitoring or nuclear heart scans to help determine whether individuals have heart disease. However, elderly people and those with orthopedic, vascular, or neurological problems often cannot exercise vigorously enough for traditional stress testing to be of value.

In a recent study, Italian investigators gave dipyridamole to a group of patients undergoing echocardiogram (sound wave) imaging of the heart. Intravenous infusion of dipyridamole changes cardiac blood flow patterns, which can cause detectable change in cardiac function or increase the heart's ability to take up radioactively labeled substances.

In the Italian study, 46 percent of those whose echocardiograms detected changes in cardiac function had cardiac problems over the next three years, compared with 6 percent of patients with no change in cardiac function. Dipyridamole can be used in a similar manner before nuclear heart scans. Recent reports suggest that the dipyridamole test may help

A healthful diet has increasingly become recognized as one of the most powerful weapons in the war on heart disease. The first statewide campaign to educate the public about nutrition and the heart was launched by New York; here, dietitian Corinne Giannini of the Niagara County program discusses the importance of sensible eating.

physicians identify the risk of cardiac complications in other groups with limited exercise capacity, such as people who have just had heart attacks. The test might help physicians select individuals who would benefit most from aggressive, but somewhat risky, measures like bypass surgery or angioplasty.

Angioplasty Alternatives

Angioplasty, the inflatable balloon dilation of coronary artery obstructions, has become as widely used as coronary artery bypass surgery. However, there is a tendency for blockages to recur following angioplasty.

Research teams have taken a variety of technical approaches to prevent this problem, with some promising results. Metal stents, or supports that hold the artery open, can be inserted at the site of narrowing and have been successful in more than 90 percent of patients in whom they have been implanted, even after the failure of routine angioplasty. Catheters have been developed that shave away fatty deposits bit by bit. Laser catheters that vaporize such deposits and catheters that break them up with microwaves have also been investigated. These techniques largely remain experimental as their safety and benefits compared to routine angioplasty are evaluated.

Drug Update

In March 1990 the results of a study comparing bloodclot-busting drugs showed no difference in effectiveness during heart attacks between the drug most commonly used in the United States, tissue plasminogen activator (TPA) and the drug most commonly used in Europe, streptokinase. TPA, a genetically engineered product, costs $2,200 per dose; streptokinase, a protein derived from certain bacteria, costs $76 to $186 per dose. Investigators found the drugs equally effective in preventing death, heart failure, and second heart attacks during coronary care unit stays.

Some medical scientists criticized the study because the blood-thinning drug heparin was not administered promptly after TPA, as is the U.S. practice, but 12 hours after hospital admission. The critics felt that the delayed use of heparin may have reduced TPA's effectiveness, making it appear no better than streptokinase.

The effectiveness of digitalis, aspirin, and hydrochlorothiazide, drugs widely used for cardiovascular disease for many years, continues to be studied.

The effect of digitalis on the heart was described over 200 years ago (it can help the heart to beat more steadily and forcefully) but its usefulness in patients without irregular heart beats has been considered unproven. New studies now provide convincing evidence that digoxin (Lanoxin), a digitalis-like preparation, is effective against chronic heart failure. In a study of 230 heart failure patients, subjects were given either digoxin, a promising experimental drug called milrinone, both drugs, or a placebo. Those receiving digoxin therapy could tolerate more exercise and experienced fewer problems requiring medical attention compared to those switched from digoxin to a placebo. In addition, digoxin worked as well as or better than milrinone and was more easily tolerated.

Aspirin has received much attention as a cardiovascular "wonder drug." The final report of the Physicians' Health Study, a highly publicized trial of aspirin to prevent heart disease, was published in 1989. During the trial one aspirin tablet or a placebo was given every other day to over 22,000 initially healthy male physicians, 40 to 80 years of age. After about 5 years, the risk of heart attack was reduced by an impressive 44 percent.

Some words of caution about the study are warranted. Aspirin did not reduce rates of heart-disease-related or overall death, and it was associated with a slight increase in strokes. A similar, but smaller, study of British physicians taking a higher dose of aspirin showed no benefit.

Hydrochlorothiazide (sold under many brand names), a widely prescribed diuretic or "water pill" used to treat high blood pressure, also made national news. Because diuretics have reduced stroke and kidney failure rates more effectively than heart attack rates, researchers investigated the possibility that diuretics have adverse effects on heart disease that counteract the benefit of reduced blood pressure. A Swedish study showed that hydrochlorothiazide caused increased cholesterol and glucose levels in 50 hypertensive patients, suggesting, but not proving, that the drug contributes to the risk of developing diabetes and heart disease.

However, hydrochlorothiazide may have desirable side effects as well. Long-term use of hydrochlorothiazide and other diuretics that reduce the amount of calcium excreted in urine was associated with 50 percent fewer hip fractures in a study of elderly Canadians. No other antihypertensive therapy showed a similar protective effect. This finding is not trivial, since hip fractures are a major health hazard in the elderly, often leading to prolonged, complicated hospitalizations and death. These findings reinforce the growing consensus among physicians that different blood pressure medications are suited to different types of patients.
    MICHAEL J. KOREN, M.D.
    JEFFREY FISHER, M.D.

LIVER

Advances in Understanding Hepatitis • Liver Transplants in Children • First U.S. Living Donor

New Hepatitis Viruses

In the last 15 years our knowledge of hepatitis viruses has increased significantly. Previously, it was thought that only two viruses—designated A and B—accounted for all cases of hepatitis. But as tests for hepatitis A and B were developed, it became apparent that other viruses must also be causing the disease. Hepatitis caused by viruses other than A and B was designated as non-A, non-B hepatitis.

The first such virus to be identified was found through studying the livers of patients with hepatitis B. At first the new virus was thought to be a particle of the hepatitis B virus, but further studies determined it was a separate virus; it was then called hepatitis D virus. This virus only infects patients who also have hepatitis B virus in their blood. The combination of the two viruses can cause more severe hepatitis or chronic hepatitis (which involves continuing liver damage) than the hepatitis B virus alone.

Research on a large outbreak of hepatitis in India suggested that the cause was yet another virus of the non-A, non-B group. This virus is transmitted through fecal contamination of water and food and has caused large outbreaks of hepatitis in developing countries; it carries a high mortality rate in pregnant women. These features helped to identify it as an infection different from hepatitis A; the virus has been designated hepatitis E virus. Cases of hepatitis E seen thus far in the United States appear to have been acquired during travel to countries where the infection is common.

In 1989 the virus responsible for most of the cases of hepatitis acquired following blood transfusions was discovered; it was named hepatitis C virus. An antibody test for hepatitis C has been submitted to the U.S. Food and Drug Administration for approval. (The test detects the antibodies that the body produces in response to the virus but does not test for the virus itself.) If the test goes into general use, infected people will be identified and prevented from donating blood for transfusion. In studies of New York City blood donors, up to 1.6 percent tested positive for hepatitis C antibody. Hepatitis C antibody is also found in patients not directly exposed to blood or blood products, suggesting that person-to-person contact can also spread the infection. Up to two-thirds of patients with hepatitis C develop chronic hepatitis.

It appears that still more hepatitis viruses remain

to be discovered. Cases of hepatitis not caused by hepatitis A, B, C, D, or E have already been identified.

Treatment. While most patients with hepatitis recover within a few weeks, some continue to be infected by the virus. This occurs in 5 to 10 percent of people with hepatitis B infection, up to 67 percent of hepatitis C cases, and in the majority of patients with hepatitis D. It does not happen with hepatitis

As her husband, John, looks on, Teresa Smith kisses her 21-month-old baby Alyssa after surgery in which a section of Teresa's liver was transplanted to her ailing child. The November 1989 operation was the first liver transplant using a living donor performed in the United States.

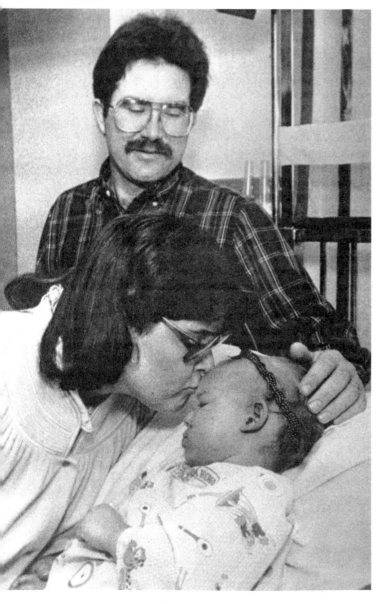

A or E infections. Because continuing infection with these viruses may lead to cirrhosis and/or liver cancer, treatment is needed to eradicate the virus from the liver. Recent studies have indicated that treatment with a genetically engineered form of alpha-interferon—a protein normally secreted by white blood cells to fight viral infections—can benefit some patients. This treatment works best for hepatitis C. When chronic hepatitis C patients receive injections of alpha-interferon, 50 percent improve, and their liver functions return to normal. However, therapy must be continued three times a week for at least 12 months to decrease the risk of relapse and reoccurrence of liver injury. Although daily treatment with alpha-interferon may not completely eradicate the hepatitis B virus, it does seem to stop growth of new virus in up to one-third of patients; their liver functions improve as well. Some investigators think that treatment of hepatitis B virus carriers with cortisone-like drugs before giving them alpha-interferon will make the response even better. Unfortunately, alpha-interferon does not appear to be very promising for hepatitis D patients. Even when these patients are treated with high doses of alpha-interferon every day for 12 months, very few get better.

Alpha-interferon must be given by injection into tissue beneath the skin. It frequently causes side effects, especially during the first few weeks of treatment; patients feel as if they have the flu, with muscle and joint aches, fever, chills, nausea, headache, and impaired concentration. These symptoms usually lessen after a few weeks.

Transplant Advances

The 1980s were a decade of significant advances in organ transplantation, specifically in liver transplantation. This was partly a result of improved drug therapy to suppress the immune system, so that patients' bodies would not reject transplanted organs, and partly due to better surgical techniques. Liver transplantation is no longer considered an experimental therapy for the treatment of liver disease, such as cirrhosis in its terminal stages.

The limited availability of donor livers for children with chronic liver disease, however, remains a problem in pediatric liver transplantation. Children with end-stage liver disease often die while awaiting a donor, in part because only 50 percent of potential childhood donors have organs removed for donation. (The death of a child is difficult for parents and medical personnel alike and can lead to a reluctance to discuss organ donation.)

To compensate for this lack of childhood donors, other techniques have been utilized for treating children with liver disease. The normal liver is separated into two major lobes, the right and left, with the left lobe divided by a ligament into the medial and left lateral segments. Because, in transplants in children, the size of the donated liver must be matched to the size of the child, donor livers from adults have been made smaller by surgically splitting them into right and left lobes and transplanting them into two different children. In very small children, only the left lateral segment of the left lobe may be transplanted.

This technique of splitting livers for multiple donations has been utilized in several medical centers. There are, however, potential problems. The left lateral segment of the liver has small blood vessels that must be sewn to the recipient's blood vessels and bile ducts that must be sewn to the bowel. These procedures increase the risk of bile leaks and infection and of problems with blood vessels, such as clotting. Because these transplants have only been done for the past two years, their longevity and successful function remain to be established.

First U.S. Living Donor. In November 1989, in a widely publicized operation, doctors at the University of Chicago Medical Center removed the left lateral segment of a woman's liver and transplanted it into her 21-month-old daughter. The child, Alyssa Smith, suffered from a condition known as biliary atresia, a usually fatal defect in the ducts that carry bile away from the liver. Her mother, Teresa, had her spleen removed during the operation because of a surgical accident, but can function without it. Her liver will grow back to its normal size (the liver is the only major body organ that rejuvenates itself); Alyssa's liver should grow as she does.

This was the first liver transplant from a living donor performed in the United States, although other such operations have been performed in Australia, Brazil, and Japan. A second liver transplant in the United States from a live donor was performed by University of Chicago surgeons in December 1989 when a 16-month-old Tennessee girl received a portion of her father's liver; by the spring of 1990, three additional transplants of this type had been performed, and a number of others were scheduled.

The removal of a portion of their liver puts living donors at risk for potential complications, such as infection, bleeding, and bile leaks. It is a controversial approach and has not been uniformly endorsed by all transplant centers. Even though its long-term success remains to be studied, considering the shortage of adult organs available for transplant, the use of living donors may offer new hope for children with liver disease.

See also the Spotlight on Health article ORGAN DONATION: WHY IT'S IMPORTANT.

ROWEN K. ZETTERMAN, M.D.

MEDICAL TECHNOLOGY

Improved Healing After Pelvic Surgery •
New Filter to Prevent Blood Clots •
Detecting HPV Infections

Postsurgical Adhesions

The Interceed Absorbable Adhesion Barrier was approved by the U.S. Food and Drug Administration (FDA) in September 1989 for use in gynecologic pelvic surgery. The device is a biodegradable knitted fabric made of treated cellulose that is intended to prevent the formation of adhesions—abnormal fibrous bands that appear between tissues and/or organ surfaces. The new device was developed by Johnson & Johnson Patient Care, Inc.

Adhesions are a common problem following gynecologic pelvic surgery. Experience has shown that roughly 75 to 80 percent of women who undergo surgical procedures related to fertility will develop adhesions. When adhesions do occur, women may be unable to conceive, or may suffer from bowel obstruction or from chronic pain.

The Interceed Barrier works by physically separating the tissue surfaces that have undergone surgical trauma until healing has occurred. The product comes as a sheet measuring 3 x 4 inches that is applied dry in one layer after the surgeon has completely controlled any bleeding. After the barrier is positioned, it is irrigated with a small amount of sterile solution so that it adheres to the surgical area. Eight hours after implantation, Interceed Barrier becomes a gelatinous substance that forms a protective coat over the raw tissue surfaces. It can no longer be identified as a knitted fabric after 24 hours, and it is totally absorbed by the body in less than 28 days.

A recent study evaluated the use of the Interceed Barrier in 74 of the 122 women who had been treated with it. All the women had adhesions on both sides of the pelvis resulting from a variety of causes. In all cases, the adhesions were removed by various surgical techniques, and bleeding was completely controlled. Then one side of the pelvis was treated with the Interceed Barrier while the other side was left untreated for comparison purposes. The treated and untreated sides were selected randomly. Between 10 and 14 days after surgery, adhesion formation was evaluated by looking through a laparoscope (a telescopic instrument that is inserted into the abdomen through a small incision). Of the 74 patients, 53 had significantly more adhesions on the control side than on the side treated with the Interceed Barrier. Clinical tests showed no evidence of any problems caused by the presence of the barrier in the abdominal area, presumably because the barrier is absorbed by the body and broken down into natural products such as glucose.

Preventing Pulmonary Embolism

A pulmonary embolism is a blood clot that has lodged in a pulmonary artery, thereby obstructing blood supply to the lungs. This is a significant medical problem in the United States, occurring in about 630,000 people annually and causing about 150,000 deaths. Anticoagulants are the first step in treating patients with pulmonary embolism, but not everyone can benefit from this therapy, which may itself produce severe side effects, such as bleeding.

The Bird's Nest inferior vena cava filter, a device designed to prevent pulmonary embolism in patients who cannot be given anticoagulant therapy, was approved by the FDA in April 1989. Developed by Cook, Inc., of Bloomington, Ind., it may also be used for high-risk patients who have deep vein clots, to prevent these clots from moving to the lungs.

A vena cava filter is a blood-straining device that works by trapping emboli in the inferior vena cava (the large vein that carries blood from the lower part of the body to the heart) before they reach the lungs. The filter can be inserted into the vena cava under local anesthesia. The body of the Bird's Nest filter is constructed of four 25-centimeter strands of stainless steel wire that are preshaped into a crisscrossing maze

that resembles a bird's nest. A pair of short-angled hooks at each end of the filter fixes the device to the wall of the inferior vena cava so that it remains in place. The filter is preloaded in a Teflon catheter so that it can be positioned with the help of a wire pusher, usually in about five minutes.

The Bird's Nest filter offers an advantage over existing straining devices because it is much easier to use. Problems with other filters have included significant blood loss, failure of insertion, and dislodgement of the filter. There have been no significant problems with the Bird's Nest filter; however, the device migrated in five patients before the anchoring hooks were redesigned.

The filter has been used in clinical tests in 568 patients since 1982. Follow-up information was obtained for 440 of these patients, who had had the filter in place for more than six months. In only 12 of them did the clinical evidence suggest a recurrence of pulmonary embolism; 13 others had experienced blockage to blood flow in the inferior vena cava.

A Diagnostic Test for HPV

ViraPap, a diagnostic device for human papillomavirus (HPV) infections associated with cervical cancer was approved by the FDA in December 1988. It is manufactured by Life Technologies, Inc., of Gaithersburg, Md. HPV infections have a strong association with cervical cancer. With over a million new cases reported each year, HPV is one of the fastest spreading

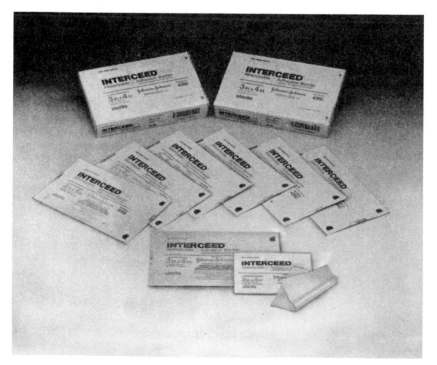

Adhesions, one of the most common side effects of gynecological pelvic surgery, may now become less common thanks to the development of the Interceed Absorbable Adhesion Barrier. It is made of a biodegradable fabric that creates a protective coating over raw tissue surfaces and then is absorbed by the body in less than 28 days.

sexually transmitted diseases. Women with the highest risk are those who have had multiple sexual partners, those who experienced first sexual intercourse at an early age, those who have had a prior sexually transmitted infection, and those whose immune system is impaired. The Pap smear test may provide unclear or borderline results for these women since it detects abnormal cells but not the virus itself. In these cases ViraPap can serve as an adjunct to the Pap smear in establishing a diagnosis.

ViraPap is the first commercially available device that can detect the genetic material (DNA) unique to any of seven specific human papillomavirus types that can infect the human cervix. Although there are more than 60 types of HPV, only a few are associated with infections of the anal and genital areas. For instance, types 6 and 11 are usually found in benign condyloma (a wartlike growth) and genital warts. Types 16, 18, 31, 33, and 35 are more closely associated with advanced cervical tumors and invasive cervical cancer. Before these DNA probes were developed, none of the principal seven HPV types could be identified through routine laboratory testing.

The ViraPap test is intended not for general screening but for use in women at high risk for HPV. It is performed on cervical samples and requires only that the physician take an additional cervical swab immediately after the Pap smear specimen is taken. It can also be performed on cervical scrapes and on fresh or frozen biopsy specimens. Clinical tests show that the test accurately detects the most common genital HPV types 95 percent of the time.

If the ViraPap test is positive but the Pap smear is negative, a repeat Pap smear is recommended.

VIRGINIA S. COWART

MEDICATIONS AND DRUGS

*Treating Heart Attacks and Hypertension •
New Cancer Drugs • Heartburn Relief •
New Drug for Schizophrenia*

Cardiovascular Drugs

Blood Clot Dissolver. Anistreplase, brand name Eminase, received U.S. Food and Drug Administration (FDA) approval in November 1989 for use as soon as possible after the first symptoms of a heart attack. Anistreplase, a derivative of a natural clot-dissolving enzyme complex, was designed specifically to exert a longer-lasting action than the body's own enzyme system. Its prolonged anticlotting effect keeps new clots from forming after the drug's rapid initial action breaks up the main coronary thrombus, or clot, that set off the heart attack.

Another advantage claimed for this product over the two previously available drugs of the class called thrombolytic (clot-dissolving) agents is the ease and convenience with which it is administered. While the earlier drugs require relatively complicated infusion pump systems for delivering a steady drip of their solutions into the circulatory system, anistreplase is injected rapidly into an arm vein with a simple small syringe. Thus, it can be used routinely in hospital emergency rooms and ambulances rather than only in specially equipped coronary care units or catheterization laboratories.

Anistreplase reopens over 70 percent of blocked coronary arteries within 90 minutes of its administration. By thus restoring blood flow to oxygen-starved heart muscle areas, it prevents permanent muscle damage and loss of pumping power. In one clinical trial the drug, injected within six hours of the start of heart attacks, cut the death rate almost in half by preventing such complications as congestive heart failure and cardiac arrest.

As with other substances that prevent thrombi from forming or that break up formed clots, bleeding is this drug's most common complication. However, when patients are properly selected and carefully monitored, the benefit-to-risk ratio is acceptable. To avoid heart rhythm irregularities and sudden steep drops in blood pressure, patients' heart action and blood pressure are monitored continuously.

Calcium Channel Blockers. Calcium channel blockers, which dilate, or widen, blood vessels, are used mainly for relief of severe chest pain in angina pectoris and for reducing hypertension, or high blood pressure. However, one new drug of this class was approved for an entirely different purpose—protecting nerve cells from destruction following brain hemorrhage.

Nimodipine, the first drug ever found effective for reducing the risk of severe disability and death from certain types of strokes, became available as the brand-named product Nimotop. Administered to patients who have suffered subarachnoid hemorrhages, in which brain blood vessels spill blood into the space between two of the three membranes that surround the brain, this calcium channel blocker counteracts the brain artery spasms responsible for brain cell damage that can lead to paralysis, loss of sensory perception, coma, and death. It does so by maintaining normal blood flow following surgical repair of the wall of the brain artery whose rupture caused the hemorrhage.

For best results, nimodipine treatment should be started within four days of the beginning of bleeding into the brain. It is taken as capsules, or if the patient cannot swallow or is unconscious, the contents of the capsules are washed into the stomach by way of a nasogastric tube. Drug treatment is then given every four hours for 21 consecutive days. This three-week period includes the dangerous ten days when post-surgical complications are most likely to occur.

Because nimodipine widens narrowed brain blood vessels much more readily than it dilates the outlying arteries that keep blood pressure normal, it does not ordinarily cause a severe drop in pressure. However, blood pressure is carefully monitored to detect the start of any possibly deep decline. Flushing, headache, and fluid retention sometimes occur, but these minor side effects do not require treatment to be stopped.

Other new calcium blocker products include one entirely new drug called nicardipine (Cardene) and two longer-acting dosage forms of nifedipine and diltiazem, drugs previously available only as capsules that required several doses daily.

Nicardipine was approved for use in both angina pectoris and high blood pressure. Its ability to dilate blood vessels relieves anginal chest pains in two ways. Widening of the coronary arteries increases the flow of oxygenated blood to deprived heart muscle areas. Drug-induced dilation of the general arterial system, into which the heart has to pump blood, reduces the heart's work load by lessening resistance to the outflow of blood from the heart. This reduction of resistance in the arterioles of the abdomen and elsewhere in the body causes abnormally high blood pressure to drop down to more normal levels.

The most common side effects of nicardipine are headache, flushing, a feeling of weakness, and swelling of the feet. This calcium blocker sometimes slows the heart and weakens cardiac contractions, especially when it is prescribed together with a beta adrenergic blocker drug. This action makes it unsafe for patients prone to periodic episodes of congestive heart failure. Paradoxically, this drug can sometimes speed up a patient's heart rate and set off anginal chest pains instead of preventing them or lessening their severity.

Nifedipine became available late in 1989 as Procardia XL extended release tablets. This new dosage form for treating angina pectoris and high blood pressure delivers a slow steady flow of the drug from the gastrointestinal tract into the circulatory system over a period of 24 hours. Unlike the previously available capsules, which produced a series of peaks and valleys of the drug in blood plasma after each of the several daily doses, this new once-a-day tablet keeps nifedipine at a steady, therapeutically effective level without the peaks that cause such side effects as facial flushing, dizziness, and heart palpitations.

Diltiazem, now available as Cardizem SR sustained release capsules, is also claimed to cause fewer adverse effects when taken twice daily to treat high blood pressure. By minimizing such discomforting side effects as headaches, dizziness, weakness, and swelling of the feet, this new dosage form helps people stay on the drug. Long-continued treatment usually succeeds in keeping mild to moderate hypertension under control. This, in turn, helps to prevent the damage that sustained elevated blood pressure can inflict on vital organs such as the kidneys, brain, and heart.

Beta blockers. Carteolol (Cartrol) and penbutolol (Levatol), two new beta adrenergic blocking drugs, were approved for use in treating high blood pressure. Each can be prescribed for use alone in mild to moderate cases or be given together with a diuretic or other antihypertension drug. Both these drugs have certain similar properties that, it is claimed, give them advantages over most other beta blockers. Because, for example, their pressure-reducing effects last close to 24 hours, patients need take only a single daily dose. Both are also less likely to cause patients' heart rates to slow excessively. Neither drug causes blood levels of cholesterol or other fatty substances to rise, as occurs with some other high blood pressure drugs.

Carteolol and penbutolol, like all beta blockers, block nerve impulses that stimulate the heart and must not be taken by patients with pulse rates below 50 beats per minute. Caution is required in high blood pressure patients who have had an episode of heart failure; these patients are advised to call their doctor at the first sign that they may again be going into heart failure. And because carteolol and penbutolol also block nerve impulses that dilate the bronchioles, they must not be used by patients with bronchial asthma. Caution is also necessary in patients with chronic bronchitis or emphysema to avoid setting off bronchial tube spasms. Patients are warned not to stop taking any beta blocker without first consulting their doctors. Abruptly discontinuing drugs of this type can cause chest pains or even a heart attack in people with previously unrecognized coronary artery disease.

Cancer Treatments

Flutamide (Eulexin) was approved for use in combination with previously available leuprolide (Lupron) for treating men with advanced prostate gland cancer. Adding this new drug to patients' daily treatment programs keeps them from relapsing for a longer time than when they receive leuprolide alone. Also, by taking daily injections of leuprolide and oral doses of flutamide simultaneously, men with the most severe

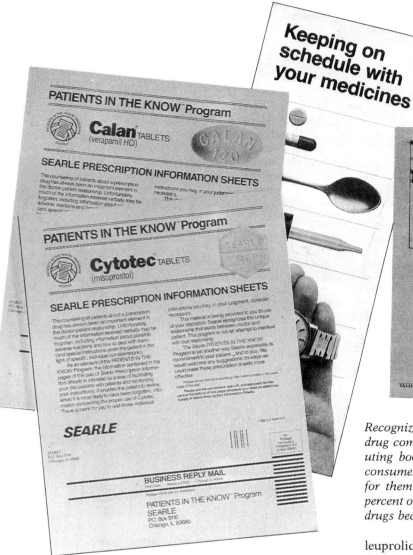

Recognizing that an informed patient is a better patient, drug companies and other organizations began distributing booklets, pamphlets, and fact sheets to educate consumers about the medications their doctors prescribe for them. It has been estimated that from 50 to 75 percent of patients do not receive the full benefits of their drugs because they do not follow instructions closely.

grade of this disease live, on average, about 25 percent longer than those who get only leuprolide.

The two drugs act in different ways to deprive prostate cancer cells of the growth-stimulating effects of male sex hormones, or androgens. Leuprolide supresses the testicular secretion of testosterone, the main male sex hormone. Flutamide blocks receptor sites for testosterone and other androgens on cells of prostate tumor tissues, including cancer cells that have spread beyond the gland to the bones. The combined effects of leuprolide and flutamide stop the disease's progress and relieve bone pain and other symptoms for the longest periods achieved so far by any drug therapy.

The side effects of these two drugs together are mostly the same as those of leuprolide alone—hot flashes, swelling of male breast tissue, impotence, nausea, and vomiting. Diarrhea occurs three times as often when flutamide is taken at the same time as

leuprolide. However, this symptom is usually so mild that in the largest clinical trial of this combination, no patients stopped taking their medication because of diarrhea.

Ifosfamide (Ifex) was approved for treating the 20 to 25 percent of patients with cancer of the testis who are either not cured by the current highly successful combination chemotherapy or who suffer a relapse after an initial complete remission. While useful against advanced testicular cancer when given alone, ifosfamide is recommended for use in combination with the very effective drug cisplatin (Platinol), and either etoposide (VePesid) or vinblastine (Velban). Results of recent clinical trials in patients with widespread recurrent tumors indicate that some patients with previously incurable disease responded to such so-called salvage, or last-ditch, treatment of metastatic testicular cancer.

The most common toxic effect of ifosfamide has been irritation and inflammation of the bladder followed by the appearance of blood in the urine. This can now be prevented by administering mesna (Mesnex), a recently approved agent that neutralizes the drug-derived bladder toxin that is responsible for this reaction.

Mesna does not, however, prevent other types of toxicity caused by ifosfamide, including the suppression of bone marrow production of white blood cells, platelets, and hemoglobin. To avoid the dangers of such drug-induced deficiencies, a blood sample is tested before administration of each dose of ifosfamide. If the laboratory reports that counts of blood cells are too low, the drug is withheld until counts rise to safer levels. Some patients receiving ifosfamide show symptoms of central nervous system toxicity, including drowsiness, confusion, and, occasionally, coma. If these symptoms develop, the drug is discontinued until they disappear. Other adverse effects of ifosfamide include hair loss, nausea, and vomiting.

Carboplatin (Paraplatin) was approved for relief of symptoms of advanced ovarian cancer in women who suffer a relapse following remission after a first course of chemotherapy. This new drug, a close chemical relative of the first-line drug cisplatin (Platinol), is just as effective as the parent compound but causes fewer and milder adverse effects. It does not, for example, cause the distressing bouts of vomiting that occur with cisplatin. Similarly, carboplatin does not damage sensory and motor nerve fibers, which can cause disturbances of feeling in the hands and feet, hearing loss, and difficulty in walking, as cisplatin sometimes does.

Another advantage of the new drug is the ease with which it can be administered. The entire dose may be infused into a vein in 15 to 30 minutes instead of the 6 to 8 hours required with cisplatin, which has to be given with large amounts of fluid to protect the patient's kidneys. Thus, carboplatin can be given during an office visit or in other outpatient facilities rather than in a hospital.

The new drug's main drawback is its greater tendency to suppress bone marrow function and lower circulating blood cell counts. Patients must be monitored closely for signs of infection caused by low white cell counts and for bleeding tendencies resulting from reduction in blood platelets. However, bone marrow suppression is reversible when the drug is withheld for a while. Symptoms of infection can be controlled by antibiotics, and transfusions of the various blood cell components can be given to counteract symptoms caused by their lack.

Treating Digestive System Disorders

Misoprostol, marketed as Cytotec, is the first drug approved by the FDA for preventing stomach ulcers in arthritis patients being treated with regular high doses of aspirin or any of the many other medications known as nonsteroidal anti-inflammatory drugs (NSAIDs). Given to patients taking these antiarthritic drugs, misoprostol markedly reduces development of gastric ulcers. It is especially beneficial for elderly arthritics and for other patients at high risk, including those with a history of prior ulcers who are prone to suffer serious complications.

Misoprostol is a synthetic prostaglandin similar to the natural hormonelike substances produced locally in nearly all body tissues, including the linings of both the stomach and the joints. While aspirin and other NSAIDs benefit arthritic patients by inhibiting production of prostaglandins involved in causing joint inflammation, these drugs can deplete prostaglandins that help protect the stomach lining from its own acids or other ulcer-producing substances.

Taken orally after each meal and at bedtime, misoprostol replaces the prostaglandins lost from the stomach lining because of the action of NSAIDs. This lets arthritic patients continue NSAID therapy even when they are thought to be at high risk of developing such complications as sudden severe gastrointestinal bleeding or perforation of the stomach wall.

Misoprostol is well tolerated by most patients. Diarrhea is its most common side effect, but this and other abdominal symptoms are seldom severe enough to require discontinuing the drug. However, because it can cause miscarriages, misoprostol must not be taken during pregnancy.

Omeprazole (Losec) received FDA approval for short-term use in treating gastroesophageal reflux disease (GERD) and severe erosive esophagitis. GERD is a chronic disorder in which the acidic contents of a person's stomach back up into the esophagus, the tube that carries food and liquid from the mouth to the stomach. This causes chronic heartburn that is harder to relieve than the burning feeling beneath the breastbone that many people sometimes suffer after overeating. The continuous backward flow of irritating gastric acid also inflames the lining of the esophagus and makes it wear away. This erosive esophagitis is often followed by formation of esophageal ulcers and scar tissue that narrow the passageway and make swallowing difficult.

Omeprazole, the first of a new class of drugs for suppressing secretion of stomach acid, acts differently from such previously available antisecretory medications as ranitidine (Zantac) and other histamine H_2-receptor antagonists. It acts by inhibiting an enzyme system responsible for pumping acid out of the stomach cells that produce it. Because less acid becomes free to flow back into the esophagus, erosions and ulcers heal within four to eight weeks. Results of clinical trials indicate that healing and complete relief of heartburn occur faster and in a higher proportion of patients, including many who had not responded well to treatment with H_2 antagonists. Omeprazole was also approved for long-term use in treating Zollinger-Ellison syndrome, in which excessive stomach acid leads to stomach and duodenal ulcers.

Omeprazole comes as a capsule containing tiny granules specially coated to keep the drug from being destroyed by stomach acids. Release of the drug from these granules is delayed until they enter the intestine. The drug is then absorbed into the bloodstream and carried back to the stomach lining's acid-producing cells. Patients are told to take their daily dose before eating by swallowing the capsule whole and never opening, chewing, or crushing it.

Ethanolamine oleate (Ethamolin)—in use in Canada for several years—received FDA approval for controlling bleeding from varicose veins in the esophagus of patients with cirrhosis of the liver. In that disease, common in alcoholics, high pressure is transmitted from the liver's blood vessels to those of the esophagus. Often the veins of the esophagus become twisted and swollen with excess blood, and their walls burst.

Ethanolamine is used both to control sudden massive bleeding and to prevent recurrences of bleeding episodes, thereby saving lives. It is relatively safe in the hands of a doctor experienced in delivering small amounts of drug solution through a needle guided directly into a bleeding vein by an endoscope, an instrument passed through the mouth so the doctor can look down the esophagus. About 10 to 15 percent of patients develop complications from the ethanolamine solution. Too large an amount may cause ulcers of the esophagus that can scar and narrow the passageway or even cause its walls to perforate. Leakage of the fluid into the lungs may lead to pneumonia, especially in elderly patients with heart and lung disease as well as cirrhosis of the liver.

Drugs for Mental Disorder

Clozapine (Clozaril), the first major new drug in 20 years for treating schizophrenia, received FDA approval for treating patients with severe symptoms of this mental illness who had not been helped by any of the previously available antipsychotic medications. This drug, first introduced in Europe during the 1970s and already employed in 30 countries, had previously been denied FDA approval because it was no more effective than earlier therapy but capable of causing more life-threatening toxicity. Now, however, the agency has agreed that the benefits obtained by many patients justify clozapine's use in selected cases.

Results of several recently reported studies have proved clozapine's superiority over chlorpromazine (Thorazine in the United States; Chloropromanyl, Lagartil, and Novochlropromazine in Canada) and other conventional antipsychotic drugs in the treatment-resistant minority—about 200,000 people whose condition did not improve when treated with less toxic drugs. Some studies have shown that many of these mentally ill patients, when treated with clozapine, stopped hearing voices and having the delusions, or false beliefs, that led them to behave abnormally. In addition, patients who were too emotionally and socially withdrawn to function outside a mental institution have often recovered enough to be released from hospitals and have become able to live on their own in society.

The most serious toxic reaction to clozapine results from damage to patients' bone marrow. This leads to a drop in the white blood cells that help protect against infection. Between 1 and 2 percent of patients taking the drug have developed a dangerous blood disorder called agranulocytosis that can cause death if not detected early and controlled.

To reduce this risk, the drug's producers have set up a special distribution system, in which doctors have to enroll their patients. This system assures that every patient has a blood sample drawn and tested weekly. The next week's supply of this drug is dispensed only after a lab report shows that the patient's white blood cell count is not significantly reduced.

Another adverse effect of clozapine is the risk of seizures in some patients when the dose required to control their symptoms has to be raised. Other side effects include drowsiness, increased salivation, a rise in pulse rate, and a drop in blood pressure. Patients are warned to report flulike symptoms such as fever or sore throat immediately, as these may be early signs of infection caused by agranulocytosis. Patients are also advised not to drive or to undertake potentially hazardous activities while their dose of clozapine is being adjusted upward to optimal levels.

Bupropion (Wellbutrin) received FDA approval for treating mental depression. This drug, which differs chemically from all other classes of antidepressant drugs, is as effective as the others but does not cause the kinds of side effects most commonly seen with such standard drugs as the tricyclic antidepressant amitriptyline (Elavil). Thus, bupropion may prove most useful for patients whose depression does not respond to conventional medications or who are unable to tolerate such side effects of these drugs as sudden drops in blood pressure when they stand up or the development of rapid irregular heartbeats.

Bupropion has, however, its own side effect pattern that calls for care, especially during the early dosage adjustment period. Patients often show signs of central nervous system stimulation such as restlessness, insomnia, and agitation. Seizures occur much more often than with other antidepressant drugs. To avoid these adverse effects, the doctor must carefully select the kinds of patients for whom to prescribe the drug. Starting off with several small doses daily, the dosage should be raised only gradually to the lowest level that produces improvement.

Depressed patients with insomnia should not take this drug at bedtime. Those with a history of head injuries or previous seizures should not be treated with bupropion at all. It is also contraindicated in people with such eating disorders as bulimia (uncontrolled eating binges) and anorexia nervosa (severe self-starvation to avoid gaining weight), because adolescents with these conditions have proved most prone to suffer seizures while receiving bupropion.

Drugs for Arthritis

Flurbiprofen (Ansaid), a nonsteroidal anti-inflammatory drug (NSAID) first introduced abroad in the 1970s and already available in Canada and about 70 other countries, finally received FDA approval for the relief of signs and symptoms in osteoarthritis and rheumatoid arthritis. Flurbiprofen seems to be about as effective as aspirin and other NSAIDs when taken several times a day in recommended doses.

This chemical relative of ibuprofen (Motrin, Advil, Nuprin, and other brand names) is claimed to cause fewer side effects than the parent drug or aspirin, but one British study found more frequent serious reactions with flurbiprofen than with ibuprofen. Among its gastrointestinal adverse effects are dyspepsia, abdominal pain, diarrhea, nausea, and vomiting. As with all other drugs of this class, its label—in accordance with a recent FDA ruling—is now required to carry a warning reporting that up to 4 percent of patients on long-term treatment suffer serious reactions such as stomach ulcers and gastrointestinal bleeding. Other reported side effects include headache, visual and hearing abnormalities, tremors, anxiety, nervousness, and insomnia. Tissue swelling from retained fluid sometimes develops. This drug's adverse effects on the kidneys are similar to those seen with other NSAIDs and caution is required in patients with impaired kidney, liver, or cardiac function.

Methotrexate, a potentially very toxic drug long reserved mainly for use in leukemia and several kinds of cancer, became available in a new oral dosage form for use in cases of severe rheumatoid arthritis that have failed to respond to other, safer antirheumatic drugs. Now marketed as Rheumatrex, this drug is taken only once weekly, and patients must be warned not to make the mistake of taking it daily. The small initial dose is raised gradually to optimal levels over a period of several weeks. Three to six weeks are

usually needed for signs of improvement to appear, such as the relief of joint inflammation, swelling, stiffness, and pain. Improvement may then continue during the next three months of weekly therapy.

Patients must be fully informed about the symptoms of methotrexate toxicity, and they must be told to call their doctor promptly if any of these develop. Close monitoring by frequent laboratory tests detects early signs of drug-induced damage to patients' bone marrow, liver, or kidneys. This drug must not be taken during pregnancy, as it can cause fetal deformity or fetal death.

Drugs for Skin Disorders

Mometasone furoate (Elocon), a synthetic corticosteroid of moderate potency, was approved by the FDA to relieve moderate to severe symptoms of certain steroid-responsive skin disorders. Applied only once a day to affected areas as a thin film of cream or ointment or a few drops of lotion, this drug exerts a rapid and prolonged anti-inflammatory effect. It relieves redness, itching, and scaling in psoriasis, eczema, and seborrheic dermatitis (a severe form of dandruff marked by the scaling of crusty patches of scalp). Lotion is the preferred dosage form for application to the scalp and other hairy areas.

Mometasone may cause mild tingling, stinging, burning, and itching in a small proportion of patients. Signs of skin atrophy such as shininess and thinning are seen in even fewer cases. Because its use does not require dressing or bandages, very little of the drug tends to be absorbed through the skin into the bloodstream to cause a reduction in adrenal gland secretions. However, youngsters who require treatment of diaper area skin should not wear plastic pants or tight-fitting diapers, as this tends to increase absorption of steroids.

Oxiconazole (Oxistat), an antifungal agent that stops the spread of ringworm infections, received FDA approval for use in a cream that is applied to affected skin areas once each evening. Athlete's foot should be treated for a month to clear the condition and keep it from recurring. Two weeks of treatment is considered enough to control fungal infections of the smooth skin of the upper body and those localized on the skin of the upper inner thighs. A small minority of patients complain of drug-induced itching, burning, or redness. Such reactions may require that treatment be discontinued. Care is needed to avoid contact of the cream with patients' eyes.

Drug for Anesthesia

Propofol (Diprivan), a new intravenous anesthetic approved by the FDA for producing and maintaining loss of consciousness during surgery, is said to have a unique combination of actions. Its sleep-producing effects come on very quickly—within 40 seconds of the start of an injection. Recovery is also rapid, with most patients waking in the recovery room alert and clearheaded within eight minutes. Of course, when propofol is supplemented for added pain relief with a narcotic drug or nitrous oxide gas and with a general inhalation anesthetic, recovery may take longer.

Results of clinical studies in the United States and Canada and from worldwide experience with about 7 million patients have shown mainly mild and transient side effects. Still, anesthesiologists must be prepared to ventilate a patient's lungs with oxygen if breathing suddenly stops and to counteract a steep drop in blood pressure or a slowing of the heart rate. Burning or stinging pain can occur at local injection sites in small veins on the back of the hand, but pain is minimal when injections are made into the larger veins in the forearm or the inside bend of the elbow.

Propofol injections are not recommended for use during obstetrical procedures, including cesarean sections, as the drug has not yet been proved safe for the fetus. Children and nursing mothers are not considered good candidates for this anesthetic. Nor is it employed in patients with poor brain blood flow or with increased pressure within the skull.

Infection Fighter

The antibiotic cefixime (Suprax) received FDA approval. Cefixime is an antibiotic of the third-generation cephalosporin class, a group active against strains of bacteria that are resistant to treatment with first-generation and second-generation drugs of the cephalosporin family. Unlike the half dozen third-generation drugs available up to now, cefixime does not have to be given by injection. Taken by mouth once a day—or sometimes divided into two daily doses—this antibiotic has proved especially effective for treating such respiratory tract infections as sore throat, tonsillitis, and bronchitis. Children with middle ear infections who swallow an oral suspension of cefixime have been cured or markedly improved at the end of a ten-day course of treatment. This antibiotic's usefulness in these infections stems from its high activity against the most common respiratory-disease-causing bacteria—*Streptococcus pneumoniae* and strains of *Haemophilus influenzae* and *Branhamella catarrhalis*—that are resistant to most other cephalosporins and penicillins because of their ability to produce the antibiotic-destroying enzyme beta-lactamase.

Most of cefixime's side effects are mild and transient. The gastrointestinal tract is the main site of such adverse reactions, which include diarrhea, abdominal

pain, nausea, and vomiting. Caution is required when this antibiotic is prescribed for patients with a history of colitis or other gastrointestinal diseases. It must not be given to patients known to be allergic to cephalosporin antibiotics or to penicillin.

Keeping Kidney Stones From Forming

Tiopronin (Thiola) became available for use in preventing formation of kidney stones made up of the amino acid cystine. Such stones form as the result of an inherited disorder that affects only about 10,000 Americans. Thus, tiopronin received FDA approval as an "orphan" drug—one that the agency helps pharmaceutical companies market for treating relatively rare diseases.

Cystine stones form from crystals that precipitate in the urine when a person's kidneys excrete more of the amino acid than can stay in solution. Tiopronin works by reducing the urinary concentration of cystine to below the level of its solubility. It is reserved for patients who are resistant to conservative treatment measures such as drinking large amounts of fluid to increase the volume of urine and taking potassium citrate to make the urine more alkaline and better able to keep cystine in solution.

The adverse effects of tiopronin occur less often and are less severe than those of the previously available drug penicillamine (Cuprimine, Depen). Still, patients must be watched for signs of dangerous drops in circulating white blood cells and platelets and for the development of severe muscle weakness. Less serious side effects include nausea and vomiting, diarrhea, and abdominal pain.

Patients take this drug three times a day at least one hour before or two hours after meals. To determine the lowest possible doses, simple urinalysis tests for cystine are conducted.

See also the Spotlight on Health article THE ROLE OF THE PHARMACIST.

MORTON J. RODMAN, PH.D.

MENTAL HEALTH

Therapies for Depression • Support Groups and Cancer Survival • Genetic Research on Psychiatric Illness • Psychological Effects of AIDS

Treating Depression

A long-awaited report on a study of the effectiveness of psychotherapy in treating depression was released in November 1989. The subjects of the study were 250 depressed outpatients assigned for 16 weeks to

The Mental Shocks
of Natural Disasters

The natural disasters of 1989 served to underscore the fact that such events involve damage to not only physical health but also the psychological well-being of survivors. After Hurricane Hugo tore into South Carolina, state mental health officials sent scores of psychiatrists and social workers to affected areas to help victims cope with lingering fears and anxieties. Left, therapist Linda Austin, whose own house was damaged by the storm, "talks through" her experiences. Survivors of the California earthquake, above, also suffered emotional aftershocks and needed support and counseling. Typical reactions ranged from initial euphoria at having survived to anger at the misery caused by the damage to denial of the seriousness of the earthquake danger in the region.

one of four types of weekly treatments. The treatments were supportive contact with a therapist (but no formal therapy) plus imipramine, a widely used antidepressant medication; supportive contact with a therapist (but no formal therapy) plus a placebo, or inactive drug; interpersonal psychotherapy designed to help patients understand and correct problems in relating to other people; and cognitive behavior therapy designed to help patients correct their excessively negative views of themselves. The results were surprising in that all of the treatments worked about equally well and all reduced depression.

There was some evidence that the interpersonal psychotherapy and the drug therapy were more effective than the cognitive behavior therapy, although the differences were not large. This was especially true in the most severely depressed third of the sample. These patients, sufficiently impaired in mood and energy that they were unable to function at home or work, did best with medication, with interpersonal psychotherapy coming in second.

However, among the less seriously depressed portion of the sample—patients who felt sad much of the time but were able to carry on with work and home duties—the four treatments were roughly equivalent. The study demonstrated that, although medication is important when symptoms are severe, supportive professional contact is clearly useful in treating depression as are the two major forms of psychotherapy.

Group Support and Cancer Survival

Can psychological treatment affect disease processes? A study published in October 1989 provided evidence that group support can indeed prolong the survival of cancer patients. Eighty-six women with breast cancer that had spread to other organs were assigned randomly for a one-year period either to weekly support groups as well as their usual cancer care (the treatment group) or to the cancer care alone (the control group). After the initial year, the treated patients were less anxious and depressed. They also had half the pain of the control group, due in part to having been trained in self-hypnosis for pain control. When the researchers later followed up on what had happened to the group as a whole, they discovered that those assigned to the treatment group lived an average of 37 months after the study began, as compared with 19 months for the control group. Thus, survival time was nearly doubled for those who participated in the psychotherapeutic treatment. Nonetheless, most of the patients (81 of 86) did eventually die of cancer.

Several factors might have contributed to the differences in survival time. It may be that because the patients in the treatment group were less depressed

and better able to control pain, they ate better or were more active physically, thereby enabling their bodies to fight the illness better. Perhaps the group experience encouraged patients to communicate with their doctors more effectively—resulting in more vigorous treatment of the disease and better treatment compliance—or helped them to cope better with stress and its deleterious effects on the body. There may, as well, be other psychological factors influencing the way the immune system fights disease that were affected by the group support. Perhaps the study created an intense and supportive social network that repaired the social isolation often suffered by cancer patients. There is growing evidence that social relations are an important factor in health status. A 1988 review of research in the field concluded that a relative lack of social relations are a major risk factor for health. The recently bereaved have higher death rates than those who have not suffered such losses. Married cancer patients live longer than unmarried cancer patients, all other things being equal.

The breast cancer study provides no evidence that any of these factors were involved in survival differences, but all are possible explanations. There does seem to be growing evidence from this and other studies that social support and psychotherapeutic treatment not only improve the quality of life of cancer patients but may extend life as well.

Prevalence of Mental Illness

Data from the largest study ever of the extent of mental illness in the United States indicate that approximately 15 percent of adults suffer from mental illness or a substance abuse disorder at any given time. Furthermore, 32 percent of the population are likely to have such a problem during their lifetime.

The study found the most common mental illnesses (7 percent) to be anxiety disorders. These include phobias, in which individuals develop specific irrational fears that inhibit their activities, panic attacks, in which patients have sudden and overwhelming feelings of anxiety and physical discomfort, and obsessive-compulsive disorder, in which people are beset with unpleasant thoughts (obsessions) that lead them to act in irrational and repetitive ways (compulsions). Disorders of mood such as depression and manic-depressive illness were the next most common, accounting for 5 percent. In general, women had higher rates of many disorders than men, and younger people more than older individuals. The study, based on interviews with more than 18,000 people, indicates that many more people have mental illnesses than receive effective treatment for it. *(See also the feature article* WHY AM I GOING THROUGH THIS DOOR AGAIN?*)*

Genetics and Psychiatric Illness

In 1989 follow-up research cast doubt on the results of a 1987 study that appeared to have located a gene responsible for manic-depressive illness, a major psychiatric disorder characterized by extreme mood shifts. In the original study researchers analyzed genetic material from 81 members of a large Old Order Amish family group with a high incidence of manic depression. (The Old Order Amish make an ideal community for genetic research because their roughly 15,000 members are descended from only about 30 couples and therefore represent a gene pool in which variation is limited.) Researchers found that family members with manic depression carried specific, recognizable variants of two particular genes on chromosome 11. Neither of these genes appeared to cause the illness, but the correlation strongly suggested that a gene involved in manic depression must lie nearby.

With these marker genes to indicate where the gene for manic depression should be found, other researchers attempted to find that gene itself. Not only did they fail to find it, however, but the addition of new subjects to the study and new information about some of the original subjects greatly reduced the probability that the conclusions of the original study were accurate.

Similarly, further studies have found no link between schizophrenia and two marker genes on chromosome 5 that had been identified in a 1988 study of British and Icelandic families.

There is already considerable evidence for some genetic predisposition to both manic depression and schizophrenia. However, science has yet to clarify the exact genetic basis of any major psychiatric illness. Problems in such research include the complex nature of these illnesses and the difficulty in agreeing on the exact diagnosis of family members studied.

Psychological Effects of AIDS

Studies have shown that individuals infected with the human immunodeficiency virus (HIV), which causes AIDS, frequently become depressed and often suffer considerable social isolation as friends and family avoid them because they fear infection. Now researchers have made a somewhat surprising finding about the relationship between level of depression and stage of HIV infection.

There are three stages in the development of HIV infection. The first is characterized by the presence of the virus in the bloodstream. At the time this is documented, most individuals have no symptoms but are frightened and upset at the news that they are infected. The second stage, AIDS-related complex, is identified by poor immune system function and other symptoms such as fever, night sweats, and persistent diarrhea. The third stage, full-blown AIDS, is characterized by serious immune system failure, infections, and certain tumors. AIDS is uniformly fatal. Investigators were therefore somewhat surprised to find that patients with the milder forms of the illness, HIV infection and AIDS-related complex, were more depressed and anxious than those with AIDS. It may well be that the change from normal life to a confrontation with a life-threatening illness is more stressful than adapting to a worsening of the disease at a later time.

See also the feature article How the Arts Are Used in Therapy *and the Spotlight on Health article* Those Winter Blues.

David Spiegel, M.D.

NUTRITION AND DIET

A Diet for Good Health • Oat Bran and Psyllium • New Fat Substitute • Nutrition and the Immune System

The Diet and Health Connection

In March 1989 a comprehensive report examined the relationship between aspects of the American diet and the development of chronic diseases. The report, entitled *Diet and Health: Implications for Reducing Chronic Disease Risk*, reflected a growing consensus among scientists that certain eating patterns increase one's risk for potentially life-threatening conditions. Issued by the Committee on Diet and Health of the National Research Council (the research arm of the U.S. National Academy of Sciences), the report concluded that diets high in fat—particularly saturated fat—and cholesterol increase the chances for developing heart disease. It also concluded that high-fat diets are linked with cancer of the colon, prostate, and breast.

The report contained recommendations on the type of diet to be followed to minimize such risks (see the box on page 307). Key recommendations included holding down intake of fat and cholesterol, so as to avoid—or bring down—high levels of cholesterol in the blood. High blood cholesterol can contribute to the development of coronary heart disease—the leading cause of death in the United States.

Further support for such a preventive approach came in a report issued in February 1990 by the National Cholesterol Education Program of the U.S. National Heart, Lung, and Blood Institute, which urged that all Americans—including children aged

PERRIER: THE BUBBLE BURSTS

The fizzy French water in the little green bottles, the chic drink of choice to replace alcoholic beverages, suffered a severe loss of sparkle when, in January 1990, the laboratory of the Mecklenburg County Environmental Protection Department in Charlotte, N.C., found traces of benzene, a recognized carcinogen, in bottles of the imported beverage.

The manufacturer, believing at first that the contamination had been caused by improper cleaning of bottling equipment, halted all production in early February, and well over 70 million bottles of Perrier were recalled from U.S. and Canadian stores and restaurants. When benzene was also found in samples from Denmark and the Netherlands a few days later, the recall became worldwide. The number of bottles withdrawn reached 160 million, worth some $70 million.

The problem, it turned out, was actually bubbling up from the source. The company eventually determined that workers at the spring in Vergeze had failed to change the filters that remove the benzene that occurs naturally in the gas that carbonates the water.

Medical experts pointed out that the actual health risk was small, and the company was commended for the candor and speed with which it met the crisis (the firm even set up a hotline for anxious consumers). But had the cachet of the so-called Yuppie drink gone flat? The company, which began selling newly bottled Perrier in March, certainly hoped not—but was taking no chances. The reintroduction of Perrier in the United States was accompanied by an extensive advertising campaign stressing that "the problem has been fixed," and the familiar pear-shaped bottles had new labels prominently featuring the words "nouvelle production."

two and over—eat diets that are low in total fat, saturated fat, and cholesterol.

More Help From Labels. Help in following guidelines for a healthful diet may be on the way for U.S. consumers. In March 1990, U.S. Secretary of Health and Human Services Louis Sullivan announced a plan to extend mandatory nutrition labeling to cover almost all packaged foods. The plan—which the government hoped to put into effect by late 1991—would require labels to carry more specific information than at present, such as the amount of cholesterol and saturated fat in each serving and the number of calories per serving derived from fat. In an effort to reduce misleading or exaggerated claims, the plan would also set uniform definitions for terms such as "low fat" and "high fiber."

A Controversial View. In a 1989 book called *Heart Failure*, Thomas J. Moore—a writer, not a scientist—claimed that research data do not support the recommendation that people eat less fat and cholesterol to help prevent heart disease. However, Moore discussed findings from selected studies only, ignoring large amounts of data that did demonstrate that lowering blood cholesterol stops or slows the progress

Above: High-fiber oat bran muffins are a popular weapon in the war against high cholesterol. Below: It is sometimes possible to combine a visit to the local supermarket—such as the one shown here in Houston—with a test to measure cholesterol levels.

of atherosclerosis (hardening of the arteries), which can lead to a heart attack. (*See also the Spotlight on Health article* TREATING HIGH CHOLESTEROL.)

New RDAs

Another important publication of the National Research Council, the 10th edition of *Recommended Dietary Allowances*, came out in the fall of 1989. The recommended dietary allowances, or RDAs, are the amounts of protein, vitamins, and certain minerals that if taken in daily (on average) will meet the needs of practically all healthy people. (There are separate RDAs for people of different ages, including children, for men and women in some cases, and for pregnant and breast-feeding women.)

The Food and Nutrition Board, which prepares the RDAs, emphasized that the recommendations made in the 10th edition should be used in conjunction with those in the *Diet and Health* report. Taken together, the two publications form a basis for planning nutritionally adequate diets that will diminish the chances of developing major chronic diseases.

The 1989 RDAs differ from those of the 9th edition (published in 1980) only in the case of nutrients for which new scientific information has become available. The adult RDAs were lowered for several nutrients, including folate (also called folacin and folic acid), vitamins B$_6$ and B$_{12}$, and the minerals magnesium, iron, and zinc. The most drastic decrease was for folate, based upon data indicating that adequate amounts of folate can be obtained from diets furnishing half the 1980 RDA. The highest 1989 RDAs for folate are for pregnant women (400 micrograms a day) and for women who are breast-feeding (280 micrograms). The recommended amounts can be obtained by proper food choices, without using diet supplements. Foods such as spinach, turnip and mustard greens, romaine lettuce, parsley, beef liver, dried beans, and wheat germ are all excellent folate sources.

Recently the media reported on studies that associated multivitamin/folate supplements taken during early pregnancy with a reduction in the occurrence of spinal cord defects in infants. This publicity may have led people to believe that women should take such supplements before and during pregnancy; however, the studies failed to agree as to whether this is a useful practice. Also, it was not shown that any decrease in these birth defects was actually due to folate.

The RDA for calcium remained as it was in 1980 except that the age range for the highest RDA—1,200 milligrams—was changed from 11-18 years to 11-24 years. This was to allow for completion of bone calcification, which appears to occur at a later age than was formerly believed. Supplements that provide more calcium than specified in the RDAs are not recommended for normal, healthy people. The RDA for iron for nonpregnant women in their reproductive years was reduced from 18 to 15 milligrams, based on new estimates that this amount is adequate.

RDAs were set for the first time for vitamin K, essential for normal blood clotting. This vitamin is obtained from many foods—green leafy vegetables, in particular—and also synthesized in the body. Vitamin K deficiency is rare.

In the 10th edition, minimum daily requirements were set for the first time for sodium and potassium—500 milligrams and 2,000 milligrams, respectively. These levels are for normal, healthy persons who are not involved in heavy physical activity. The RDA committee of the Food and Nutrition Board noted that the *Diet and Health* report recommended that salt intake be no higher than 6,000 milligrams a day (2,400 milligrams of sodium), or roughly a teaspoon of table salt, and that a daily intake of 3,500 milligrams of potassium (available from fruits and vegetables) appears to aid in preventing strokes.

Challenging Oat Bran

A recent study challenged the apparently widely held belief among consumers that simply eating oat bran can be a shortcut to lowering blood cholesterol. The researchers reported that the blood cholesterol levels of a group of 20 subjects were lowered by 7 to 8 percent when they added to their usual diets either high-fiber oat bran or low-fiber refined white flour or farina cereal. All of the subjects, who had normal blood cholesterol levels to begin with, also ate more polyunsaturated fat and less saturated fat and cholesterol during the study than they had before. The researchers concluded that these changes accounted for their lower blood cholesterol levels and that people can expect to lower their blood cholesterol with diets rich in oat bran only if their intake of dietary fat decreases to compensate for the oat bran calories. Some scientists—and the Quaker Oats Company, a major manufacturer of oat cereal—criticized the study, pointing to its small sample and the fact that the participants started with lower-than-average cholesterol levels for the American population. Nonetheless, the wide publicity it attracted may help consumers gain perspective on oat bran. Scientists know that oat bran contains soluble fiber, which can lower blood cholesterol, but only if it is part of a healthful diet low in saturated fat and cholesterol.

Cereals With Psyllium

Recently, a bizarre twist occurred in the controversy over what health claims manufacturers should be allowed to make for processed foods. Procter & Gamble asked the U.S. Food and Drug Administration (FDA) to require General Mills to remove its new breakfast cereal, Benefit, from the market. Benefit contained psyllium, a plant whose seeds are high in soluble fiber, and the package boasted that Benefit reduced cholesterol. The Kellogg Company has also marketed two breakfast cereals—Heartwise and Bran Buds—that contain psyllium but has not made cholesterol-reducing claims for them. Until 1989, psyllium was used chiefly in laxatives, including one from Procter & Gamble called Metamucil. But because Metamucil is classified as a drug, the FDA did not allow Procter & Gamble to advertise that it will lower blood cholesterol, since carefully controlled clinical trials had not yet documented that psyllium has that effect. Under regulations in force in 1989, drug manufacturers had to conduct extensive tests to back up any claims they made for their products, but food manufacturers were not required to supply any evidence for their claims. (An FDA proposal to tighten the regulation of health benefits claimed for food products was under review within the government in early 1990.) Procter & Gamble charged that Benefit, like Metamucil, should be classified as a drug and as such should not be allowed to carry health claims. Meanwhile, in late 1989, General Mills discontinued Benefit, citing weak sales.

Psyllium contains about five times more soluble fiber than oat bran. Some recent studies do suggest that psyllium can lower blood cholesterol levels.

Fat Substitute

In February 1990 the FDA approved for use in frozen dessert products the first fat substitute to become available to American consumers. Called Simplesse, the new food additive is made from egg-white and milk proteins and is also lower in calories than regular fat. An ice cream-like frozen dessert made with Simplesse would have virtually no fat (compared to 5 grams in a 4-ounce portion of regular ice cream). In addition, it would have about two-thirds the cholesterol of regular ice cream and about 10 percent fewer calories. The Simplesse product would be made with regular sugar.

Although initially approved only for frozen desserts, Simplesse may eventually also be used in such products as mayonnaise, cheeses, margarine, and yogurt. Since it breaks down when heated, it cannot be used in baked or fried goods.

Pending before the FDA in early 1990 was an application for approval of another fat substitute, known as Olestra. This fat substitute remains stable when heated, and it could be used in products such as cakes and potato chips.

Pesticides in Food

For the past six years consumers surveyed in the United States have ranked pesticides as the most serious threat to food safety. This perception differs markedly from the position of the FDA, which considers contamination of food by microorganisms (bacteria, for example) to be far more hazardous than pesticides and other chemicals used in agriculture. The FDA estimates that between 6.5 and 33 million Americans—3 to 14 percent of the population—become ill each year as a result of contamination of food by microorganisms, and about 9,000 of these people die. By contrast—using a worst-case scenario—pesticide residues in foods may lead to 6,000 cases of cancer a year, or 2 per 100,000 people, according to the U.S. Environmental Protection Agency (EPA).

Why do perceptions of food hazards diverge so widely? A major reason is that the dangers of pesticides and other agricultural chemicals have been more highly dramatized in the media than those of microorganism contamination. For example, in early 1989 the Natural Resources Defense Council (NRDC)—a private nonprofit environmental group—received wide media attention when it charged that consumption of apples and apple products containing the growth regulator Alar increased the risk of cancer—particularly in infants and children, who might develop cancer in later years. In early 1989 the EPA announced it was considering banning Alar based on preliminary evidence that a cancer-causing substance called UDMH, produced from Alar during heat processing of apple juice and applesauce, constituted an unacceptable risk, but the EPA said there was no immediate danger from eating apples and apple products. Meanwhile, sales of these items plummeted, and Alar's manufacturer voluntarily stopped selling it to U.S. apple producers—and eventually halted almost all sales worldwide.

Consumer anxiety about pesticides and other agricultural chemicals in fresh produce prompted several supermarket chains in California and other parts of the United States to employ private firms to test produce items for pesticide residues and to certify that they were residue-free. Many supermarkets have also begun to sell some organically grown produce—produce grown without the application of chemical pesticides. A few states and some private organizations, such as the California Certified Organic Farmers, have programs for certifying that organically grown foods meet specified standards. (Certification is important to prevent fraudulent labeling of foods as organically grown.) The spread of all these programs makes it likely that U.S. government standards on testing for pesticides and on certifying organically grown foods may be needed.

The furor over pesticides provides an example of the problems consumers face in evaluating food safety. It may be helpful to realize that a single study rarely if ever establishes that a given dietary practice will be either detrimental or beneficial. Several experiments, done by different investigators, are needed to validate a scientific finding. And it is well to remember that the food and chemical industries, like other groups with vested interests, selectively publicize those studies whose results are to their benefit.

See also the feature article PESTICIDES AND FOOD ADDITIVES.

Nutrition and the Immune System

Scientists have long recognized that what people eat influences the functioning of their immune systems and that there is therefore a relationship between diet and the occurrence and severity of infections. At present, however, little reliable data are available on the influence of individual nutrients on specific immune system functions in humans or on the mechanisms by which nutrition and immunity are interrelated. Some research scientists suggest that using tests of immunocompetence (which measure how well a person's immune system is functioning) together with traditional methods of assessing a person's nutritional status may help single out individuals most likely to benefit from the addition of nutritional supplements to their diet. Such individuals may include those debilitated by severe illness or trauma, premature infants and full-term infants of low birth weight, and some elderly people. It should be noted, however, that some tests of immunocompetence are without merit and may be used by poorly qualified individuals to promote supplement sales.

Generalized malnutrition—in which intake of both calories and most nutrients are low—increases the likelihood that an individual will contract infectious diseases. However, some microorganisms compete with host cells for nutrients and therefore may fail to multiply (and cause disease) in malnourished people. Diseases like malaria and tuberculosis have been known to flare up in some malnourished population groups only after these people have been fed a nutritious diet.

Susceptibility to infection differs depending on whether malnutrition is the result of an overwhelming infection or trauma or the result of starvation. The adequacy of the immune system depends on the body's ability to synthesize the large numbers of proteins required to maintain that system. In starving people the body adapts to food deprivation so as to avoid tearing down body proteins and is thereby able to protect the immune system until starvation reaches advanced stages. In severe illness or trauma the

A HEALTHFUL DIET

Recommendations From the 1989 *Diet and Health* Report

- Keep total fat intake to 30 percent of calories or less.
- Keep consumption of saturated fats (fats derived mainly from animal sources, including dairy products and red meat) to 7-10 percent of total calories.
- Take in no more than 300 milligrams of cholesterol a day.
- Carbohydrates should account for more than 55 percent of total calories.
- Protein should account for 15 percent of calories.
- Maintain appropriate body weight by balancing food intake with physical activity.
- For those who drink alcohol, limit intake to less than 1 ounce of pure alcohol a day (two cans of beer, or two small glasses of wine, or two average-size cocktails).
- Daily salt intake should not exceed 6 grams.
- Maintain adequate calcium intake.
- Avoid taking any supplements that provide more than the recommended dietary allowances of vitamins and minerals. (The preferred way to obtain adequate amounts of nutrients is to consume a wide variety of foods and take no supplements.)

To Achieve the Above Goals:

- Eat fish, poultry without skin, lean meats, and legumes (especially dried beans) rather than fatty meats.
- The size of portions of meat, poultry, and fish should be 2-3 ounces.
- Substitute low-fat or nonfat dairy products for whole milk dairy products.
- Limit consumption of oils, fats, and fried or fatty foods.
- Eat no more than three or four egg yolks a week.
- Eat five or more servings a day of vegetables and fruits, especially green and yellow vegetables and citrus fruits.
- Eat six or more servings daily of cereals, breads, and legumes.
- Limit the use of salt in cooking and avoid adding it at the table. Also limit consumption of salty processed foods such as potato chips, canned and dried soups, and salt-preserved or salt-pickled foods. Read labels to determine the amounts of sodium or salt in foods.

higher metabolic rate due to fever increases nutrient needs, but at the same time the appetite fails; body proteins then are broken down and the destruction of amino acids (the building blocks of which proteins are made) accelerates. As a result, the body's ability to synthesize new proteins rapidly diminishes, the immune system becomes impaired, and new infectious diseases rapidly develop.

Definite deficiencies of many nutrients, including linoleic acid, an essential fatty acid, the trace elements iron, zinc, copper, selenium, and iodine, and vitamins A, E, C, B_6, B_{12}, and folate all depress the functioning of the immune system. Paradoxically, excessive intakes of many of these substances, including linoleic acid and zinc, also adversely affect the immune system. Extremely high iron intakes can overwhelm the immune system by causing excessive growth of bacteria that require iron. In addition, excessive intakes of vitamins A and B_6 and of all trace elements can be toxic. Healthy people who routinely eat a wide variety of foods will not develop deficiencies and do not need supplements to maintain their immune systems.

See also the feature article DIET ROUNDUP *and the Spotlight on Health article* VITAMIN PILLS AND OTHER SUPPLEMENTS.

ELEANOR R. WILLIAMS, PH.D.

OBSTETRICS AND GYNECOLOGY

New Test for HPV Virus • Measuring Fertility Clinic Success Rates • News on French Abortion Pill

Detecting and Treating Human Papilloma Virus

In recent years, the human papilloma virus (HPV) has been associated with both precancerous cells on the cervix and cervical cancers. In December 1988 the U.S. Food and Drug Administration approved a new test to detect the presence of HPV. Called ViraPap, the test identifies the DNA unique to seven strains of HPV in a sample of cells obtained through a routine cervical swab.

In recent years the incidence of HPV has been rising at a rapid rate. One U.S. study revealed evidence of HPV infection in 2 percent of all Pap smears. Another showed HPV evidence in 16 percent of college students. A West German study found HPV present in 28 percent of pregnant women.

Only recently has medical science started to unravel the mysteries surrounding this widespread virus and its drastic consequences. With the advent of techniques to study DNA, many strains of HPV have been identified. Strains 16 and 18, both of which can be detected by ViraPap, are closely linked to many cervical cancers. Other strains cause common or plantar

warts (warts on the sole of the foot), external genital condylomas (wartlike growths), cervical dysplasias (atypical cells which can be precancerous), invasive cervical cancers, and laryngeal papilloma (warty growths in the throats of children, which may be acquired via infection from the birth canal). Pregnancy, smoking, immune deficiency, and other venereal infections, such as genital herpes, are factors that make women more susceptible to HPV infections. Men with HPV infections are at increased risk for cancer of the penis.

While there is currently no cure for HPV infection, treatment is directed at controlling the growth of the virus so that the individual's immune system can handle it. Cautery (burning with electric currents), freezing with liquid nitrogen, external application of trichloroacetic acid, and laser surgery have all been used in the treatment of genital warts. Topical treatment with the drug 5-fluorouracil (brand name, Efudex) and with injectable interferon (brand name, Intron A), a drug that has only recently become available, has shown promise in the treatment of extensive condylomas.

Typically 10 to 15 years elapses between evidence of Pap smear abnormalities and the development of invasive cervical cancer. The lifetime risk of cervical cancer has been estimated at 1 percent for the current generation of American women. But with HPV infections on the rise among sexually active teenagers, there may be a similar rise in cervical cancer rates in the coming decades. For their protection, women should get regular Pap smears at a laboratory that screens carefully for signs of HPV.

See also the Health and Medical News article MEDICAL TECHNOLOGY.

Fertility Clinics—Measuring Success

Since the birth in 1978 of Louise Brown, the world's first "test-tube baby," increasing numbers of in vitro fertilization (IVF) clinics throughout the world have been competing to offer new hope to infertile couples. However, the exaggerated claims about pregnancy rates made by some of these clinics have led to concern on the part of the U.S. Food and Drug Administration, as well as the American Fertility Society and other professional groups, that consumers are being misled.

To encourage more accurate and consistent reporting, two professional organizations, the Society for Assisted Reproductive Technology (SART) and Medical Research International, have developed a standardized form for reporting results and established the In Vitro Fertilization-Embryo Transfer Registry (IVF-ET). The pooled results of the clinics participating in the registry are published annually by the American Fertility Society. While individual clinics' results are currently not reported separately, the pooled data do

*"I feel as if I have a thousand brothers and sisters,"
said ten-year-old Louise Brown (right), the world's first
"test-tube baby," as, with one of the youngest babies,
she joined a tea party in England (above) for some 615
children conceived through in vitro fertilization. The
event marked the tenth anniversary of the founding of
the world's first center for in vitro fertilization, a procedure pioneered by Britain's Dr. Patrick Steptoe, who
died in 1988, and Professor Robert Edwards.*

give some idea of typical figures. Moreover, participating clinics are subject to outside peer review.

Fertilization Procedures. In traditional in vitro
fertilization, eggs are surgically removed from a woman's ovaries, fertilized in the laboratory with semen
from her husband or a sperm donor, and inserted into
the uterus of either the egg donor or another woman.
IVF pregnancy rates are highest in women who are
taking fertility drugs to produce multiple eggs, and
the best pregnancy rates are achieved in women under
30 whose only fertility problem is blocked fallopian
tubes. (This is because IVF bypasses the tubes altogether.) However, IVF has also been successful when
used in cases of male infertility (probably because
sperm can be combined directly with the eggs) and
unexplained infertility.

In gamete intrafallopian transfer (GIFT), a newer technique, eggs are harvested, then mixed with sperm and inserted into a woman's fallopian tube. GIFT is useful in women who have normal tubes but in whom sperm may not be reaching the eggs for various reasons. The pregnancy rates in appropriately chosen couples using this procedure are generally higher than IVF pregnancy rates. Sometimes the two procedures are combined.

Calculating Success. A success is, obviously, a pregnancy, but much confusion surrounds the definition of what constitutes a pregnancy. Many women undergoing IVF have "chemical" pregnancies, in which there is a brief rise in blood levels of the hormone measured in pregnancy tests—human chorionic gonadotropin (hCG)—followed by a rapid fall in hCG and a menstrual period. Other women have miscarriages or tubal pregnancies (in which the embryo implants in one of the fallopian tubes). But what infertile couples are interested in is the "take-home baby" rate of a clinic, not the "raw" pregnancy rate. Unfortunately, some labs have published or advertised pregnancy rates that include all of these occurrences rather than revealing their "take-home baby" rate, which is almost certainly a much lower figure. Some clinics have also made their statistics look better by varying the basis used to measure their pregnancy rate. They may base it on the total number of women undergoing IVF, the total number of cycles (a cycle is the period from fertility drug ingestion to embryo implantation) in which IVF was performed, the number of cycles in which eggs were retrieved (eliminating cycles in which no usable eggs developed), or the number of embryo transfers performed.

The IVF-ET Registry defines a clinical pregnancy as a rising level of hCG with a gestational sac (early pregnancy) detected in the uterus by ultrasound. The registry systematically reports clinical pregnancies, tubal pregnancies, actual deliveries, and multiple pregnancy rates in relation to both the number of egg retrieval cycles and the number of embryo transfers. The registry reported that, in 1989, of 13,674 egg retrievals in the 135 participating clinics, 87 percent led to embryo transfer and there were 2,243 clinical pregnancies; 14 percent of the transfers resulted in the delivery of a baby. The ectopic (outside the uterus) pregnancy rate was 5 percent, and the multiple birth rate 3.1 percent, or approximately one out of five deliveries.

Of the participating clinics, 93 percent reported at least one pregnancy. There seemed to be little relationship between clinic volume and pregnancy rates. The miscarriage rate was 24 percent overall, a little higher than in the general population. Separate figures for deliveries per number of embryos trans-

ferred revealed an overall delivery rate of 12 percent with three or fewer embryos transferred and 16 percent with four or more embryos transferred; the figures explain why most clinics transfer four embryos at a time if possible. Delivery rates of multiple births were negligible when one or two embryos were transferred, 2.8 percent with three embryos, and 4.3 percent with four or more embryos. Because the rate of multiple births rises rapidly when more than four embryos are transferred, most clinics implant only four and freeze the rest for future use or for donation to other couples. However, the delivery rate was only 8 percent for frozen embryos.

GIFT procedures resulted in a delivery rate of 21 percent of egg retrievals. Combining IVF and GIFT procedures resulted in a 20 percent delivery rate.

Standardized reporting has helped educate consumers and made them more discriminating in their choice of clinics. However, success rates may still be misleading because the system does not account for differences in patient population. A clinic that accepts older patients and couples with significant male fertility problems will have lower pregnancy rates than a clinic that takes only young couples with tubal problems. Many infertility researchers feel data should be broken down further by maternal age and infertility factors.

Ethical Issues. The IVF and GIFT procedures have led to enormous social and ethical controversies. IVF makes surrogate mothering a possibility, since a fertilized egg can be placed in a woman other than the egg donor. Legal custody and inheritance issues have already been raised over frozen embryos, and as a result many clinics are unwilling to either freeze or destroy excess embryos. And IVF costs several thousand dollars each time it is done, so its use is limited to couples with the means to pay for it.

See also the Health and Medical News article BIO-ETHICS.

RU 486 Update

A new study among French patients of the controversial RU 486 abortion pill showed the drug to be safe and effective in 96 percent of the more than 2,000 women tested. RU 486 blocks the action of progesterone, a hormone necessary for fetal survival. This causes the uterine lining—and the fertilized embryo—to slough off, in effect bringing on a menstrual period. The pill has been found to work best when followed shortly afterward by a dose of prostaglandin, a hormonelike substance that stimulates the uterus to contract. In previous studies RU 486 caused a high rate of excessive bleeding, but only one participant in the new study developed bleeding severe enough to warrant a blood transfusion.

RU 486 has been available in France since 1988, where it is approved for use only within the first seven weeks of pregnancy. In February 1990, Emile-Etienne Baulieu, the French chemist who developed the drug, announced that the manufacturer, the French firm Groupe Roussel-Uclaf (a subsidiary of the West German company Hoechst AG), was seeking approval to market RU 486 in Great Britain, the Netherlands, Finland, and Scandinavia. No attempt has yet been made to introduce RU 486 into the United States, largely because of the expression of strong resistance by antiabortion groups.

See also the feature article BREAST CANCER: DETECTION AND TREATMENT *and the Spotlight on Health articles* COPING WITH DIABETES DURING PREGNANCY *and* MENOPAUSE: A TIME OF TRANSITION.

LINDA HOLT, M.D.

PEDIATRICS

*Preventing Newborn Lung Disease •
Benefits of Bicycle Helmets • Treating
Birthmarks • Terminating Tantrums*

Steroid Lung Treatment

According to a study published in June 1989, treatment with the steroid drug dexamethasone (sold as Decadron) for six weeks can help clear up lung disease and promote brain development in selected tiny premature infants. Babies who are born two or three months early often experience a number of problems caused by their immaturity. One of the most serious—and almost inevitable—problems afflicting very small infants is lung disease. Although this condition is commonly treated by giving babies extra oxygen and putting them on mechanical respirators that breathe for them, such lifesaving measures can actually cause further damage to the lungs, leading to a chronic form of lung disease called bronchopulmonary dysplasia. Infants with this disease tend to have a variety of long-term troubles, such as frequent respiratory infections, slow growth, and delayed development.

Researchers from Syracuse, N.Y., encouraged by earlier studies suggesting that dexamethasone can help clear up lung disease in some tiny infants, designed a study to find out for sure whether the drug works. They studied 36 two-week old infants with lung disease that was not improving with additional oxygen and mechanical respiration; all of the babies had been born at least ten weeks early and weighed 2.75 pounds or less at birth. The infants were divided into three groups. The first group received dexamethasone for 42 days, the second group received

dexamethasone for 18 days, and the third group received a placebo (inactive substance). The investigators found that the infants treated with dexamethasone for 42 days needed oxygen therapy and mechanical respiration for shorter periods of time than did those in the other two groups, thus lessening their risk of developing chronic lung disease. Babies in the 42-day dexamethasone treatment group were also more likely to be developing normally at their 6-month and 15-month checkups. Infants treated with the 18-day course of dexamethasone did not appear to benefit from the medication. Dexamethasone therapy was not associated with any serious complications during the study.

Bike Helmets Work

A study published in May 1989 concluded that bicycle safety helmets can prevent serious head injuries, especially in children. Despite the popularity of bike riding, bicycle accidents are common and sometimes serious. In one recent year they resulted in 1,300 deaths and sent over 500,000 people to emergency rooms in the United States. Most of the severe or fatal accidents that befall bicycle riders involve head injuries. Although safety helmets are designed to prevent such injuries, until now there has been little proof that they actually work.

In a project carried out at five hospitals in the Seattle area, researchers compared three groups of individuals involved in bicycling accidents over a one-year period: 235 patients who were treated in emergency rooms for head injuries; 433 patients treated for other injuries not involving the head; and an additional 558 individuals who had reported one or more bicycle accidents in the preceding year, regardless of whether they were injured or treated at the time. The authors found that over 60 percent of the head injuries occurred in children, especially in those between 6 and 14 years of age. More importantly, children also accounted for about two-thirds of the severe brain injuries observed in the study.

When the investigators examined the use of safety helmets among the three groups of individuals, they discovered that only 7 percent of the patients with head injuries were wearing bike helmets when they had their accidents, compared with nearly 25 percent of the individuals in the other two groups. From their observations, the researchers calculated that wearing a helmet reduced the risk of head injury by nearly 90 percent. They concluded that bicycle safety helmets are effective in preventing head injuries but, unfortunately, are not being used enough. They recommended a campaign to increase the use of bicycle helmets, especially by children, who sustain most of the serious head injuries.

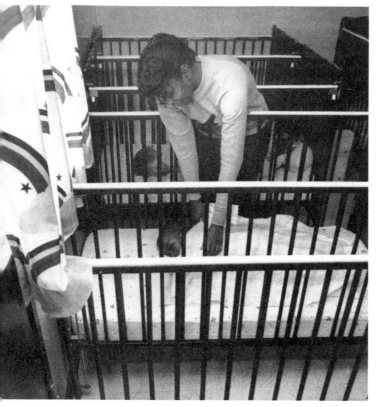

More than half of the children in day-care centers in the United States get a cytomegalovirus infection at some time, but without showing any symptoms. The infection may be more serious in the adults looking after them.

Day-Care Concern

According to a recent study in Richmond, Va., day-care workers are at risk for catching a potentially serious viral infection from the children they tend. As day-care centers have become facts of American life, there has been increasing awareness that such centers can be breeding grounds for a variety of contagious diseases. Although most of the illnesses that are spread in day-care centers—like colds and diarrhea—are not very serious, certain infections are more worrisome. One such infection is caused by cytomegalovirus. Although most viruses are not choosy about whom they infect, cytomegalovirus seems to prefer young children in day-care centers. It is estimated that over half of all youngsters in day-care centers have a cytomegalovirus infection some time during the first few years of life. Part of the reason infection is so widespread in day-care centers is that it seldom causes any symptoms in infants and pre-schoolers; this allows the virus to spread from one child to another without being noticed. The real worry about cytomegalovirus is that infections in

pregnant women can lead to significant birth defects in their newborn infants. Since many day-care workers are women in their childbearing years, taking care of infected youngsters could be a risky proposition.

In the Richmond study, researchers evaluated over 600 women who worked at 34 day-care centers over a two-year period. They found that 11 percent of the susceptible day-care workers became infected with cytomegalovirus each year. The risk of acquiring the infection was five times higher in these day-care workers than in another group of women who worked in a hospital. Day-care employees who took care of children less than two years old were more likely to catch cytomegalovirus infections than were those caring for older children. Finally, when the viruses of infected women were examined in the laboratory, they were usually found to be the same types as those the children at the centers had. These results show that day-care workers can catch cytomegalovirus infection from youngsters in their care, especially children less than two years of age.

Treating Port-Wine Stains

A recent article from researchers at Boston University Medical Center reported that children with disfiguring birthmarks of the face can be treated successfully with a new form of laser therapy. The port-wine stain is a relatively common type of birthmark caused by abnormal dilation of blood vessels under the skin. This leads to a purplish discoloration of the skin, resembling a wine spill. Because these birthmarks typically occur on the face, they can be quite disfiguring, especially large ones. Of the many treatments used in the past, therapy with the argon laser had been the most successful. The laser works by penetrating the skin and being absorbed by the hemoglobin, or oxygen-carrying pigment, in the red blood cells contained within the abnormal blood vessels. The laser's concentrated energy heats up and destroys the dilated vessels.

Unfortunately, argon laser therapy tends to cause more scarring in children than it does in adults. Recently, a new kind of laser has become available, called the flashlamp-pulsed tunable dye laser. Since early experience with the new device suggested that it caused less scarring than the argon laser, physicians from Boston decided to test it in children.

The study included 35 children between three months and 14 years of age with port-wine stains on their heads or necks. The birthmarks varied in size from less than 1 square inch to over 30 square inches. After an average of 6.5 treatments to each area, all patients were rid of their birthmarks. Only two patients had minor scarring; in both cases, the treated area had been injured soon after laser therapy. About half the children experienced some darkening of the skin, which disappeared over three to four months. The findings of this study demonstrate that the tunable dye laser is the best tool yet for treating disfiguring port-wine stains in children.

Treating Tantrums

A 1989 Little Rock, Ark., study reported that bedtime tantrums can be reduced either by engaging children in pleasant activities at bedtime or by ignoring their behavior entirely. As many parents can attest, putting young children to bed at night is no picnic. Although some children give in without too much fuss, others engage in full-blown toddler warfare.

Two common approaches to reducing bedtime tantrums are positive routines and graduated extinction. With the first strategy, children are initially allowed to stay up until they fall asleep naturally, while parents engage in a series of enjoyable activities (positive routines), such as rubbing the children's backs or kissing them. Each week, parents begin the routines earlier and earlier until they are finally completed at the desired bedtime. Graduated extinction is an alternative to simply ignoring a tantrum. With this technique, parents put the child to bed at the usual time. When tantrums occur, parents ignore the behavior for a specific amount of time before attending to the child. Each week they ignore the tantrums for a longer period of time, up to a maximum of 60 minutes. Although each strategy seems to make sense, no previous studies had compared the two techniques to see which one, if any, worked better.

In the new study, 36 children (20 girls and 16 boys) who had at least one bedtime tantrum three times a week were enrolled. Their ages ranged from 18 months to 48 months. They were divided into three groups: the first group was treated with positive routines, the second with graduated extinction, and the third group received no specific treatment. The researchers found that each of the two techniques reduced the number and duration of tantrums and that both strategies worked better than simply waiting for a child to "grow out of it." Interestingly, parents of children in the positive routine group also reported an improvement in levels of marital satisfaction, suggesting that treating tantrums may have some added bedtime benefits to offer.

Phenobarbital and IQ

According to a study published in February 1990, using the drug phenobarbital to treat fever-induced seizures in children can be hazardous to their intelligence. A seizure is a sudden, dramatic event that occurs when the brain's normal electrical activity becomes disorganized. The electrical chaos, in turn, can lead to a loss of consciousness, difficulty in breathing, and violent jerking movements of the arms and legs. The most common type of seizure in children is known as a febrile seizure, in which a high fever serves as a trigger for the seizure. Between 4 and 5 percent of all children experience a febrile seizure some time in their first five years of life. Although seizures are usually frightening to watch, brief febrile seizures seldom cause any long-term problems. On the other hand, some children have certain risk factors (such as lengthy or multiple seizures) that increase their chances of developing epilepsy, a disease in which people have recurrent seizures without a known cause. It has been widely accepted for a long time that the daily use of phenobarbital can prevent febrile seizures in children who have had an initial episode. It can also cause a number of undesirable side effects, however, such as drowsiness, hyperactivity, and behavior changes. Nonetheless, this medication is widely used to prevent febrile seizures, with the assumption that the value of preventing seizures outweighs the adverse effects of the medication.

Investigators from the University of Washington and the National Institutes of Health conducted a study to examine the pros and cons of giving phenobarbital to selected children who had had febrile seizures. The researchers enrolled 217 children between 8 months and 36 months of age who had experienced a febrile seizure in the preceding 3 months and who had one or more risk factors that increased their chances of having more seizures. Half of the children were treated with a standard dose of phenobarbital, and the other half received a placebo; treatment was given for two years, after which it was gradually discontinued over a two-month period. The investigators found that after two years, the average IQ was 8.4 points lower in children treated with phenobarbital than in those given a placebo; six months later, after the medication had been stopped, children in the phenobarbital group still had slightly lower average IQ scores compared with subjects in the placebo group. Furthermore, seizures recurred just as often in the phenobarbital-treated children as in those receiving a placebo. These sobering results suggest that phenobarbital can impair intellectual functioning without offering much protection against recurrent seizures.

See also the feature articles CHILDREN'S FEARS *and* IS YOUR CHILD ON DRUGS OR ALCOHOL? *and the Spotlight on Health articles* CHOOSING A PEDIATRICIAN, FEEDING YOUR BABY: THE FIRST YEAR, HEAD LICE, RAISING TWINS: DOUBLE TROUBLE?, TEACHING GOOD HEALTH, *and* WHAT ARE GROWING PAINS?

RAYMOND B. KARASIC, M.D.

PUBLIC HEALTH

*Lyme Disease Update • Measles
Outbreaks • Death by Tanning*

Infectious Diseases

Infectious diseases making the headlines in 1989 included relatively new ones, such as Lyme disease, and old ones, such as measles, that are making a comeback.

In the 1960s healthcare authorities generally believed infectious diseases to be under such good control that there was no need to worry much about epidemics. Reasons given for continued concern, despite the optimism of the moment, included the growing world population (population density promotes the spread of infectious diseases and increases problems of waste disposal); urbanization; rapid mobility; declining immunity levels; increasing resistance of bacteria to antibiotics and insects to insecticides; changing lifestyles; diseases endemic in wild animal populations, such as rabies and plague; and lack of public concern. One item not discussed was perhaps the most important: the possibility of new epidemic diseases. At that time, such a thing was almost unthinkable, especially because smallpox was on the way to being eradicated. Nobody was prepared for the devastating new diseases that have appeared since 1975, including Lyme disease, Legionnaires' disease, toxic shock syndrome, and, in 1981, the new epidemic called AIDS.

Two questions are now worrying epidemiologists: How many more new diseases are just beyond the horizon? How many of the relatively well-known but recently controlled diseases are poised to make a comeback? The first question cannot be answered with any certainty, but in recent years a second virus that sometimes can cause AIDS and a retrovirus that can cause a type of leukemia have been discovered, making epidemiologists cautious about the future. The second question is being asked about diseases such as malaria, streptococcal infections, measles, pneumococcal pneumonia, rabies, and yellow fever.

Discussion of the "greenhouse effect" and how it might increase the earth's average temperature also worries epidemiologists. If the world temperature rises, the United States and other countries in northern climates might be plagued by certain diseases that are now essentially excluded from these areas because the insects or arthropods that spread them do not survive the cold.

Dengue Fever. Of special concern in this regard is dengue fever, a disease that seldom now occurs and is seldom discussed in the United States. Dengue fever, also known as breakbone fever because it causes severe joint and muscle pain as well as fever, headache, rash, and flu-like symptoms, has the potential for spread in the southern United States. Moreover, in recent years it has become more severe in the Caribbean where a fatal form called hemorrhagic fever, which causes internal bleeding, has appeared.

Dengue fever is caused by a virus spread by the *Aedes aegypti* mosquito, which is found in many areas of Central and South America and also to some extent in the southern United States. *A. aegypti* also spreads the dreaded yellow fever. In the early 1960s, after the mosquito had been eradicated in Central and South America, U.S. President John F. Kennedy promised to try to eradicate *A. aegypti* because it was being "exported" (in old tires and the like) from the United States back to Central and South America. The U.S. effort failed, both because of questionable methods and because the United States gave up when it became apparent that it would be an extensive and costly job. Now the United States is vulnerable to importing dengue fever, and even possibly yellow fever, from south of its borders.

Streptococcal Infections. When a microorganism changes and becomes less capable of producing serious disease, healthcare authorities may mistakenly conclude that the decline in the number of reported cases is caused by antibiotics. The resurgence of a previously well-controlled health problem then comes as a shock. A case in point is infections caused by streptococcal bacteria. In decades past this variety of bacteria produced such feared diseases as scarlet fever and rheumatic fever, which causes damage to heart valves and to the kidneys. These diseases have been rare in recent decades, but a more virulent form of the streptococcus bacterium has been causing them again recently, especially in the western United States. Sometimes young healthy patients with these infections have died rapidly, despite the use of antibiotics. Similar reports have been received from Great Britain and Scandinavia.

Lyme Disease. Between 1980 and 1989 over 21,000 cases of Lyme disease were reported to the U.S. Centers for Disease Control. They came mostly from three areas—the Northeast, the Wisconsin-Minnesota area, and the California-Oregon area, but cases have been reported from most of the U.S. states. The disease is also common in Europe and has been reported in other countries, including the Soviet Union, China, Japan, and Australia, among others. If it were not for AIDS, Lyme disease would be the most feared of the new infectious diseases. Yet in areas where Lyme disease is not a severe problem, it is difficult to get people to take the danger seriously.

There seems little doubt that the disease is spreading rapidly throughout the United States and is becoming an increasingly serious problem in areas that have already had many cases, as higher and higher proportions of tiny Ixodes ticks are found to be carrying the causative organism, a spirochete named *Borrelia burgdorferi.*

The tick has a two-year life cycle—as larva, nymph, and adult—and feeds on people as a nymph or an adult. It generally acquires the spirochete from feeding as a nymph on the white-footed mouse and as an adult on the white-tailed deer.

The greatest danger to people is when the nymphs feed between May and July, although a tick bite may cause infection before or after these dates. A tick must remain attached to a person for more than 24 hours to transmit the infection, so that daily removal of all ticks should be adequate protection against the disease. The first sign of Lyme disease may be a small, red bite mark where the tick was, but the mark is often missed. Usually the mark is followed in a few days by a spreading red rash that may be darker at the rim, making it look somewhat like a ring. The disease may involve pain in the joints, headache, chills and fever, and fatigue; later, some patients may develop inflammation of the heart, arthritis, and other symptoms. If not adequately treated with antibiotics—and the sooner the better—the disease may become chronic. There is some evidence that untreated infection in pregnant women can damage their fetuses.

Prevention is possible by avoiding wooded areas known to harbor ticks or by wearing protective clothing and using insect repellents (those containing the chemical deet help when applied to clothing and exposed skin), followed by careful searches for the ticks after returning indoors.

Unfortunately, there is no reliable test on the market to identify people who have Lyme disease, but new tests are being developed, as are potential vaccines. For the present it is important to be aware of the possibility of contracting Lyme disease, to avoid risky activity or take proper precautions, and to see a physician quickly if any symptoms develop. So far no means has been found to reduce the number of infected ticks in the wild.

Measles. Outbreaks of measles increased in the United States in 1989. Chicago was fighting a measles epidemic in August, even before schools began. There the health department set up walk-in immunization centers so that schools could begin on time. The risk in Chicago, as in other cities with high rates, especially Los Angeles and Houston, tended to be highest in blacks and Hispanics, whose immunization rates have been low.

Most of the U.S. states had some measles in 1989, and the total number of U.S. cases exceeded 17,000. This has produced a general realization that the strategy of eradicating measles by vaccination pursued

Cases of Lyme disease, transmitted by ticks, continued to rise in the United States and elsewhere. Here, Connecticut public health officials Phyllis Erlandson and Tom Galotti spread a white flannel flag in the woods near Stamford to capture ticks and determine the rate of infection in the area.

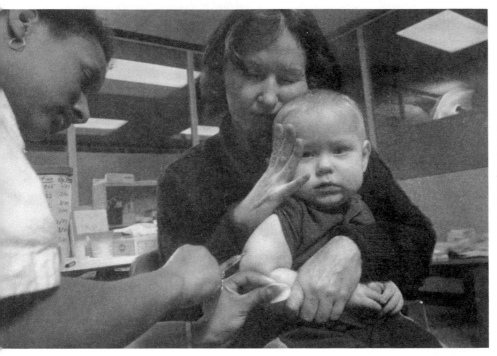

A Texas toddler submits to a measles vaccination in Houston, where a significant outbreak of the disease took place in the winter of 1988-1989. U.S. health officials originally hoped that measles would be eliminated by 1982.

since 1963, when the first measles vaccine went on the market, is not working well. Healthcare officials had originally predicted that measles would be eradicated from the United States by 1982.

The early vaccination programs (especially the immunization of children against measles before their first birthday) did not always produce good immunity. Also, the immunity produced by the vaccine does not appear to last as long as the immunity produced by natural infection. Moreover, the current vaccine has a lower rate of success than the original vaccine in preventing disease (between 2 percent and 10 percent of those who are vaccinated fail to make antibodies). Therefore, two doses of the measles vaccine are needed for effective protection. This is recommended for all persons who have not had measles. In fact, a booster measles shot is recommended for everyone under 32 years of age. Measles continues to be a serious disease, especially in the very young or in adults.

Death From a Tanning Booth

In May 1989 a 45-year-old woman died of burns covering over 70 percent of her body that she received from 25 minutes in a tanning booth. Apparently the woman had been taking psoralen, which is used to treat psoriasis but which makes the skin vulnerable to damage from light. Psoralen is not the only drug that makes the skin more sensitive to light: some antibiotics and some blood-sugar-lowering medica-

tions do the same thing. Before going into the sun or into tanning booths, people should be sure that any medications they are taking do not endanger them in this way. In 1989 both the American Medical Association and the U.S. National Institutes of Health recommended that people avoid tanning machines altogether because they are a dangerous source of the ultraviolet radiation that can cause cancer and other ills. Limiting exposure to other sources of ultraviolet radiation, especially the sun, was also recommended.

Mysterious Blood Illness

For many people the idea that "if some is good, more is better" makes sense, but it does not make sense to the body. Most anything we take into our bodies becomes toxic in excessive amounts. L-tryptophan is an amino acid that is essential in the diet. However, in 1989 the Centers for Disease Control linked its use as a dietary supplement to an unusual and occasionally fatal blood disease. It is possible that the disease was caused by a contaminant introduced during manufacturing rather than by L-tryptophan itself. Whatever the case, in November 1989 the U.S. Food and Drug Administration requested the recall of some products containing L-tryptophan and in March 1990 sought the recall of nearly all products containing the supplement.

See also the Spotlight on Health article NEW PROBLEMS OF POLIO VICTIMS *and the Health and Medical News article* AIDS. JAMES F. JEKEL, M.D., M.P.H.

RESPIRATORY SYSTEM

Tuberculosis on the Rise • Asthma Deaths Increase • Cystic Fibrosis Test Developed

Tuberculosis Developments

Cases on Upswing. In 1989 the U.S. Centers for Disease Control, responding to an alarming increase in tuberculosis rates in prisons, issued guidelines for prevention and control of the disease among prison populations. The rise in cases among inmates was perhaps the most dramatic sign of a disquieting trend in the United States. Considered a disease of the past by many, tuberculosis began a comeback in the United States in the late 1980s. Some 22,000 cases were reported in each of 1987 and 1988, and millions more Americans were believed to be infected without showing symptoms of the disease.

The comeback appeared to be linked in large part to the spread of the human immunodeficiency virus (HIV) and acquired immune deficiency syndrome (AIDS). In large urban areas, the groups experiencing the greatest increases in tuberculosis were the same as those with large numbers of AIDS patients, namely blacks and Hispanics between 25 and 44 years of age. (By contrast, tuberculosis among non-Hispanic whites has largely become a disease of the elderly.)

About a quarter of those affected in 1987 and 1988 were born outside the United States, most in countries with a higher prevalence of tuberculosis. The problem of tuberculosis among immigrants to the United States is compounded by the fact that these individuals are more likely to be infected with strains of the disease-causing organism that are resistant to the drugs usually prescribed first.

In most patients, tuberculosis primarily affects the lungs, although the disease may involve a number of organs. When the infection is focused in the respiratory tract, it is transmissable from person to person by infectious droplets released into the air by coughing. Patients generally become noncontagious within two weeks of starting effective treatment. But if undetected, the disease can easily be passed on, particularly in the relatively closed communities of nursing homes, shelters for the homeless, and prisons.

The majority of new cases of tuberculosis arise in individuals who were infected in the past and have carried the inactive infection for some time. Most cases develop in the first year or two after infection, but the disease may remain latent for many years. The presence of diseases like AIDS that compromise the immune system appears to provoke reactivation of the dormant disease. Cases of inactive tuberculosis may be identified by a skin test, even when no evidence of disease is visible on an X ray of the chest. The development of tuberculosis can then usually be prevented by administration of isoniazid (brand name, INH), one of several drugs used to treat active tuberculosis. Current efforts to further reduce the incidence of tuberculosis focus on preventive therapy for high-risk infected individuals who have not yet developed tuberculosis and early identification and treatment of individuals with active disease. Screening efforts need to be most intensive in high-risk populations.

Blacks More Susceptible? A report published in early 1990 indicated that blacks are more susceptible to tuberculosis than whites. When more than 25,000 residents of racially integrated nursing homes who were free of infection when they entered the homes had repeat skin testing months later, twice as many blacks as whites showed evidence of infection. Since the study participants were exposed to roughly the same living conditions, the researchers theorized that a genetic difference may enable whites to fend off the tuberculosis bacterium better than blacks. The study also showed, however, that blacks and whites, once infected, had the same chance of developing active tuberculosis.

Increase in Asthma Deaths

The sudden death from asthma, in May 1989, of the 52-year-old chancellor of the New York City school system, Dr. Richard Green, focused national attention on the growing number of asthma deaths in the United States. Asthma is a common disease characterized by wheezing and shortness of breath. The symptoms are caused by constriction of muscle in the walls of air passages, inflammation, and excess mucus production by the walls, resulting in narrowed bronchial tubes. The severity of narrowing during an attack may lessen over time, either spontaneously or as the result of treatment. Since 1977, reported asthma deaths in the United States have approximately doubled; it is estimated that around 4,000 people died of asthma in 1989. The increase in U.S. asthma deaths has been greatest among people over age 65. Several other countries, including Canada, the United Kingdom, Denmark, Sweden, Australia, and New Zealand, have also reported a rise in total asthma deaths.

Several explanations have been offered for the rising asthma mortality rate. Diagnostic confusion may be one. Older patients, particularly smokers, may have chronic obstructive pulmonary disease (COPD)—the obstructed airflow that occurs in chronic bronchitis and emphysema—rather than asthma, or they may have both. Misdiagnosis of either disease or uncertainty about the cause of death when both are present could inflate asthma mortality statistics.

Another possibility is that asthma is becoming more

Nancy Sander, founder of a support group for parents of children with asthma, looks on as her daughter, Brooke, uses a pocket-size inhaler. Parents have organized to help children cope with the emotional problems resulting from their illness.

prevalent and severe, perhaps because of environmental or other unknown factors. There are few data to support this theory, other than isolated reports from some urban medical centers that both total asthma admissions and the percentage of asthma admissions requiring intensive care have risen.

Finally, the possibility that increased asthma mortality is related either to undertreatment or overtreatment needs to be considered. A number of drugs and drug combinations are used to manage asthma. The primary class of drugs, called bronchodilators, are medications that widen the airways, and they include theophylline compounds, beta-adrenergic drugs, and anticholinergic drugs. Another type of drug, cromolyn sodium, does not widen airways but prevents them from narrowing in the first place. Corticosteroids may be used to reduce inflammation. A combination of these drugs may be prescribed for the most effective

treatment. It is necessary to follow a physician's orders carefully, since high doses of theophylline and the beta-adrenergic drugs used together may induce abnormal cardiac rhythms, especially in older individuals with underlying heart disease.

But not taking enough medication can be as risky as taking too much. A major concern about asthma treatment is that patients and physicians sometimes underestimate the severity of the disease. This may lead to overreliance on less powerful medications like theophylline and beta-adrenergics when corticosteroids are needed to help abort an acute attack or when hospitalization is necessary for closer observation, in case mechanical ventilation is needed. Some people may even fail to consult a physician at all and rely solely on over-the-counter products, which may not contain the optimal dose or drug for a given person.

Implantable Lung Aid

Experimental use of an implantable device intended to assist the lungs in exchanging oxygen and carbon dioxide was approved in early 1990 by the U.S. Food and Drug Administration. Permission was given for doctors to test the device for safety in ten patients with little chance of survival. Use of the device was not expected to extend the patients' lives.

Called the intravascular oxygenator, the device is not a permanent lung replacement but a temporary aid that can be used for up to seven days to give damaged lungs time to heal. It consists of a bundle of very fine, hollow, synthetic fibers that is inserted into the inferior vena cava, the body's main vein. The bundle is attached to two external tubes: one delivers oxygen to the blood, and the other removes carbon dioxide—a process normally achieved solely by the lungs. In February 1990 the device was used for the first time in a human. The patient died in a few days, although apparently not because of use of the device. The device's significance remains unclear.

Cystic Fibrosis Advances

Genetic Discovery. The discovery in August 1989 of the gene defect responsible for many cases of cystic fibrosis was cause for celebration. Within months the FDA had cleared for marketing a test to detect the gene defect, which occurs in about 70 percent of all those who are carriers of the disorder.

Cystic fibrosis, in which the body produces excessive amounts of thick, sticky mucus that interferes with the functioning of many organs, is the most common fatal inherited disease of Caucasians, among whom it occurs about once in every 2,000 live births. About 5 percent of the white population are carriers of the disorder, which is transmitted as a recessive trait, meaning that a child must receive a defective gene from each parent to inherit the disease. Most people with the disease do not live past their 20s. The test approved by the FDA will be useful in prenatal screening for those with a family history of the disease. However, as not all the gene defects for cystic fibrosis have been discovered yet, some couples with a negative test could still give birth to a child with the disease.

Improved Treatment. A major problem for people with cystic fibrosis is lung infections. When the disease is present, chloride ions, components of salt, do not move normally across cell membranes and consequently water stays inside the cells. Lacking water, lung passages dry out, and the mucus in the lungs becomes thick and sticky and clogs the bronchial tubes, setting the stage for recurrent infections. Once respiratory infections develop, pulmonary function deteriorates more rapidly. The treatment of such infections is difficult because the bacteria that cause them are resistant to many antibiotics and because the patient's lung defenses are impaired. However, drug therapy for infections has been made more convenient. Intravenous antibiotics, formerly administered mainly in hospitals, can now often be given at home. And some oral antibiotics have been found effective against the "pseudomonas" organisms responsible for many lung infections.

See also the feature article PNEUMONIA.

DAVID FREDERICK, M.D.

SEXUALLY TRANSMITTED DISEASES

Progress in Vaccines • Gonorrhea Treatment Changes • Antibiotics, Chlamydia, and Pregnancy

Cases and Consequences

Sexually transmitted diseases (STDs) remain a significant health problem in all parts of the world. In the United States in 1990, according to estimates by the U.S. Centers for Disease Control, 1.5 million new cases of gonorrhea were expected, along with 110,000 cases of syphilis, 4 million cases of genital chlamydia infection, 500,000-1,000,000 cases of genital warts, 200,000-500,000 cases of genital herpes, 3 million cases of trichomonal infection, and 200,000 cases of hepatitis B. Also, 1.2 million new cases of urethritis (inflammation of the urethra) and 1 million new cases of mucopurulent cervicitis (inflammation of the cervix) not caused by either chlamydia or gonococcal bacteria were expected. In addition, approximately 1.5 million

people in the United States are infected with the human immunodeficiency virus (the virus that causes AIDS), which is often sexually transmitted.

Sixty-three percent of all U.S. cases of sexually transmitted diseases occur among persons less than 25 years of age, and 2.5 million American teenagers contract STDs annually. Sexually transmitted diseases occur more frequently in lower socioeconomic groups. This is true even after correcting for reporting bias. (Up to 80 percent of cases of sexually transmitted diseases are reported by the public STD clinics that tend to serve the poor; these clinics report scrupulously, while private physicians tend to underreport.)

Sexually transmitted diseases are difficult to control because of many factors. One factor is that many infected people have no symptoms. Another is that many government health departments do not have the resources needed to locate and treat the sexual partners of patients with sexually transmitted diseases. Despite the magnitude of the STD problem, the public and the media have focused on AIDS, which continues to overshadow other sexually transmitted diseases. In 1989 the U.S. National Institutes of Health allotted $604 million for research on AIDS but only $60 million for the study of other sexually transmitted diseases.

The most serious health consequences of sexually transmitted diseases are those that affect women and those that affect fetuses and infants. These consequences include pelvic inflammatory disease, infertility, ectopic (tubal) pregnancy, cervical cancer, and adverse pregnancy outcome—including death of the fetus, infant pneumonia, mental retardation, and immune deficiencies. The contribution of genital infections to male infertility is not known.

Vaccines

Other than for hepatitis B, there are no effective vaccines for the prevention of sexually transmitted diseases. However, vaccines are currently being developed for genital herpes, and French researchers are working on an oral vaccine designed to prevent recurrent vaginal yeast infections. Approximately three-fourths of women have at least one yeast infection during their childbearing years. Researchers in the United States have made progress toward developing a chlamydia vaccine.

Genital Warts

An estimated 12 million Americans suffer from genital warts, making genital warts one of the most common STDs in the United States. These warts are caused by the human papilloma virus (HPV), and more than 60 types of this virus have been identified.

Some types of HPV have been associated with cancer. A new test of genetic material (DNA) can now detect the more risky types of HPV in the cells and tissues of the genital area. It is possible that this test will complement the Pap smear in the early diagnosis of cervical cancer.

Using another biochemical technique, Dutch scientists have detected HPV in the urine of men with warts. Such studies may help clarify how the virus is transmitted.

Change in Gonorrhea Treatment

In September 1989, for the first time, no form of penicillin or penicillin derivative was included among the preferred antibiotics listed by the Centers for Disease Control for the treatment of gonorrhea. This change in the recommendations resulted from a continued increase in the number of strains of gonococcal bacteria that are able to destroy penicillin by means of an enzyme called beta-lactamase. In some areas of the United States, up to 40 percent of strains of gonococci produce beta-lactamase—and are thus penicillin resistant.

Chlamydia and Pregnancy

Physicians at the University of Tennessee in Memphis successfully tested two antibiotics—erythromycin and sulfisoxazole—for the treatment of pregnant patients infected with chlamydia. Chlamydia infections in pregnant women may result in premature birth, death of the infant, or low birth weight. The most effective antibiotic against chlamydia, tetracycline, cannot be given to pregnant women because of possible damage to the unborn child. Erythromycin and sulfisoxazole may be given during pregnancy and appear to be effective in eradicating chlamydia.

Self-Examination for STDs

In conjunction with five major medical and health associations (including the American Academy of Family Physicians), the Burroughs Wellcome drug company has produced a pamphlet, *The Genital Self-Examination Guide*, which teaches people to monitor themselves for STDs. People are told how to examine parts of their body and what signs and symptoms might indicate the presence of a sexually transmitted disease. The booklet advises people to visit a doctor immediately if they detect any suspicious signs and symptoms. The pamphlet is free and available in English or Spanish by calling 1-800-234-1124.

See also the Spotlight on Health article CHLAMYDIA: THE MOST COMMON VENEREAL DISEASE *and the Health and Medical News article* AIDS.

ROBERT C. NOBLE, M.D.

SKIN

Improved Treatment for Scabies • New Use for Interferon • Melanoma Marker • Laser Therapy for Warts—More Harm Than Good?

New Treatment for Scabies

A new antiscabies drug was approved by the U.S. Food and Drug Administration in 1989. The new medication is a 5 percent permethrin skin cream, marketed under the trade name Elimite.

Since biblical times, the agony of patients suffering from scabies, also called the "seven year itch," has been well documented. Scabies is a skin disease that results from an infestation of the skin by a small mite, *Sarcoptes scabiei*. The insect, which is too small to be seen, is most often acquired by simple skin-to-skin contact with another infested individual. On rare occasions, it can be acquired indirectly by contact with infected bedding or clothing. In both cases, the mite penetrates the skin surface of its new host, where it lays its eggs, from which new mites eventually hatch. As a result of this infestation, patients develop itching of a severity unrivaled by any other known disease. The itching is sufficient to disrupt sleep and normal daily activities. A few people have even been driven by the intense itching to attempt suicide.

The standard therapy for scabies has been a 1 percent lindane lotion, better known by its trade name Kwell. Unfortunately, increasing numbers of patients are now proving unresponsive to Kwell therapy—treatment failures as high as 35 percent have been reported. It is believed that the increased incidence of scabies and the widespread use of lindane have favored the development of mites that are resistant to the drug.

Comparative studies have demonstrated that the new permethrin cream is safer, more effective, and more convenient than lindane. Permethrin and related chemicals have been widely used as insecticides by veterinarians and in agriculture for many years. There does not appear to be any significant risk of a toxic reaction in humans—when the cream is applied to the skin, no active permethrin is absorbed into the body because permethrin is rapidly broken down by enzymes in the skin. Studies have documented that a single head-to-toe application of permethrin cream is significantly more effective than lindane. In addition, permethrin is easy to use, is odorless, and does not stain clothing.

Unfortunately, if permethrin therapy becomes widely used, the scabies mite may develop a resistance to permethrin. Thus, the continued development of safe and effective drugs to combat resistant strains will be necessary.

Controlling Scar Production

Experimental use of interferon offers the hope of effective therapy for patients afflicted with a tendency to uncontrolled production of scar tissue. People with this tendency respond to simple skin injuries with large tumor-like scars known as keloids. It has long been established that a cell called the fibroblast is the key in both normal healing and the altered healing that leads to keloid formation. In normal individuals, healing following a skin injury results from increased growth and activity of fibroblasts. In response to the injury these cells produce large amounts of collagen and other substances that are the major constituents of scar tissue. Once the wound has been repaired, the fibroblasts turn off, leaving a normal scar. In a patient who produces keloids, the fibroblasts appear to be turned on properly, but they are overactive—and they fail to turn off properly after their job is done. The result is a continuously enlarging tumor-like mass of scar tissue rather than a normal scar.

The most widely used therapy for keloids is the injection of certain steroids into the tumorous scar. Because this therapy is relatively ineffective, a new approach has been needed. Experiments have shown that normal fibroblast activity can be dramatically reduced by exposure to interferon, a substance that is important to the body's natural defense against viral infection. Fibroblasts obtained from enlarging keloids and grown in the laboratory continue their pattern of accelerated growth and activity. However, when they are exposed to interferon, their excessive growth and activity stops. The production of collagen returns to normal.

Interferon has also been tested on patients suffering from enlarging keloids. Although the results of these human studies are still preliminary, the early indications are promising. Not only has the injection of interferon into keloids halted their progressive enlargement, but their size has actually been significantly reduced. The side effects of this therapy have been minimal. Carefully controlled human studies of this new use for interferon are now in progress.

Perhaps even more exciting is the fact that the findings may also lead to other therapeutic advances. Early clinical trials of interferon for patients suffering from scleroderma—a potentially lethal disease characterized by generalized excessive scar tissue production—are now in progress, and the preliminary results are again promising.

Genetic Marker For Melanoma

Researchers reported that they had identified a gene that makes one susceptible to malignant melanoma, the most lethal form of skin cancer. The identification

What to do if you know the sun is bad for your skin but you don't like to handle slippery, sandy bottles of lotion? There are now available at some beaches vending machines called the Sun Center where, for 50 cents, savvy sunbathers can use a hose to spritz themselves with a 40-second dose of sunscreen.

of this genetic marker should be an important advance in the early recognition of melanoma-prone individuals. More importantly, this finding may lead to new understanding of how and why malignant melanoma develops.

The finding evolved from ongoing studies of families with an extraordinarily high rate of melanoma. Individuals in these rare families who have unusual moles, called dysplastic nevi, have a lifetime risk for melanoma development approaching 100 percent. Previously, melanoma-prone individuals could be identified only by a positive family history and by an atypical pattern of moles. The genetic marker provides a further way of identifying individuals at high risk for melanoma, thus increasing the chances that melanoma will be diagnosed at an earlier stage, when cure is a virtual certainty.

Scientists can also study the effects of ultraviolet radiation (a constituent of sunlight) and of other carcinogens on the melanoma gene's functioning. Eventually, it may even be possible to repair the gene in order to prevent the development of melanoma. Certainly, further study of this gene promises to greatly advance understanding of how genetic information leads to the development of human cancer.

Setback in Therapy for Warts

In the continuing battle to develop new and effective treatments for the common wart, physicians suffered a setback. It was discovered that laser treatments to remove warts (which are caused by a virus) may actually produce an increased risk of wart infection for patients, physicians, and nurses. Potentially infectious wart virus (papilloma virus) was detected in the vapor of smoke that develops during carbon dioxide laser treatment of warts. Because the smoke vapor may be inhaled by anyone present, the potential exists for spread of the virus. This may explain why laser operators have occasionally reported the development of warts in unusual places, such as their nostrils. There is particular concern when the laser is used to treat genital warts, which are caused by a subtype of the wart virus that has a preference for mucous membranes.

The potential of these inhaled virus particles to seed new wart lesions in the mucous membranes of the mouth is especially disconcerting because of increasing evidence that human wart viruses contribute to the development of cancers of the mouth and larynx (voice box). It is feared that the persistent inhalation of laser vapor containing wart virus could not only cause a susceptibility to warts but eventually lead to a higher risk of oral and laryngeal cancer.

Studies suggest that the risk of infection can be greatly reduced by the use of surgical masks and a smoke removal system. However, the use of the carbon dioxide laser for the treatment of warts has been discontinued by many surgeons.

EDWARD E. BONDI, M.D.

SMOKING

Marketing Cigarettes to Blacks • Liability Verdict Thrown Out • New Public Smoking Restrictions

New Products

In the face of a steady decline in Americans' consumption of cigarettes, tobacco companies continued their search for new products in the hope of increasing sales.

Poor sales, however, led R. J. Reynolds to withdraw the widely touted Premier "smokeless" cigarette from test marketing in February 1989. RJR Nabisco, which owns Reynolds, had spent a reported $800 million to develop what it had described as a "cleaner" cigarette.

In May, Philip Morris announced the marketing of two new "ultra low nicotine" cigarettes, Merit Free and Next. R. J. Reynolds announced it would introduce a new cigarette brand aimed specifically at blacks. Test marketing of the new product, known as Uptown, was to begin in February 1990 in Philadelphia, a city with a 40 percent black population. But the market test was abruptly canceled in January 1990 after the U.S. secretary of health and human services, Dr. Louis Sullivan, denounced R. J. Reynolds for "promoting a culture of cancer" among blacks.

Smoking and Minorities

In addition to targeting black smokers with a new brand, tobacco companies continued to aim advertising specifically at black communities. Detroit's city planning commission found more billboards advertising cigarettes and tobacco products in low-income, predominantly black neighborhoods than in other parts of the city; similar trends were reported in other parts of the United States. Statistics showing a high number of black smokers reflected the apparent success of this strategy. The U.S. Department of Health and Human Services said that in 1987 (the last year for which statistics were available), 40.3 percent of black men over age 20 smoked, compared with 30.7 percent of white men, and 27.9 percent of black women smoked, compared with 27.3 percent of white women. Blacks now account for 13 percent of all American smokers. The rate of lung cancer among black men is 58 percent higher than among white men, and blacks lose twice as many years of life as whites because of smoking-related diseases.

Advertising and Promotion

While tobacco companies found new ways to advertise their products and themselves, those opposed to smoking sought to restrict such promotion.

In November 1989, R. J. Reynolds mailed 78-second videotapes to smokers, advertising its low-tar Now cigarette. Philip Morris promoted its Parliament Light brand by giving away compact disks with songs by several popular singers along with specially designed three-packs of the cigarettes.

Philip Morris paid $600,000 to the U.S. National Archives for the right to use its name in a two-year series of print and broadcast advertisements celebrating the 200th anniversary of the Bill of Rights in 1991. While there was to be no mention of company

Accusing R. J. Reynolds of promoting a "culture of cancer" among black Americans, U.S. Secretary of Health and Human Services Louis W. Sullivan successfully stalled the tobacco company's plan to test-market a new menthol cigarette called Uptown, targeted specifically at blacks.

products in the commercials, some observers saw them as an extension of Philip Morris's "smokers' rights" campaign and as a subtle protest against existing and proposed restrictions on advertising of tobacco products. Critics also noted that the ads provide a way for the company to use its name on television, where tobacco advertising has been banned since 1971.

Philip Morris and the Liggett Group were accused of having violated federal law when movies displaying their products were shown on television. Although no federal law governs the use of cigarettes in movies, Representative Thomas A. Luken (D, Ohio) complained that when the 1980s feature films *Superman II* and *Supergirl* were shown on television without the surgeon general's warning on the health hazards of smoking, the tobacco companies were in violation of the Federal Cigarette Labeling and Advertising Act. When the James Bond movie *Licence to Kill* was released in mid-1989, the health warning appeared in the closing credits. A spokesman for the producer said that the filmmaker's sense of social responsibility, rather than Luken's complaint, had prompted the warning. Philip Morris was reported to have paid the filmmaker $350,000 for featuring Lark cigarettes.

Australia joined Canada, Norway, Finland, Italy, Portugal, Singapore and Ireland in totally banning tobacco ads. The minister of health announced late in the year that such ads would no longer be allowed in newspapers or magazines; broadcast advertising of tobacco products was eliminated in 1976.

Smokeless Tobacco

The use of smokeless tobacco among teenage boys and young adult men is a significant and growing problem in the United States, according to reports issued in 1989 by the National Cancer Institute, physician groups, and academic researchers. The rate of smokeless tobacco use is highest among white males aged 12 to 25 who live in nonmetropolitan areas. States with the highest rates of smokeless tobacco use among young men include West Virginia (23.1 percent), Mississippi (16.5 percent), Wyoming (15.8 percent), Arkansas (14.7 percent), Montana (13.7 percent), and Kentucky (13.6 percent). On college campuses, 22 percent of male students use smokeless tobacco, although only 13 percent smoke cigarettes. Only 2 percent of female college students said they use snuff or chewing tobacco, while 16 percent said they smoke.

Less than 1 percent of women use smokeless tobacco, compared to 5.5 percent among men. Overall, use is highest in the South and lowest in the Northeast.

The American Academy of Otolaryngology, which represents ear, nose, and throat doctors, states that use of smokeless tobacco causes cancer of the mouth and throat, tooth decay, and gum disease. A study by dental researchers from the University of California, San Francisco, found that nearly half the baseball players who used smokeless tobacco at least once a week had signs of damage in their mouths, compared with 2 percent for nonusers.

Current Research

Additional evidence of the association between smoking and both heart disease and cancer was presented during 1989. Early in the year, a Harvard Medical School researcher reported that heart disease patients who smoke are three times more likely to suffer from chest pains (angina) and painless restricted flow of blood to the heart than are nonsmokers. Episodes of chest pain last longer in smokers, and their frequency and duration increase as the number of cigarettes smoked goes up.

Smoking cigarettes with reduced tar and nicotine delivery does not lower a person's risk of heart attack, according to a report published in June. Boston University researchers found that the number of cigarettes smoked rather than the type affected an individual's risk of heart attack, apparently because smokers who switch to reduced tar and nicotine cigarettes often compensate by increasing the number of puffs per cigarette, how deeply they inhale, or the number of cigarettes they smoke.

Cigarette smoking can be a factor in the buildup of plaque (fatty deposits) in the arteries, according to researchers from the Bowman Gray School of Medicine, in Winston-Salem, N.C. They reported that carotid atherosclerosis—hardening of the main neck arteries—may progress more slowly in those who quit smoking than in those who continue.

Women who smoke and those who are exposed to someone else's smoke—so-called passive smokers—appear to be at increased risk of developing cervical cancer, according to a report published in the *Journal of the American Medical Association*. The report said the risk was even higher for female smokers who are also passively exposed to smoke.

Liability Verdict Overturned

In January 1990 a federal appeals court threw out damages of $400,000 awarded earlier to the husband of a New Jersey woman who had died of lung cancer after smoking for 40 years and ordered a new trial. While tobacco interests claimed victory, antismoking forces stressed that the court's reinstatement of broader claims that were not fully considered at the first trial may make it easier for smokers and their families to win future lawsuits.

Restricting Public Smoking

The trend toward limiting smoking in public places continued during 1989. The U.S. Congress banned smoking in the passenger cabin and toilets of airliners on virtually all domestic flights, the only exceptions being flights beginning or ending in Hawaii or Alaska that last for more than six hours.

Canada's even more restrictive airline policy, which bans smoking on any Canadian airline flight—domestic or international—was supposed to go into effect on December 31, 1989. Implementation of the new policy, however, was postponed for six months to give both smokers and airlines more time to prepare.

The list of U.S. communities placing limits on smoking in public places grew to include Greensboro, N.C., whose voters chose, by a narrow margin, to ban smoking in elevators and large retail stores and to require nonsmoking sections in restaurants seating more than 50 people. The vote was considered an important victory by antismoking advocates because Lorillard Tobacco is a major employer in the area.

In Virginia, another tobacco-producing state, the General Assembly in March 1990 passed a bill banning smoking in some public places and requiring no-smoking areas in government buildings, large restaurants and stores, and educational and healthcare centers. If the governor signed the bill into law, the only states lacking statewide public smoking laws would be North Carolina, Tennessee, Alabama, Louisiana, Missouri, and Wyoming.

New York became the 11th state to pass comprehensive smoking restriction legislation. Under the new law, every restaurant with more than 50 seats must have a nonsmoking area of 70 percent of its capacity, or enough seats to meet customer demand. In addition, businesses must adopt a written policy providing smoke-free work areas for nonsmokers.

Smoking—by teachers as well as students—was banned in all New Jersey school buildings. The statewide legislation mandated a $25 fine for violators, but some districts adopted stricter penalties, including the withholding of salary increases for third-time offenders.

The Minnesota legislature sent a message to merchants who sell tobacco to minors by upgrading the offense to a gross misdemeanor, punishable by a $3,000 fine and up to a year in jail.

BARBARA SCHERR TRENK

TEETH AND GUMS

Baby Bottle Tooth Decay • Plastic Sealants • Diagnosing and Treating Gum Disease

Tooth Decay in Children

Problems From Baby Bottles. Thanks largely to the widespread use of fluoride—in drinking water, children's dietary supplements, toothpastes, mouth rinses, and gels—50 percent of U.S. children aged 5 to 17 are now free of decay in their permanent teeth. By and large the "baby teeth" of younger children are doing very well too, but recent surveys have shown that many young children are still prone to a special problem known as baby bottle tooth decay (or, more formally, nursing bottle caries). The decay caused by this condition follows a very characteristic pattern— the four upper front teeth are affected most, and the lower front teeth least. In severe cases the upper back teeth are also affected.

As the name implies, the culprit is the child's bottle—in particular, letting the child have bottles well past the usual age of weaning (about 6 months) or while falling asleep. When the child drinks from the bottle, the nipple rests against the palate, while the tongue extends over the lower front teeth and protects them. Thus the fluid from the bottle will pool mainly around the upper front teeth, especially during sleep. Breathing through the mouth and the reduced flow of saliva during sleep intensify the reaction between sugar in the fluid and decay-producing bacteria on the teeth. Although milk or milk formulas do not contain especially high levels of sugar, under the special circumstances of prolonged contact these levels are enough to produce decay. The problem is magnified if parents add table sugar or honey to the milk or use condensed milk. Equally harmful is permitting the child to fall asleep with a bottle containing fruit juice, a carbonated soda, or a sweetened beverage such as Kool-Aid, or using a pacifier with the nipple dipped in honey.

In a study published in 1989, baby bottle tooth decay was found in 24 percent of children enrolled in Head Start programs in four southwestern states. (The children ranged in age from three to six.) Native American children had the highest prevalence (38 percent), followed by Hispanic children (29 percent), Caucasian children (20 percent), and black children (18 percent). Different cultural patterns of feeding and weaning had a major influence on the extent of the problem among the different ethnic groups. Dental organizations are now conducting a broad-based education campaign to help prevent this type of decay.

Campaign for Plastic Sealants. In the 50 percent of American children who still have decay in their permanent teeth, the most vulnerable areas are the chewing surfaces of the back teeth, the molars and the premolars, or bicuspids. These surfaces are characterized by irregular pits and fissures that trap food and bacteria and are protected only to a limited degree by fluoride. They can be made virtually decay-proof, however, by plastic sealants that are painted on by a dentist or hygienist. With the new materials and techniques now available, these sealants can last more than ten years and are therefore very cost effective.

The U.S. National Institute of Dental Research recently announced that despite years of urging by various health agencies, only 8 percent of those ex-

A condition known as baby bottle tooth decay occurs when a child habitually falls asleep while sucking a bottle, giving the sugar in the milk or juice plenty of time to combine with bacteria in the mouth.

amined in its 1986-1987 survey of almost 40,000 schoolchildren had had sealant applied to one or more teeth. Questionnaires and surveys suggest that the surprisingly low rate is due to low public awareness of and limited insurance coverage for this procedure and to insufficient use of it by general dentists. Specialists in dentistry for children are much more likely to encourage its use. Dental and public health organizations are currently campaigning to publicize the value of sealants and urge parents to request them.

Gum Disease

A Problem for Young People. Although the association between the more serious forms of gum disease (periodontitis) and aging is well known, few people are aware that older children and adolescents can be affected by a very destructive form of the disease, known as localized juvenile periodontitis. It attacks the lower front teeth and the four first molars (the molars closer to the front of the mouth). If not detected and treated properly, it can result in tooth loss at an early age. Because there have been no recent national surveys of the prevalence of this condition in the United States, a clear picture of its incidence and distribution is not available. But a 1989 survey of patients 10 to 20 years old visiting dental clinics in Alabama found that 1.8 percent of the black children and adolescents were suffering from localized juvenile periodontitis, compared with 0.26 percent of the Caucasians. This difference in incidence is more dramatic than that seen in some earlier surveys. Consistent with all previous surveys, however, females were much more likely than males to have the disease, accounting for 70 percent of the cases. The disease is known to run in families, and genetic studies are clearly needed.

In treating localized juvenile periodontitis, dentists now prescribe the antibiotic tetracycline (taken in capsule form), in addition to providing local periodontal treatment—scraping (also called scaling) and smoothing tooth roots. The use of tetracycline has dramatically improved the results of treatment. In some cases, however, the destructive infection is still not arrested. Notable success in these situations has been reported with a combination of two antibiotics, metronidazole and amoxicillin, taken over a seven-day period.

Local Tetracycline Therapy for Adults. Taking capsules of tetracycline for prescribed periods (in addition to having local periodontal treatment) has not been as effective against severe periodontal disease affecting adults as it has been against localized juvenile periodontitis. The reason is that the offending bacteria are different in the two forms of the disease. A recently completed study has shown, however, that tetracycline can significantly help adult patients provided the concentration in the periodontal pockets (the spaces between the tooth roots and surrounding gum and other tissue) is high enough to really "knock out" the infection. This concentration can be accomplished by localized administration of tetracycline: the antibiotic is incorporated into special thread-like fibers that are inserted into the pockets and maintained in place for ten days by use of a colorless adhesive or dressing. Using new diagnostic methods, the researchers showed that at the end of this period the levels of the monitored bacterial species were markedly lower and the depths of the periodontal pockets were significantly reduced, meaning that supporting tissue had become reattached to the teeth. The combination of tetracycline fiber treatment and thorough scaling and smoothing of root surfaces thus shows promise in reversing the course of periodontal disease. This treatment also has little effect on the levels of tetracycline circulating in the blood—and, therefore, there is little danger that it will produce resistance to antibiotics in the bacteria that inhabit the mouth.

New Diagnostic Aids. On the basis of several years of clinical testing, the U.S. Food and Drug Administration recently approved a new probing device that detects early warning signs of periodontal disease by identifying "hot spots" under the gums. This device, called a thermocouple probe, measures the temperature of the periodontal pocket relative to the normal temperature of the tissue under the tongue. In general, diseased pockets are around 0.65°C warmer than healthy sites. The pocket of each tooth is measured in sequence, and a computer built into the probe determines the difference between the measured temperature and the reference temperature under the tongue. On a tabletop console a light represents each tooth. When the pocket for that tooth is probed, the light will turn red, green, yellow, or orange, depending on the temperature differential. Red signals a "hot spot" that requires immediate attention. Green indicates health, while yellow and orange identify intermediate differentials that suggest better home care is required.

Even the traditional diagnostic method of measuring the depth of periodontal pockets with a probing instrument is being upgraded by new devices that take advantage of fiber-optic and computer technology. These new probes, either plastic or metal depending on the system, automatically measure the depth of the pocket and the level of attachment between tooth and supporting tissue; they then transfer the information to a computer module that can display it and print it out, as well as store it for future comparisons.

Also becoming available is a hand-held probe for measuring tooth mobility, an indirect indicator of the attachment level. Each tooth is tapped, and the time required for it to return to its original position is determined. The procedure is simple, painless, and fast: a typical examination takes about ten minutes.

Mouth Protectors

One of the unheralded benefits of preventive dentistry has been the marked reduction in injuries to teeth during contact sports that has resulted from the widespread use of plastic mouth protectors. Promoted by the American Dental Association, these devices have been in use for nearly 30 years and are now worn by an estimated 3 million athletes, who are thereby protected from up to 200,000 injuries a year. Many authorities believe that the mouthpieces not only prevent dental injuries but also reduce the severity of concussions.

Unfortunately, however, not every athlete who could benefit from wearing a mouth protector exercises this ounce of prevention. For example, the National Collegiate Athletic Association requires football players at member schools to wear the protector, but not all of these college athletes do so. A new rule going into effect for the 1990 football season mandates that all NCAA football players wear colored mouth protectors, so that officials can readily see whether the protective device is being used. Eventually the colored protectors are expected to replace clear plastic ones among all players of contact sports.

Dental Care Before Cancer Treatment

A 1989 conference convened by the U.S. National Institutes of Health strongly recommended that whenever possible, cancer patients slated for chemotherapy or for radiation therapy around the head and neck have a dental examination and any necessary oral care beforehand. Cancer therapy often causes dental and oral complications so severe that they can interfere with the treatment. Dental care for those facing cancer treatment should include a cleaning and scaling of the teeth, the filling of cavities, and the application of fluoride and the prescription of antibacterial rinses or antibiotics where needed to prevent or reduce complications from the cancer therapy.

The Value of Teeth

The American Association of Endodontists, a professional group whose members specialize in root canal treatment, recently asked over a thousand adults this question: "A very wealthy person wants to buy one of your front teeth. The removal would be painless. What is the least amount of money you would accept?" The average amount came out to be $309,000. Thirteen percent of the respondents wanted a million dollars, and nearly half of those over 65 said they would not sell a front tooth for any price.

See also the Spotlight on Health article COSMETIC DENTISTRY. IRWIN D. MANDEL, D.D.S.

WORLD HEALTH NEWS

AIDS Update • Shanghai Flu Deaths • Meningitis Epidemic in Ethiopia • One-Fifth of World's Population in Poor Health

AIDS Trends

Growing Numbers. In 1989 the World Health Organization predicted that approximately nine times as many people in the world would develop AIDS in the 1990s as did in the 1980s, when the estimated number of cases totaled a half million (the number of officially reported cases was about a third of that). The organization called for increased international cooperation to fight the disease. About half of the cases appearing in the new decade will involve people infected with the human immunodeficiency virus (HIV), the virus that causes AIDS, before 1990.

Looking at just the reported cases of AIDS, one might conclude that the problem is concentrated in the United States and central Africa, but the disease is a rapidly growing concern in most other parts of the world as well. By the end of 1989 over 150 countries had reported AIDS cases, and the rates of infection were rising rapidly in many, such as Thailand and Brazil. In Bangkok, Thailand, for example, the proportion of intravenous drug users who are infected—drug users contract the virus by sharing contaminated needles—increased from 1 percent in 1987 to over 40 percent in 1989. HIV infection was reported to have been found in 70 of Thailand's 73 provinces. Comparable rises have been seen in high-risk groups in Brazil, including homosexual and bisexual men and female prostitutes. The disease is appearing in urban India and West Africa. Two of the hardest-hit areas outside the United States and Africa are South America and the Caribbean.

Heterosexual Transmission. While experts are concerned by the increasing numbers of people infected with HIV, they are even more troubled by the male-to-female ratio found in some areas. In the United States and other countries where male homosexuality and intravenous drug abuse appear to be responsible for most of the virus transmission, there are approximately ten times as many AIDS cases among males as among females—a ratio of 10 to 1. However, in Africa, where the virus is transmitted mostly by heterosexual activity, the ratio is almost 1 to 1. Epidemiologists consider the male-to-female ratio a crude indicator of the extent of the virus's introduction into the heterosexual population and of the efficiency of a country's heterosexual practices in transmitting AIDS. The male-to-female ratio in some areas in or near the Caribbean is less than 2 to 1. It is 1.8 to 1 in the Bahamas, 1.7 to 1 in Honduras, and 1.5 to 1 in French Guiana. The ratio in Trinidad, while somewhat higher, is still only 4 to 1. Although the disease is nowhere nearly as prevalent in the region as in central Africa, the possible development there of a similar pattern of heterosexual transmission is cause for concern.

Cuba's Quarantine Approach. The most severe governmental response to the AIDS epidemic has occurred in Cuba, which in 1986 set up a massive program to test people for HIV infection. This screening program, which began by focusing on groups at high risk of infection, was intended to eventually encompass the country's entire population. All persons who screen positive are quarantined in special areas. The government says it guarantees continuance of the individuals' salaries, but visits to families, while permitted, are generally chaperoned.

The Cuban approach is a modern equivalent of the

leper colony. Outside Cuba this policy has been criticized for many reasons, most notably because it severely restricts individual rights and freedoms. Doubts have been voiced about the policy's effectiveness, in part because of the problem of false negatives— the screening tests fail to detect the presence of infection in some cases. Other concerns about the policy have included the erroneous detention of people because of false-positive blood tests and the prohibitive economic cost.

Children in Romania. In February 1990 the World Health Organization sent an emergency team to Romania to verify reports of an epidemic of AIDS among children in the country's crowded orphanages and clinics. After testing children in certain hospitals and orphanages in three cities, including the capital, Bucharest, the team found that 700 children were infected with HIV and 50 others had AIDS. A principal cause of the problem was the Romanians' use of the antiquated medical practice of giving small amounts of blood ("microtransfusions") to infants to strengthen them. Blood obtained from just one person infected with HIV could thus expose numerous babies to the virus. The use of contaminated needles and syringes probably also aided the spread of infection; Romania has a shortage of needles, and those reused are not always properly sterilized. A contributing factor was official neglect of the AIDS problem. Until December 1989 and the overthrow of President Nicolae Ceausescu, the existence of the epidemic was not acknowledged by the Romanian authorities. When two Romanian doctors uncovered a high infection rate in June 1989, the Ministry of Health instructed them to stop testing children for HIV.

See also the Health and Medical News article AIDS.

Influenza Epidemic

Great Britain in late 1989 suffered a massive epidemic of the "Shanghai flu," a strain of influenza first identified in China. Hospitals and clinics were filled to overflowing, and dozens of people died from the disease. The outbreak exhausted the nation's supply of vaccine. The infection also produced large numbers of cases in other countries of Europe and elsewhere in the world, including the United States. (In January 1990 the U.S. Centers for Disease Control declared the existence of a flu epidemic, said to be the most widespread in the country since 1984-1985.)

Meningitis

Ethiopia in 1989 was again beleaguered by public health problems. Famine continued to rage, and early in the year the country suffered an epidemic of a particularly dangerous strain of bacteria-caused meningitis. Symptoms often developed less than a day after exposure. The disease's progression was so rapid that, without treatment, many people died within two days of being exposed.

The area most badly hit was Wollaita, a densely populated district about 100 miles south of the capital, Addis Ababa. More than 10,000 persons were estimated to have died in Wollaita, where the government set up some 20 temporary hospitals. One village reported that 15 percent of its population had died from the disease. The heaviest toll was among children of ages 3 to 18.

While Ethiopia regularly has meningitis outbreaks during the dry season, this epidemic was far worse than usual. The affected population may have built up less antibody resistance than people in areas such as the capital city, where meningitis has been more common.

To help deal with the epidemic, a number of nations and organizations sent vaccines, antibiotics, needles, and syringes to Ethiopia. Officials tried simultaneously to treat the ill and to vaccinate those who were still well. Other nations hit by the meningitis epidemic included Kenya, Nigeria, Somalia, and Sudan. However, the problem was most severe in Ethiopia.

Lassa Fever

The first known U.S. case of Lassa fever in a decade occurred in 1989. The victim was a man who had recently returned from Africa, where he had contracted the disease. One of a group of infections that cause internal bleeding and are sometimes called hemorrhagic fevers, this virus-caused illness is extremely dangerous. Seldom seen in the United States but common in parts of Africa, Lassa fever is named after the town in Nigeria where it was discovered. The disease causes as many as 300,000 infections and 5,000 deaths each year in tropical Africa and is the primary public health problem in many areas.

The virus—which belongs to a type not often seen in the United States, the arenaviruses—is carried by wild rodents. Humans usually pick it up from dust, food, or household effects contaminated by the infected animals with their urine but can also get it from an infected person. The virus is extremely dangerous to work with in the laboratory.

Epidemic of Asthma

In a fascinating study, researchers in Spain identified the cause of a series of outbreaks of asthma in Barcelona. Since the cases seemed to be clustered near the harbor, the scientists focused their efforts there. They discovered that the outbreaks occurred when ships were unloading soybeans and the wind was blowing in the direction of densely populated areas. The unloading was found to release a large amount of soybean dust, which caused the asthma.

State of the World's Health

The World Health Organization released a report in September 1989 stating that approximately 1 billion people, or about 20 percent of the world's population, are malnourished, diseased, or in some other way in poor health. Much could be done to reduce death and disease through relatively inexpensive steps such as immunization. It would cost just $1 billion dollars a year to vaccinate most of the unimmunized children of the world against diphtheria, whooping cough, tetanus, measles, polio, and tuberculosis. Also, a modest $50 million could prevent about 2 million of the 4 million annual deaths from diarrheal diseases among children. About 1 million lives are already being saved each year by the relatively new technique of oral rehydration treatment, which requires nothing more than water being added to packets of a mixture of sugar and salts.

People with certain diseases need some kind of professional medical care, but the costs of the treatment involved are often reasonable; pneumonia and tuberculosis, for example, can be treated with antibiotics. Diseases that so far are difficult and expensive to control include malaria, schistosomiasis, and sexually transmitted diseases.

The World Health Organization pointed with pride to the success of the smallpox eradication program. Since 1977, when smallpox was declared eradicated, at least 20 million deaths and countless cases of nonfatal illness have been prevented.

JAMES F. JEKEL, M.D., M.P.H.

The infants at right are among hundreds of babies and older children in Romania recently found to have AIDS or to be infected with the AIDS virus. Romanian authorities had formerly refused to acknowledge the existence of the epidemic, which resulted primarily from poor sterilization of needles and syringes and the old-fashioned practice of giving blood transfusions to new-borns. The couple below, carrying a coffin and grave marker, are going to a Bucharest hospital to collect the body of their baby, dead of AIDS.

Contributors

Authors of articles in the Spotlight on Health and Health and Medical News sections

Beutler, Ernest, M.D. Chairman, Department of Molecular and Experimental Medicine, Scripps Clinic and Research Foundation; Clinical Professor of Medicine, University of California, San Diego. BLOOD AND LYMPHATIC SYSTEM.

Boettcher, Iris F., M.D. Director of Geriatrics, Butterworth Hospital; Medical Director, Grand Valley Health Centre, Grand Rapids, Mich. AGING AND THE AGED (coauthor).

Bondi, Edward E., M.D. Associate Professor, Department of Dermatology, University of Pennsylvania. SKIN.

Bosl, George, M.D. Head, Division of Solid Tumor Oncology Service, Director, Hematology/Oncology Fellowship Training Program, Memorial Sloan-Kettering Cancer Center, New York City. TESTICULAR CANCER (coauthor).

Carleton, Susan. Writer specializing in health and medicine. ELECTROLYSIS.

Cohen, Lynne. Ottawa-based medical writer. GOVERNMENT POLICIES AND PROGRAMS (CANADA).

Cowart, Virginia. Principal, Medical Information Service; Contributing Editor, *Physician and Sports Medicine.* MEDICAL TECHNOLOGY.

Davis, Sharon Watkins, M.P.A. Director, Cancer Information Service, Project Coordinator, Community Clinical Oncology Program, Fox Chase Cancer Center, Philadelphia. CANCER (coauthor).

Engstrom, Paul F., M.D. Vice President for Population Science, Fox Chase Cancer Center, Philadelphia; Professor of Medicine, Temple University Medical School. CANCER (coauthor).

Fisher, Jeffrey, M.D. Associate Professor of Clinical Medicine, Division of Cardiology, New York Hospital-Cornell Medical Center, New York City. HEART AND CIRCULATORY SYSTEM (coauthor).

Frederick, David, M.D. Assistant Professor of Medicine, University of Connecticut School of Medicine; Medical Director, Respiratory Therapy, University of Connecticut Health Center. RESPIRATORY SYSTEM.

Hager, Mary. Correspondent, Washington Bureau Staff, *Newsweek.* HEALTHCARE COSTS AND INSURANCE.

Holt, Linda Hughey, M.D. Chairman, Department of Obstetrics and Gynecology, Rush North Shore Medical Center, Skokie, Ill.; Assistant Professor, Rush-Presbyterian-St. Luke's Medical Center, Chicago. OBSTETRICS AND GYNECOLOGY.

Jekel, James F., M.D., M.P.H. Professor of Epidemiology and Public Health, Yale University School of Medicine. AIDS; PUBLIC HEALTH; WORLD HEALTH NEWS.

Jovanovic-Peterson, Lois, M.D. Senior Scientist, Sansum Medical Research Foundation, Santa Barbara, Calif.; Clinical Associate Professor, University of Southern California; Adjunct Associate Professor, University of California, Irvine; Medical Director, Diabetes Center, Cottage Hospital, Santa Barbara. COPING WITH DIABETES DURING PREGNANCY (coauthor).

Karasic, Raymond B., M.D. Assistant Professor of Pediatrics, University of Pittsburgh. PEDIATRICS.

Katz, Paul R., M.D. Fellowship Coordinator, Division of Geriatrics, State University of New York, Buffalo; Medical Director, Nursing Home Care Unit, Buffalo Veterans Administration Medical Center. AGING AND THE AGED (coauthor).

Koren, Michael J., M.D. Fellow in Cardiology, Cornell University Medical College; Clinical Instructor, New York Hospital-Cornell Medical Center, New York City. HEART AND CIRCULATORY SYSTEM (coauthor).

Lin, Kant Y., M.D. Resident, Division of Plastic Surgery, Hospital of the University of Pennsylvania. HAND PROBLEMS (coauthor).

Mandel, Irwin D., D.D.S. Professor of Dentistry, Director, Center for Clinical Research in Dentistry, Columbia University School of Dental and Oral Surgery, New York City. TEETH AND GUMS.

Maugh, Thomas H., II, Ph.D. Science Writer, Los Angeles *Times.* GENETICS AND GENETIC ENGINEERING.

McLellan, A. Thomas, Ph.D. Director of Clinical Research, Psychiatry Service, Philadelphia Veterans Administration Medical Center; Associate Professor, Department of Psychiatry, University of Pennsylvania. DRUG ABUSE (coauthor).

Meyerhoff, Michael K., Ed.D. Executive Director, The Epicenter Inc. (The Education for Parenthood Information Center), Wellesley Hills, Mass. RAISING TWINS: DOUBLE TROUBLE?

Moreno, Jonathan D., Ph.D. Professor of Pediatrics and of Medicine, Director, Division of Humanities in Medicine, State University of New York Health Science Center, Brooklyn. BIOETHICS.

Moses, Hamilton, III, M.D. Associate Professor, Department of Neurology, The Johns Hopkins Medical Institutions; Vice President for Medical Affairs, The Johns Hopkins Hospital. BRAIN AND NERVOUS SYSTEM.

Motzer, Robert J., M.D. Clinical Assistant Physician, Solid Tumor Service, Department of Medicine, Memorial Sloan-Kettering Cancer Center, New York City. TESTICULAR CANCER (coauthor).

Navarro, Luis, M.D. Senior Clinical Instructor in Surgery, Mount Sinai School of Medicine, City University of New York. WHAT TO DO ABOUT VARICOSE VEINS.

Noble, Robert C., M.D. Professor of Medicine, Division of Infectious Diseases, University of Kentucky College of Medicine. CHLAMYDIA: THE MOST COMMON VENEREAL DISEASE; SEXUALLY TRANSMITTED DISEASES.

O'Brien, Charles P., M.D., Ph.D. Chief, Psychiatry Service, Philadelphia Veterans Administration Medical Center; Professor and Vice Chairman, Department of Psychiatry, University of Pennsylvania. DRUG ABUSE (coauthor).

Osterman, A. Lee, M.D. Department of Orthopaedic Surgery, Hospital of the University of Pennsylvania. HAND PROBLEMS (coauthor).

Owen, Richard R., M.D. Medical Director, Sister Kenny Institute, Minneapolis. NEW PROBLEMS OF POLIO VICTIMS.

Pelot, Daniel, M.D. Associate Clinical Professor, Division of Gastroenterology, Department of Medicine, University of California, Irvine. DIGESTIVE SYSTEM.

Peterson, Charles M., M.D. Director of Research, Medical Director, Sansum Medical Research Foundation, Santa Barbara, Calif.; Clinical Professor of Medicine, University of Southern California School of Medicine. COPING WITH DIABETES DURING PREGNANCY (coauthor).

Repka, Michael X., M.D. Assistant Professor, The Johns Hopkins University; Consultant, Howard University, Washington, D.C.; Consultant, Sinai Hospital, Veterans Administration Medical Center, Baltimore. EYES.

Rodman, Morton J., Ph.D. Professor of Pharmacology, Rutgers University, New Brunswick, N.J. MEDICATIONS AND DRUGS.

Rotherham, James A. Staff Director, U.S. House of Representatives Subcommittee on Domestic Marketing, Consumer Relations, and Nutrition. GOVERNMENT POLICIES AND PROGRAMS (UNITED STATES).

Smith, Pat Costello. Free-lance writer and editor; member, National Association of Science Writers. THAT RINGING IN THE EARS.

Spiegel, David, M.D. Associate Professor of Psychiatry and Behavioral Sciences, Stanford University School of Medicine. MENTAL HEALTH.

Stach, Brad A., Ph.D. Director, Audiology and Speech Pathology Service, The Methodist Hospital, Houston; Assistant Professor, Baylor College of Medicine. HEARING AIDS.

Stewart, Jan, R.N. Illinois Director to National Association of School Nurses; Board of Directors for Illinois School Nurses. HEAD LICE.

Szer, Ilona S., M.D. Associate Chief, Division of Pediatric Rheumatology, Floating Hospital for Infants and Children, Boston; Associate Director, Affiliated Children's Arthritis Centers of New England; Assistant Professor of Pediatrics, Tufts University School of Medicine. WHAT ARE GROWING PAINS?

Terman, Jiuan Su, Ph.D. Research Scientist, New York State Psychiatric Institute. THOSE WINTER BLUES (coauthor).

Terman, Michael, Ph.D. Associate Professor, Department of Psychiatry, College of Physicians and Surgeons, Columbia University; Director, Light Therapy Unit, New York State Psychiatric Institute; Board of Directors, Society for Light Therapy and Biological Rhythms. THOSE WINTER BLUES (coauthor).

Thro, Ellen. Science writer specializing in environmental and medical topics. ENVIRONMENT AND HEALTH (coauthor).

Trenk, Barbara Scherr. Writer specializing in health issues. THE ROLE OF THE PHARMACIST; SMOKING; VOLUNTEERS: THEIR KEY ROLE.

Utian, Wulf H., M.D., Ph.D. Professor and Chairman, Department of Obstetrics and Gynecology, University Hospitals of Cleveland; Chairman, Department of Reproductive Biology, Case Western Reserve University School of Medicine. MENOPAUSE: A TIME OF TRANSITION.

Weinstein, Alan R., D.D.S. Affiliate Faculty Member, Division of Maxillofacial Prothetics, University of Cincinnati College of Medicine; Affiliate Member, Children's Hospital Medical Center, Cincinnati. COSMETIC DENTISTRY.

Williams, Eleanor R., Ph.D. Associate Professor, Department of Human Nutrition and Food Systems, University of Maryland. FEEDING YOUR BABY: THE FIRST YEAR; NUTRITION AND DIET; VITAMIN PILLS AND OTHER SUPPLEMENTS.

Winick, Myron, M.D. President and Professor, University of Health Sciences, The Chicago Medical School. TREATING HIGH CHOLESTEROL.

Woody, George E., M.D. Chief, Substance Abuse Treatment Unit, Philadelphia Veterans Administration Medical Center; Clinical Professor, Department of Psychiatry, University of Pennsylvania. DRUG ABUSE (coauthor).

Worner, T. M., M.D. Director, Alcoholism Services, The Long Island College Hospital, Brooklyn, N.Y.; Associate Professor of Clinical Medicine, Downstate Medical Center; Professor of Medicine, Mount Sinai School of Medicine, City University of New York. ALCOHOLISM.

Zetterman, Rowen K., M.D. Chief, Section of Digestive Disease and Nutrition, University of Nebraska Medical Center. LIVER.

Index

Page number in *italics* indicates the reference is to an illustration.

A

Photo/Art Credits